HARVARD LAW SCHOOL

International Tax Program

BIBLIOGRAPHY ON TAXATION

IN DEVELOPING COUNTRIES

BIRD

BIBLIOGRAPHY ON TAXATION
IN DEVELOPING COUNTRIES

INTERNATIONAL
TAX PROGRAM

HARVARD
LAW SCHOOL

BIBLIOGRAPHY

ON

TAXATION

IN

DEVELOPING

COUNTRIES

Compiled by
Richard M. Bird

assisted by
Juan M. Terán C.

THE LAW SCHOOL OF HARVARD UNIVERSITY

CAMBRIDGE   1968

PREFACE

In 1962, the Harvard Law School International Tax Program published a pamphlet entitled *Bibliography on Taxation in Underdeveloped Countries*. Since that time, the literature on taxation and development has grown considerably, and the present bibliography has more than twice as many entries as the first one. Every attempt has been made to include in the new bibliography all relevant materials that have appeared over the last five years.

This bibliography, like the first one, has been designed as a reference tool for those interested in the fiscal problems of developing countries. In order to make this compilation even more useful to researchers and practitioners, a subject classification has been introduced. The classification scheme is explained in detail in the Note following the Introduction.

Bibliography on Taxation in Developing Countries was compiled by Richard M. Bird, Lecturer on Economics at Harvard University and a member of the staff of the International Tax Program, with the assistance of Juan M. Terán C., a graduate student in law. It was prepared under the general direction of Elisabeth A. Owens, Lecturer on Law at Harvard Law School and Research Director of the Tax Program. Gretchen Hovemeyer and Susan Singer, of the editorial staff of the Tax Program, provided advice on matters of style and prepared the materials for publication.

Comments from those who used the first bibliography were helpful to the compilers of the present work. The International Tax Program is contemplating the possibility of publishing supplements from time to time and would again welcome corrections, additions, and suggestions for improvements.

This pamphlet is one of several works published by the International Tax Program on the general subject of taxation and the developing countries. Others include *Papers and Proceedings of the Conference on Agricultural Taxation and Economic Development* (1954), *Tax Incentives for Industry in Less Developed Countries* (1963), *Tax Burden on Indian Agriculture* (1966), *A General Theory of Tax Structure Change During Economic Development* (1966), and World Tax Series volumes on Brazil, Colombia, India, and Mexico. The Program's three most recent publications in this area are *Taxes and Tax Harmonization in Central America* (1967), *Readings on Taxation in Developing Countries* (The Johns Hopkins Press, revised edition, 1967), and *Financing Urban Development in Mexico City* (Harvard University Press, 1967).

The International Tax Program was founded in 1952 to conduct research in comparative taxation and to provide specialized training for foreign officials and students. It is part of the Harvard Law School's broad program in International Legal Studies.

OLIVER OLDMAN
Professor of Law and
Director of the
International Tax Program

CONTENTS

INTRODUCTION

This bibliography has been prepared as a research tool for persons studying and attempting to solve the domestic tax problems of developing countries. Although it is improbable that any bibliography covers its subject completely, this pamphlet does bring together references to much of the postwar literature on taxation in the underdeveloped areas of the world. Of the more than 4,600 references that have been gathered, almost two thirds are in English. There are a number of references in French and Portuguese, but most of the foreign materials are in Spanish.

The "developing countries" covered in this bibliography include most countries in the world other than the United States, Canada, Australia, New Zealand, western European countries (except Spain, Portugal, and Greece), and the centrally planned economies of the Soviet type. A few arbitrarily selected items on the Union of Soviet Socialist Republics, Yugoslavia, mainland China, and Mongolia have been listed, however. In the case of the Union of South Africa, where the tax literature is largely like that for the developed economies of Australia and the United Kingdom, only the few references that deal with native taxation have been included. Similar considerations governed the selection of materials on Rhodesia. The forthcoming World Tax Series volume on Japan will provide a detailed and comprehensive examination of the present Japanese tax tystem, and therefore only those references which are of special interest to students of the less developed countries have been listed.

A wide variety of materials have been brought together in this bibliography: books, articles, theses, institutional and private group reports, and publications of governmental and international agencies and organizations, for example. No special effort has been made to seek out English translations of foreign tax laws, but those chanced upon have been included. Similarly, direct translations into foreign languages of articles originally written in English have not been included. The number of references to such primary sources as government publications of tax laws in the native language or official statistical compilations is small; such materials can in most cases be obtained from a country's finance ministry or central bank, or from an international lending agency. On the other hand, a special effort has been made to list tax reports and studies prepared by institutions and private groups.

One of the aims in compiling this bibliography has been to give complete bibliographical information for all entries and to present that information in as uniform a manner as possible. The diversity of the materials covered and of the sources from which the references were drawn complicated this task, however, and the results are far from perfect. One of the primary problems was the availability of some of the materials listed, and it must be emphasized here that the compilers did not have access to everything listed in the bibliography. In a few instances, student seminar papers of particular interest which are on file at the Harvard Law Library have been cited. A few documents known to be of restricted circulation have been deliberately included—United Nations and government reports and theses, for example. Materials such as these may not be readily accessible to all potential users of the bibliography, but it may still be of interest to learn of their existence. Many other confidential studies—the often extremely useful annual country reports of the International Monetary Fund and the World Bank, for example—have not been cited as a rule.

In the case of collections of articles and the like, only those articles which were known to be of special interest or which referred to particular countries have been listed separately from the collection as a whole. In a few cases, journals, tax services, and other periodical publications which were known to be good sources of current information on the tax system of a particular country have been listed, even though many of the items appearing in these sources appear separately.

The original purpose in preparing this bibliography was to provide a research tool for students of the tax problems associated with economic development. A considerable amount of the analytical material (most of I : General References) should in fact prove useful for this purpose. A great many of the references are purely descriptive, however, and simply outline the provisions of the tax law in a particular country. The high proportion of descriptive material in this bibliography is probably a fair reflection of the existing literature. Many of these descriptive items are brief, but they should provide a useful starting point for research on the tax system of a particular underdeveloped country. For tax lawyers, investors, businessmen, and others concerned primarily with foreign tax laws, it is the descriptive rather than the analytical material that will be most valuable.

RICHARD M. BIRD
Lecturer on Economics

NOTE ON CLASSIFICATION SCHEME

The materials have been classified, first, as "General References" or "Country References" and, second, according to subject matter. The General References deal with tax problems common to many developing countries rather than to a particular country. Included here are materials on the financial problems of development and on such nontax sources of finance as multiple exchange rates. Chapters in texts on economic development and similar works have been listed if they were known to be of special interest in connection with tax problems.

The Country References are materials dealing with the fiscal systems of particular developing countries. Certain of the 134 "country" designations do not refer to actual states, however. Some of them refer to areas that are considered integral parts of other countries for many purposes (Sarawak and the Ryukyu Islands, for example). Political circumstances account for other country designations: references to prewar Chinese taxation are listed under "China (Mainland)," for example. Classifying the Country References was a complicated task in another sense. Many of the developing countries have become independent, changed their names, merged, or split up in recent years. It was particularly difficult in the case of Africa to be sure that colonial materials had been listed under the correct country heading.

Both the General References and the Country References have been organized according to a subject classification scheme in order to simplify use of the bibliography. The 18 classifications are listed below. Where the scope of a section is not fully evident from its title, or where the material in a section varies from country to country, a brief comment has been added.

1. General.
2. Fiscal policy for development.
3. Comparative tax structures.
4. Income taxation. Also material on the taxation of particular industries.
5. Direct taxes on expenditure and wealth. Includes taxes on estates, inheritances, and gifts. For real property taxes, see 10.
6. Sales and excise taxes. Also stamp taxes.
7. Taxes on foreign trade.
8. Tax aspects of foreign investment. Material on international tax treaties and related matters, as well as some references to tax incentives for foreign investors.
9. Local finance. Includes items dealing with problems of federal finance.
10. Property tax. Also real property transfer taxes (except stamp taxes) and special assessments.
11. Taxation of agriculture.
12. Tax incentives.

13. Tax administration. Also other aspects of the tax policy process.

14. Legal aspects of taxation. Intended for a class of items, particularly common in the Latin countries, dealing with judicial, constitutional (other than federal), and philosophical aspects of tax law.

15. Nontax methods of financing development.

16. Technical assistance. Items on general aspects of foreign advisory groups in the fiscal field.

17. Tax harmonization. Deals with tax problems of common markets and other forms of economic union.

18. General reference materials.

When an item was known to refer to more than one country, a separate entry has been made for each country. Often, however, classification decisions have been based on the limited information revealed by the title of the book or article. It is possible, therefore, that some entries listed under a specific country heading may in fact have broader application. Similarly, each item within a country has been classified according to what appeared to be its main subject. Thus, it may be advisable to refer to several related subject classifications for references on a particular topic (for example, both 10 and 11 for the taxation of agriculture and both 8 and 12 for tax incentives). In this connection, classifications 1 and 2 should also be consulted as a rule.

GENERAL REFERENCES

1
GENERAL

Asociación Argentina de Estudios de Derecho Fiscal. *Jornadas internacionales de derecho fiscal.* Depalma, Buenos Aires, 1961, 250pp.

Basch, A. *Financing economic development.* New York, 1964.

Bird, R., and Oldman, O. (eds.). *Readings on taxation in developing countries.* The Johns Hopkins Press, Baltimore, 1964, xii/556pp.; revised edition, 1967, xii/545pp.

Chelliah, R. *Fiscal policy in underdeveloped countries, with special reference to India.* The Macmillan Company, New York, 1960, 168pp.

Hicks, U. *Development finance: Planning and control.* Oxford University Press, London, 1965, 187pp.

Institut International de Finances Publiques. *Les Aspects financiers, fiscaux et budgétaires du développement des pays sous-développés.* W. P. Van Stockum et Zoon, The Hague, 1952, 276pp.

Joint Tax Program, Organization of American States, Inter-American Development Bank, and Economic Commission for Latin America. *Fiscal policy for economic growth in Latin America.* Published for The Joint Tax Program by The Johns Hopkins Press, Baltimore, 1965, x/462pp.

Jornadas latinoamericanas de derecho tributario—IV, Buenos Aires, 1964. Ediciones Contabilidad Moderna, Buenos Aires, 1966, 657pp.

Peacock, A., and Hauser, G. (eds.). *Government finance and economic development.* Organisation for Economic Co-operation and Development, Paris, 1965.

Prest, A. *Public finance in underdeveloped countries.* Weidenfeld and Nicolson, London, 1962, 164pp.

Tripathy, R. *Public finance in underdeveloped countries.* World Press Private Ltd., Calcutta, 1964, x/288pp.

Van Philips, P. *Public finance and less developed economy with special reference to Latin America.* Martinus Nijhoff, The Hague, 1957, 185pp.

2
FISCAL POLICY FOR DEVELOPMENT

Adler, J. "The fiscal and monetary implications of development programs," *American economic review, papers and proceedings,* vol. 42, May 1952, pp. 584-600.

Adler, J. "Fiscal policy in a developing country." In: International Economic Association, *Economic development with special reference to East Asia,* pp. 287-321. New York, 1964. Reprinted in: R. Bird and O. Oldman (eds.), *Readings on taxation in developing countries,* pp. 31-58. The Johns Hopkins Press, Baltimore, 1964.

Adler, J. "Fiscal problems in economic development." In: Institut International de Finances Publiques, *Les Aspects financiers, fiscaux et budgétaires du développement des pays sous-développés.* W. P. Van Stockum et Zoon, The Hague, 1952.

Adler, J. "La Politique fiscale dans le développement économique," *Civilisations,* vol. 2, 1952, pp. 525-534.

Adler, J. *Recursos financieros y reales para el desarrollo.* Centro de Estudios Monetarios Latino Americanos, México, 1961, vi/148pp.

Ahmad, Z. "Taxation and economic development." In: State Bank of Pakistan, Research Department, *Selected papers on Pakistan economy.* Karachi, 1958.

Amaya, A. "Política fiscal y política monetaria de los paises subdesarrollados," *Boletín de la Facultad de derecho y ciencias sociales* (Córdoba), vol. 27, January-September 1963, pp. 443-482; vol. 27, October-December 1963, pp. 193-299.

Andic, S., and Andic, F. "Problems of economic and fiscal policy in underdeveloped countries," *Finanzarchiv,* vol. 16, no. 3, March 1956, pp. 472-486.

Antonelli, M. *La política fiscal y del desarrollo económico.* Thesis, Facultad de Ciencias Económicas de la Universidad, Buenos Aires, 1958, 223pp.

Aubrey, H. "The role of the state in

1

economic development," *American economic review, papers and proceedings,* vol. 41, May 1951, pp. 266-273.

Baer, W., and Kerstenetzky, I. (eds.). *Inflation and growth in Latin America.* Published for the Economic Growth Center, Yale University, by Richard D. Irwin, Inc., Homewood, Ill., 1964, pp. 482-508.

Barrère, A. "Structure fiscale et développement économique," *Colectânea de estudos,* no. 15, 1962, pp. 67-171. Also in: *Economia e finanças,* vol. 29, no. 3, 1961, pp. 954-1060.

Bauer, P. *Economic analysis and policy in underdeveloped countries.* Duke University Press, Durham, N. C., 1957, chapter 3.

Bauer, P. "Lewis' theory of economic growth: A review article," *American economic review,* vol. 46, September 1956, pp. 637-638.

Bauer, P., and Yamey, B. *The economics of underdeveloped countries.* University of Chicago Press, Chicago, 1962, chapters 11, 13.

Bernstein, E. "Financing economic growth in underdeveloped economies." In: W. Heller (ed.), *Savings in the modern economy.* University of Minnesota Press, Minneapolis, Minn., 1953.

Bernstein, E. "General problems of financing development programs," *Journal of finance,* vol. 12, May 1957, pp. 167-177.

Bloch, H. "Economic development and public finance." In: B. Hoselitz (ed.), *The progress of underdeveloped areas,* pp. 248-258. University of Chicago Press, Chicago, 1952.

Bloch, H. "Finances publiques et développement économique: La Politique fiscale des pays sous-développés," *Revue de science et de législation financières,* vol. 45, 1953, pp. 5-17.

Bloch, H. "The relation of tax policy to economic growth." In: Tax Institute of America, Inc., *The limits of taxable capacity,* pp. 171-182. Princeton, N.J., 1953.

Blough, R. *Taxation and economic development.* Paper presented before the first Annual Conference of Executives of the Peruvian Institute of Business Administration at Paracas, Peru, 16 September 1961, 7pp. (mimeo).

Borkar, V. *Public finance and full employment with special reference to underdeveloped areas.* University of Bombay Publications, Economic Series No. 9, Vora and Co., Bombay, 1959, vi/179pp.

Borkar, V. "Public finance and full employment (with special reference to underdeveloped systems)," *Journal of the University of Bombay,* vol. 24, January 1956, pp. 37-38.

Brahmananda, P. "Towards an optimal tax policy in retrogressive economy," *Journal of the University of Bombay,* vol. 23, July 1954, pp. 1-27.

Buchanan, N., and Ellis, H. *Approaches to economic development.* Twentieth Century Fund, New York, 1955, chapter 15.

Burchardt, F. "Some aspects of fiscal policy in a period of economic development." In: Ministry of National Planning, *Conference papers on current economic problems of Burma 1951.* Rangoon, 1951.

Butter, J. "Problems of colonial financial policy," *East African economics review,* vol. 2, July 1955, pp. 24-38.

Carson, C. "Financing Latin American industrialization." In: A. Whitaker (ed.), *Inter-American affairs, 1943.* New York, 1944.

Chelliah, R. *Fiscal policy in underdeveloped countries with special reference to India.* Allen & Unwin, London, 1960.

Claro Valdes, R. *La política fiscal y el desarrollo económico.* Editorial Universitaria, S.A., Santiago, 1959, 186pp.

Cole, D. "Problems of measuring the incidence of the tax system." In: Joint Legislative-Executive Tax Commission (Philippines), *Taxation and socio-economic growth,* pp. 122-129. Manila, 1960.

Colin, J. "Política económica y política fiscal," *Revista de economía* (México), vol. 12, February 1949, pp. 52-54.

Coombs, H. "Economic development and financial stability," *Economic record,* November 1955.

Cramer, D. *The relationship between monetary, fiscal, and external policies and their effects upon income and prices in Latin America.* Ph.D. thesis, Louisiana State University, Baton Rouge, La., 1958.

Czarkowski, J. "Some aspects of financing economic growth in underdeveloped countries," *Folia oeconomica cracovi-ensia*, vol. 1, no. 4, 1962 (Polish text, English and Russian summaries).

Davin, L. "De l'impôt propulseur de croissance," *Economie appliquée*, vol. 12, July-September 1959.

Davis, T. *La inflación y las finanzas públicas*. Trabajo presentado en la Primera Jornada de Estudios Fiscales, Santiago, June 1957.

De Carbon, L. "Financement interne et financement externe des pays en voie de développement," *Revue de science financière*, vol. 53, 1961, pp. 83-99.

Dehem, R. "Le Rôle des finances publiques dans la croissance économique," *Cahiers économiques de Bruxelles*, no. 8, October 1960.

Delors, J. "Politique des revenus et stratégie du développement," *Revue d'économie politique*, vol. 75, no. 3, May-June 1965.

"Design of fiscal policy for increasing government saving," *Economic bulletin for Asia and the Far East*, vol. 13, December 1962, pp. 27-49.

De Vries, E. "Financial aspects of economic development." In: United Nations, *Formulation and economic appraisal of development projects*, vol. 1, pp. 273-415. Sales No. 1951.II.B.4, New York, 1951.

Dischamps, J. "Le Problème du financement du développement économique," *Annales africaines*, no. 2, 1962, pp. 337-346.

Ducros, B. "Dépenses publiques, formation et emploi des révenues en pays sous-développés," *Revue économique de Madagascar*, January-July 1966, pp. 45-60.

Due, J. *Policy for financing economic development*. Paper presented at the Second Inter-regional Seminar on Development Planning sponsored by the United Nations Department of Economic and Social Affairs, 1966. Part reprinted in: R. Bird and O. Oldman (eds.), *Readings on taxation in developing countries*, pp. 33-43. The Johns Hopkins Press, Baltimore, revised edition, 1967.

Ellis, H. "The financing of economic development in underdeveloped areas," *Indian economic journal*, vol. 3, January 1956, pp. 256-268.

Enke, S. *Economics for development*. Prentice-Hall, Inc., Englewood Cliffs, N.J., 1964, chapter 13.

Farer, T. (ed.). *Financing African development*. The MIT Press, Cambridge, Mass., 1965.

Fisher, F. *Tax reform in Latin America*. United States Agency for International Development, Bureau of Latin American Affairs, Washington, 1962. Supplement, 1962.

Fitts, N. "The role of the Alliance for progress in Latin American tax policies." In: Tax Institute of America, Inc., *Tax policy and United States investment in Latin America*, pp. 217-232. Princeton, N.J., 1963.

Fliegers, S. "The financing of Latin America's economic development," *Journal of international affairs*, vol. 9, 1955, p. 56.

Gerelli, E. "Analisi degli aspetti fiscali delle politiche stabilizzatrici nei paesi sottosviluppati," *Politica degli scambi*, vol. 3, no. 13, January-February 1963, pp. 5-28; vol. 3, no. 14, March-April 1963, pp. 5-21.

Gerelli, E. "Politiche fiscali e commercio estero dei paesi sottosviluppati," *Giornale degli economisti e annali de economia*, vol. 19, nos. 9-10, September-October 1960; vol. 19, nos. 11-12, November-December 1960.

Ghosh, A. "Fiscal problem of growth with stability," *Calcutta review*, January 1959, pp. 21-56. Also reprinted by Calcutta University Press, Calcutta, 1959, 56pp.

Ghosh, A. "Stability and fiscal policy in underdeveloped countries," *Indian economic journal*, vol. 3, April 1956, pp. 373-393.

Ghosh, S. "Counter-inflationary fiscal, monetary and direct control measures in an underdeveloped country," *Public finance*, vol. 14, 1959, pp. 151-162.

Gill, P. "Future taxation policy in independent East Africa," *East African economics review*, vol. 9, June 1962, pp. 1-15.

Gini, C. "Dificultades financieras y evolución económica," *Económica* (Buenos Aires), vol. 1, July-September 1954, pp. 33-48.

Giorgetti, A. "Politica tributaria e sviluppo economico," *Risparmio*, vol. 9, no. 12, December 1961, pp. 2408-2419.

Goode, R. "Taxation and economic development," *Proceedings of the National tax association 1953*, vol. 46, pp. 225-236.

Goode, R. "La tributación y el desarrollo económico," *Boletín del Banco central del Ecuador*, vol. 29, January-February 1956, pp. 342-343.

Guchtengere, A. de, and Degrege, G. "La Formation intérieure de resources financières dans le développement économique," *Industria* (Milan), vol. 11, December 1957, pp. 749-755.

Guésé, P. "Méthode d'analyse des conséquences économiques de la fiscalité et règles particulières aux territoires sous-développés," *Public finance*, vol. 10, 1955, pp. 178-211.

Habbu, R. "Role of financial and fiscal measures in economic planning," *Indian journal of economics*, vol. 32, April 1952, pp. 421-432.

Hamza, S. "Taxation vs. direct controls in underdeveloped countries," *Égypte contemporain*, vol. 53, no. 309, July 1962, pp. 5-18.

Harberger, A. "Aspectos de una reforma tributaria en América Latina," *Economía latinoamericana*, November 1963, pp. 127-149.

Harberger, A. "Issues of tax reform for Latin America." In: Joint Tax Program, Organization of American States, Inter-American Development Bank, and Economic Commission for Latin America, *Fiscal policy for economic growth in Latin America*, pp. 110-134. Published for The Joint Tax Program by The Johns Hopkins Press, Baltimore, 1965.

Hart, A. *Fiscal policy in Latin America*. Paper presented at Conference on Key Problems of Economic Policy in Latin America, University of Chicago, Chicago, Ill., 1966, 56pp. (duplicated).

Hicks, U. "Financial responsibility and self government: Problems of maturing colonies," *The banker*, vol. 106, October 1956, pp. 629-636. Also in: *Journal of African administration*, vol. 9, October 1957, pp. 196-199.

Hicks, U. *Public finance*. James Nisbet & Co. Ltd. and Cambridge University Press, London, 1955, chapter 18.

Hicks, U. "The search for revenue in underdeveloped countries," *Revue de science et de législation financières*, vol. 44, 1952, pp. 6-43.

Higgins, B. *Economic development*. W. W. Norton & Co., New York, 1959, chapters 19-24.

Higgins, B. "Políticas de estabilización en los paises subdesarrollados," *El trimestre económico*, vol. 26, January-March 1959, pp. 103-123.

Higgins, B., and Malenbaum, W. "Financing economic development," *International conciliation*, no. 502, March 1955, pp. 275-339.

Hooley, R. "Tax policy and private business investment." In: Joint Legislative-Executive Tax Commission (Philippines), *Taxation and socio-economic growth*, pp. 114-121. Manila, 1960.

Inter-American Council of Commerce and Production. *Modalidades del momento en materia de política fiscal*. Montevideo, 1947, 72pp.

Iversen, C. "Fiscal policy in underdeveloped countries." In: Institut International de Finances Publiques, *Stabilité financière intérieure et balance des paiements*. Paris, 1955.

Jevons, H. "The finance of economic development," *Indian journal of economics*, vol. 2, November 1919, pp. 564-608.

Jha, D. "Fiscal policy and the economic development of under-developed countries," *Indian journal of economics*, vol. 37, July 1956, pp. 75-98.

Kahn, R. "The pace of development." In: *The challenge of development*. Hebrew University, Jerusalem, 1958.

Kaldor, N. "The role of taxation in economic development." In: Joint Tax Program, Organization of American States, Inter-American Development Bank, and Economic Commission for Latin America, *Fiscal policy for economic growth in Latin America*, pp. 70-86. Published for The Joint Tax Program by The Johns Hopkins Press, Baltimore, 1965.

Kaldor, N. *The theory of economic development and its implications on economic and fiscal policy*. Lecciones dadas en el Curso de Capacitiación de la CEPAL, 1956 (mimeo).

Kaldor, N. "Will underdeveloped countries learn to tax?" *Foreign affairs*, vol. 41, no. 2, January 1963, pp. 410-419.

Kalecki, M. "The problem of financing economic development," *Indian econo-*

mic review, vol. 2, February 1955, pp. 1-22

Kindleberger, C. *Economic development.* McGraw-Hill, Inc., New York, 2nd edition, 1964, chapter 11.

Kinoshita, K. "The role of fiscal policy in the economic development of backward countries," *Osaka economic papers,* September 1958, pp. 14-30.

Krause, W. *Economic development.* Wadsworth Publishing Company, Inc., San Francisco, 1961, pp. 213-224.

Krivine, D. (ed.). *Fiscal and monetary problems in developing states.* Frederick A. Praeger, New York, 1967, 404pp.

Kulkarni, N. "The role of fiscal and financial measures in relation to planning," *Indian journal of economics,* vol. 32, January 1952, pp. 225-236.

Kurihara, K. "Capital theory, corporate taxation, and capacity expansion," *Kyklos,* vol. 19, no. 2, 1966, pp. 219-230.

Kurihara, K. "The fiscal role of government in economic development," *Indian journal of economics,* vol. 37, July 1956, pp. 39-47.

Leaming, G. "Taxation and economic growth in a developing area: The example of Latin America," *Arizona review of business and public administration,* vol. 12, June 1963, pp. 10-17.

Lecaillon, J. "Problèmes économiques et financiers de l'Amérique Latine," *Revue de science financière,* vol. 53, 1961, p. 664.

Leduc, G. "Aperçus sur la situation des finances publiques dans les états africains d'expression française," *Pénant: Revue de droit des pays l'Afrique,* vol. 75, 1965, pp. 447-456.

Lewis, S., Jr. *Taxation and growth in the dual economy: An evaluation of tax devices in under-developed countries.* Ph.D. thesis, Stanford University, Stanford, Calif., 1963.

Lewis, W. *The theory of economic growth.* Richard D. Irwin, Inc., Homewood, Ill., 1955, pp. 396-408.

Lim, T. "Redistribution of income in underdeveloped territories." In: A. Peacock (ed.), *Income distribution and social policy,* pp. 268-290. Jonathan Cape, London, 1954.

Lindholm, R. "Accelerated development with a minimum of foreign aid and eco-nomic controls," *Social and economic studies,* vol. 9, March 1960, pp. 57-67.

Malhotra, M. *The finance of underdeveloped countries.* Suneja Book Centre, New Delhi, 1954, 61pp.

Malkani, H. "The role of fiscal and financial measures in economic planning," *Indian journal of economics,* vol. 32, January 1952, pp. 249-256.

Mapa, P., Jr. *Development financing in a developing economy.* Ph.D. thesis, Harvard University, Cambridge, Mass., 1962.

Martner G., G. *Significado y funciones de la política fiscal en un país subdesarrollado.* Trabajo presentado en la Primera Jornada de Estudios Fiscales, Santiago, June 1957.

Masoin, M. "La política fiscal más apropiada en países en desarrollo." In: Asociación Argentina de Estudios de Derecho Fiscal, *Jornadas internacionales de derecho fiscal,* pp. 121-161. Depalma, Buenos Aires, 1961.

Matthai, J. "Public finance and development," *Indian journal of economics,* vol. 5, July 1924, pp. 31-37.

Matus R., C. *Análisis de algunos problemas de teoría y política fiscal.* Thesis, Santiago, 1955.

Matus R., C. "Política fiscal en países desarrollados," *Economía* (Santiago), vol. 18, 1958, pp. 37-48.

Matus R., C. *Política fiscal y desarrollo económico.* Ministerio de Hacienda, Santiago, 1957, 13pp.

Matus R., C. "Teoría y política fiscal," *Economía* (Santiago), vol. 15, April 1955, pp. 1-14.

"Measures for mobilizing domestic saving for productive investment," *Economic bulletin for Asia and the Far East,* vol. 13, December 1962, pp. 1-26.

Meier, G., and Baldwin, R. *Economic development.* John Wiley & Sons, Inc., New York, 1957, pp. 383-391.

Melady, T., Jr. *Taxation as factor in development of underdeveloped countries.* Abstract of dissertation, Catholic University of America Press, Washington, 1954, 14pp.

"Memorandum supplied for the record on tax reform in Latin America since the act of Bogotá." In: United States Congress, House of Representatives, Committee on Foreign Affairs, *Hearings on* the foreign assistance act of 1962, 87th Congress, 2d Session, pp. 473-504. Washington, 1962.

Misra, J. "The role of taxation in economic planning," *Indian journal of economics,* vol. 32, January 1952, pp. 237-248.

"Mobilization of domestic resources for economic development and the financial institutions in the ECAFE region," *Economic bulletin for Asia and the Far East,* vol. 1, August 1950, pp. 20-28.

Moscarella, J. "Aspects fiscaux du développement économique de l'Amérique Centrale," *Revue de science financière,* vol. 49, 1957, pp. 450-474.

Naqvi, N. "Role of finance in relation to economic development," *Federal economic review* (Pakistan), January-July 1958, pp. 11-19.

Natarajan, V. "Fiscal policy as an instrument of planning," *Mysore economic review,* vol. 41, June-July 1955, pp. 3-4.

Nathan, R. "Taxation as a tool for development." In: Middle East Institute, *Developmental revolution,* pp. 213-225. Washington, 1963.

Navarrete, A., Jr. "Los problemas del desarrollo económico y su financiamiento en la Décima conferencia interamericana de Caracas," *Investigación económica,* vol. 14, no. 3, 1954, pp. 365-372.

Navarrete, I. de. "El proceso de desarrollo económico y la política fiscal," *Investigación económica,* vol. 15, no. 2, 1955, pp. 229-247.

Nurkse, R. *Problems of capital formation in underdeveloped countries.* Oxford University Press, New York, 1957, pp. 99-103, 142-152.

Nusbaumer, J. "Tax measures to stimulate monetization of the subsistence sector in developing countries," *Finanzarchiv,* vol. 26, no. 1, March 1967, pp. 8-48.

Ojha, P. "Taxable capacity in a developing economy," *Indian economic journal,* vol. 2, January 1955, pp. 263-273.

Ojha, P. "Taxable capacity in underdeveloped countries," *Journal of the University of Bombay,* vol. 24, July 1955, pp. 22-41.

Pal, S. "Some aspects of monetary and fiscal policies for economic growth in underdeveloped countries," *Indian jour-*

nal of economics, vol. 37, July 1956, pp. 125-137.

Panikkar, K. "Fiscal policy and partial planning in underdeveloped countries," *Indian journal of economics,* vol. 32, January 1952, pp. 193-206.

Parizeau, J. "Le Problème du financement intérieur." In: G. Balandier (ed.), *Le Tiers monde: Sous développement et développement,* pp. 305-330. Presses Universitaires de France, Paris, 1956.

Pathak, H. "Towards an optimum tax system and economic development," *Vidya,* vol. 1, 1956, pp. 34-40.

Patil, R. "Planning and fiscal and monetary action," *Indian journal of economics,* vol. 32, January 1952, pp. 269-278.

Peacock, A. *Analytical concepts of fiscal policy with special reference to developed countries.* Centro de Estudios de Estadística Económica, Lisbon, 1962.

Peacock, A. "Fiscal policy for economic development in theory and practice." In: A. Peacock (ed.), *Public finance as an instrument for economic development,* pp. 7-17. Organisation for Economic Co-operation and Development, Paris, 1965.

Peacock, A. (ed.). *Public finance as an instrument for economic development.* Organisation for Economic Co-operation and Development, Paris, 1965, 112pp.

Pinto S.C., A. "Fines y medios de la política fiscal en los paises poco desarrollados," *Panorama económico* (Santiago), vol. 8, no. 106, August 1954, pp. 554-558. Also in: *El trimestre económico,* vol. 21, April-June 1954, pp. 185-194.

Please, S. "Saving through taxation— Reality or mirage?" *Finance and development,* vol. 4, March 1967, pp. 24-32.

"Política tributaria en Centroamérica," *El trimestre económico,* vol. 24, January-March 1957, pp. 33-67.

Prakash, O. "Taxation policy in a transitional economy," *Indian journal of economics,* vol. 37, July 1956, pp. 3-14.

Prebisch, R. "Economic development or monetary stability: The false dilemma," *Economic bulletin for Latin America,* vol. 6, March 1961, pp. 1-25.

Prest, A. "The fiscal structure of underdeveloped countries," *Colectânea de estudos*, no. 12, 1961, pp. 9-111.

Prest, A. "El papel de las finanzas públicas en el desarrollo," *Etudes*, vol. 283, September 1954, pp. 13-26.

Ray, N. "The role of taxation in planned economic development," *Asian economic review*, vol. 1, November 1959, pp. 79-89.

Remba, O. "Public finance and private enterprise in the Middle East," *Middle Eastern affairs*, vol. 10, no. 12, December 1959, pp. 382-393.

Reviglio, F. "Social security: A means of savings mobilization for economic development," *International monetary fund staff papers*, vol. 14, July 1967, pp. 324-365.

Ruiz Novoa, A. "Las finanzas públicas y su relación con el desarrollo económico," *Economía colombiana*, vol. 7, October 1955, pp. 53-62.

Sáenz, J. "El principio de lucrecio, o algunos aspectos monetarios y fiscales del desarrollo," *El trimestre económico*, vol. 25, October-December 1958, pp. 621-637.

Salinas Lozano, R. "Política fiscal y desarrollo económico," *Investigación económica*, vol. 12, no. 2, 1952, pp. 152-166.

Sánchez Masi, L. "Estrategia de la política fiscal del desarrollo," *Investigación económica*, vol. 24, no. 95, 1964, pp. 43-62.

Sant'Ana e Silva, S. de. "A política fiscal e o desenvolvimento econômico," *Revista do serviço público*, vol. 18, February 1955, pp. 231-244.

Sant'Ana e Silva, S. de. "Política fiscal dos países subdesenvolvidos," *Revista do serviço público*, vol. 16, June 1953, pp. 11-15.

Saper, J., and Sweeney, T. "The fiscal problems of less developed countries," *Finance and development*, vol. 2, December 1965, pp. 230-235.

Schenk, W. "Tecnología, formación de capital y política fiscal gubernamental," *Economía salvadoreña*, vol. 4, 1954, pp. 141-149.

Schlesinger, E. *The role of assigned tax revenues in a development program*. Report No. EC-25, International Bank for Reconstruction and Development, Washington, 12 January 1954, 7pp. (mimeo).

Schlesinger, E. *Taxation and economic progress in primary-producing countries*. Ph.D. thesis, Harvard University, Cambridge, Mass., 1950.

Schmölders, G. "A theory of incentive taxation in the process of economic development," *Il politico*, vol. 31, no. 4, December 1966, pp. 788-800.

Sethi, J. "Fiscal policy and economic development—A perspective," *Indian economic journal*, vol. 8, October 1960, pp. 126-146.

Shoup, C. "Taxes and economic development," *Finanzarchiv*, vol. 25, no. 3, November 1966.

Singer, H. "Financing economic development programs," *Revista brasilera de economía*, September 1950.

Singh, B. "Some aspects of fiscal policy in underdeveloped economies," *Indian journal of economics*, vol. 38, July 1957, pp. 83-88.

Slesinger, R. "Fiscal policy considerations for underdeveloped countries," *Kyklos*, vol. 15, no. 3, 1962, pp. 624-634.

"Some financial aspects of development programmes in Asian countries," *Economic bulletin for Asia and the Far East*, vol. 3, November 1952, pp. 1-12.

Somers, H. "Problemas fiscales de paises en desarrollo," *Impuestos*, vol. 23, 1965, pp. 201-214.

Sommerfeld, R. "Tax reform and the Alliance for progress," *Iowa business digest*, vol. 33, August 1962, pp. 22-30.

Sommerfeld, R. *Tax reform and the Alliance for progress*. Published for the Institute of Latin America Studies by the University of Texas Press, Austin, Texas, 1966, xiv/217pp.

"Sources of financing Latin American foreign investment and economic development," *Inter-American bar association 11th conference*. Miami, 1959.

Stammer, D. "British colonial public finance," *Social and economic studies*, vol. 16, June 1967, pp. 191-205.

"Statement of conclusions XXth congress of the international chamber of commerce—Report on fiscal conditions for economic growth, presented to the congress," *Bulletin for international fiscal documentation*, vol. 19, 1965, pp. 289-293.

Stevenson, C. "La financiación del desarrollo económico en los territorios no autónomos," *Mundo financiero,* vol. 10, 1955, pp. 13-15.

Stewart, E. *Developing a theory of optimum taxation for underdeveloped countries.* Ph.D. thesis, Columbia University, New York, 1962.

Tarantino, J. *Finanzas públicas y desarrollo económico.* Ediar Soc. Anon. Editores, Buenos Aires, 1961.

"Tax reforms needed in Latin America," *Comments on Argentine trade,* vol. 40, 1960, p. 77.

"Taxation and economic development," *State bank of Pakistan bulletin,* December 1956, pp. 14-18.

"Taxation and economic development—A summary of the discussion of an ECAFE working party, in September 1953," *Central bank of Ceylon bulletin,* November 1953, p. 10.

"Taxation and economic development in Asian countries," *Economic bulletin for Asia and the Far East,* vol. 4, November 1953, pp. 1-15. Reprinted in: H. Wald and J. Froomkin (eds.), *Papers and proceedings of the conference on agricultural taxation and economic development,* pp. 86-109. Harvard Law School International Program in Taxation, Cambridge, Mass., 1954.

Tixier, G. "Les Finances publiques et la politique budgétaire des états de l'Afrique de l'Ouest," *Pénant: Revue de droit des pays l'Afrique,* vol. 72, 1962, pp. 205-217.

Tixier, G. "La Politique budgétaire des états de l'Afrique de l'Ouest," *Annales africaines,* no. 1, 1962, pp. 256-266.

Tixier, G. "La Politique budgétaire des états de l'Afrique de l'Ouest," *Pénant: Revue de droit des pays l'Afrique,* vol. 73, 1963, pp. 315-325.

United Nations. *Domestic financing of economic development.* Sales No. 1951.II.B.1, New York, 1951, pp. 6-8, 26-39.

United Nations. "A draft report on programme of revenue analysis and on problems of revenue policy relating to economic development in Latin America." Prepared by H. Bloch, 1954, 103pp. (duplicated).

United Nations. *Measures for the economic development of under-developed countries.* Sales No. 1951.II.B.2, New York, May 1951, pp. 38-40.

United Nations. *Methods of financing economic development in under-developed countries.* Sales No. 1949.II.B.4, New York, 1949, pp. 14-18, 27-28, 84-93, 118-119, 134-135.

United Nations. *Mobilization of domestic capital.* Sales No. 1953.II.F.4, Bangkok, 1953, pp. 4-6, 38-41, 49-50, 135-138.

United Nations. *Mobilization of domestic capital in certain countries of Asia and the Far East.* Sales No. 1951.II.F.3, Bangkok, 1951, pp. 68-70, 230-239.

United Nations. *Mobilization of domestic capital: Report and documents of the first working party of experts.* Sales No. 1953.II.F.2, Bangkok, 1952, pp. 32-37, 48-49, 66-67.

United Nations. *Taxes and fiscal policy in under-developed countries.* Sales No. 1955.II.H.1, New York, 1954, 123pp. Part reprinted in: R. Bird and O. Oldman (eds.), *Readings on taxation in developing countries.* The Johns Hopkins Press, Baltimore, 1964, pp. 3-30; revised edition, 1967, pp. 5-32.

United Nations. *World economic survey, 1957.* Sales No. 1958.II.C.1, New York, 1958, pp. 95-101.

United Nations. *World economic survey, 1965.* Sales No. 1966.II.C.3, New York, 1966, Part I.

United Nations, Department of Economic Affairs. "Methods of increasing domestic savings." 1949.

United Nations, Economic Commission for Asia and the Far East. "Taxation as an instrument of development policy." 1953.

United Nations, Fiscal and Financial Branch, Department of Economic and Social Affairs. "An introductory note on a methodology for revenue forecasting in developing countries." Doc. No. IBRW.1/L.10, 20 August 1964, 7pp. (mimeo).

United Nations, Fiscal and Financial Branch, Department of Economic and Social Affairs. "Tax revenue forecasting in developing countries." Doc. No. E/CN.11/BRW.4/L.12, 1966, 24pp. (mimeo).

United Nations, Fiscal Division, Department of Economic Affairs. "Some aspects of the tax systems in certain ECAFE countries in relation to economic development." Doc. No.

ECAFE/I & T/FED.2/6, 11 October 1954.

Urquidi, V. "El papel de la política fiscal y monetaria en el desarrollo económico," *El trimestre económico,* vol. 18, October-December 1951.

Urrutia Mandez, L. "La política fiscal y los modelos de crecimiento económico," *Investigación económica,* vol. 24, no. 95, 1964, pp. 429-440.

Valdés-Costa, R. "Tendances actuelles de la politique fiscale en Amérique Latine," *Revue de science financière,* vol. 56, 1964, pp. 47-66.

Vankudre, S. "The role of fiscal policy in economic planning," *Indian journal of economics,* vol. 32, January 1952, pp. 207-224.

Wai, U. "Taxation problems and policies of underdeveloped countries," *International monetary fund staff papers,* vol. 9, November 1962, pp. 428-445.

Wallich, H. "Fiscal policy and the budget." In: S. Harris (ed.), *Economic problems of Latin America.* New York, 1944.

3
COMPARATIVE TAX STRUCTURES

Abdel-Rahman, A. "The revenue structure of the CFA (Communauté financière africaine)," *International monetary fund staff papers,* vol. 12, no. 1, March 1965, pp. 73-116.

Berolzheimer, J. *Problems of international comparisons of public finance.* International Cooperation Administration, Washington, 149pp. (duplicated).

Brochier, H. "Structures nationales et systèmes fiscaux," *Revue de science et de législation financières,* vol. 44, 1952, pp. 171-192.

"Les Budgets des états d'Afrique Équatoriale (exercice 1961)," *Banque centrale des états de l'Afrique Équatoriale et du Cameroun bulletin mensuel,* vol. 56, April 1961, pp. 177-189.

Burns, A. *Comparative economic organization.* Prentice-Hall, Inc., New York, 1955, pp. 691-702.

Commerce Clearing House, Inc., Tax Research Department. *Tax systems.* New York, 13th edition, 1952, 522pp.

Crockett, J. "Tax pattern in Latin America," *National tax journal,* vol. 15, March 1962, pp. 93-104. Reprinted in: R. Bird and O. Oldman (eds.), *Readings on taxation in developing countries,* pp. 153-168. The Johns Hopkins Press, Baltimore, 1964.

Desai, R. "La capacidad fiscal de los paises en desarrollo," *Información,* vol. 37, 1966, pp. 147-178.

Drachsler, M. "Latin American investment climate: A comparative survey of legal and economic features," *International markets,* January 1954, p. 19.

Due, J. "Collecting taxes south of the Sahara: Eight African revenue systems," *Challenge,* vol. 12, October 1963, pp. 8-11.

Due, J. *Taxation and economic development in Tropical Africa.* The MIT Press, Cambridge, Mass., 1963, 172pp.

Ehrhard, J. *Finances publiques d'outre-mer.* Eyrolles, Paris, 1960, 264pp.

Ferreisa, R., and Costillo, L. *Estudio comparado de legislación sobre impuestos en América.* Asociación Comercio, Peru, 2 volumes, n.d.

"Finances publiques des pays africains," *Bulletin économique pour l'Afrique,* vol. 1, no. 2, June 1961, pp. 1-29.

Foosaner, S. "Contrasting systems of Latin American taxation," *Inter-American bar association 10th conference.* Buenos Aires, 1958.

Foosaner, S. "Taxes, around the world," *Inter-American bar association 12th conference,* pp. 152-163. 1963.

Ford, E. "Practical aspects of taxation in Latin America," *Taxes,* vol. 18, 1941, p. 539.

"Government budgets of Middle East countries," *Quarterly bulletin of economic development,* no. 13. United Nations Relief and Works Agency for Palestine Refugees, Beirut, 1956, 333pp. (mimeo).

Hailey, W. *An African survey.* Oxford University Press, London, 1957.

Heckerling, P. "Latin American tax systems," *Kentucky law journal,* vol. 52, 1964, pp. 609-630.

Hinrichs, H. "Determinants of government revenue shares among less-developed countries," *Economic journal,* vol. 75, September 1965, pp. 546-556.

Hinrichs, H. *A general theory of tax structure change during economic devel-*

opment. Harvard Law School International Tax Program, Cambridge, Mass., 1966, xvi/154pp. Part reprinted in: R. Bird and O. Oldman (eds.), *Readings on taxation in developing countries,* pp. 104-111. The Johns Hopkins Press, Baltimore, revised edition, 1967.

Hinrichs, H., and Bird, R. "Government revenue shares in developed and less developed countries," *Canadian tax journal,* vol. 11, 1963, pp. 431-437.

Institut International de Finances Publiques. *L'Importance et la structure des recettes et des dépenses publiques en fonction du développement économique.* Bruylant, Brussels, 1960, 348pp.

International Chamber of Commerce. *Taxation and developing nations.* Paris, 1959, 27pp.

Japan Tax Association. *Asian taxation 1965.* Tokyo, 1966, 148pp.

Kurowski, L. "Les Finances dans les états socialistes," *Revue de science financière,* vol. 53, 1961, pp. 597-663.

Lecaillon, J. "Le Financement des pays sous-développés (l'exemple des territoires dépendant des pays membres de l'OECE)," *Revue de science et de législation financières,* vol. 44, 1952, pp. 408-423.

Lewis, S., Jr. "Government revenue from foreign trade: An international comparison," *Manchester school,* vol. 31, January 1963, pp. 36-45.

Martin, A., and Lewis, W. "Patterns of public revenue and expenditure," *Manchester school,* vol. 24, September 1956, pp. 203-232. Reprinted in: R. Bird and O. Oldman (eds.), *Readings on taxation in developing countries.* The Johns Hopkins Press, Baltimore, 1964, pp. 91-115; revised edition, 1967, pp. 71-95.

Musgrave, R. *Fiscal systems.* Yale University Press, New Haven, Conn., forthcoming.

"1963 South and Central American taxes," *Foreign tax law weekly bulletin,* vol. 14, no. 20, 1963, pp. 4-7.

Pan American Union. *Financing of economic development in Latin America.* Washington, 1958, 343pp.

Pan American Union, Division of Economic Research. *Fiscal receipts, expenditures, budgets and public debts of Latin American republics.* Washington, 1954, 180pp.

Plasschaert, S. *Taxable capacity in developing countries.* Report No. EC-103, International Bank for Reconstruction and Development, Washington, February 1962, 59pp. (mimeo).

Prest, A. *A fiscal survey of the British Caribbean.* H.M. Stationery Office, London, 1957.

"Public finance." In: United Nations, *Review of economic conditions in the Middle East, 1951-52,* pp. 73-83. Sales No. 1953.II.C.1, New York, 1953.

"Public finance in African countries," *Economic bulletin for Africa,* vol. 1, June 1961, pp. 1-28.

Siddiqi, S. *Public finance in Islam.* Muhammenad Ashraf, Lahore, 1958, 242pp.

"Tableau des principaux impôts en vigueur le 31 décembre 1965 dans les pays de l'Afrique Équatoriale," *Problèmes d'outre-mer,* 1 March 1966, pp. 1-12.

Tanigawa, K. "Asiatic characteristics in taxation system," *Asian affairs,* vol. 2, 1957, pp. 385-397.

Tanzi, V., and McCustion, G. "Determinants of government revenue shares among less-developed countries: A comment," *Economic journal,* vol. 77, June 1967.

"Tax potential and economic growth in the countries of the ECAFE region," *Economic bulletin for Asia and the Far East,* vol. 17, September 1966, pp. 29-48. Reprinted in: R. Bird and O. Oldman (eds.), *Readings on taxation in developing countries,* pp. 96-103. The Johns Hopkins Press, Baltimore, revised edition, 1967.

Thorn, R. "The evolution of public finances during economic development," *Manchester school,* vol. 35, January 1967, pp. 19-53.

United Nations. *Economic survey of Asia and the Far East, 1960.* Sales No. 1961.II.F.1, Bangkok, 1961, Part II, pp. 53-119. Part reprinted in: R. Bird and O. Oldman (eds.), *Readings on taxation in developing countries,* pp. 116-152. The Johns Hopkins Press, Baltimore, 1964.

United Nations. *Economic survey of Europe in 1959.* Sales No. 1960.II.E.1, Geneva, 1960.

United Nations. *Economic survey of Latin America 1955.* Sales No. 1956.II.G.1, New York, 1956, pp. 111-176.

United Nations. *La política tributaria y el desarrollo económico en Centroamérica.* Sales No. 1957.II.G.9, New York, 1957, 152pp.

United Nations. *Special study on economic conditions and development in non-self-governing territories.* Sales No. 1952. VI.B.2, New York, 1952, 415pp.

United Nations, Committee on Information from Non-Self-Governing Territories. "The structure of tax revenue in non-self-governing territories." Doc. No. A/AC.35/L.161, 28 July 1954.

United Nations, Economic and Social Council, Fiscal Commission. "Review of fiscal developments, 1951-1952." Doc. No. E/CN.8/74, 16 December 1952, 42pp.

United Nations, Economic Commission for Asia and the Far East. "The tax structures in underdeveloped countries." 1954.

United Nations, Economic Commission for Latin America. "Derechos aduaneros y otros gravámenes y restricciones a la importación en países latinoamericanos, y sus niveles promedios de incidencia." Doc. No. E/CN.12/554, 21 March 1961, 75pp.

United Nations, Economic Commission for Latin America. "Estudio preliminar de las medidas gubernamentales que influyen en las inversiones privadas extranjeras en América Latina." Doc. No. E/CN.12/C.1/12/Add.1, 1959, 82pp.

United Nations, Economic Commission for Latin America. "Public finance development in Latin America." Doc. No. E/CN.12/217/Add.13, 15 April 1951, 75pp.

Wéralski, M. "La Pression fiscale dans les pays capitalistes et dans les pays socialistes," *Revue de science financière,* vol. 54, 1962, pp. 24-40.

Williamson, J. "Public expenditure and revenue: An international comparison," *Manchester school,* vol. 29, January 1961, pp. 43-56.

Yoingco, A., and Trinidad, R. *Fiscal systems and practices in Asian countries.* Frederick A. Praeger, New York, 1967.

4

INCOME TAXATION

Cosciani, C. "Los impuestos directos en los países en desarrollo." In: Asociación Argentina de Estudios de Derecho Fiscal, *Jornadas internacionales de derecho fiscal,* pp. 25-67. Depalma, Buenos Aires, 1961.

Cosciani, C. "Progressive taxation in underdeveloped countries," *Banca nazionale del lavoro quarterly review,* no. 55, December 1960, pp. 303-316.

Due, J. "The African personal tax," *National tax journal,* vol. 15, December 1962, pp. 385-398.

Due, J. "Income taxation in Tropical Africa," *British tax review,* July-August 1962, pp. 225-240; September-October 1962, pp. 368-376.

Eichelgruen, G. "Income tax in British colonies," *Economic journal,* vol. 58, March 1948, pp. 128-132. Also in: *Bulletin for international fiscal documentation,* vol. 2, 1948, pp. 175-179.

Fujita, S. "Political ceiling on income taxation," *Public finance,* vol. 16, 1961, pp. 183-198.

Gandolfi, A. "Réflexions sur l'impôt de capitation en Afrique noire," *Revue juridique et politique d'outre-mer,* vol. 16, no. 2, April-June 1962, pp. 235-262.

Goode, R. "A new method of taxing capital gains and losses." In: R. Bird and O. Oldman (eds.), *Readings on taxation in developing countries,* pp. 197-199. The Johns Hopkins Press, Baltimore, revised edition, 1967.

Goode, R. "Reconstruction of foreign tax systems," *Proceedings of the National tax association 1951,* vol. 44, pp. 212-222. Reprinted in: R. Bird and O. Oldman (eds.), *Readings on taxation in developing countries.* The Johns Hopkins Press, Baltimore, 1964, pp. 169-179; revised edition, 1967, pp. 121-131.

Hanson, H. "The income tax in South America," *Taxes,* vol. 14, 1936, p. 341.

Hicks, U. "Direct taxation and economic growth," *Oxford economic papers* (new series), vol. 8, October 1956, pp. 302-317.

Higgins, B. *Business taxation and regulation of profits in underdeveloped countries.* Unpublished paper, 1954, 11pp.

Irizarry y Puente, J. *Latin American business taxes.* Pan American Union, Washington, 1953, 256pp./supps.

Jetha, N. "Company taxation in East Africa," *British tax review,* January-February 1965, pp. 42-56.

Lassudrie-Duchêne, B., and Richet, O.

"Amortissement fiscal et formation du capital dans les économies en voie de développement," *Revue de science financière*, vol. 55, 1963, pp. 235-248.

Laufenburger, H. "La autonomía del derecho fiscal y el impuesto a las sociedades." In: Asociación Argentina de Estudios de Derecho Fiscal, *Jornadas internacionales de derecho fiscal*, pp. 163-198. Depalma, Buenos Aires, 1961.

Llaneza, J. "Theoretical and practical bases and problems of a progressive system of taxation," *Far Eastern law review*, vol. 7, March 1960, p. 652.

Morselli, E. (ed.). *Enquête sur l'imposition des revenus industriels, commerciaux et professionels*. Cedam Casa Editrice, Dr. A. Milani, Padova, 1954, 519pp.

Oldman, O., and Temple, R. "Comparative analysis of the taxation of married persons," *Stanford law review*, vol. 12, May 1960, pp. 585-605.

Organization of Petroleum Exporting Countries. *Taxation economics in crude production*. Geneva, 1965, 19pp.

Pepper, H. "Instant tax: An appraisal of enforcement methods with regard to current collection of direct taxes on income," *Bulletin for international fiscal documentation*, vol. 20, 1966, pp. 247-257, 323-332.

Polanyi, G. "The taxation of profits from Middle East oil production: Some implications for oil prices and taxation policy," *Economic journal*, vol. 76, December 1966, pp. 768-785.

Prest, A. "Corporate income taxation in Latin America." In: Joint Tax Program, Organization of American States, Inter-American Development Bank, and Economic Commission for Latin America, *Fiscal policy for economic growth in Latin America*, pp. 234-272. Published for The Joint Tax Program by The Johns Hopkins Press, Baltimore, 1965.

Shirley, D. "Income taxes for lesser developed nations?" *National tax journal*, vol. 12, September 1959, pp. 265-269.

Tanzi, V. "Personal income taxation in Latin America: Obstacles and possibilities," *National tax journal*, vol. 19, June 1966, pp. 156-162.

Tanzi, V., and Aschheim, J. "Saving, investment, and taxation in underdeveloped countries," *Kyklos*, vol. 18, no. 2, 1965, pp. 205-226.

United Nations. *Economic measures in favour of the family*. Sales No. 1952. IV.6, New York, 1952, 175pp.

United Nations, Commission on the Status of Women. "Tax legislation applicable to women." Doc. No. E/CN.6/344, 26 January 1959, 36pp.

United Nations, Economic and Social Council, Fiscal Commission. "Corporate tax problems." Doc. No. E/CN.8/66, 25 November 1953, 142pp. Part reprinted in: R. Bird and O. Oldman (eds.), *Readings on taxation in developing countries*. The Johns Hopkins Press, Baltimore, 1964, pp. 199-214; revised edition, 1967, pp. 139-154.

Yoingco, A., and Trinidad, R. "A comparative study of the individual income tax structures of selected Asian countries," *Philippine economic journal*, vol. 2, no. 2, 1963, pp. 132-168.

Young, A. "Depreciation and depletion, an inter-American comparison," *Taxes*, vol. 30, 1952, p. 298.

5

DIRECT TAXES ON EXPENDITURE AND WEALTH

Goode, R. "Taxation of savings and consumption in underdeveloped countries," *National tax journal*, vol. 14, December 1961, pp. 305-322. Reprinted in: R. Bird and O. Oldman (eds.), *Readings on taxation in developing countries*. The Johns Hopkins Press, Baltimore, 1964, pp. 259-280; revised edition, 1967, pp. 231-252.

Jarach, D. "Taxes on net wealth, inheritances, and gifts." In: Joint Tax Program, Organization of American States, Inter-American Development Bank, and Economic Commission for Latin America, *Fiscal policy for economic growth in Latin America*, pp. 197-233. Published for The Joint Tax Program by The Johns Hopkins Press, Baltimore, 1965.

Tanabe, N. "The taxation of net wealth," *International monetary fund staff papers*, vol. 14, March 1967, pp. 124-168. Part reprinted in: R. Bird and O. Oldman (eds.), *Readings on taxation in developing countries*, pp. 281-296. The

Johns Hopkins Press, Baltimore, revised edition, 1967.

Ugoh, S. "Income versus expenditure taxes in economic growth," *Nigerian journal of economic and social studies,* vol. 4, no. 3, November 1962.

6

SALES AND EXCISE TAXES

Borkar, V. "The role of indirect taxes in development planning," *Indian journal of economics,* vol. 32, January 1952, pp. 279-284.

Brochier, H. "Les Problèmes de l'impôt indirect dans les pays en voie de développement," *Revue de science financière,* vol. 57, 1965, pp. 369-385.

Dosser, D. "Indirect taxation and economic development." In: A. Peacock and G. Hauser (eds.), *Government finance and economic development,* pp. 127-142. Organisation for Economic Cooperation and Development, Paris, 1965.

Due, J. "Administrative criteria in the establishment of sales and excise structure." In: Joint Tax Program, Organization of American States, Inter-American Development Bank, Economic Commission for Latin America, *Problems of tax administration in Latin America,* pp. 412-436. Published for The Joint Tax Program by The Johns Hopkins Press, Baltimore, 1965.

Due, J. "Estructura y administración de la imposición sobre las ventas," *Investigación fiscal,* no. 19, July 1967, pp. 71-91.

Ghose, D. "The case for indirect taxation in underdeveloped countries," *Asian economic review,* vol. 2, May 1960, pp. 316-328.

Khatkhate, D. "Commodity taxation, deficit financing and inflationary pressures," *Economia internazionale,* vol. 16, no. 1, February 1963, pp. 53-60.

Masoin, M., and Morselli, E. (eds.). *Impôts sur transactions, transmissions et chiffre d'affaires.* Archives Internationales de Finances Publiques No. 2, Cedam Casa Editrice, Dr. A. Milani, Padova, 1959, 437pp.

Morag, A. *Indirect taxes, inflation, and development: A re-appraisal of indirect taxation in underdeveloped countries.* Ph.D. thesis, Johns Hopkins University, Baltimore, 1954.

Pepper, H. "General notes on turnover taxation, especially in respect of developing countries," *Bulletin for international fiscal documentation,* vol. 20, 1966, pp. 67-82, 103-114.

Rab, A. "Resources for economic development: Excise taxation in developing countries." In: A. Qureshi (ed.), *The third five year plan and other papers,* pp. 135-144. Pakistan Economic Association, Lahore, 1965.

United States Department of the Interior. *World retail prices and taxes on gasoline, kerosene, and motor lubricating oils, 1960.* Washington, 1961, 27pp.

7

TAXES ON FOREIGN TRADE

Due, J. "Customs, excise and export duties in Tropical Africa," *Canadian tax journal,* vol. 11, March 1963, pp. 142-150.

"Estructura de los impuestos sobre la exportación de café en Centroamérica." In: United Nations, Economic Commission for Latin America, *La política tributaria y el desarrollo económico en Centroamérica,* pp. 139-141. Sales No. 1957.II.G.9, New York, 1957.

Goode, R., Lent, G., and Ojha, P. "Role of export taxes in developing countries," *International monetary fund staff papers,* vol. 13, November 1966, pp. 453-503.

Jackson, F. "Political aspects of export taxation," *Public finance,* vol. 12, 1957, pp. 291-296.

Jacquot, M. "Les Aspects douaniers de l'association des pays africains et malgache a la C.E.E.," *Pénant: Revue de droit des pays l'Afrique,* vol. 74, 1964, pp. 331-344.

Kling, M. "Taxes on 'external' sector: An index of political behavior in Latin America?" *Midwestern journal of political science,* vol. 3, 1959, p. 127.

Korteweg, S. "Financing development through tariff revenue," *International development review,* vol. 6, no. 1, 1964, pp. 3-6.

Latin American Free Trade Association. *Derechos aduaneros y gravámenes de efectos equivalentes aplicables a la importación de mercaderías vigentes en los paises de la ALALC al 15 de abril de 1963.* Montevideo, May 1963 (mimeo).

Levin, J. *The export economies.* Harvard

University Press, Cambridge, Mass., 1960, chapters 6, 7. Part reprinted in: R. Bird and O. Oldman (eds.), *Readings on taxation in developing countries.* The Johns Hopkins Press, Baltimore, 1964, pp. 453-466; revised edition, 1967, pp. 341-354.

MacBean, A. *Export instability and economic development.* Harvard University Press, Cambridge, Mass., 1966, chapters 10, 11.

Marcus, E. "Countercyclical weapons for the open economy," *Journal of political economy,* vol. 62, December 1954, p. 499.

Mieszkowski, P. "The comparative efficiency of tariffs and other tax-subsidy schemes as a means of obtaining revenue or protecting domestic production," *Journal of political economy,* vol. 74, December 1966, pp. 587-599.

Nurkse, R. "Trade fluctuations and buffer policies of low-income countries," *Kyklos,* vol. 11, 1958, pp. 141-154, 244-265.

Reubens, E. "Commodity trade, export taxes and economic development," *Political science quarterly,* vol. 71, March 1956, pp. 42-70.

Rothwell, K. "Taxes on exports in underdeveloped countries," *Public finance,* vol. 18, nos. 3-4, November 1963, pp. 310-327.

Shere, L. *Sugar taxation in the Caribbean and Central American countries.* Pan American Union, Washington, December 1952.

Staley, C. *Export taxes, a problem in international trade and economic development.* Ph.D. thesis, Massachusetts Institute of Technology, Cambridge, Mass., 1956.

Staley, C. "Export taxes in Ceylon," *Public finance,* vol. 14, 1959, pp. 249-265.

8
TAX ASPECTS OF FOREIGN INVESTMENT

Aharoni, Y. *The foreign investment decision process.* Harvard University Graduate School of Business Administration, Division of Research, Boston, 1966, xvii/362pp.

American Management Association, International Management Division. *Taxation of business income from foreign operations.* AMA Management Report No. 2, New York, 1958, 203pp.

Baker, R. "International trade and investment: An imperfect alliance of taxation and policy," *Taxes,* vol. 31, 1953, p. 120.

Barlow, E., and Wender, I. *Foreign investment and taxation.* Harvard Law School International Program in Taxation, Cambridge, Mass., 1955, xxv/481pp.

Barnes, W., *et al.* "Tax factors affecting Latin American investment: A panel discussion," *Report of the proceedings of the inter-American investment conference,* pp. 185-220. New Orleans, 1955.

Blough, R. "General analyses of issues facing management." In: Tax Institute of America, Inc., *Taxation and operations abroad,* pp. 70-82. Princeton, N.J., 1960.

Brandon, M. "Legal deterrents and incentives to private foreign investments," *Grotius society,* vol. 43, 1957, pp. 39-60.

Brown, W. "Treaty, guaranty, and tax inducements for foreign investment," *American economic review, papers and proceedings,* vol. 40, May 1950.

Carroll, M. "Tax measures abroad to spur foreign trade and investments," *Commercial and financial chronicle,* vol. 178, 26 November 1953, p. 12.

Conference on legal problems of trade and investment in Latin America. Columbia University, New York, 1963, 295pp.

Dale, W. *Private United States venture capital for investment in newly developing countries.* International Development Center, Stanford Research Institute, Menlo Park, Calif., 1958, 29pp.

Diamond, W. "Economic problems of foreign trade and investment in underdeveloped countries," *Ohio state law journal,* vol. 17, 1956.

Diamond, W. *Tax laws of selected countries applicable to American enterprises.* Fallon Law Book Company, New York, 1954, 20pp. (mimeo).

Ecker-Racz, L. "Tax stimulants to foreign investment," *Proceedings of the National tax association 1949,* vol. 42, pp. 142-160. Also in: *New York university 8th institute on federal taxation,* 1949, p. 142.

Friedmann, W., and Pugh, R. (eds.). *Legal aspects of foreign investment.* Little, Brown & Co., Boston, 1959, 812pp.

Gal-Edd, I. *Relief of double taxation from the point of view of developing countries*. Lecture at the University of Copenhagen, Jerusalem, July 1967, 22pp. (mimeo).

Gibbons, W. *Tax factors in basing international business abroad*. Harvard Law School International Program in Taxation, Cambridge, Mass., 1957, 177pp.

Hellawell, R. "United States income taxation and less developed countries: A critical appraisal," *Columbia law review*, vol. 66, December 1966, pp. 1393-1427.

International Chamber of Commerce. *Avoidance of double taxation*. Paris, 1955, 35pp.

International Chamber of Commerce. *Settlement of difficulties and disputes arising out of double taxation agreements*. Paris, 1959, 19pp.

International Confederation of Free Trade Unions. *Foreign investments in economically underdeveloped countries*. Brussels, 1960, 108pp.

Irizarry y Puente, J. "Currency depreciation in Latin America—Its character and effect on foreign taxpayers," *Taxes*, vol. 33, 1955, pp. 52-67.

Juano, M. de. "Participación necesaria de los paises latinoamericanos en la celebración de tratados tributarios internacionales," *Juris*, vol. 26, 1965, pp. 371-386.

Kirk, M. "Formation and operation of foreign subsidiaries and branches, including the extent to which foreign subsidiaries are entitled to special treatment under the law of their incorporation or under international law," *International bar association conference report*, vol. 8, July 1960, p. 323.

Kuhn, R. "United States tax policy with respect to less developed countries," *George Washington law review*, vol. 32, December 1963, pp. 261-287.

Kust, M. "Tax treaties with underindustrialized countries." In: C. Shaw (ed.), *Legal problems in international trade and investment*, pp. 197-212. Oceana, Dobbs Ferry, N.Y., 1962.

Lachmann, K. "Foreign tax havens for Canadian business." In: Canadian Tax Foundation, *Report: 1957 conference*, pp. 135-146. Toronto, 1958.

"Laws and regulations affecting foreign investment in Asia and the Far East," *Economic bulletin for Asia and the Far East*, vol. 8, May 1957, pp. 1-7.

Littell, N. "Improvements in legal climate for investments abroad," *Virginia law review*, vol. 38, October 1952, pp. 729-744.

"Local tax consequences of forms of business organization." In: *Conference on legal problems of trade and investment in Latin America*, pp. 199-222. Columbia University, New York, 1963.

Marcus, E., and Marcus, M. *Investment and development possibilities in Tropical Africa*. Bookman Associates, New York, 1960, 286pp.

Mersan, C. "Medidas fiscales destinadas a facilitar las inversiones de capitales extranjeros," *Cahiers de droit fiscal international*, vol. 41, 1959, p. 289.

"Mesures unilatérales à éviter la double imposition, particulièrement en ce qui concerne les aspects fiscaux des relations entre pays exportateurs de capitaux et pays en cours de développement," *Cahiers de droit fiscal international*, vol. 44, 1961, pp. 1-277.

Mikesell, R. *Foreign investments in Latin America*. Pan American Union, Washington, 1955.

National Planning Association. *Private investment in underdeveloped countries*. Special Report No. 30, Washington, 1951, 9pp.

Oldman, O. "Tax policies of less developed countries with respect to foreign income and income of foreigners." In: Tax Institute of America, Inc., *Taxation of foreign income by the United States and other countries*, pp. 74-88. Princeton, N.J., 1966. Reprinted in: R. Bird and O. Oldman (eds.), *Readings on taxation in developing countries*, pp. 199-206. The Johns Hopkins Press, Baltimore, revised edition, 1967.

Organisation for Economic Co-operation and Development. *Fiscal incentives for private investment in developing countries*. Paris, 1965, 118pp.

Organisation for European Economic Co-operation. *Taxation systems applicable to investments in the overseas countries of O.E.E.C.* Paris, 2 volumes, 1960-1961, 98/166pp.

Pan American Union. *Model of a conven-*

tion for the mitigation of double taxation with respect to taxes on income. Washington, 1959, 79pp.

Pomeranz, M. "Taxation of United States investments in Latin America," *Virginia law review,* vol. 44, February 1958, pp. 205-228.

Popkin, W. "Less developed countries and the revenue act of 1962," *Indiana law journal,* vol. 40, 1964, pp. 1-20.

Price Waterhouse & Co. *Information guide for doing business in Central America.* New York, 1967.

Quinn, T., Jr. "Tax advantages of less developed country corporations," *Taxes,* vol. 43, 1965, pp. 556-562.

Raymond, A. "Tax aspects of joint ventures and oil operations in Latin America." In: Southwestern Legal Foundation, *Proceedings of the 1962 institute on private investments abroad and foreign trade,* pp. 63-108. Matthew Bender & Co., Albany, N.Y., 1962.

Richman, P. *Taxation of foreign investment income—An economic analysis.* The Johns Hopkins Press, Baltimore, 1963, ix/140pp.

Riofrio Villagómez, E. "Doble imposición international. Base para su prevención a fin de alentar las inversiones extranjeras en los paises latinoamericanos." In: *Jornadas latinoamericanas de derecho tributario—IV, Buenos Aires, 1964,* pp. 49-144. Ediciones Contabilidad Moderna, Buenos Aires, 1966.

Sahwell, A. *Investment of foreign capital in the Arab states.* American Friends of the Middle East, New York, 1956, 55pp.

Schreiberg, S. "The United States private investor and the Central American common market." In: United States Congress, Joint Economic Committee, *Hearings before the Subcommittee on inter-American economic relationships on Latin American development and western hemisphere trade,* 89th Congress, 1st Session, pp. 260-289. Washington, 1965.

Shere, L. "Taxation of American business abroad," *New York university 7th institute on federal taxation,* 1949, pp. 812-828.

Short, R. "Tax treaties with developing countries," *Canadian tax journal,* vol. 14, 1966, pp. 171-179.

Slowinski, W., and Janetatos, J. "Tax

planning for trading with and doing business in Central and South America," *Bulletin of the section of taxation, American bar association,* vol. 18, no. 3, 1965, pp. 72-81.

Southwestern Legal Foundation. *Proceedings of fifth annual institute on oil and gas law and taxation as it affects oil and gas industry.* Matthew Bender & Co., Albany, N.Y., 1954, 658pp.

Southwestern Legal Foundation. *Proceedings of the 1959 institute on private investments abroad and foreign trade.* Matthew Bender & Co., Albany, N.Y., 1959, 690pp.

Southwestern Legal Foundation. *Proceedings of ninth annual institute on oil and gas law and taxation as it affects oil and gas industry.* Matthew Bender & Co., Albany, N.Y., 1958, 652pp.

Swanson, H. "Tax problems confronting American foreign trade," *Export trade and shipper,* 12 August 1967. Reprinted in: *Taxes,* vol. 36, 1958, pp. 58-62.

Tax Institute of America, Inc. *Tax policy on United States investment in Latin America.* Princeton, N.J., 1963, xii/275pp.

Tax Institute of America, Inc. *Taxation and operations abroad.* Princeton, N.J., 1960, 308pp.

Tax Institute of America, Inc. *Taxation of foreign income by the United States and other countries.* Princeton, N.J., 1966, xii/340pp.

"Tax sparing and U.S. investment in Latin America." In: Commerce Committee for the Alliance for Progress, *Proposals to improve the flow of United States private investment to Latin America,* pp. 1-11. United States Department of Commerce, Washington, 1963.

"Unilateral measures for the avoidance of double taxation, especially as regards fiscal aspects of the relationship between capital-exporting countries and countries in the process of development," *Cahiers de droit fiscal international,* vol. 43, 1961, pp. 7-112.

United Nations. *The effects of taxation on foreign trade and investment.* Sales No. 1950.XVI.1, Lake Success, New York, February 1950, 87pp.

United Nations. *Foreign capital in Latin*

America. Sales No. 1954.II.G.4, New York, 1955, 164pp.

United Nations. *Foreign investment laws and regulations of the countries of Asia and the Far East.* Sales No. 1951.II.F.1, New York, 1951, 89pp.

United Nations. *Investment laws and regulations in Africa.* Sales No. 65.II.K.3, New York, 1965.

United Nations. *United States income taxation of private United States investment in Latin America.* Sales No. 1953.XVI.1, New York, January 1953, pp. 41-42, 47-48, 67ff.

United Nations, Economic and Social Council. "Financing of economic development: Recent governmental measures affecting the international flow of private capital." Doc. No. E/2766, 2 June 1955, 66pp.

United Nations, Economic and Social Council. "The promotion of the international flow of private capital." Doc. No. E/3325, 26 February 1960, pp. 46-58.

United Nations, Economic and Social Council. "A survey of policies affecting private foreign investment." Doc. No. E/1614/Rev. 1, 8 March 1950.

United Nations, Economic and Social Council. "Taxation in capital-exporting and capital-importing countries of foreign private investment." Doc. No. E/2865, 23 May 1956.

United Nations, Economic and Social Council. "Taxation in capital-exporting and capital-importing countries of foreign private investment." Doc. No. 3074, 3 June 1958.

United Nations, Economic and Social Council, Fiscal Commission. "Taxation in capital-exporting and capital-importing countries of foreign private investment in Latin America." Doc. No. E/CN.8/69, 5 December 1952, 99pp.

United Nations, Economic Commission for Latin America. "Economic and legal status of foreign investment in selected countries of Latin America." Doc. No. E/CN.12/166, 12 April 1950, and Addenda.

United Nations, Economic Commission for Latin America. "Tributación en los paises exportadores e importadores de capital, de las inversiones privadas extranjeras en América Latina." Doc. No. E/CN.12/298, 6 April 1953, 150pp.

United Nations, Economic Commission for Latin America, Trade Committee. "Government policies affecting private foreign investment in a Latin American regional market." Doc. No. E/CN.12/C.1/12, 28 March 1959, pp. 12-21.

United States Department of Commerce. *Trade and investment in Central America.* Washington, 1965, 88pp.

United States Department of Commerce, Bureau of Foreign Commerce. *Factors limiting U.S. investment abroad. Part I: Survey of factors in foreign countries.* Washington, 1953.

van Hoorn, J., Jr., et al. *Fiscal measures in capital-exporting countries for the purpose of encouraging investments in countries in the process of development.* International Fiscal Association, Paris, 1963.

9

LOCAL FINANCES

Cameron, I., and Cooper, B. *The West African councillor.* Oxford University Press, London, 2d edition, 1961, chapters 8-10.

Colonial Local Government Advisory Panel. "Principles of local government finance in Africa," *Journal of African administration,* vol. 8, October 1956, supp., 28pp.

Due, J. "Tropical African contributions to federal finance," *Canadian journal of economics and political science,* vol. 30, no. 1, February 1964, pp. 49-61.

Froomkin, J. "Fiscal management of municipalities and economic development," *Economic development and cultural change,* vol. 3, July 1955, pp. 309-320. Also in: *Journal of African administration,* vol. 8, January 1956, pp. 15-26. Reprinted in: R. Bird and O. Oldman (eds.), *Readings on taxation in developing countries.* The Johns Hopkins Press, Baltimore, 1964, pp. 386-401; revised edition, 1967, pp. 412-427.

Hicks, U. *Development from below: Local government and finance in developing countries of the Commonwealth.* Oxford University Press, London, 1961, xiii/549pp.

Hicks, U., Carnell, F., Newlyn, W., Hicks,

J., and Birch, A. *Federalism and economic growth in underdeveloped countries.* Allen & Unwin, London, 1963, chapters 4, 5.

Robson, P. "Federal finance." In: C. Leys and P. Robson (eds.), *Federation in East Africa.* Oxford University Press, London, 1965.

Robson, P. "Patterns of federal finance in the newer federations," *Finanzarchiv,* vol. 21, no. 3, April 1962, pp. 415-428.

Tripathy, R. *Federal finance in a developing country.* The World Press Private Ltd., Calcutta, 1960.

10

PROPERTY TAX

Brown, H., *et al.* (eds.). *Land value taxation around the world.* Robert Schalkenbach Foundation, New York, 1955, 216pp.

Due, J. "Taxation of property in developing economies: The African experience," *Land economics,* vol. 39, February 1963, pp. 1-14.

Hicks, J. "Unimproved value rating—The case of East Africa." In: J. Hicks, *Essays in world economics,* pp. 237-244. Oxford University Press, London, 1959.

Lent, G. "The taxation of land value," *International monetary fund staff papers,* vol. 14, March 1967, pp. 89-123.

Schlesinger, E. *The use of special assessments to finance development projects.* International Bank for Reconstruction and Development, Washington, 15 July 1953, 12pp. (mimeo).

Strasma, J. "Market-enforced self-assessment for real estate taxes," *Bulletin for international fiscal documentation,* vol. 19, 1965, pp. 353-363, 397-414.

11

TAXATION OF AGRICULTURE

Barranclough, S., and Domike, A. "Agrarian structure in seven Latin American countries," *Land economics,* vol. 12, no. 4, November 1966, pp. 414-415.

Carroll, T. "The land reform issue in Latin America." In: A. Hirschman (ed.), *Latin American issues: Essays and comments,* pp. 191-194. Twentieth Century Fund, New York, 1961.

Dalisay, A. "The place of agriculture in tax policy." In: Joint Legislative-Executive Tax Commission (Philippines), *Taxation and socio-economic growth,* pp. 11-27. Manila, 1960.

Dickinson, W., Jr. "Land and tax reform in Latin America," *Editorial research reports,* 13 December 1961, pp. 897-914.

Fitchett, D. "Land taxation and land reform in underdeveloped countries: A comment," *Economic development and cultural change,* vol. 10, part 1, 1962, pp. 210-213.

Jacoby, E. "Problems of land taxation." In: Food and Agricultural Organization of the United Nations, *Information on land reform,* no. 2. Rome, 1965.

Jacoby, E. "Taxation of the agricultural population in underdeveloped countries," *Monthly bulletin of agricultural economics and statistics,* vol. 1, no. 2, June 1952.

Jarach, D. *El impuesto a la renta normal potencial de la tierra.* Cuadernos de Finanzas Públicas No. 5, Unión Panamericana, Washington, 1966, 30pp.

Johnson, V., and Barlowe, R. *Land problems and policies.* McGraw-Hill, Inc., New York, 1954.

Johnston, B., and Mellor, J. "The role of agriculture in economic development," *American economic review,* vol. 51, September 1961, pp. 566-593.

"Land and tax reform in the less developed countries." Papers presented at a conference sponsored by the Committee on Taxation, Resources and Economic Development and the Land Tenure Center of the University of Wisconsin, Madison, August 1963.

Leduc, G. "La Fiscalité agricole dans les pays en voie de développement," *Revue juridique et politique indépendance et coopération,* vol. 19, 1965, pp. 521-530.

Lewis, S., Jr. "Taxation of agriculture and economic development." In: B. Johnston and H. Southworth (eds.), *Agriculture and economic development.* Cornell University Press, Ithaca, N.Y., 1967. Part reprinted in: R. Bird and O. Oldman (eds.), *Readings on taxation in developing countries,* pp. 465-477. The Johns Hopkins Press, Baltimore, revised edition, 1967.

Lindholm, R. "Analysis of the land use and land taxation policies of non-communist underdeveloped areas," *Economic development and cultural change,* vol. 8, April 1960, pp. 252-256.

Lindholm, R. "Land taxation and economic development," *Land economics,* vol. 41, no. 2, May 1965, pp. 121-130.

Moral-López, P. "Tax legislation as an instrument to assist in achieving the economic and social objectives of land reform." In: Food and Agricultural Organization of the United Nations, *Information on land reform,* no. 2, pp. 2-11. Rome, 1965.

Morley, L. "Expropriation in Latin America," *Editorial research reports,* 13 January 1960, pp. 21-38.

Prud'homme, R. *Fiscalité agricole pour pays sous-développés.* Thesis, Centre d'Etudes des Relations Sociales, Paris, 1962, 381pp.

Raup, P. "The contribution of land reforms to economic development: An analytical framework," *Economic development and cultural change,* vol. 12, October 1963, pp. 1-21.

Rowling, C. "Analysis of factors effecting changes in land tenure in Africa," *Journal of African administration,* vol. 4, October 1952, supp.

Rulliere, G. "Fiscalité agricole et développement économique," *Revue de science financière,* vol. 51, 1959, pp. 221-250.

Rulliere, G. "La tributación agrícola y el desarrollo económico," *Revista de economía latinoamericana,* April-June 1967, pp. 75-108.

Stewart, C., Jr. "Land reform as fiscal policy for agrarian nations," *Social research,* vol. 32, Spring 1965, pp. 98-109.

"Taxation and development of agriculture in under-developed countries, with special reference to Asia and the Far East," *Economic bulletin for Asia and the Far East,* vol. 9, June 1958, pp. 2-16.

United Nations. *Land reform.* Sales No. 1951.II.B.3, New York, 1951, pp. 43-48.

United Nations. *Progress in land reform.* Sales No. 1954.II.B.3, New York, 1954, pp. 261-267.

United Nations, Department of Economic Affairs, Fiscal Division. "An introductory survey of taxation of agriculture in underdeveloped countries." May 1953, 56pp.

United Nations, Department of Economic Affairs, Fiscal Division. "Tax burden on the rural population." 1951, 74pp.

United Nations, Economic Commission for Latin America. "Analysis of some factors which act as an obstacle to the increase of agricultural production." Doc. No. E/CN.12/306, 9 April 1953.

Wald, H. "El sistema impositivo en la agricultura de las economías en proceso de desarrollo," *El trimestre económico,* vol. 27, April-June 1961, pp. 247-263.

Wald, H. *Taxation of agricultural land in underdeveloped economies.* Harvard University Press, Cambridge, Mass., 1959, 231pp.

Wald, H. "Taxation of agriculture in Latin America." In: Tax Institute of America, Inc., *Tax policy on United States investment in Latin America,* pp. 19-30. Princeton, N.J., 1963.

Wald, H., and Froomkin, J. (eds.). *Papers and proceedings of the conference on agricultural taxation and economic development.* Harvard Law School International Program in Taxation, Cambridge, Mass., 1954, 439pp.

12
TAX INCENTIVES

Ahooja, K. "Development legislation in Africa," *Journal of development studies,* vol. 2, 1966, pp. 297-322.

Bird, R. "Tax-subsidy policies for regional development," *National tax journal,* vol. 19, June 1966, pp. 113-124.

Bryce, M. *Industrial development.* McGraw-Hill, Inc., New York, 1960, pp. 75-92.

Bryce, M. *Policies and methods for industrial development.* McGraw-Hill, Inc., New York, 1965, chapters 12-15.

Bulhoes, A. de. "Arrecadação e fiscalização das rendas públicas federais," *Revista do serviço público,* vol. 17, May 1955, pp. 279-298.

Earle, A. "Incentives to private investment as an aspect of development programmes," *Social and economic studies,* vol. 2, July 1953.

Escuela Superior de Administración Pública América Central. *Informe del seminario sobre el proyecto de convenio centroamericano de incentivos fiscales al desarrollo industrial.* San José, 1962, 255pp.

Florin, R. "Les Régimes spéciaux instaurés par les pays sous développés en faveur des investissements privés étrangers," *Steuer revue,* vol. 20, 1965, pp. 530-543.

Fontaneau, P. *La Detaxation des investissements.* Algiers, 1956.

Froomkin, J. "Some problems of tax policy in Latin America," *National tax journal,* vol. 10, December 1957, pp. 370-379.

Gal-Edd, I. *Export incentives through tax legislation. I: National policy aspects. II: International aspects.* Lectures at the University of Copenhagen, Jerusalem, July 1967, 17/9pp. (mimeo).

Garner, R. "Tax incentives for development investment," *American journal of economics and sociology,* vol. 18, July 1959, pp. 379-380.

Harris, B. "Note on tax exemptions and development," *National tax journal,* vol. 8, December 1955, pp. 393-399.

Heller, J., and Kauffman, K. *Tax incentives for industry in less developed countries.* Harvard Law School International Program in Taxation, Cambridge, Mass., 1963, xii/288pp.

Kahabka, J. *Tax incentives for private industrial investment in less developed countries.* Report No. EC-102, International Bank for Reconstruction and Development, Washington, 30 January 1962, 87pp. (mimeo).

Kauffman, K. "Income tax exemption and economic development," *National tax journal,* vol. 13, June 1960, pp. 141-162; vol. 13, September 1960, pp. 252-269.

Kövary, R. *Investment policy and investment legislation in underdeveloped countries.* Taplinger Publishing Co., Inc. (Rangoon University Press), New York, 1960, 124pp.

Lent, G. "Tax incentives for investment in developing countries," *International monetary fund staff papers,* vol. 14, July 1967, pp. 249-323. Also in: *Finance and development,* vol. 4, September 1967, pp. 195-201.

Loyrette, J. "Les Codes d'investissement," *Pénant: Revue de droit des pays l'Afrique,* vol. 73, 1963.

Mendive, P. "Tax incentives in Latin America," *Economic bulletin for Latin America,* vol. 9, March 1964, pp. 103-116.

Norberg, C. "Industrial incentive legislation in Latin America." In: Washington Foreign Law Society, *A symposium on the law of Latin America,* pp. 47-67. Washington, 1959.

Organisation for Economic Co-operation and Development, Fiscal Committee. *Fiscal incentives for private investment in developing countries.* Paris, 1965, 115pp.

Pan American Union, Department of Economic Affairs. *Tax incentives for industrial development in Latin America.* CIES/1138, Add.3, Washington, 1967, 80pp.

Pincus, J. *The industrial development laws of Central America.* International Co-operation Administration, Washington, 1961.

Prest, A. "Taxes, subsidies and investment incentives." In: A. Peacock and G. Hauser (eds.), *Government finance and economic development,* pp. 113-126. Organisation for Economic Co-operation and Development, Paris, 1965.

Ross, S. "Foreign governments' tax incentives for investment." In: Southwestern Legal Foundation, *Proceedings of the 1959 institute on private investments abroad and foreign trade,* pp. 285-336. Matthew Bender & Co., Albany, N.Y., 1959.

United Nations, Economic and Social Council. "The promotion of the international flow of private capital: Fourth report of the Secretary General." Doc. No. E/3905 and E/3905/Add.1, 26 May 1964, 143/27pp.

United Nations, Economic Commission for Asia and the Far East. "The use of taxation techniques as incentive to private investment in Far Eastern countries." Doc. No. ECAFE/I & T/FED/19, 18 September 1953.

United Nations, Economic Commission for Latin America. "Incentivos fiscales para incrementar la afluencia internacional de capitales privados destinados al desarrollo económico de los paises insuficientemente desarrollados." Prepared by E. Malaccorto, April 1953 (mimeo).

United Nations, Economic Commission for Latin America, Committee on Economic Co-operation of the Central American Isthmus. "Industrial promotion laws in Central America." Prepared by K. Lachmann, 1960, 141pp. (mimeo).

van Hoorn, J., Jr. *Tax treatment of research and development.* Organisation for Economic Co-operation and Development, Paris, 1962, 280pp.

Vogel, H. "Tax incentives for industrial development." In: Organisation for Economic Co-operation and Development, *Methods of industrial development with reference to less developed areas,* chapter 12. Paris, 1962.

Wolfe, J. "Industrial expansion and optimal tax policies," *Canadian tax journal,* vol. 4, 1956, pp. 211-213.

Yoingco, A., and Trinidad, R. "Some tax incentives and export promotion in selected Asian countries," *Economic research journal* (Philippines), vol. 12, December 1965, pp. 166-180; vol. 13, March 1966, pp. 285-297.

13

TAX ADMINISTRATION

Alderfer, H. *Public administration in newer nations.* Frederick A. Praeger, New York, 1966, chapter 6.

"Conferencia interamericana sobre administración tributaria," *Boletín de la Dirección general impositiva* (Argentina), vol. 16, November 1961, pp. 15-39.

"Conferencia sobre administración de impuestos," *Revista de derecho financiero y de hacienda pública* (Madrid), vol. 12, 1962, pp. 129-138.

Davis, R. *Observations of a tax advisor.* International Cooperation Administration, Washington, December 1958, 12pp. (typewritten).

Escuela Superior de Administración Pública América Central. *Informe del seminario regional sobre administración fiscal 5 a 9 de octubre de 1964.* San José, 1965, 133pp.

Hart, A. *An integrated system of tax information: A model and a sketch of possibilities of practical application under Latin American conditions.* Columbia University School of International Affairs, New York, 1967, 142pp.

Inter-American Economic and Social Council. *The Alliance for progress: Its first year 1961/1962.* Washington, 1962, pp. 45-51.

Joint Tax Program, Organization of American States, Inter-American Development Bank, and Economic Commission for Latin America. *Problems of tax administration in Latin America.* Published for The Joint Tax Program by The Johns Hopkins Press, Baltimore, 1965, 574pp.

Liker, A. "The legal and institutional framework of tax administration in developing countries," *University of California at Los Angeles law review,* vol. 14, 1966, pp. 240-346.

Morag, A. "Some economic aspects of two administrative methods of estimating taxable income," *National tax journal,* vol. 10, June 1957, pp. 176-185.

Japan Tax Association. *Proceedings of the special meeting of the Japan tax association on tax system and administration in Asian countries, April 8th to 16th.* Tokyo, 1964, 282pp.

Public Administration Service. *Modernizing government revenue administration.* Chicago, 1961, 92pp.

Riggs, F. "Public administration: A neglected factor in economic development." In: B. Hoselitz (ed.), *Agrarian societies in transition: Annals of the American academy of political science,* vol. 305, 1956, pp. 70-80.

Sharef, Z. "Posibles soluciones para problemas de administración tributaria en paises en desarrollo," *Revista de ciencias económicas* (Buenos Aires), vol. 50, January-June 1962, pp. 81-89.

Surrey, S. "Tax administration in underdeveloped countries," *University of Miami law review,* vol. 12, Winter 1958, pp. 158-188. Reprinted in: R. Bird and O. Oldman (eds.), *Readings on taxation in developing countries.* The Johns Hopkins Press, Baltimore, 1964, pp. 503-533; revised edition, 1967, pp. 492-523.

United Nations, Department of Economic and Social Affairs. *Manual of income tax administration, discussion draft.* Prepared by the Harvard Law School International Tax Program in consultation with the United Nations Secretariat, New York, 1967, xi/440pp. (mimeo).

United Nations, Economic and Social Council, Fiscal Commission. "Procedures available for the review of initial tax assessments." Doc. No. E/CN.8/59, 7 May 1951.

United Nations, Economic and Social Council, Fiscal Commission. "Report on the technical assistance conference on comparative fiscal administration." Doc. No. E/CN.8/67, ST/TAA/M/3, 5 December 1952, 138pp.

United Nations, Technical Assistance Administration, Special Committee on Public Administration. "Standards and techniques of public administration." Doc. No. ST/TAA/M/1.

14

LEGAL ASPECTS OF TAXATION

Allorio, E. "Lo contencioso tributario." In: Asociación Argentina de Estudios del Derecho Fiscal, *Jornadas internacionales de derecho fiscal*, pp. 199-242. Depalma, Buenos Aires, 1961.

Bielsa, R. "Lineamiento general de un método para el derecho fiscal." In: Asociación Argentina de Estudios del Derecho Fiscal, *Jornadas internacionales de derecho fiscal*, pp. 27-92. Depalma, Buenos Aires, 1962.

Carámbula, A. "Admisión fiscal de deudas," *Revista internacional del notariado*, vol. 13, no. 49, 1961, pp. 15-50.

Forns, J. "La necesidad de un concepto jurídico del seguro como presupuesto para evitar la doble imposición fiscal." In: *International congress on insurance law*, vol. 1, pp. 421-430. Giuffrè, Milan, 1963.

Programa Conjunto de Tributación de la Organización de los Estados Americanos y del Banco Interamericano de Desarrollo. *Reforma tributaria para América Latina. III: Modelo de código tributario*. Unión Panamericana, Washington, 1967, 162pp.

15

NONTAX METHODS OF FINANCING DEVELOPMENT

"The application of multiple exchange rates in selected Asian countries," *Economic bulletin for Asia and the Far East*, vol. 5, November 1954, pp. 19-38.

Baldwin, R. "Exchange rate policy and economic development," *Economic de-velopment and cultural change*, vol. 9, July 1961, pp. 598-604.

Bernstein, E. "Some aspects of multiple exchange rates," *Ekonomi dan keuangan Indonesia*, vol. 6, May 1953.

Bernstein, E. "Some economic aspects of multiple exchange rates," *International monetary fund staff papers*, vol. 1, September 1950, pp. 224-237.

Bernstein, E., and Patel, I. "Inflation in relation to economic development," *International monetary fund staff papers*, vol. 2, November 1952, pp. 363-398.

Bronfenbrenner, M. "The appeal of confiscation in economic development," *Economic development and cultural change*, vol. 3, April 1955, pp. 201-218. Reprinted in: A. Agarwala and S. Singh (eds.), *The economics of underdevelopment*, pp. 472-494. Oxford University Press, Bombay, 1958.

Bruton, H. *Principles of development economics*. Prentice-Hall, Inc., Englewood Cliffs, N.J., 1965, pp. 160-169.

"Deficit financing for economic development with special reference to ECAFE countries," *Economic bulletin for Asia and the Far East*, vol. 5, November 1954, pp. 1-18.

Hanson, A. *Public enterprise and economic development*. Routledge & Kegan Paul Ltd., London, 1959, chapter 3.

"Inflation and the mobilization of domestic capital in underdeveloped countries of Asia," *Economic bulletin for Asia and the Far East*, vol. 2, February 1952, pp. 21-34.

Morag, A. *On taxes and inflation*. Random House, New York, 1965, chapter 7.

Prakash, S. "Deficit financing in underdeveloped countries," *Indian journal of economics*, vol. 44, October 1963, pp. 103-112.

Reviglio, F. "Social security: A means of savings mobilization for economic development," *International monetary fund staff papers*, vol. 14, no. 2, July 1967, pp. 324-368.

Schlesinger, E. *Multiple exchange rates and economic development*. Princeton University Press, Princeton, N.J., 1952, 76pp.

United Nations. *World economic survey, 1965*. Sales No. 1966.II.C.3, New York, 1966, Part I.

United Nations, Economic Commission

for Asia and the Far East. "Inflation and mobilization of domestic capital." Doc. No. E/CN.11/I & T/WP.1/L.6, 22 October 1951.

Woodley, W. "Multiple currency practices," *Finance and development,* vol. 3, June 1966, pp. 113-119.

Woodley, W. "The use of special exchange rates for transactions with foreign companies," *International monetary fund staff papers,* vol. 3, October 1953, p. 255.

16
TECHNICAL ASSISTANCE

Andic, S., and Peacock, A. "Fiscal surveys and economic development," *Kyklos,* vol. 19, no. 4, 1966, pp. 620-642.

Bloch, H. "Fiscal advisory functions of United Nations technical assistance," *International organization,* vol. 11, Spring 1957, pp. 248-260.

Bloch, H. "U. N. technical assistance in public finance," *Proceedings of the National tax association 1951,* vol. 44, pp. 202-207.

Bronfenbrenner, M., and Kogiku, K. "The aftermath of the Shoup tax reforms," *National tax journal,* vol. 10, September 1957, pp. 236-254; vol. 10, December 1957, pp. 345-360.

Ganjei, N. "Contribution of tax missions in the developing countries." In: Central Treaty Organization, *Symposium on tax administration,* pp. 137-146. Office of United States Economic Coordinator for CENTO Affairs, American Embassy, Ankara, 1965.

Ganjei, N. "Contribution of tax missions in underdeveloped countries," *Proceedings of the National tax association 1955,* vol. 48, pp. 208-217.

Herzel, W. "Administrative problems faced by tax missions," *Proceedings of the National tax association 1955,* vol. 48, pp. 220-226.

Joint Tax Program, Organization of American States, and Inter-American Development Bank. *Annual report—1966.* Pan American Union, Washington, 1967.

Moss, H. "Experiences under the U.S. foreign tax assistance program," *Proceedings of the National tax association 1967.*

Schlesinger, E. "Tax policy recommendations of technical assistance missions." In: Joint Tax Program, Organization of American States, Inter-American Development Bank, and Economic Commission for Latin America, *Fiscal policy for economic growth in Latin America,* pp. 425-452. Published for The Joint Tax Program by The Johns Hopkins Press, Baltimore, 1965. Part reprinted in: R. Bird and O. Oldman (eds.), *Readings on taxation in developing countries,* pp. 528-536. The Johns Hopkins Press, Baltimore, revised edition, 1967.

Surrey, S., and Oldman, O. "Tax survey missions and related problems." In: International Cooperation Administration, *Review of mutual cooperation in public administration in 1958.* Washington, 1959.

United States Treasury Department, Internal Revenue Service. *Background report on reforms in tax administration through the Alliance for progress and the Foreign tax assistance program.* Washington, 1967 18pp. (mimeo).

17
TAX HARMONIZATION

Belassa, B. *The theory of economic integration.* Richard D. Irwin, Inc., Homewood, Ill., 1961, chapter 11.

Bird, R. "The possibility of fiscal harmonization in the Communist bloc," *Public finance,* vol. 19, 1964, pp. 201-227.

"Convenio centroamericano sobre equiparación de gravámenes a la importación y el protocolo sobre preferencia arancelaria centroamericana," *Boletín informativo* (ODECA), no. 26, 1961, pp. 83-134.

Cosciani, C. "Fiscal problems of a common market." In: Joint Tax Program, Organization of American States, Inter-American Development Bank, and Economic Commission for Latin America, *Fiscal policy for economic growth in Latin America,* pp. 359-382. Published for The Joint Tax Program by The Johns Hopkins Press, Baltimore, 1965.

Due, J., and Robson, P. "Tax harmonization in the East African common market." In: C. Shoup (ed.), *Fiscal harmonization in common markets,* vol.

2, pp. 553-605. Columbia University Press, New York, 1967.

Escuela Superior de Administración Pública América Central. *Informe del seminario sobre el proyecto de convenio centro-americano de incentivos fiscales al desarrollo industrial.* San José, 1962, 255pp.

Gillim, M. "The fiscal aspects of the Central American common market." In: C. Shoup (ed.), *Fiscal harmonization in common markets,* vol. 2, pp. 479-523. Columbia University Press, New York, 1967.

Gillim, M. "Some fiscal aspects of the Latin American free trade association." In: C. Shoup (ed.), *Fiscal harmonization in common markets,* vol. 2, pp. 524-552. Columbia University Press, New York, 1967.

Gnazzo, E. "Aspectos fiscales de la integración económica latinoamericana." In: *Integración económica de América Latina.* Cuaderno No. 27, Instituto de la Hacienda Pública, Montevideo, 1960.

González Casal, R. "Zonas de libre comercio y trato nacional en materia de impuestos internos," *Revista de la Facultad de ciencias económicas y administración* (Montevideo), July 1962, pp. 21-67.

Joint Tax Program, Organization of American States and Inter-American Development Bank. *La administración tributaria en Centroamérica y el proyecto de armonización fiscal.* Pan American Union, Washington, 1966.

Latin American Free Trade Association. *Armonización de los tratamientos aplicados a las inversiones privadas extranjeras en los países de la Asociación latinoamericana de libre comercio.* Montevideo, April 1964 (mimeo).

Lomas, P. "The report of the East African economic and fiscal commission," *East African economics review,* vol. 8, June 1961, pp. 14-23.

Massad, C., and Strasma, J. *La zona de libre comercio en América Latina: Algunos problemas por resolver.* Instituto de Economía, Universidad de Chile, Santiago, 1961.

Pitta e Cunha, P. de. "Problemas fiscais da Associaçao europeia de comercio livre." Reprinted from: *Boletim da Direcção-geral das contribuições e impostos,* 1960, 84pp.

Protocolo al convenio centroamericano sobre equiparación de gravámenes a la importación," *Boletín informativo* (ODECA), no. 26, 1961, pp. 213-244.

Secretaría de Hacienda y Crédito Público, Dirección General de Estudios Hacendarios (México). *La Asociación latinoamericana de libre comercio.* México, 3 volumes, 1960-1961. I: *Conceptos generales y documentos.* II: *Estadísticas.* III: *Aspectos fiscales.*

Shoup, C. "Tax problems of a common market in Latin America," *Tax policy,* vol. 29, no. 11, November 1962. Also in: Tax Institute of America, Inc., *Tax policy on United States investment in Latin America,* pp. 181-188. Princeton, N.J., 1963. Reprinted in: R. Bird and O. Oldman (eds.), *Readings on taxation in developing countries,* pp. 497-502. The Johns Hopkins Press, Baltimore, 1964.

Strasma, J. *Diferencias de tributación, costos comparativos, y "armonización" dentro del area latinoamericana de libre comercio.* Instituto de Economía, Universidad de Chile, Santiago, 1963, 48pp. (mimeo).

Strasma, J. "Reform finance and a Latin American common market: Some harmonization problems in tax policy." Research Paper No. 11, Land Tenure Center, University of Wisconsin, Madison, Wisc., 1965, 38pp.

United Nations, Economic Commission for Africa. "Co-ordination of industrial incentives and legislation." Doc. No. E/CN.14/RES/140 (VII), 1965.

United Nations, Economic Commission for Latin America. "Cuestiones fiscales, de política comercial y metodología relacionadas con la formación del mercado común centroamericano." Doc. No. E/CN.12/497, 28 March 1959.

United Nations, Economic Commission for Latin America. "Política comercial y libre comercio en Centroamérica." Doc. No. E/CN.12/368, 1955, 175pp.

Watkin, V. *Taxes and tax harmonization in Central America.* Harvard Law School International Tax Program, Cambridge, Mass., 1967, xiii/519pp.

Wionczek, M. "El financiamiento de la integración económica de América Latina," *El trimestre económico,* vol. 27, January-March 1960, pp. 15-33.

18

REFERENCE MATERIALS
Sources of Laws

Board of Inland Revenue (Great Britain). *Income taxes outside the United Kingdom 1966.* H. M. Stationery Office, London, 8 volumes, 1967.

Business International Corporation. *Investing, licensing and trading in 50 countries.* New York, 8th edition, 1964, 431pp.

Commerce Clearing House, Inc. *Tax treaties.* Chicago, loose-leaf, 1952-.

Diamond, W. *Foreign tax and trade briefs.* Fallon Law Book Company, New York, loose-leaf, 1951-.

International Bureau of Fiscal Documentation. *Tax news service.* Amsterdam, bimonthly, 1965-.

Morgan Guaranty Trust Co. *Doing business abroad.* New York, loose-leaf, 1963-.

United Nations, Department of Economic Affairs. *International tax agreements.* New York, loose-leaf, 1948-.

Periodicals

Association Internationale de Droit Financier et Fiscal. *Cahiers de droit fiscal international.* Amsterdam, 1939-.

Associazione fra le Società Italiane per Azioni. *Rassegna della stampa.* Rome, monthly, January 1956-.

Bank of London and Montreal Limited. *Economic review.* London, fortnightly.

Commercial Relations and Exports Department (Great Britain). *Overseas economic surveys.* H.M. Stationery Office, London, published every few years for most countries.

Finanzarchiv. J.C.B. Mohr (Paul Siebeck), Tübingen, quarterly.

Foreign Tax Law Association. *Foreign tax law weekly bulletin.* St. Petersburg, Fla., weekly.

International Bureau of Fiscal Documentation. *Bulletin for international fiscal documentation.* Amsterdam, monthly, 1946-.

International Monetary Fund. *International financial news survey.* Washington, weekly, July 1948-.

International Monetary Fund and International Bank for Reconstruction and Development. *The fund and bank review: Finance and development.* Washington, quarterly, June 1964-.

National Tax Association. *National tax journal.* Harrisburg, Pa., quarterly, 1948-.

Public finance. The Hague, quarterly, 1946-.

Revista de derecho financiero y de hacienda pública. Editorial de Derecho Financiero, Madrid, quarterly, June 1951-.

Revue de science financière. Librairie Générale de Droit et de Jurisprudence, Paris, quarterly, 1903-. Titled *Revue de science et de législation financières,* 1903-1955.

Rivista di diritto finanziario e scienza delle finanze. A. Giuffrè, Milan, quarterly, 1937-.

United States Department of Commerce. *Foreign commerce weekly.* Washington, weekly, 1940-. Also titled *International commerce.*

United States Department of Commerce, Bureau of Foreign Commerce. *World trade information service.* Washington, 1954-1961.

United States Department of Commerce, Bureau of International Commerce. *Overseas business reports.* Washington, 1962-.

Bibliographies

Bird, R., and Oldman, O. (eds.). *Readings on taxation in developing countries.* The Johns Hopkins Press, Baltimore, revised edition, 1967, pp. 535-545.

Harvard Law School Library. *Annual legal bibliography.* Cambridge, Mass., annual, 1961-.

Harvard Law School Library. *Current legal bibliography.* Cambridge, Mass., monthly (except July-September), October 1960-.

Owens, E. *Bibliography on taxation of foreign operations and foreigners.* Harvard Law School International Tax Program, Cambridge, Mass., 1968.

Surrey, W., and Shaw, C. *A lawyer's guide to international business transactions.* Joint Committee on Continuing Legal Education, Philadelphia, Pa., 1963.

United Nations Educational, Scientific and Cultural Organization. *International bibliography of economics.* Paris, annual, 1952–.

United States Department of State, Office of External Research. *External research lists: 2.25 (Asia), 4.25 (Middle East), 5.25 (Africa), 6.25 (American republics), and 7.25 (international affairs).* Washington, annual.

COUNTRY REFERENCES

ADEN

4

"Aden." In: Board of Inland Revenue (Great Britain), *Income taxes outside the United Kingdom 1966,* vol. 1, pp. 1-25. H. M. Stationery Office, London, 1967.

"The income tax law of Aden Colony," *Foreign tax law semi-weekly bulletin,* vol. 6, nos. 35-40, 1955, pp. 1-19.

AFGHANISTAN

1

Public Administration Service. *Present revenue structure of the royal government of Afghanistan.* Special Report No. 35, United States Operations Mission to Afghanistan, Kabul, 1959, 31pp.

United States Department of Commerce. *Basic data on the economy of Afghanistan.* Washington, 1966, 8pp.

Wilber, D. (ed.). *Afghanistan.* Human Relations Area Files, New Haven, Conn., 1956, pp. 168-181.

2

The five year economic development plan of Afghanistan. n.p., Kabul, 1956, chapter 8.

Public Administration Service. *Long range tax objectives.* Special Report No. 60, United States Operations Mission to Afghanistan, Kabul, 1960.

4

Hinrichs, H. "Certainty as criterion: Taxation of foreign investment in Afghanistan," *National tax journal,* vol. 15, June 1962, pp. 139-154.

10

Public Administration Service. *Utilization and taxation of land.* Special Report No. 67, United States Operations Mission to Afghanistan, Kabul, 1961.

12

Royal Afghan Embassy. *Law encouraging the investment of private foreign capital in Afghanistan.* Washington, 1965.

13

Public Administration Service. *A proposed plan of organization for the Revenue department, Ministry of finance of the royal government of Afghanistan.* Special Report No. 25, United States Operations Mission to Afghanistan, Kabul, 1950, 22pp.

Public Administration Service. *A proposed revenue administration improvement program for Afghanistan.* United States Operations Mission to Afghanistan, Kabul, 1958, 42pp. (mimeo).

ALGERIA

1

Brochier, M. "Aménagements fiscaux en Algérie," *Bulletin for international fiscal documentation,* vol. 15, 1961, pp. 328-335; vol. 16, 1962, pp. 1-8.

Brochier, M. "Fiscalité algérienne," *Bulletin for international fiscal documentation,* vol. 16, 1962, pp. 9-15.

Guide pratique des impôts en Algérie et au Sahara. Louis Broët, Paris, looseleaf.

Piquart, M. "Partie de la fiscalité algérienne," *Nouvelles réalités algériennes,* vol. 3, January-March 1957.

United States Department of Commerce. *Basic data on the economy of Algeria.* Washington, 1965, 16pp.

2

Fontaneau, P. "Fiscalité et développement de Sahara," *Public finance,* vol. 13, 1958, pp. 225-239.

3

Brochier, E. "Fiscalités française, algérienne, marocaine et tunisienne," *Bulletin for international fiscal documentation,* vol. 9, 1955, pp. 271-285.

Caniot, A. "Fiscalité comparée: Algérie-Tunisie-Maroc," *Bulletin for international fiscal documentation,* vol. 6, 1952, pp. 203-219.

4

"La Déclaration en 1965 des bénéfices industriels et commerciaux réalisés en

Algérie," *Problèmes d'outre-mer,* 1 March 1965.

"La Déclaration en 1966 des bénéfices industriels et commerciaux réalisés en Algérie," *Problèmes d'outre-mer,* 15 February 1966, pp. 26-34; 15 March 1966, pp. 1-11.

6

Brochier, E. "Les Nouveaus tarifs d'enregistrement en Algérie," *Bulletin for international fiscal documentation,* vol. 14, 1960, pp. 1-4.

7

United States Department of Commerce. *Foreign trade regulations of the Republic of Algeria.* Washington, 1964, 6pp.

8

United States Department of Commerce. *Establishing a business in Algeria and departments of Sahara.* Washington, 1960, 12pp.

9

Caniot, A. "La Réforme des finances locales en Algérie," *Bulletin for international fiscal documentation,* vol. 6, 1952, pp. 65-75.

12

"Tax exemptions for private capital," *Foreign tax law weekly bulletin,* vol. 10, no. 21, 1959, pp. 8-9.

18

Diamond, W. *Foreign tax and trade briefs.* Fallon Law Book Company, New York, loose-leaf, 1951-.

ANGOLA

1

Organisation for European Economic Co-operation. *Taxation systems applicable to investments in the overseas countries of O.E.E.C.* Paris, 2 volumes, 1960-1961, 98/166pp.

United States Department of Commerce. *Basic data on the economy of Angola.* Washington, 1961, 20pp.

United States Department of Commerce. *Preparing shipments to Angola.* Washington, 1963, 8pp.

7

United States Department of Commerce. *Foreign trade regulations of Angola.* Washington, 1967, 8pp.

8

United States Department of Commerce. *Establishing a business in Angola.* Washington, 1960, 10pp.

12

Gersdorff, R. "La Formation de capitaux par des mesures fiscales dans l'empire portugais," *Public finance,* vol. 15, 1960, pp. 31-50 (English summary).

Gersdorff, R. *Mesures pour encourager la formation de capitaux privés dans l'empire portugais.* Polygraphischer Verlag, Zurich, 1958.

ANTIGUA

4

"Antigua." In: Board of Inland Revenue (Great Britain), *Income taxes outside the United Kingdom 1966,* vol. 1, pp. 27-44. H. M. Stationery Office, London, 1967.

ARGENTINA

1

Alemann, R. "Tax policies in Argentina." In: Tax Institute of America, Inc., *Tax policy on United States investment in Latin America,* pp. 57-63. Princeton, N.J., 1963.

Amaya, A. "Función social de los impuestos," *Boletín de la Facultad de derecho y ciencias sociales* (Córdoba), vol. 24, July-December 1960, pp. 167-216; vol. 25, January-June 1961, pp. 103-142.

Andreozzi, M. *Derecho tributario argentino.* Tip. Edit. Argentina, Buenos Aires, 2 volumes, 1951.

"Argentina amends tax laws," *Foreign commerce weekly,* vol. 55, no. 17, 1956.

"Argentina taxation: Present structure and procedure," *Comments on Argentine trade,* vol. 39, 1959, p. 14.

Argentine Embassy. *Argentine tax system: Summary.* Washington, 1962, 35pp.

Arthur Andersen & Co. *Tax and trade guide: Argentina.* Buenos Aires, 1965, 86pp.

Atchabahian, A. "Concepto y determinabilidad de la presión tributaria," *Impuestos*, vol. 20, 1962, pp. 385-399.

Atchabahian, A. "Les Tarifs d'impôts dans la République Argentine." In: E. Morselli and L. Trotabas, *Enquête sur la tarifs d'impôts*, pp. 33-64. CEDAM, Padova, 1964.

Berardo, C. "La hacienda pública y su control (noticia histórica acerca de su evolución en nuestro país)," *Revista de la Facultad de ciencias económicas* (Buenos Aires), vol. 1, nos. 1-5, 1948, pp. 171-235.

Bielsa, R. *Estudios de derecho público. II: Derecho fiscal.* Depalma, Buenos Aires, 1951.

Business International. *Argentina today: Conditions and prospects for profit.* New York, 1967, 42pp.

Cardinale, J. "Legal and general considerations involved in business operations in Argentina," *Export trade and shipper*, 19 December 1955, pp. 7-9.

"Changes in tax laws," *Comments on Argentine trade*, vol. 41, 1961, p. 13.

"Estudios sobre las últimas modificaciones al régimen impositivo." In: Cámara Argentina de Sociedades Anónimas, *La sociedad anónima actual*, series 3, vol. 5, pp. 167-183. Buenos Aires, 2d edition, 1960.

"Exposición de motivos sobre las recientes reformas al régimen impositivo vigente." In: Cámara Argentina de Sociedades Anónimas, *La sociedad anónima actual*, series 5, vol. 7, pp. 83-93. Buenos Aires, 2d edition, 1961.

Freytes, R. "Nuevas reformas impositivas: El decreto-ley no. 11.452/62," *Impuestos*, vol. 20, 1962, pp. 486-498.

Freytes, R. "Los recientes decretos-leyes en materia impositiva," *Impuestos*, vol. 21, 1963, pp. 513-522.

Freytes, R. "Las recientes reformas impositivas: Exposición comentario de la ley 16.450," *Impuestos*, vol. 20, 1962, pp. 97-121.

Freytes, R. "Las reformas impositivas del decreto 8723/62," *Impuestos*, vol. 20, 1962, pp. 433-445.

García Belsunce, H. *Estudios financieros.* Ed. Abeledo-Perrot, Buenos Aires, 1966, 516pp.

García Belsunce, H. "Los recargos cambiarios del decreto 11.918/58: Problemas constitucionales derivados de su aplicación," *Revista jurídica argentina: La ley*, vol. 103, July-September 1961, pp. 952-960.

García Vázquez, E. "Crítica a las últimas reformas impositivas," *Revista de ciencias económicas* (Buenos Aires), vol. 46, April-June 1958, pp. 181-194.

García Vázquez, E. "Notas sobre la evolución del régimen impositivo argentino," *Revista de ciencias económicas* (Buenos Aires), vol. 49, January-March 1961, pp. 21-40.

García Vázquez, E. "Observaciones al régimen impositivo nacional," *Revista de ciencias económicas* (Buenos Aires), vol. 49, April-June 1961, pp. 157-166.

García Vázquez, E., et al. *Curso del Colegio de graduados en ciencias económicas.* Buenos Aires, 2 volumes, 1956.

"General tax law modifications," *Comments on Argentine trade*, vol. 30, 1954, pp. 18-21.

Giuliani Fonrouge, C. "Cuatro reformas impositivas y su enseñanza," *Impuestos*, vol. 23, 1965, pp. 169-179.

Giuliani Fonrouge, C. *Derecho financiero.* Depalma, Buenos Aires, 2 volumes, 1962, 958pp.

Giuliani Fonrouge, C. "La ley 16.656 de reformas impositivas," *Impuestos*, vol. 23, 1965, pp. 1-10.

Giuliani Fonrouge, C. "Reformas de los impuestos internos," *Derecho fiscal*, vol. 4, July 1954-June 1955, pp. 557-562.

Giuliani Fonrouge, C. "Unificación de impuestos internos," *Derecho fiscal*, vol. 4, July 1954-June 1955, pp. 417-420.

González, B. "Nuevas modificaciones al régimen impositivo," *Derecho fiscal*, vol. 12, July 1962-June 1963, pp. 417-427.

González, F. "Creación de nuevos gravámenes y otras modificaciones al régimen impositivo," *Derecho fiscal*, vol. 12, July 1962-June 1963, pp. 249-269.

González, F. "Latest taxation reforms," *Review of the River Plate*, vol. 125, 30 January 1959, pp. 19-25.

Grivot, A. "The tax system of the Republic of Argentina." In: Tax Institute of America, Inc., *Tax policy on United States investment in Latin America*, pp. 64-75. Princeton, N.J., 1963.

Jarach, D. *Curso superior de derecho tributario.* Ed. Cima, Buenos Aires, 2 volumes, 1958.

Jarach, D. "Desarrollo del derecho tributario argentino," *Revista de derecho financiero y de hacienda pública* (Madrid), vol. 8, 1958, pp. 797-815.

Jarach, D. *Estudio sobre las finanzas argentinas, 1947-1957.* Depalma, Buenos Aires, 1961, 95pp.

Jarach, D. "La reciente reforma impositiva: Examen crítico de algunos de sus aspectos," *Derecho fiscal,* vol. 8, July 1958-June 1959, pp. 1-16.

Juano, M. de. *Curso de finanzas y derecho tributario.* Ediciones Molachino, Rosario, 2 volumes, 1963-1964, 466/766pp.

Krieger Vasena, A. "Modificaciones al régimen impositivo," *Boletín de la Dirección general impositiva,* vol. 8, February 1958, pp. 121-124.

Krieger Vasena, A. "Reformas impositivas," *Boletín de la Dirección general impositiva,* vol. 7, August 1957, pp. 93-97.

Laufenburger, H. "Acerca de los proyectos de reforma fiscal," *Selección de temas de finanzas públicas* (Montevideo), 1st quarter 1957, pp. 30-34.

López, A. "Algunas consideraciones en torno a la última reforma impositiva," *Derecho fiscal,* vol. 5, July 1955-June 1956, pp. 485-503.

López, A. "Las modificaciones al régimen impositivo nacional introducidas por la ley no. 16.450," *Derecho fiscal,* vol. 11, July 1961-June 1962, pp. 337-379.

López, A. "Modifications in tax laws," *Review of the River Plate,* vol. 110, 5 October 1951, pp. 27-30.

López, A. "Modifications of the Argentine taxation laws," *Review of the River Plate,* vol. 108, 29 August 1950, pp. 18-21.

López, A. "Modifications proposed by the tax reform," *Comments on Argentine trade,* vol. 34, 1955, p. 13.

López, A. "New modifications of the Argentine taxation system," *Review of the River Plate,* vol. 108, 18 August 1950, pp. 17-21.

López, A. "Novedades en materia impositiva," *Derecho fiscal,* vol. 7, July 1957-June 1958, pp. 233-245.

López, A. "Tax reform: A general review of the proposed modifications," *Review of the River Plate,* vol. 116, 10 December 1954, pp. 29-31.

López, A. "Taxation in Argentina: Present position and procedures," *Review of the River Plate,* vol. 126, 21 September 1959, pp. 35-37; vol. 126, 30 September 1959, pp. 41-42; vol. 126, 10 October 1959, pp. 40-41; vol. 126, 20 October 1959, pp. 39-40. Reprinted in: *Comments on Argentine trade,* vol. 39, 1959, pp. 14-18.

López, A., and González, F. "Latest changes in Argentine taxation regulations," *Review of the River Plate,* vol. 115, 29 January 1954, pp. 19-21.

López, A., and González, F. "Las reformas impositivas introducidas por ley no. 15.273," *Derecho fiscal,* vol. 9, July 1959-June 1960, pp. 369-423.

López Agnetti, E. "La ley impositiva no. 16,451," *Información,* vol. 35, 1964, pp. 71-80.

López Agnetti, E. "Sobre la reforma impositiva," *Información,* vol. 38, 1967, pp. 143-150.

Losada, D. "Algunos aspectos de la reforma impositiva del año 1956," *Revista de ciencias económicas* (Buenos Aires), vol. 44, October-November-December 1956, pp. 323-341.

Martínez, F. *Derecho tributario argentino.* Universidad de Tucumán, 1956, 202pp.

Marval and O'Farrell. *Outline of Argentina corporation, tax, labour and foreign investment laws.* Talleres Gráficos Rado, Buenos Aires, 4th edition, 1955, 79pp.

Marval and O'Farrell. *Practical outline of Argentina law.* Talleres Gráficos "Optimus," Buenos Aires, 5th edition, 1960, 110pp.

Marval and O'Farrell. "Tax reforms," *Comments on Argentine trade,* vol. 35, 1956, p. 43.

"Mensaje y proyecto remitidos por el poder ejecutivo nacional con fecha 29/11/65," *Impuestos,* vol. 23, 1965, pp. 714-768.

Ministerio de Hacienda de la Nación. *Conferencia de Ministros de haciendas.* Buenos Aires, annual, 1946–.

"Modificaciones al código fiscal y ley impositiva, año 1963," *Boletín Colegio de escribanos de la provincia de Buenos Aires,* vol. 13, 1963, pp. 1035-1041.

"Las modificaciones al régimen impositivo sancionadas por la ley 14.789." In: Cámara Argentina de Sociedades Anónimas, *La sociedad anónima actual,* series 6, vol. 8, pp. 23-55. Buenos Aires, 1960.

"Modification to Argentine tax laws," *Review of the River Plate,* vol. 127, 10 June 1960, pp. 32-34.

Morselli, E. "Capacidad contributiva," *Revista de ciencias económicas* (Buenos Aires), vol. 42, January-February 1954, pp. 3-12.

"New Argentine legislation revises most taxes," *Foreign commerce weekly,* vol. 61, no. 9, 1959.

New York University School of Law. *Outline of the tax law of Argentina.* New York, 1949 (processed).

"Nuevas normas impositivos de aplicación." In: Cámara Argentina de Sociedades Anónimas, *La sociedad anónima actual,* series 4, vol. 6, pp. 117-130. Buenos Aires, 2d edition, 1960.

Oderigo, E. "Temas para las próximas modificaciones tributarias (ley 11.682, t.o. 1960 y modif.)," *Impuestos,* vol. 22, 1964, pp. 562-568.

Pan American Union. *A statement of the laws of Argentina in matters affecting business.* Washington, 3d edition, 1963, 323pp. Supplement, 1965, 56pp.

Patterson, E. "Finances of national government of Argentina," *Journal of finance,* vol. 8, March 1963, pp. 66-67. Abstract of Ph.D. thesis.

Patterson, E. *The finances of the national government of Argentina.* Ph.D. thesis, Texas, 1951.

Patterson, E. "The tax system of the Argentine national government," *National tax journal,* vol. 5, September 1952, pp. 261-276.

Price Waterhouse & Co. *Information guide for doing business in Argentina.* New York, 1966.

Programa Conjunto de Tributación de la Organización de los Estados Americanos y del Banco Interamericano de Desarrollo. *Sistemas tributarios de América Latina: Argentina.* Unión Panamericana, Washington, 1966, 104pp.

"El proyecto de reformas impositivas, elevado por el poder ejecutivo al Congreso nacional el 31/8/64," *Impuestos,* vol. 22, 1964, pp. 393-422.

Pugliese, M. "Problems of public finance in the Argentine Republic," *Taxes,* vol. 18, 1940, pp. 494-496.

Raimondi, C. "Nuevas modificaciones al régimen impositivo nacional," *Derecho fiscal,* vol. 12, July 1962-June 1963, pp. 97-115.

Rampoldi, L. "La capacidad contributiva en los antecedentes argentinos," *Impuestos,* vol. 15, 1957, pp. 4-8. Also in: *Revista fiscal y financiera,* vol. 16, April 1957, pp. 153-157.

"Recientes modificaciones al régimen impositivo dictadas por el poder ejecutivo nacional." In: Cámara Argentina de Sociedades Anónimas, *La sociedad anónima actual,* series 5, vol. 7, pp. 68-82. Buenos Aires, 2d edition, 1961.

"Reformas impositivas—Años 1967," *Información,* vol. 38, 1967, pp. 89-120.

"Reformas introducidas al régimen impositivo nacional por la ley no. 15.273." In: Cámara Argentina de Sociedades Anónimas, *La sociedad anónima actual,* series 7, vol. 9, pp. 142-235. Buenos Aires, 1961.

"Régimen impositivo de la República Argentina," *Boletín informativo* (Banco Provincial de Buenos Aires), February 1960, pp. 11-14.

"Revision of tax law," *Foreign tax law weekly bulletin,* vol. 9, no. 37, 1959, pp. 8-9.

Roig, R. "Comentarios al decreto no. 6480/62 y a la resolución general no. 793 (I.E.I.N.J.)," *Información,* vol. 33, 1962, pp. 451-460.

Schaffroth, A. "Interpretación de las leyes impositivas," *Impuestos,* vol. 15, 1957, pp. 167-173.

Siri, E. "Mensaje sobre el plan impositivo," *Revista de la municipalidad de la ciudad de Buenos Aires,* vol. 10, August 1948, pp. 15-60.

"Sistema impositivo y la presión tributaria," *Información,* vol. 35, 1964, pp. 646-669.

Soler, A. *Los principios fundamentales de los sistemas impositivos.* Universidad Nacional del Litoral, Rosario, 1940.

Surrey, S., and Oldman, O. "Report of preliminary survey of the tax system of Argentina," *Public finance,* vol. 16, 1961, pp. 155-182, 313-342.

Tarantino, J. "Economía internacional y reforma tributaria en Latinoamérica y en la República Argentina," *Boletín de la Facultad de derecho y ciencias sociales* (Córdoba), vol. 26, May-September 1962, pp. 55-90.

"Tax reform indispensable for economic growth," *Review of the River Plate,* vol. 128, 12 October 1960, pp. 25-26.

"Unification of taxes proposed," *Foreign tax law weekly bulletin,* vol. 10, no. 2, 1959, pp. 1-5.

United States Department of Commerce. *Basic data on the economy of Argentina.* Washington, 1966, 36pp.

United States Department of Commerce. *Federal tax system of Argentina.* Washington, 1961.

Velázquez, A. "Reformas impositivas: Comentario de la ley 16,656," *Información,* vol. 36, 1965, pp. 103-150.

Vieiro, R. "Algunas reformas impositivas," *Información,* vol. 33, 1962, pp. 123-134.

Vieiro, R. "Los impuestos internos y las reformas impositivas," *Impuestos,* vol. 23, 1965, pp. 129-142.

Vieiro, R. "Modificaciones impositivas recientes," *Impuestos,* vol. 23, 1965, pp. 69-102.

2

Andreozzi, M. "Algunos aspectos del derecho tributario en la República Argentina," *Revista de la Facultad de derecho* (Tucumán), vol. 10, 1954, pp. 19-78.

Atchabahian, A. "La economía y las finanzas argentinas en 1963," *Revista de derecho financiero y de hacienda pública* (Madrid), vol. 14, 1964, pp. 985-996.

Atchabahian, A. "Las finanzas públicas y el nivel y distribución de la renta en la República Argentina, desde 1947 a 1957," *Impuestos,* vol. 19, 1961, pp. 69-75.

Blanco, E. *La política presupuestaria, la deuda pública y la economía nacional.* Ministerio de Hacienda de la Nación, Buenos Aires, 1956, 55pp.

Boccia, A. "Funciones de la política fiscal," *Revista de la Facultad de ciencias económicas de la Universidad de Cuyo,* vol. 12, April 1960, pp. 42-59.

Brodersohn, M. "Elasticidad—Ingreso del impuesto a la renta en Argentina," *Desarrollo económico,* vol. 3, no. 4, January-March 1964.

Caplan, B. "Las finanzas públicas en el plan económico 1952," *Revista de la Facultad de ciencias económicas de la Universidad de Cuyo,* vol. 4, May-August 1952, pp. 33-40.

García Freyre, J. "El aumento de los impuestos y sus efectos sobre la economía nacional," *Revista de ciencias económicas* (Buenos Aires), vol. 44, January-February 1956, pp. 3-18.

García Martínez, C. *La inflación argentina.* Editorial Kraft, Buenos Aires, 1965.

García Vizcaino, J. "El equilibrio del presupuesto: Un imperativo de política económica," *Revista jurídica argentina: La ley,* vol. 113, January-March 1964, pp. 971-985.

Givorgri, C. "La política fiscal adecuada al desarrollo económico," *Revista de economía* (Argentina), vol. 12, no. 18, 1961-1962, pp. 9-38.

González, N. "La financiación del desarrollo económico con recursos nacionales," *Revista de desarrollo económico,* vol. 2, no. 3, April-June 1959, pp. 103-126.

Herschel, F. "Instrumentos y métodos de la política fiscal," *Impuestos,* vol. 13, 1955, pp. 203-209.

Herschel, F. "Política fiscal y desarrollo económico en la República Argentina," *Revista de la Universidad de Buenos Aires,* vol. 7, no. 1, January-March 1962, pp. 54-98.

Herschel, F., and Itzcovich, S. "Fiscal policy in Argentina," *Public finance,* vol. 12, 1957, pp. 97-115, 208-228.

Hinrichs, H. "Lessons of the Argentine revenue sharing experience." In: United States Congress, Joint Economic Committee, 90th Congress, 1st Session, *Revenue sharing and its alternatives: What future for fiscal federalism?* vol. 1, pp. 562-591. Joint Committee Print, Washington, 1967.

Krieger Vasena, A. "Política fiscal, inflación y desarrollo económico." In: Asociación Argentina de Estudios de Derecho Fiscal, *Memoria anual de ejercicio,* pp. 54-80. Buenos Aires, 1963.

López, A. "Los fondos de inversión ante las leyes fiscales," *Derecho fiscal,* vol. 9, July 1959-June 1960, pp. 173-178.

López Agnetti, E. "El producto bruto como instrumento de análisis económico de los impuestos," *Información,* vol. 36, 1965, pp. 801-815.

Lopez Frances, M. *La política financiera y el ciclo económico.* La Plata, 1952, 30pp.

Mancini, J. "Algunos aspectos de la evolución de la renta nacional," *Lecciones y ensayos* (Buenos Aires), no. 27, 1964, pp. 47-58.

Ministerio de Hacienda, Economía y Previsión, Dirección General de Estadística e Investigaciones. *Capacidad contributiva y presión tributaria.* La Plata, 1958, 19pp.

"Normas jurídico-financieras para una política fiscal de desarrollo económico." In: Federación Argentina de Colegios de Abogados, *Sexta conferencia nacional de abogados, La Plata, 1959,* pp. 159-198. Abeledo-Perrot, Buenos Aires, 1963.

Pinedo, F. "Función de los impuestos en la reconstrucción de la economía nacional," *Información,* vol. 31, 1960, pp. 5-15.

Rennie, R. "Argentine fiscal policy," *Inter-American economic affairs,* vol. 1, no. 1, 1947, pp. 51-76.

"Repercusión de las obligaciones de la legislación fiscal y trabajista sobre los costos de producción," *Revista de ciencias económicas* (Buenos Aires), vol. 42, November-December 1954, pp. 347-359; vol. 43, January-February 1955, pp. 15-47.

"Sistema impositiva, presión tributaria y las inversiones," *Información,* vol. 36, 1965, pp. 469-503.

"Sistema impositiva y la presión tributaria," *Información,* vol. 36, 1965, pp. 263-274.

Stanford Research Institute. *The economic impact of taxes on Argentina's industrial and resource development.* Vol. 1: *Taxation and economic development in Argentina.* Vol. 2: *The Argentine tax system, description and evaluation.* Menlo Park, Calif., 1963, 136/148pp.

United Nations. *El desarrollo económico de la Argentina.* Sales No. 59.II.G.3, New York, 1959.

3

"Análisis comparativo de la tributación en la Argentina, el Brasil, Chile y México." In: United Nations, *Las inversiones privadas extranjeras en la zona latinoamericana de libre comercio,* pp. 31-33. Sales No. 1960.II.G.5, México, 1960.

Gómez Oyarzan, C. *El impuesto a la renta en Chile y en Argentina.* Thesis, Universidad de Concepción, 1955, 98pp.

4

"Activo fijo. Reemplazo," *Impuestos,* vol. 15, 1957, pp. 165-166.

"Amendments to the Argentine tax laws and law on revaluations of assets: Summary," *Comments on Argentine trade,* vol. 39, 1960, p. 35.

Arecha, W. "Tasa de reparto y tasa de dividendo," *Jurisprudencia argentina,* vol. 1962-II, March-April 1962, pp. 11-15.

Audisio, A. "Régimen impositivo de los contratos petroleros," *Revista jurídica argentina: La ley,* vol. 112, October-December 1963, pp. 930-943.

Balbi, R. "El reintegro al balance impositivo por disminución de la capacidad productiva," *Información,* vol. 34, 1963, pp. 671-681.

Benson, J. "How Argentina taxes corporations," *Taxes,* vol. 25, 1947, p. 1092.

Blanco, E. *Los valores mobiliarios frente a la reforma impositiva de 1956.* Ministerio de Hacienda, Buenos Aires, 1956, 22pp.

Caceres Bernal, J. *Manual práctico de réditos.* Basilea, Buenos Aires, 1962, 223pp.

"El capital de los auxiliares de comercio en el impuesto a los beneficios extraordinarios," *Impuestos,* vol. 18, 1959, pp. 236-238.

Cholvis, F. *La revaluación de los bienes activos.* Editorial Prometo, Buenos Aires, 1954, 174pp.

Chouhy, A. "El contribuyente frente a la doble imposición en materia de impuestos internos," *Derecho fiscal,* vol. 9, July 1959-June 1960, pp. 1-5.

"Comentario al decreto del p.e. no. 5438/60, reglamentario de la revaluación impositiva de los activos," *Información,* vol. 31, 1960, pp. 367-392.

Consejo Federal de Inversiones. *Política fiscal en la Argentina—Titulo primero: Impuestos sobre la ingresos.* Buenos Aires, 1962, xiv/173pp.

Cosciani, C. "El impuesto directo en el cuadro de un sistema tributario," *Impuestos,* vol. 21, 1963, pp. 1-19.

Duwaran, R. "The Argentine income tax," *Taxes,* vol. 20, 1942, p. 275.

"La empresa como objeto del impuesto a los beneficios extraordinarios," *Impuestos,* vol. 14, 1956, pp. 9-11.

Foreign Tax Law Association. *Argentine income tax service.* Centerport, L.I., N.Y., loose-leaf, 1952-1955.

García Vázquez, E. "Algunos efectos de los impuestos sobre las utilidades en la economía del país," *Impuestos,* vol. 20, 1962, pp. 289-299.

García Vázquez, E. "Aspectos de la imposición a sociedades anónimas," *Revista de ciencias económicas* (Buenos Aires), vol. 42, January-February 1954, pp. 19-26.

García Vázquez, E. "La revaluación de activos con fines fiscales," *Revista de ciencias económicas* (Buenos Aires), vol. 47, October-November-December 1959.

García Vázquez, E. "Tratamiento impositivo del aporte de la distribución de bienes," *Revista de ciencias económicas* (Buenos Aires), vol. 40, July-August 1952, pp. 289-295.

Giuliani Fonrouge, C. "Taxes affecting industrial and commercial enterprises in Argentina," *Bulletin for international fiscal documentation,* vol. 5, 1951, pp. 265-272.

González, F. "Modificación del decreto reglamentario del impuesto a los réditos," *Derecho fiscal,* vol. 13, July 1963-June 1964, pp. 297-307.

González, F., and Raimondi, C. "Las ganancias de inflación y los impuestos," *Derecho fiscal,* vol. 11, July 1961-June 1962, pp. 497-510.

Gustavino, L. *Impuesto a los réditos: Régimen vigente para agentes de retención y agentes de información.* 1966.

Gutiérrez Kirchner, A. "¿Puede abolirse el impuesto a la renta de las empresas?" *Informacion,* vol. 36, 1965, pp. 840-853.

Herrendorf de Baccetti, O. "El escribano como agente de retención del impuesto a las ganancias eventuales," *Revista notarial* (La Plata), no. 742, 1962, pp. 819-828.

Herschel, F. "Aspectos económicos del impuesto a los réditos," *Selección contable,* May 1954, pp. 253-265.

Herschel, F. "Métodos de la imposición de las sociedades anónimas en el derecho fiscal comparado," *Impuestos,* vol. 14, 1956, pp. 180-187.

Hirsch, H. "Major summaries of company taxation in 1965," *Bulletin for international fiscal documentation,* vol. 19, 1965, pp. 273-276.

"El impuesto a los beneficios extraordinarios: Su creación y efecto en la actualidad," *Impuestos,* vol. 15, 1957, pp. 261-263.

"Impuesto a los réditos: Declaración patrimonial-réditos derivados de sociedades entre conyugues," *Impuestos,* vol. 15, 1957, p. 204.

"Income tax in Argentina," *Accountants journal* (England), vol. 41, July 1949, pp. 135-136.

"Indice analítico y por materias de la ley no. 15.272 sobre revaluación de activos y sus reglamentaciones impositiva y contable." In: Cámara Argentina de Sociedades Anónimas, *La sociedad anónima actual,* series 7, vol. 9, pp. 381-398. Buenos Aires, 1961.

"Individualización de tenedores de valores mobiliarios y retención de impuesto a los réditos." In: Cámara Argentina de Sociedades Anónimas, *La sociedad anónima actual,* series 4, vol. 6, pp. 71-83. Buenos Aires, 2d edition, 1960.

Iturrioz, E. "Renta gravable declarada para el impuesto a los réditos," *Revista de economía y estadística* (Córdoba) (n.s.), vol. 10, nos. 1-2, 1966, pp. 75-87.

Jarach, D. *Impuesto a los réditos.* Ed. Cima, Buenos Aires, n.d., 516pp.

Jarach, D. "El nuevo proyecto de revaluación de activos," *Derecho fiscal,* vol. 9, July 1959-June 1960, pp. 243-261.

La Rosa, R. *Impuesto a las actividades lucrativas.* Ed. Contabilidad Moderna, Buenos Aires, 1954.

López, A. " 'Blanqueo' de capitales e impuesto a los incrementos no justificados. Normas complementarias del decreto no. 6.480/62," *Derecho fiscal,* vol. 12, July 1962-June 1963, pp. 49-74.

López, A. *Impuesto a los beneficios extraordinarios.* Ed. Contabilidad Moderna, Buenos Aires, 4th edition, 1956.

López, A. *Impuesto a los réditos.* Ed. Contabilidad Moderna, Buenos Aires, 2 volumes, 1955.

López, A. "Las ultimas modificaciones del régimen impositivo nacional: Impuesto a los réditos," *Revista de ciencias económicas* (Buenos Aires), vol. 42, November-December 1954, pp. 391-400.

López, A., González, F., and Raimondi, C. "Impuesto a los réditos. Ultimas modificaciones del decreto reglamentario y otras disposiciones," *Derecho fiscal,* vol. 10, July 1960-June 1961, pp. 193-210.

López, A., and Raimondi, C. "Impuesto a los beneficios extraordinarios," *Derecho fiscal,* vol. 10, July 1960-June 1961, pp. 211-213.

López Agnetti, E. "Las reformas reglamentarias de ganancias eventuales y réditos," *Información,* vol. 35, 1964, pp. 1-24.

Losada, D. "El nuevo régimen de ajuste automático de amortizaciones y deducciones especiales por ventas de inmuebles y automotores del decreto-ley 6670/63," *Impuestos,* vol. 21, 1963, pp. 431-440.

Martín, J. "Imposición de los réditos de la sociedad conjugal," *Impuestos,* vol. 25, 1967, pp. 169-182.

Martínez, F. "Las sociedades de capital ante el impuesto a los réditos," *Revista jurídica* (Tucumán), no. 2, 1957, pp. 27-33.

Marval and O'Farrell. *Memorandum on company and company taxation law in Argentina.* Buenos Aires, 3d edition, 1951, 20pp.

Mayer, J. "El impuesto a los réditos y el fracaso del plan de desarrollo," *Jurisprudencia argentina,* vol. 1962-III, May-June 1962, pp. 19-26.

Mayer, J. "La nueva reforma de la ley de réditos, el sacrifico de la clase media, impuesto a los réditos o impuesto al petróleo," *Jurisprudencia argentina,* vol. 1960-V, September-October 1960, pp. 59-65.

"Middle class and income tax," *Foreign tax law weekly bulletin,* vol. 11, no. 9, 1960.

Ministerio de Hacienda. *Impuesto a las actividades lucrativas.* Buenos Aires, 1955, 309pp.

Ministerio de Hacienda de la Nación. *Impuesto a los beneficios extraordinarios.* Buenos Aires, 1952, 21pp.

Molinari, A. "Realización de bienes del activo fijo y los resultados consiguientes ante las disposiciones legales de los impuestos a los réditos y eventuales," *Impuestos,* vol. 23, 1965, pp. 431-438.

Morales, C., Jr. "Influencia de la contabilidad en la imposición de la contribución sobre ingresos," *Revista de ciencias económicas* (Buenos Aires), vol. 43, July-August 1955, pp. 251-262.

New income tax laws of Argentina. La Facultad, Buenos Aires, 1949, 272pp.

"Normas para la revaluación de bienes a los efectos impositivos y/o contables." In: Cámara Argentina de Sociedades Anónimas, *La sociedad anónima actual,* series 7, vol. 9, pp. 280-302. Buenos Aires, 1961.

Oderigo, E. "Restitución al balance impositivo de las deducciones efectuadas por inversiones en bienes," *Impuestos,* vol. 22, 1964, pp. 316-335.

Palmer, W. *Argentine income tax guide.* Palmer Editorial, Buenos Aires, 1961, 120pp.

Parola, J. "Reforma a la ley de impuesto a los réditos," *Información,* vol. 36, 1965, pp. 179-201.

Pereiro, V. "Revaluación de activos (ley no. 14.789)," *Derecho fiscal,* vol. 9, July 1959-June 1960, pp. 49-65.

Perrell, G. "Taxation of income in Argentina," *Foreign tax law weekly bulletin,* vol. 2, no. 10, 1951, pp. 3-14.

Rabinovich, M. *Impuesto a los réditos: Exposición y comentario.* Ed. Contabilidad Moderna, Buenos Aires, 1957, 513pp.

Raimondi, C. "Impuesto para aprendizaje: Algunos aspectos vinculados con su reciente reforma," *Derecho fiscal,* vol. 4, July 1954-June 1955, pp. 1-10.

Raimondi, C. "Imputación de réditos y gastos al año fiscal. Sistema de lo devengado," *Derecho fiscal,* vol. 12, July 1962-June 1963, pp. 193-205.

"Regulates assets' revaluation," *Foreign tax law weekly bulletin,* vol. 11, no. 8, 1960.

Reig, E. "Considérations sur l'imposition des gains de capital," *Revue de science financière,* vol. 54, 1962, pp. 232-257.

Reig, E. "Fuente argentina en el impuesto a los réditos," *Revista de ciencias económicas* (Buenos Aires), vol. 49, July-August-September 1961, pp. 221-243.

Reig, E. *El impuesto a los réditos.* Ed. Contabilidad Moderna, Buenos Aires, 1961, 685pp.

Reig, E. "Objeto del impuesto argentino a los réditos," *Revista de ciencias económicas* (Buenos Aires), vol. 46, October-November-December 1958.

Reig, E. *Objeto del impuesto argentino a los réditos (concepto de rédito).* Instituto de Finanzas Argentinas, Universidad de Buenos Aires, Buenos Aires, 1959, 26pp.

"Retención del impuesto a los réditos en el régimen del anonimato del tenedor de acciones." In: Cámara Argentina de Sociedades Anónimas, *La sociedad anónima actual,* series 6, vol. 8, pp. 111-123. Buenos Aires, 1960.

Risueño, M. *Argentina: Summary of various taxes affecting commercial and industrial operations.* Arthur Young & Company, Buenos Aires, June 1961, 13pp.

Schwartzman, L. "Tratamiento impositivo contable de la construcción por le régimen de la propiedad horizontal," *Derecho fiscal,* vol. 9, July 1959-June 1960, pp. 297-309.

Scotti, N. "La 'fuente' en la tercera categoría de réditos. Bienes de cambio en el exterior y diferencias de cambio," *Derecho fiscal,* vol. 8, July 1958-June 1959, pp. 89-97.

Scotti, N. "Réditos y emergencia: Paralelo entre la sociedad del exterior y la constituida en el país," *Información,* vol. 36, 1965, pp. 245-249.

Tarantino, J. "El impuesto a las actividades lucrativas y los honorarios de abogados y procuradores," *Impuestos,* vol. 20, 1962, pp. 212-222.

Tarantino, J. "Opción de las formas jurídicas y la evasión legal del impuesto," *Boletín de la Facultad de derecho y ciencias sociales* (Córdoba), vol. 22, July-December 1958, p. 351.

Valls, M. *Sistema tributario de la minería en la República Argentina.* Consejo Federal de Inversiones, Buenos Aires, 1962, 40pp.

Vieiro, R. "Aspectos prácticos del régimen de imposición a las sociedades de capital y sus accionistas," *Impuestos,* vol. 23, 1965, pp. 527-537.

Vieiro, R. "Deducción adicional en la enajenación de bienes inmuebles," *Impuestos,* vol. 24, 1966, pp. 1-11.

Vieiro, R. "Impuesto a los réditos: Aplicación práctica," *Revista de la Facultad de ciencias económicas* (Buenos Aires), vol. 6, nos. 59-60, 1953, pp. 1265-1354.

Vieiro, R. "El impuesto a los réditos y las sociedades de capital," *Revista de ciencias económicas* (Buenos Aires), vol. 48, October-November-December 1960, pp. 341-358.

Vieiro, R. "Reseña sobre el régimen de imposición a las sociedades de capital y sus accionistas," *Impuestos,* vol. 23, 1965, pp. 475-493.

Vieiro, R. *Revaluación impositiva.* Depalma, Buenos Aires, 1960, 120pp.

5

Giuliani Fonrouge, C. "Impuesto sucesorio en las transferencias de padres a hijos," *Derecho fiscal,* vol. 1, July 1951-June 1952, pp. 241-242.

Herschel, F. "El impuesto al gasto," *Impuestos,* vol. 15, 1957, pp. 103-107. Reprinted in: *Revista fiscal y financiera,* vol. 16, June 1957, pp. 75-91.

"Impuesto substitutivo al gravamen a la transmisión gratuita de bienes: Deducción en el impuesto los réditos," *Impuestos,* vol. 16, 1958, p. 43.

"Impuesto substitutivo de transmisión gratuita de bienes: Sociedad anónima en formación," *Impuestos,* vol. 14, 1956, pp. 29-30.

"El impuesto substitutivo del gravamen a la transmisión gratuita de bienes y su incidencia respecto al impuesto a los réditos." In: Cámara Argentina de Sociedades Anónimas, *Le sociedad anónima actual,* series 6, vol. 8, pp. 404-414. Buenos Aires, 1960.

Martínez, F. "El impuesto territorial en los supuestos de condominio e indivisión hereditaria, y la autonomía financiera de las provincias," *Jurisprudencia argentina,* vol. 1956-IV, October-November-December 1956, pp. 46-48.

Rechter, I. "Reglamentación de las reformas introducidas por la ley 16.450 al impuesto substitutivo del gravamen a la transmisión gratuita de bienes," *Impuestos,* vol. 21, 1963, pp. 267-277.

Schaffroth, A. "La presunción fiscal de gratuitidad en transmisión de bienes a título oneroso," *Impuestos,* vol. 15, 1957, pp. 251-255. Reprinted in: *Revista fiscal y financiera,* vol. 18, May 1958, pp. 49-67.

Sole Villalonga, G. "Discusión de una propuesta: El impuesto sobre el gasto personal," *Información,* vol. 37, 1966, pp. 85-118.

Vieiro, R. *Impuesto substitutivo del gravamen a la transmisión gratuita de bienes.* Oresme, Buenos Aires, 1953.

Vieiro, R. *Incrementos patrimoniales de*

origen justificado. Depalma, Buenos Aires, 1962, 109pp.

6

Biondi, M. *La ley nacional de sellos.* Buenos Aires, 1950.

Chalupowicz, I. "Impuesto a las actividades lucrativas e impuesto de sellos en las operaciones de las entidades de ahorro y préstamo para la vivienda, el la capital federal y en la provincia de Buenos Aires," *Derecho fiscal,* vol. 13, July 1963-June 1964, pp. 420-436.

Coni, R. "Fundamento ético del impuesto de sellos," *Revista notarial* (La Plata), no. 749, 1963, pp. 1240-1252.

Cuello, R. "El impuesto a las ventas en Argentina," *Investigación fiscal,* no. 19, July 1967, pp. 147-160.

Foti, N., and Corso, J. "Impuesto a las ventas en el mercado interno: Cambio de tasa dispuesto por el art. 3 de la ley 15.798," *Impuestos,* vol. 20, 1962, pp. 122-127.

González, F., and Raimondi, C. "Contabilización del impuesto a las ventas y su incidencia en la determinación de la renta imponible," *Derecho fiscal,* vol. 11, July 1961-June 1962, pp. 193-207.

"Impuesto sustitutivo del gravamen a la transmisión gratuita de bienes. Comentario sobre las modificaciones introducidas por la ley 16.450 y decreto reglamentario no. 3.804/63," *Información,* vol. 34, 1963, pp. 449-476.

Jarach, D. "L'Impôt sur les ventes dans la République Argentine." In: M. Masoin and E. Morselli (eds.), *Impôts sur transactions, transmissions et chiffre d'affaires,* pp. 51-79. Archives Internationales de Finances Publiques No. 2, Cedam Casa Editrice, Dr. A. Milani, Padova, 1959.

Jarach, D. "Impuesto sobre el patrimonio y las sucesiones y donaciones," *Información,* vol. 37, 1966, pp. 561-592.

Larraud, R. "El impuesto de sellos en Uruguay y Argentina," *Revista notarial* (La Plata), no. 755, 1964, pp. 1221-1254.

López Agnetti, E. "Comentario sobre las reformas impositivas a la ley del impuesto de sellos (ley 16,450)," *Información,* vol. 33, 1962, pp. 1-13.

López Agnetti, E. "El empuje inflacionario del impuesto indirecto," *Información,* vol. 38, 1967, pp. 78-82.

Lugones, E. "Impuesto de sellos: Operaciones monetarias que devenguen interés sujetas a las prescripciones del capítulo IV del titulo II de la ley de sellos (t.o. en 1961), artículos 33 y 34," *Impuestos,* vol. 22, 1964, pp. 569-578.

Rabinovich, M. *Impuesto de sellos de la capital federal y territorios nacionales.* Ed. Contabilidad Moderna, Buenos Aires, 1954.

Raimondi, C. "Impuesto a las ventas y para aprendizaje. Modificación del decreto reglamentario," *Derecho fiscal,* vol. 10, July 1960-June 1961, pp. 289-293.

Raimondi, C. "Impuesto de sellos sobre depósitos monetarios en la provincia de Buenos Aires," *Derecho fiscal,* vol. 9, July 1959-June 1960, pp. 201-205.

Rapoport, J. *Manual práctico de la ley de sellos nacional.* Artes Gráficas Alfonso Ruiz, Buenos Aires, 1952, 535pp.

"Reforma del impuesto nacional a las ventas," *Impuestos,* vol. 22, 1961, pp. 179-194.

Reig, E. *El impuesto a las ventas.* Ed. Contabilidad Moderna, Buenos Aires, 5th edition, 1959.

Reig, E. "Lineamientos fijados por el decreto ley 6691/63 para la reestructuración del impuesto a las ventas," *Derecho fiscal,* vol. 13, July 1963-June 1964, pp. 233-243.

Reig, E. "Note explicative sur les propositions de réforme de l'impôt argentin sur les ventes." In: M. Masoin and E. Morselli (eds.), *Impôts sur transactions, transmissions et chiffre d'affaires,* pp. 77-80. Archives Internationales de Finances Publiques No. 2, Cedam Casa Editrice, Dr. A. Milani, Padova, 1959.

Vieiro, R. "Nueva reglamentación del impuesto a las ventas," *Impuestos,* vol. 24, 1966, pp. 481-496.

7

Amaya, A. "El impuesto a la exportación en Argentina," *Impuestos,* vol. 15, 1957, pp. 70-74.

"Decreto 6232/65: Reintegro de impuestos —Productos manufacturados—Exportaciones no tradicionales," *Información,* vol. 35, 1965, pp. 615-616.

Figueredo, R. "Reformas a la legislación aduanera," *Impuestos,* vol. 25, 1967, pp. 261-269.

La Rosa, R. "Valor de las mercaderías de

importación para el pago de los recargos (decreto ley 8158/61)," *Derecho fiscal,* vol. 11, July 1961-June 1962, pp. 145-156.

"Reintegro de impuestos a exportadores," *Boletín de la Dirección general impositiva,* vol. 19, July 1963, pp. 173-182.

United States Department of Commerce. *Foreign trade regulations of Argentina.* Washington, 1966, 8pp.

United States Department of Commerce. *Import tariff system of Argentina.* Washington, 1963, 3pp.

8

"Doble imposición: Acuerdos para evitarla—Acuerdo por notas reversales con Japon—Su aprobación," *Información,* vol. 38, 1967, pp. 16-17.

García Freyre, J. "Las inversiones de empresas extranjeras en el país y la doble imposición internacional," *Selección contable,* June 1957, p. 423.

Hoefs, R. *El impacto de los impuestos de Estados Unidos en sus inversores en América Latina y el de los impuestos latinoamericanos en esos inversores.* Asociación Argentina de Derecho Fiscal, Buenos Aires, 1964, 30pp.

Martín, J. "Tratamiento fiscal de las regalias y otros pagos al extranjero por asistencia técnica," *Impuestos,* vol. 23, 1965, pp. 403-412.

Rechter, I. "Tratamiento impositivo de las sumas pagadas al exterior en concepto de asesoramiento," *Impuestos,* vol. 20, 1962, pp. 145-150.

Stalsky, H. "El problema de la doble imposición en las relaciones entre Argentina y Alemania," *Boletín de la Cámara de comercio argentino-alemana,* May 1960, pp. 130-133.

United States Department of Commerce. *Establishing a business in Argentina.* Washington, 1966, 36pp.

Valdés Costa, R. "Régimen impositivo de las inversiones extranjeras en América Latina," *Impuestos,* vol. 25, 1967, pp. 93-97.

9

Amaya, A. "Los municipios y los recursos del régimen de coparticipación," *Impuestos,* vol. 18, 1960, pp. 65-69.

Amaya, A. "Separación impositiva entre la nación y las provincias," *Derecho*

fiscal, vol. 6, July 1956-June 1957, pp. 337-360.

Anteproyecto de ley sobre régimen impositivo municipal (Buenos Aires). Ed. Oficial, Buenos Aires, 1948, 125pp.

Bielsa, R. "El poder fiscal en la esfera municipal: Tasas e impuestos—Examen crítico de la distinción," *Impuestos,* vol. 20, 1962, pp. 193-211.

Cima, A. "Los poderes concurrentes de la nación y de las provincias en materia impositiva," *Boletín de la Facultad de derecho y ciencias sociales* (Córdoba), vol. 26, January-April 1962, pp. 321-354.

Figueredo, R. "El convenio sobre impuesto a las actividades lucrativas del 24 de agosto de 1953 y la denuncia de la provincia de entre rios," *Derecho fiscal,* vol. 8, July 1958-June 1959, pp. 469-474.

Forino, S. "Superposición tributaria entre tasas comunales y los impuestos a las actividades lucrativas," *Derecho fiscal,* vol. 13, July 1963-June 1964, pp. 57-74.

Giuliani Fonrouge, C. "Inter-governmental fiscal relations in Republic of Argentine," *Bulletin for international fiscal documentation,* vol. 4, 1950, pp. 299-317.

González, F. "Las últimas modificaciones al régimen tributario de la provincia de Buenos Aires," *Revista del notariado,* vol. 68, no. 682, 1965, pp. 585-605.

González Arzac, F. "La constitución nacional y las facultades impositivas de las provincias en la nueva jurisprudencia de la Corte suprema de la nación," *Revista de desarrollo económico,* vol. 2, no. 2, January-March 1959, pp. 265-273.

Hayzus, J. *Tax relations between governmental units in the Argentine Republic.* Sección Publicaciones del Seminarios de Ciencias Jurídicas y Sociales, Facultad de Derecho de la Universidad de Buenos Aires, Buenos Aires, 1940, 68pp.

"Los impuestos municipios en la provincia de Buenos Aires," *Impuestos,* vol. 17, 1959, pp. 117-118.

La Rosa, R. "Coparticipación y distribución de impuestos entre la nación y las provincias (ley no. 14.799)," *Derecho fiscal,* vol. 8, July 1958-June 1959, pp. 421-433.

López, A., González, F., and Raimondi, C. "Las últimas modificaciones impositivas en la provincia de Buenos Aires," *Derecho fiscal,* vol. 10, July 1960-June 1961, pp. 377-386.

López Agnetti, E. "Competencia territorial del impuesto a las actividades lucrativas," *Información,* vol. 32, 1961, pp. 931-933.

Molina, R. *Régimen financiero municipal de la ciudad de Buenos Aires.* Librería y Editorial "La Facultad," Bernabé y Cía, Buenos Aires, 1941, 417pp.

Molinas, L. "Coordinación del gobierno central con los gobiernos locales en la política fiscal del estado," *Revista de ciencias jurídicas y sociales,* vol. 23, nos. 105-106, 1961, pp. 357-372.

"Municipal taxation," *Municipal digest of the Americas,* vol. 22, no. 3-4, March-April 1961, pp. 1-2.

Patterson, E. "Argentine provincial tax system," *Inter-American economic affairs,* vol. 7, no. 3, 1953, p. 37.

Pellegrini, H. *Régimen rentístico municipal de la ciudad de Buenos Aires, ordenanza general impositiva y su reglamentación: Análisis de las reformas a la ley no. 12.704, introducidas por las leyes no. 13.487 y 13.675.* Lajouane, Buenos Aires, 1950, 131pp.

Pelosi, C. "El régimen impositivo de las comunas y su reflejo en la actividad notarial," *Revista notarial* (La Plata), no. 735, 1961, pp. 575-596.

"Política financiera de la provincia de Buenos Aires," *Impuestos,* vol. 15, 1957, pp. 33-38.

Raimondi, C. "Modificaciones impositivas en la provincia de Buenos Aires," *Derecho fiscal,* vol. 12, July 1962-June 1963, pp. 473-484.

"La reforma fiscal de la provincia de Buenos Aires," *Impuestos,* vol. 17, 1959, pp. 173-175.

"Reformas fiscales en Buenos Aires," *Impuestos,* vol. 14, 1956, pp. 209-212. Reprinted in: *Revista fiscal y financiera,* vol. 16, November 1956, pp. 21-29.

Rennie, R. *Federal-provincial aspects of Argentina fiscal policy.* Ph.D. thesis, Harvard University, Cambridge, Mass., 1947.

"El sistema impositivo de la provincia de Buenos Aires," *Revista de desarrollo económico,* vol. 1, no. 1, October-December 1958, pp. 129-199.

Souza, R. de. "Las relaciones intergubernamentales en la administración tributaria," *Revista de ciencias económicas* (Buenos Aires), vol. 50, January-June 1962.

Tarantino, J. "El código tributario para la provincia de Córdoba, sus antecedentes y críticas al anteproyecto," *Derecho fiscal,* vol. 10, July 1960-June 1961, pp. 145-160.

Tejerina, J. "El impuesto municipal a las actividades lucrativas sobre la exportación de bienes," *Impuestos,* vol. 21, 1963, pp. 487-494.

10

Darrigrandi Aguirre, G. "Del impuesto territorial en Chile, Argentina y otras legislaciones." In: Universidad de Chile, Facultad de Ciencias Jurídicas y Sociales, *Memorias de licenciados,* vol. 13, 1951, pp. 153-203. Editorial Jurídica, Santiago, 1951.

Tezanos Pinto, M. de. "Los elementos objetivos y subjetivos del impuesto inmobiliario en la República Argentina," *Revista de la Facultad de ciencias económicas* (Buenos Aires), vol. 5, nos. 45-50, 1952, pp. 1026-1081.

11

Arnaudo, A. "Productividad, tributación y reforma agraria (estudio de un caso)," *Revista de economía y estadística* (Córdoba) (n.s.), vol. 9, nos. 1-4, 1965, pp. 17-49.

"La desgravación fiscal en favor de las explotaciones agropecuarias," *Boletín de la Dirección general impositiva,* vol. 3, September 1955, pp. 203-207.

Domike, A. "Tax policy and land tenure in Argentina." In: Food and Agricultural Organization of the United Nations, *Information on land reform,* no. 2, pp. 23-37. Rome, 1965.

Gregory, W. "La tributación de la agricultura como instrumento del desarrollo," *Información,* vol. 37, 1966, pp. 1-14.

Marull, J. "Inflación y reforma agraria." In: *Seminario sobre el financiamiento de la reforma agraria.* Instituto Interamericano de Ciencias Agrícolas, San José, 1964.

Oderigo, E. "La renta normal potencial de la tierra," *Impuestos,* vol. 23, 1965, pp. 157-168.

Pereiro, V. "La deducción a los fines del impuesto a los réditos de las inversiones en automotores en las explotaciones agropecuarias," *Derecho fiscal,* vol. 13, July 1963-June 1964, pp. 569-581.

Sapolsky, L. "Los inventarios de hacienda en las explotaciones ganaderas," *Derecho fiscal,* vol. 12, July 1962-June 1963, pp. 529-555.

Sapolsky, L. "La revaluación del novillo," *Impuestos,* vol. 21, 1963, pp. 227-237.

Vieiro, R. "Aspectos impositivos de la ley de arrendamientos y aparcerías rurales (nota a la ley 16.883)," *Impuestos,* vol. 24, 1966, pp. 437-440.

12

"Argentina grants concessions to expand steelmaking capacity," *Foreign commerce weekly,* vol. 66, no. 6, 1961, p. 7.

Atchabahian, A. "Las exenciones tributarias," *Derecho fiscal,* vol. 12, July 1962-June 1963, pp. 377-391.

Augusto Vaz, D. "El sistema del descuento impositivo y los incentivos tributarios," *Impuestos,* vol. 21, 1963, pp. 541-550.

Cámara Argentina de Comercio. *La descentralización industrial y la liberación de impuestos.* Publicación No. 5, Buenos Aires, 1954, 24pp.

Froomkin, J. "Some problems of tax policy in Latin America," *National tax journal,* vol. 10, December 1957, pp. 370-379.

Jarach, D. "Amortizaciones ordinarias, extraordinarias, aceleradas: Deducción por inversiones y revaluación de activos en la política fiscal para el desarrollo económico," *Impuestos,* vol. 19, 1960, pp. 282-286.

López, A. "Los incentivos fiscales a la forestación," *Derecho fiscal,* vol. 13, July 1963-June 1964, pp. 375-384.

Pampillón, M. "Proyecto de ley sobre promoción industrial en la provincia de Buenos Aires," *Impuestos,* vol. 23, 1965, pp. 245-255.

Picado, R. "Las exenciones del art. 19 de la ley 11.682: Algunas consideraciones al respecto," *Información,* vol. 38, 1967, pp. 259-263.

Prados, H. "Comentario al decreto reglamentario de la ley de promoción industrial de la provincia de Buenos Aires," *Impuestos,* vol. 24, 1966, pp. 667-674.

Prados, H. "Comentario de la ley 7110 de promoción industrial de la provincia de Buenos Aires," *Impuestos,* vol. 24, 1966, pp. 65-77.

Raimondi, C. "Nuevo régimen de promoción industrial," *Derecho fiscal,* vol. 13, July 1963-June 1964, pp. 649-674.

Rechter, I. "Desgravaciones impositivas por inversiones vinculadas con la actividad productiva," *Impuestos,* vol. 19, 1961, pp. 327-343.

Rechter, I. "Franquicias tributarias para viviendas económicas," *Impuestos,* vol. 21, 1963, pp. 595-618.

Reig, E. "Incentivos fiscales a la donación filantrópica," *Derecho fiscal,* vol. 7, July 1957-June 1958, pp. 361-366.

13

Amaya, A. "La repetición de impuestos ilegales y el pago con protesta," *Revista jurídica* (Tucumán), no. 8, 1960, pp. 101-122.

Amorós, N. "La elusión y la evasión tributaria," *Información,* vol. 37, 1966, pp. 465-507.

Blanco, E. "Plan de pago de deudas impositivas y cancelación de multas, recargos, e intereses," *Boletín de la Dirección general impositiva,* vol. 4, January 1956, pp. 13-15.

Colegio de Graduados en Ciencias Económicas, Comité Permanente de Impuestos. "Pronunciamiento sobre medidas para evitar la evasión fiscal," *Selección de temas de finanzas públicas* (Montevideo), 1st and 2d quarters 1960, p. 29.

Estevez, A. *El Ministerio de finanzas de la nación.* Edit. Horizontes Económicos, Buenos Aires, 1951, 64pp.

Freytes, R. "Blanqueo de capitales y condonación de multas, recargos e intereses punitorios," *Impuestos,* vol. 20, 1962, pp. 337-358.

Glogauer, G. *Evasión fiscal.* Thesis, Universidad de Buenos Aires, Buenos Aires, 1960.

Haberstroh, C. *Work flow and executive processes of the Argentine tax collection office.* Bureau of Technical Assistance Operations, 1961, 31pp. (duplicated) (restricted).

Jauregui, R. "Delito de defraudación de impuestos y pena corporal," *Información,* vol. 38, 1967, pp. 151-157.

Krieger Vasena, A. "Iniciación de la campaña contra la evasión fiscal," *Boletín de la Dirección general impositiva,* vol. 6, June 1957, pp. 375-379.

López, A. "El decreto no. 6480/62. Blanqueo de capitales e impuesto a los patrimonios injustificados. Condonación de multas, recargos e intereses punitorios. Cancelación de deudas fiscales. Facultades especiales para asegurar el futuro contralor fiscal," *Derecho fiscal,* vol. 12, July 1962-June 1963, pp. 1-26.

López, A. "Los sistemas fiscales como generadores de deshonestidad," *Revista de ciencias económicas* (Buenos Aires), vol. 45, January-February-March 1957, pp. 47-56.

Ministerio de Hacienda de la Nación. *Procedimiento para la aplicación y percepción de impuestos.* Buenos Aires, 1952, 96pp.

"Organización fiscal y reforma impositiva," *Impuestos,* vol. 17, 1959, pp. 201-210.

Peire, J. *Evasión impositiva.* n.p., Buenos Aires, 1959, 44pp.

Price, Waterhouse, Peat & Co. *Condonation of penalties and moratorium for payment of taxes.* Buenos Aires, 1966, 2pp.

"Pronunciamiento sobre medidas para evitar la evasión fiscal," *Revista de ciencias económicas* (Buenos Aires), vol. 46, July-August-September 1958, pp. 311-323.

Raimondi, C. "Recargos por mora en el pago de impuestos," *Derecho fiscal,* vol. 13, July 1963-June 1964, pp. 582-591.

Villegas, H. "Jurisdicción legislativa de nación y provincias en materia de represión fiscal," *Boletín de la Facultad de derecho y ciencias sociales* (Córdoba), vol. 28, May-December 1964, pp. 323-344.

14

Amigo, R. "El conjunto económico en la legislación doctrina y jurisprudencia argentina," *Información,* vol. 38, 1967, pp. 215-258.

Araujo Falcao, A. *El hecho generador de la obligación tributaria.* Depalma, Buenos Aires, 1964.

Atchabahian, A. "La determinación impositiva en el derecho tributario del estado federal argentino," *Derecho fiscal,* vol. 13, July 1963-June 1964, pp. 465-474.

Atchabahian, A. "Nuevo precedente en lo contencioso tributario: El tribunal fiscal nacional en la Argentina," *Diritto e pratica tributaria,* vol. 32-I, 1961, pp. 425-436.

Beltrán, J. "El tribunal fiscal de la nación: Modificaciones introducidas por el decreto-ley 6692/63," *Impuestos,* vol. 21, 1963, pp. 621-625.

Bielsa, R. "Caracteres constitucionales del sistema fiscal," *Impuestos,* vol. 20, 1962, pp. 49-60.

Carámbula, A. "Programa de derecho tributario notarial," *Revista notarial* (La Plata), no. 749, 1963, pp. 1219-1239.

Castellanos, F. "Síntesis práctica de procedimiento tributario," *Impuestos,* vol. 24, 1966, pp. 598-608.

Castiglione, A. "Inconstitucionalidad del impuesto de justicia," *Revista jurídica* (Tucumán), no. 10, 1962, pp. 85-88.

Chapouille, P. "La reestructura del tribunal fiscal de la nación y la competencia que se le asigna para entender en las causas aduaneras (decreto-ley no. 6.692/63)," *Derecho fiscal,* vol. 13, July 1963-June 1964, pp. 513-524.

"Creación del tribunal fiscal: Ley no. 15.265," *Impuestos,* vol. 18, 1960, pp. 2-10.

Falbo, M. "Derecho tributario argentino y la función notarial," *Revista notarial* (La Plata), no. 762, 1965, pp. 1375-1404.

Falbo, M. "El derecho tributario y derecho notarial," *Revista notarial* (La Plata), no. 750, 1963, pp. 1529-1538.

Figueredo, R. "Extensión de actividades pro contribuyentes comprendidos en el convenio multilateral," *Derecho fiscal,* vol. 9, July 1959-June 1960, pp. 165-171.

García Belsunce, H. "Revisiones tributarias y seguridad jurídica," *Impuestos,* vol. 17, 1959, pp. 89-91.

García Vizcaino, J. *El delito de evasión fiscal.* Abeledo-Perrot, Buenos Aires, 1961, 207pp.

Godoy, N. "Interpretación de las normas jurídicas tributarias," *Impuestos,* vol. 17, 1959, pp. 147-156.

Godoy, N. "Recursos en lo contencioso tributario," *Impuestos,* vol. 18, 1960, pp. 289-297.

Giuliani Fonrouge, C., and Bello, J. (eds.). *Procedimiento impositivo.* Depalma, Buenos Aires, 1963, 416pp.

Jarach, D. *El hecho imponible.* Revista de

Jurisprudencia Argentina, S.A., Buenos Aires, 1943, 184pp.

Jarach, D. "Reformas a la ley de procedimientos," *Información,* vol. 33, 1962, pp. 217-228.

Juano, M. de. "Bases constitucionales del régimen tributario argentino." In: Universidad Nacional del Litoral, Facultad de Ciencias Jurídicas y Sociales, Instituto de Derecho Constitucional, *Estado de sitio: Bases constitucionales del régimen tributario argentino,* pp. 63-80. Santa Fé, 1961.

Linares Quintana, S. "Jurisprudencia de la Corte suprema sobre retroactividad, de las leyes fiscales," *Impuestos,* vol. 13, 1955, pp. 91-98.

Linares Quintana, S. *El poder impositivo y la libertad individual.* Edit. Alfa, Buenos Aires, 1950.

López Agnetti, E. "La inconstitucionalidad de la norma y el tribunal fiscal," *Información,* vol. 38, 1967, pp. 1-5.

López Agnetti, E. "Mecanismos de interpretación de la ley impositiva," *Información,* vol. 35, 1964, pp. 139-147, 201-216, 349-369, 425-426, 503-523, 573-578.

Lopez Aguado, A. "El principio de igualdad en materia tributaria," *Revista de la Facultad de ciencias económicas de la Universidad de Cuyo,* vol. 8, September-December 1956, pp. 77-94.

Luqui, J. "La obligación tributaria en el derecho argentino," *Revista de ciencias económicas* (Buenos Aires), vol. 41, May-June 1953, pp. 169-204.

Luqui, J. "Sistema jurídico-tributario argentino (análisis de algunos principios constitucionales)," *Revista notarial* (La Plata), no. 737, 1961, pp. 1051-1080. Also in: *Revista jurídica de Buenos Aires,* no. 4, October-December 1960, pp. 9-41.

Martín, J. "Doctrina de los fallos dictados por el tribunal fiscal de la nación en 1965," *Impuestos,* vol. 25, 1967, pp. 11-65.

Martínez, F. "El privilegio fiscal," *Derecho fiscal,* vol. 13, July 1963-June 1964, pp. 361-374.

Martínez, F. "Los sujetos de la obligación tributaria," *Revista jurídica* (Tucumán), no. 9, 1961, pp. 107-124.

Orlando, O. "Método e interpretación en

el derecho con referencia final a la interpretación de conducta de los sujetos de las relaciones jurídicas tributarias," *Revista del notariado,* vol. 67, no. 673, 1964, pp. 21-38.

"La prescripción, la presentación espontánea y los recursos en nuestra legislación fiscal." In: Cámara Argentina de Sociedades Anónimas, *La sociedad anónima actual,* series 7, vol. 9, pp. 43-78. Buenos Aires, 1961.

Sorondo, J. "Algunas reflexiones en materia de contencioso tributario," *Impuestos,* vol. 17, 1959, pp. 119-132.

Tamagno, R. "Interpretación en el derecho financiero," *Enciclopedia jurídica OMEBA,* vol. 16, 1962, pp. 573-589.

Tarantino, J. "El balance en la quiebra y en el derecho fiscal," *Impuestos,* vol. 17, 1959, pp. 176-177.

Tarantino, J. *Proyecciones de la quiebra en el derecho tributario.* Ediar Soc. Anon. Editores, Buenos Aires, 1961.

Tarantino, J. *Quiebra y tributos.* Ediar Soc. Anon. Editores, Buenos Aires, 1961, 365pp.

Tejerina, J. "Proyecto de creación de un tribunal fiscal administrativo," *Derecho fiscal,* vol. 9, July 1959-June 1960, pp. 233-242.

Tejerina, J. "Sobre la competencia del tribunal fiscal de la nación," *Derecho fiscal,* vol. 10, July 1960-June 1961, pp. 97-107.

Trigo Represas, F. "Algunos aspectos del reconocimiento judicial de la depreciación monetaria," *Jurisprudencia argentina,* vol. 1961-V, September-October 1961, pp. 8-21.

Tróccoli, A. "Los poderes tributarios en la República Argentina," *Anales de la Facultad de ciencias jurídicas y sociales* (Universidad de La Plata), vol. 22, 1962, pp. 131-180.

Vera Villalobos, E. "Cáracteres competencia y procedimiento del tribunal fiscal nacional," *Jurisprudencia argentina,* vol. 1960-V, September-October 1960, pp. 65-73.

17

Almeida, R. "La zona latinoamericana de libre comercio," *Técnicas financieras* (CEMLA), vol. 2, no. 5, May-June 1963, pp. 453-472.

Gutiérrez Kirchner, A. "El mercomún latinoamericano y la política fiscal," *Investigación fiscal,* no. 19, July 1967, pp. 15-63.

Kostzer, M. "Aspectos impositivos de la integración e económica internacional," *Impuestos,* vol. 24, 1966, pp. 199-250.

"Leyes impositivas y decretos reglamentarios: Textos ordenados y actualizados en 1956," *Boletín de la Dirección general impositiva,* vol. 5, July-August 1956, pp. 7-208.

López del Carril, N. "Meditaciones sobre la integración latinoamericana," *Impuestos,* vol. 24, 1966, pp. 336-347.

18

"Argentina law digest." In: *Martindale-Hubbell law directory,* vol. 4, pp. 2423-2441. Martindale-Hubbell, Inc., Summit, N.J., 1961.

Derecho fiscal. Ed. Contabilidad Moderna, Buenos Aires, monthly, July 1951-.

Diamond, W. *Foreign tax and trade briefs.* Fallon Law Book Company, New York, loose-leaf, 1951-.

Dirección General Impositiva. *Boletín de la Dirección general impositiva.* Buenos Aires, monthly, 1954-.

Impuestos. La Ley, S.A., Buenos Aires, monthly, 1942-.

Información. Buenos Aires, monthly, 1930-.

Irizarry y Puente, J. *Argentine federal tax law service.* Latin American Tax Law Research Institute, New York, loose-leaf, 1951-.

Ministerio de Hacienda de la Nación. *Boletín.* Buenos Aires, semimonthly, 1946-.

Palmer, W. *Income tax law translation.* Palmer Editorial, Buenos Aires, 1961, 150pp.

Review of the River Plate. Buenos Aires, three times a month.

Tax Translation Service. English translations of Argentine tax laws. Buenos Aires.

BAHAMAS

1

Price Waterhouse & Co. *Information guide for doing business in the Bahamas.* New York, 1965.

7

United States Department of Commerce. *Foreign trade regulations of the Bahamas.* Washington, 1967, 8pp.

8

Baker, R., *et al.* "Taxpayer's paradise in the Caribbean," *Vanderbilt law review,* vol. 1, 1948, p. 194.

Diamond, W. *Bahamas: New hope for increased profits for American business.* Matthew Bender & Co., New York, 1959, 12pp.

Gibbons, W. *Tax factors in basing international business abroad.* Harvard Law School International Program in Taxation, Cambridge, Mass., 1957, pp. 41-47.

Pine, S., and Sands, S. *Tax and business benefits of the Bahamas.* Prentice-Hall, Inc., Englewood Cliffs, N.J., 1964, 30pp.

Pine, S., and Sands, S. "Tax and business benefits offered by Bahamas." In: Prentice-Hall, Inc., *Tax ideas,* pp. 8841-8865. Englewood Cliffs, N.J., 1957.

Smith, C. "Tax havens," *Taxes,* vol. 37, 1959, pp. 615-629.

Stock, L. "Foreign income, deflected to the Bahamas, accumulates taxfree," *Journal of taxation,* vol. 12, 1960, pp. 250-251.

Stock, L. "Opportunities in the use of Bahamian facilities." In: Tax Institute of America, Inc., *Taxation and operations abroad,* pp. 161-169. Princeton, N.J., 1960.

18

"Bahama Islands law digest." In: *Martindale-Hubbell law directory,* vol. 4, pp. 2461-2465. Martindale-Hubbell, Inc., Summit, N.J., 1961.

Diamond, W. *Foreign tax and trade briefs.* Fallon Law Book Company, New York, loose-leaf, 1951-.

BARBADOS

1

Beasley, C. *A fiscal survey of Barbados.* H. M. Stationery Office, London, 1952.

Canadian Tax Foundation. *Taxes abroad: West Indies.* Toronto, 1961, 22pp.

Comptroller for Development and Welfare. *Financial aspects of federation in the British West Indian territories.* Barbados, 1953.

Prest, A. *A fiscal survey of the British Caribbean.* H. M. Stationery Office, London, 1957, 136pp.
Price Waterhouse & Co. *Information guide for doing business in Barbados.* New York, 1965.

4

"Barbados." In: Board of Inland Revenue (Great Britain), *Income taxes outside the United Kingdom 1966,* vol. 1, pp. 133-169. H. M. Stationery Office, London, 1967.
Foreign Tax Law Association. *Barbados income tax service.* St. Petersburg, Fla., loose-leaf, 1963–.
"Taxation of income in Barbados," *Foreign tax law weekly bulletin,* vol. 15, no. 42, 1965, pp. 11-18.

7

United States Department of Commerce. *Foreign trade regulations of Barbados.* Washington, 1967, 8pp.

8

Noyes Research Co. *Investment in the Caribbean.* Pearl River, N.Y., 1964, 132pp.

9

Hicks, U. *Development from below: Local government and finance in developing countries of the Commonwealth.* Oxford University Press, London, 1961, 552pp.
MacArthur, D. "Problems of local financing in the Caribbean." In A. Wilgus (ed.), *The Caribbean: Natural resources.* University of Florida Press, Gainesville, Fla., 1959.

12

Caribbean Commission. *The promotion of industrial development in the Caribbean.* Port-of-Spain, 1952, 173pp.

17

Seers, D. "Federation of the British West Indies: The economic and financial aspects," *Social and economic studies,* vol. 6, June 1957, pp. 197-214.

BERMUDA

7

United States Department of Commerce. *Foreign trade regulations of Bermuda.* Washington, 1967, 8pp.

8

Appleby, Sperling and Krupe. *A memorandum on the incorporation of companies in Bermuda.* Hamilton, 1959, 9pp.
Bank of N. T. Butterfield and Son, Ltd. *The advantages of incorporating private insurance companies in Bermuda.* Hamilton, 1963, 4pp.
Bank of N. T. Butterfield and Son, Ltd. *Bermuda—A jurisdiction for the corporate and private investor.* Hamilton, 1963, 130pp.
Gibbons, W. *Tax factors in basing international business abroad.* Harvard Law School International Program in Taxation, Cambridge, Mass., 1957, pp. 48-54.
Pine, S., and Graham, D. "Bermuda—A base for foreign business and investment." In: Prentice-Hall, Inc., *Tax ideas,* pp. 9241-9275. Englewood Cliffs, N.J., 1960.

18

"Bermuda law digest." In: *Martindale-Hubbell law directory,* vol. 4, pp. 2477-2483. Martindale-Hubbell, Inc., Summit, N.J., 1961.
Diamond, W. *Foreign tax and trade briefs.* Fallon Law Book Company, New York, loose-leaf, 1951–.

BOLIVIA

1

Morton, W. "La situación boliviana en cuanto al presupuesto y a los impuestos," *Revista de derecho* (La Paz), vol. 6, March 1954, pp. 49-60.
Pan American Union. *A statement of the laws of Bolivia in matters affecting business.* Washington, 1962.
Price Waterhouse & Co. *Information guide for doing business in Bolivia.* New York, 1967.
United States Department of Commerce. *Basic data on the economy of Bolivia.* Washington, 1963, 12pp.
Vásquez, E. *Nociones de finanzas generales y hacienda pública de Bolivia.* La Paz, n.d.

2

National Planning Board. *National plan of economic and social development.* La Paz, pp. 88-91, 127-133.
Strasma, J. *Tax reform in Bolivia, 1961.*

International Cooperation Administration, Washington, 1961, 30pp.

United Nations. *Report of the United Nations mission of technical assistance to Bolivia.* Sales No. 1957.II.B.5, New York, 1957, chapters 5, 6.

4

"Income tax schedule," *Foreign tax law weekly bulletin*, vol. 7, no. 44, 1957, pp. 3-4.

Murphy, E., Jr. "Hydrocarbon concessions in Venezuela and Bolivia: Considerations for the tax lawyer." In: Southwestern Legal Foundation, *Ninth Institute on oil and gas law and taxation.* Matthew Bender & Co., Albany, N.Y., 1958.

10

"Bolivia revises taxation on real estate," *Foreign commerce weekly*, vol. 61, no. 10, 1959.

12

Ministry of National Economy. *Decreelaw for the fostering, stimulating, co-operating with private investments.* La Paz, 1966, 24pp.

United States Department of Commerce. *Investment law of Bolivia.* Washington, 1961, 4pp.

13

Costa, J. *Some aspects of revenues administration in Bolivia.* International Cooperation Administration, Washington, 1957, 70pp. (mimeo).

United Nations, Technical Assistance Administration. "Organization of accounting and financial administration." Doc. No. TAA/BOL/12 (restricted), 18 July 1957.

17

Almeida, R. "La zona latinoamericana de libre comercio," *Técnicas financieras* (CEMLA), vol. 2, no. 5, May-June 1963, pp. 453-472.

Gutiérrez Kirchner, A. "El mercomún latinoamericano y la política fiscal," *Investigación fiscal*, no. 19, July 1967, pp. 15-63.

18

"Bolivia law digest." In: *Martindale-Hubbell law directory*, vol. 4, pp. 2484-2491. Martindale-Hubbell, Inc., Summit, N.J., 1961.

Diamond, W. *Foreign tax and trade briefs.* Fallon Law Book Company, New York, loose-leaf, 1951-.

Economist Intelligence Unit, Ltd. *Economic review of Peru, Bolivia, and Ecuador.* London, irregular.

Hurtado Cuéllo, J. (ed.). *Compilación general de leyes tributarias vigentes en materia de impuestos internos.* Ministerio de Hacienda y Estadística, Dirección General de Ingresos, Administración Nacional de la Renta, La Paz, 1961, 80pp.

BOTSWANA

4

"Botswana." In: Board of Inland Revenue (Great Britain), *Income taxes outside the United Kingdom 1966*, vol. 1, pp. 209-237. H. M. Stationery Office, London, 1967.

BRAZIL

1

"Additional tax established," *Foreign tax law weekly bulletin*, vol. 12, no. 11, 1961, pp. 3-6.

Almiro, A. "Reforma tributária," *Síntese política econômica social*, vol. 4, no. 15, July-September 1962, pp. 23-32. Also in: *Revista das sociedades anônimas ltda.*, vol. 7, no. 78, 1963, pp. 34-42.

Arthur Young & Co. *Brief memorandum on taxation in Brazil.* São Paulo, 1963, 30pp.

Baleeiro, A. "Problemas de taxa no Brasil," *Revista do serviço público*, vol. 16, February 1953, pp. 5-12.

Baleeiro, A. *Uma introdução à ciência das finanças.* Edição Revista Forense, Rio de Janeiro, 2 volumes, 1955.

Barbosa Nogueira, R. *Direito financeiro—Curso de direito tributário.* José Bushatsky, São Paulo, 1964.

Barbosa Nogueira, R. "Problemática do direito tributário no Brasil," *Revista forense*, vol. 194, April-June 1961, p. 461. Also in: *Revista fiscal e de legislação de fazenda*, 31 January 1961, pp. 1-9.

Besson, A. "Finalidades e formas da fiscalização do estado," *Revista do Insti-*

46   TAXATION IN DEVELOPING COUNTRIES

tuto de resseguros do Brasil, vol. 23, no. 137, 1963, pp. 57-100.

Borges Filho, A. "A reforma fiscal no Brasil," *Revista do serviço público,* vol. 25, October-November-December 1961, pp. 64-77.

Boucas, V. "Finanças do Brasil," *Revista de finanças públicas,* vol. 15, May-June 1955, pp. 4-13.

Brazilian Government Trade Bureau. *Corporations, labor and tax system in Brazil.* New York, 1945, 134pp.

de Paula Salazar, A. "Reforma tributária federal," *Sociedades anônimas,* no. 89, January 1964, pp. 28-35.

Diamond, W. *Digest of Brazilian taxes and business organizations.* Overseas Press and Consultants, New York, 1960, 63pp.

Engling, E. "Die Verbrauchsteuer als Hauptpfeiler des brasilianischen Steuersystems," *Finanzarchiv,* vol. 15, no. 2, February 1954, pp. 323-353.

Faria, S. *Problemas jurídicos e econômicos da tributação.* Salvador Livraria Progresso Editôra, Bahia, 1958, 191pp.

Froomkin, J. "Some problems of tax policy in Latin America," *National tax journal,* vol. 10, December 1957, pp. 370-379.

Fundação Getúlio Vargas. *Elementos de direito tributário.* Edições Financeiras S.A., Rio de Janeiro, 1954, 238pp.

Gil, O. "A sinceridade dos balanços face as leis mercantis e fiscais," *Revista das sociedades anônimas ltda.,* vol. 10, no. 113, 1965, pp. 5-10.

Gomes de Sousa, R. *Estudos de direito tributário.* Edição Saraiva, São Paulo, 1950, 318pp.

Gomes de Sousa, R. "O sistema tributário federal," *Revista de direito administrativo,* vol. 72, 1963, pp. 1-22.

Gomes de Sousa, R. "Tax reform in Brazil," *Bulletin for international fiscal documentation,* vol. 20, 1966, pp. 353-368.

Guimarães de Almeida, C. "Considerações sôbre o regime tributário brasileiro," *Revista de direito administrativo,* vol. 69, 1962, pp. 37-50.

Harvard Law School International Program in Taxation. *World Tax Series: Taxation in Brazil.* Prepared by H. Gumpel and R. Gomes de Sousa. Little,

Brown and Co., Boston, 1957, xxxii/373pp.

Hugon, P. *O impôsto: Teoria moderna e principais sistemas o sistema tributário brasileiro.* Edições Financeiras S.A., Rio de Janeiro, 2d edition, 1951, 280pp.

"Important tax decision," *Foreign tax law weekly bulletin,* vol. 11, no. 8, 1960.

Lopes de Sá, A. *Mercado de capitais: Sociedades anônimas, impôsto de renda (comentário sôbre a lei numero 4728, de 14/7/1965, que disciplina o mercado de capitais—Aspectos econômicos, fiscais, financeiros, tributários, administrativos e contábeis).* Editôra Atlas, S.A., São Paulo, 1965, 160pp.

Loureiro, R. *Questões fiscais.* Edição Saraiva, São Paulo, 1953, 324pp.

Ministério de Fazenda, Comissão de Reforma. *Reforma tributária nacional.* Fundação Getúlio Vargas, Rio de Janeiro, 1966.

Monteiro de Barros Filho, T. "Estructura financeira do Brasil." In H. Laufenburger (ed.), *Finanças comparadas.* Edições Financeiras S.A., Rio de Janeiro, 1953.

Pan American Union. *A statement of the laws of Brazil in matters affecting business.* Washington, 3d edition, 1961, 310pp. Supplement, 1966.

Péricles, J., and Rezende, T. *Manual de sêlo.* Biblioteca da Revista Fiscal et de Legislação de Fazenda Vol. VI, Rio de Janeiro, 6th edition, 3 volumes, 1949-1950, 1269pp.

Price Waterhouse & Co. *Information guide for doing business in Brazil.* New York, 1965.

"Reforma do sistema tributário brasileiro," *Revista brasileira dos municípios,* vol. 2, July-September 1949, pp. 489-496.

Shoup, C. *The tax system of Brazil; A report to the Getúlio Vargas foundation.* Fundação Getúlio Vargas, Comissão de Reforma do Ministério da Fazenda, Rio de Janeiro, 1965, xvi/85pp.

Silva, G. da. *Sistema tributário brasileiro.* Edições Financeiras, Rio de Janeiro, 2d edition, 1948, 293pp. Reprinted from: *Report of the Economic and financial committee of the Ministry of finance.* Rio de Janeiro, 1948.

Souza, R. de. "Actualização do conceito de taxa," *Revista de Faculdade de ciências economicas* (Universidade de Mi-

nais Gerais), January-June 1956, p. 5.
Souza, R. de. "Taxa," *Revista de direito administrativo,* vol. 71, 1963, pp. 361-390.
"Summary of recent tax amendments and case decisions," *Foreign tax law weekly bulletin,* vol. 8, no. 30, 1957.
"Tax reform bill," *Foreign tax law weekly bulletin,* vol. 12, no. 42, 1962, pp. 4-9; vol. 12, no. 43, 1962, pp. 1-5.
"Tax reform: Constitutional amendment no. 18," *Monthly bulletin of the British chamber of commerce in Brazil,* vol. 48, 1966, pp. 7-10.
Ulhôa Canto, G. de. "Brazilian taxation alternations during and after the war," *Bulletin for international fiscal documentation,* vol. 2, 1948, pp. 120-126.
Ulhôa Canto, G. de. "Impôsto," *Revista de direito administrativo,* vol. 71, 1963, pp. 344-360.
Ulhôa Canto, G. de. *Temas de direito tributário.* Alba, Rio de Janeiro, 3 volumes, 1964.
Ulhôa Canto, G. de. "Tendências revisionistas da constituição em matéria tributária." In: Instituto Brasileiro de Direito Financeiro, *Problemas de direito tributário,* pp. 65-80. Rio de Janeiro, 1962.
United States Department of Commerce. *Basic data on the economy of Brazil.* Washington, 1964, 24pp.

2

Albuquerque, P. de. *Artifícios e ficções de um plano financeiro, 1952-1955.* SMG, Imprensa do Exército, Rio de Janeiro, 1959, 127pp.
Almeida Magalhães, J. de. "Reforma tributária e progressividade da estrutura fiscal," *Desenvolvimento e conjuntura,* vol. 6, no. 11, November 1962, pp. 7-14.
"Even when times are tough, the budget is under control," *Brazilian business,* vol. 44, no. 2, 1964, pp. 30-34.
"The financial program for 1962," *Conjuntura econômica,* vol. 9, no. 6, June 1962.
Gilson, I. "Panorama financeiro do Brasil," *Revista de direito público e ciência política,* vol. 4, no. 3, September-December 1961, pp. 82-103.
Munhoz Bailão, J. *Alguns aspectos inflacionários de atual pressão tributária no Brasil.* Volume 5 of Coleção "Forum

Roberto Simonsen," Federação e Centro das Industrias do Estado de São Paulo, São Paulo, 1957, 91pp.
Pajiste, B. "As fluctuações economicas e a política fiscal," *Digesto econômico,* vol. 9, no. 98, January 1953, pp. 126-138.
Pajiste, B. *Introdução à política fiscal.* Edições Financeiras, Rio de Janeiro, 1953, 379pp.
Remy, G. "Le Financement des pays sous-développés: L'Exemple du Brésil," *Revue de l'action populaire,* no. 94, January 1956, pp. 38-49.
Sant'Anna e Silva, S. de. *A política fiscal e o desenvolvimento econômico.* Publicação Avulsa No. 98, Departamento Administrativo do Serviço Público, Serviço de Documentação, Rio de Janeiro, 1955, 16pp.
United Nations. *Análisis y proyecciones del desarrollo económico—II: El desarrollo económico del Brazil.* Sales No. 1956.II.G.2, New York, 1956, x/165pp.
United States Department of State. *Report of the Brazil-United States technical commission.* Washington, 1949, 321pp.
Villela, A. "Observações sôbre os efeitos economicos de alguns impostos," *Econômica brasileira* (Rio de Janeiro), July-December 1960, p. 117.

3

"Análisis comparativo de la tributación en la Argentina, el Brasil, Chile y México." In: United Nations, *Las inversiones privadas extranjeras en la zona latinoamericana de libre comercio,* pp. 31-33. Sales No. 1960.II.G.5, México, 1960.
Diez del Valle, M. "O sistema tributário cubano, estudo comparativo com o sistema brasileiro," *Revista de finanças públicas,* vol. 13, July-August 1953, pp. 42-45.

4

"Additional tax on profits," *Foreign tax law weekly bulletin,* vol. 10, no. 51, 1960.
Araújo Falção, A. de. "O impôsto de renda sôbre a capitalização de reservas," *Revista de direito administrativo,* vol. 77, 1964, pp. 31-55.
"Bearer shares," *Foreign tax law weekly bulletin,* vol. 11, no. 8, 1960.
Boucher, H. *Conceitos e categórias de*

direito tributário (impôsto de renda). Livraria Freitas Bastos S.A., Rio de Janeiro, 2d edition, 1955, 432pp.

Boucher, H. *Estudos de impôsto de renda e contabilidade.* Livraria Freitas Bastos, Rio de Janeiro, 1950, 460pp.

Boucher, H. *Estudos de impôsto de renda e lucros imobiliários.* Livraria Freitas Bastos, Rio de Janeiro, 1953, 329pp.

"Brazil raises 1959 income taxes," *Foreign commerce weekly,* vol. 61, no. 1, 1959. Also in: *Foreign tax law weekly bulletin,* vol. 9, no. 28, 1958.

British Chamber of Commerce in Brazil. *Brazilian income tax regulations.* Rio de Janeiro, 1965, 311pp.

Carneiro, E. (ed.). *Anotações ao regulamento do impôsto de renda.* Edições Financeiras, Rio de Janeiro, 1963, 271pp.

Carneiro, E. "Comparison of tax provisions for reserves and depreciation allowances, Brazil," *Cahiers de droit fiscal international,* vol. 21, 1952, p. 37.

Carneiro, E. "A contabilidade de custo e o impôsto de renda." *Revista das sociedades anônimas ltda.,* vol. 8, no. 89, 1964, pp. 4-13.

Carneiro, E. (ed.). *Impôsto de renda, comentários.* Edições Financeiras, Rio de Janeiro, 2d edition, 1964, 503pp.

Carneiro, E. (ed.). *A nova lei do impôsto de renda: Lei 4506 de 30-XI-1964.* Edições Financeiras, Rio de Janeiro, 1965, 33pp.

Carneiro, E., and Barbieri, C. (eds.). *Regulamento do impôsto de renda.* Revista das Sociedades Anônimas, Rio de Janeiro, 1960.

Chaves, E. *Consultor do impôsto de renda.* Publicações Associadas Paulista Limitada, São Paulo, 2 volumes, 1962, 316pp.

Chaves, N. *Dicionário de jurisprudencia do impôsto de renda.* Publicações Associadas Paulista Limitada, São Paulo, 1962, 268pp.

Costa, L. *Impôsto de renda, 1964.* Atlas, São Paulo, 1964, 124pp.

"Decree no. 24,239 of December, 1947, approves the regulations for the collection and supervision of the income tax," *Brazilian business,* March 1948, pp. 14-69.

"Decreto no. 55.866 de 25 de março de 1965: Aprova o regulamento para a cobrança e fiscalização do impôsto de renda," *Revista das sociedades anônimas ltda.,* vol. 9, no. 105, 1965, pp. 4-56.

Foreign Tax Law Association. *Brazilian income tax service.* Centerport, L.I., N.Y., 2 volumes, loose-leaf, 1953-1955.

Gomes de Sousa, R. "Family charges in Brazilian fiscal law," *Bulletin for international fiscal documentation,* vol. 2, 1948, pp. 369-379.

Impôsto de renda. Forense, Rio de Janeiro, 3d edition, 1963, 111pp.

"Income tax amendments law," *Monthly bulletin of the British chamber of commerce in Brazil,* vol. 44, 1963, pp. 5-13.

"Income tax on revenue from work," *Monthly bulletin of the British chamber of commerce in Brazil,* vol. 46, 1964, pp. 79-81.

"Income tax owed by individuals," *Foreign tax law weekly bulletin,* vol. 16, no. 38, 1966, pp. 4-6.

Lei do impôsto de renda; decreto-lei no. 47.373 de 7 de dezembro de 1959: Aprova o regulamento para o cobrança e fiscalização do impôsto de renda. Rio de Janeiro, 1959, 66pp.

Lima, A. *O impôsto de renda em análise.* Rio de Janeiro, 1959, 179pp.

"Limitation of tax deductibility of remuneration of corporate directors," *Foreign tax law weekly bulletin,* vol 9, no. 44, 1959.

MacNair, H. "Taxation of gains from sale of real estate in Brazil," *Bulletin for international fiscal documentation,* vol. 15, 1961, pp. 65-69.

Madeiros Pereira de Souza, P. *Impôsto de renda 1966.* Editôra "Revista dos Tribunais" Ltda., São Paulo, 1966, 126pp.

Magalhães, R. de. *Regime fiscal das sociedades comerciais.* Konfino, Rio de Janeiro, 1964, 310pp.

Ministério de Fazenda, Comissão de Reforma. *Evolução do impôsto de renda no Brasil.* Fundação Getúlio Vargas, Rio de Janeiro, 1966.

Ministério de Fazenda, Comissão de Reforma. *Guia geral do impôsto de renda.* Fundação Getúlio Vargas, Rio de Janeiro, 1966.

Miranda Guimarães, Y. de. *O impôsto de indústria e profissões, teoria e práctica.* Edição Saraiva, São Paulo, 1954, 202pp.

Moreira, V. "Reformas tributárias: O código do impôsto profisional," *Revista de economía* (Lisbon), vol. 14, no. 2, June 1962.

Pires, P. *Impôsto de renda: Reforma de serviços.* Sulina, São Paulo, 2d edition, 1961, 62pp.

"Regulamento do impôsto de renda: Decreto no. 51.900 de 10 abril de 1963," *Revista das sociedades anônimas ltda.,* vol. 7, no. 80, 1963, pp. 17-98.

Rezende, T. *Impôsto de renda: Anotações.* Biblioteca da Revista Fiscal et de Legislação de Fazenda Vol. XXII, Rio de Janeiro, 2d edition, 2 volumes, 1953, 933pp.

Rezende, T. *A nova legislação do impôsto de renda.* Biblioteca da Revista Fiscal e de Legislação de Fazenda Vol. XLI, Rio de Janeiro, 1963, 123pp.

Rezende, T. *A nova lei do impôsto de renda.* Biblioteca da Revista Fiscal et de Legislação de Fazenda Vol. XXXVI, Rio de Janeiro, 1959, 132pp.

Rezende, T. *Novo regulamento do impôsto de renda.* Biblioteca da Revista Fiscal e de Legislação de Fazenda Vol. XXVIII, Rio de Janeiro, 2 volumes, 1960, 260/181pp.

Rezende, T., and Castro Viana, J. *Consolidação das leis do impôsto de renda.* Biblioteca da Revista Fiscal e de Legislação de Fazenda Vol. XXIX, Rio de Janeiro, 2 volumes, 1955, 572pp.

Rodríguez Sainz, A. "Esquema del impuesto sobre la renta," *Revista de derecho financiero y de hacienda pública* (Madrid), vol. 13, 1963, pp. 1079-1108.

Roque, G. de la. *Conheça o impôsto de renda!* Souza Lopes, São Paulo, 1964, 193pp.

"Salary and income tax," *Conjuntura econômica,* vol. 3, no. 7, July 1956, p. 51.

Silva e Serpa, A. de. "Tributação das actividades comerciais e industriais," *Boletin da Direção-geral das contribuições e impôstos,* vol. 16, 1960, pp. 524-544.

Soares, A. "Evolução do impôsto de renda no Brasil," *Observador econômico e financeiro,* vol. 16, February 1952, pp. 58-62.

Sousa, R. de. *Consolidação das leis do impôsto de renda.* Editôra Paulista, São Paulo, 1966, 448pp.

Sousa, R. de. *Impôsto de renda.* Edições Financeiras, Rio de Janeiro, 1955.

"Tax allowance for remuneration paid to

officers," *Foreign tax law weekly bulletin,* vol. 16, no. 35, 1966, pp. 1-7.

Ulhôa Canto, G. de. "Taxes affecting industrial and commercial enterprises in Brazil," *Bulletin for international fiscal documentation,* vol. 4, 1950, pp. 66-79.

5

Araujo, P. de. *O impôsto sôbre a transmissão da propriedade.* Fundação Getúlio Vargas, Rio de Janeiro, 1954, 379pp.

Moreira, V. "Reformas tributárias: O código do impôsto de capitais," *Revista de economía* (Lisbon), vol. 14, no. 3, September 1962.

6

Araujo, R. "Fusão e incorporação são categorias autónomas do direito privado e como tais não sofrem a incidência do impôsto de vendas e consignações," *Revista académica* (Faculdade de Direito de Recife), vol. 61, 1963, pp. 99-114.

Araújo Falção, A. de. *O novo impôsto do sêlo explicado.* Branco, Rio de Janeiro, 1959, 192pp.

Conselho do Desenvolvimento. *Revisão do impôsto único sôbre combustíveis líquidos.* Rio de Janeiro, 1956, 104pp.

Gil, O. "O impôsto do sêlo e a conversão de forma das ações nas sociedades anônimas," *Revista de direito administrativo,* vol. 71, 1963, pp. 391-402.

Gil, O. *Impôsto sôbre vendas e consignações.* Edições Financeiras, Rio de Janeiro, 1954.

"Incidência e exigibilidade do impôsto de consumo." In: M. Reale, *Nos quadrantes do direito positivo,* pp. 399-410. Gráfica-Editora Michalany, São Paulo, 1960.

Jucá, J. "A nova lei do sêlo," *Revista das sociedades anônimas ltda.,* vol. 10, no. 109, 1965, pp. 39-44.

Ministério de Fazenda, Comissão de Reforma. *Dicionário do impôsto de consumo.* Fundação Getúlio Vargas, Rio de Janeiro, 1966.

Ministério de Fazenda, Comissão de Reforma. *Regulamento e documentação subsidiária do impôsto de consumo.* Fundação Getúlio Vargas, Rio de Janeiro, 1966, 430pp.

Pinto, G. "Tributação da alcada do Instituto do açúcar e do alcool, *Revista de finanças públicas,* vol. 12, November-December 1952, pp. 6-10.

"Proposed new ad valorem tax on petroleum products," *Foreign tax law weekly bulletin,* vol. 7, no. 28, 1956.

"Recolhimiento ao tesouro nacional das taxas terminais, pelas emprêsas concessionárias de serviços de telecomunicação." In: Ministério das Relações Exteriores, *Pareceres dos consultores jurídicos do Ministério das relações exteriores (1935-1945),* pp. 421-431. Rio de Janeiro, 1961.

"Reform of the excise tax," *Conjuntura econômica,* vol. 9, no. 11, September 1962.

Rego, R. *O nôvo impôsto do sêlo federal.* Forense, Rio de Janeiro, 1965, 209pp.

Rezende, T. *Impôsto sôbre vendas e consignações.* Biblioteca da Revista Fiscal et de Legislação de Fazenda, Rio de Janeiro, 1955, 468pp.

Rezende, T., and Péricles, J. *Manual do impôsto de consumo.* Biblioteca da Revista Fiscal et de Legislação de Fazenda Vol. XXIV, Rio de Janeiro, 9 volumes, 1951-1956.

"Sales impost not due on foreign sales," *Foreign tax law weekly bulletin,* vol. 11, no. 9, 1960.

"Sales tax and increasing of capital," *Foreign tax law weekly bulletin,* vol. 7, no. 44, 1957.

"Sole tax on lubricants and gaseous fuels," *Monthly bulletin of the British chamber of commerce in Brazil,* vol. 46, 1964, pp. 208-212.

"Sole tax on minerals," *Monthly bulletin of the British chamber of commerce in Brazil,* vol. 46, 1964, pp. 203-205.

Souza, R. de. *O impôsto sôbre vendas e consignações no sistema tributário brasileiro.* Edições Financeiras, Rio de Janeiro, 1956, 424pp.

Ulhôa Canto, G. de. "L'Impôt sur les ventes et consignations au Brésil." In: M. Masoin and E. Morselli (eds.), *Impôts sur transactions, transmissions et chiffre d'affaires,* pp. 95-115. Archives Internationales de Finances Publiques No. 2, Cedam Casa Editrice, Dr. A. Milani, Padova, 1959.

7

British Chamber of Commerce in Brazil. *The Brazilian customs tariff.* Rio de Janeiro, 1960, 153pp.

Ministério de Fazenda, Comissão de Reforma. *Impôsto de importação.* Fundação Getúlio Vargas, Rio de Janeiro, 1966.

United States Department of Commerce *Foreign trade regulations of Brazil* Washington, 1967, 8pp.

8

American Chamber of Commerce for Brazil. *Summary of taxes more likely to be handled by a foreign company operating in Brazil.* Rio de Janeiro, 1963, 13pp.

Brazilian Embassy. *A guide to investing in Brazil.* Washington, 1966, 74pp.

Carolin, J., Pinheiro Neto, J., and Buckeridge, T. *Memorandum on the setting up of an organization in Brazil.* Bank of London & South America Ltd., London, 1960, 60pp.

Dale, W. *Brazil: Factors affecting foreign investment.* International Industrial Center, Stanford Research Institute, Menlo Park, Calif., 1959, 75pp.

Foundation for the Advancement of International Business Administration. "Taxation of foreign source income: A forum," *Brazilian business,* May 1959, p. 18.

Giese, M. "U.S. foreign income tax credit. II: Brazilian taxes and their tax credit status," *Chicago bar record,* vol. 37, 1956, pp. 273-276.

Gumpel, H. "Brazil." In: American Management Association, *The taxation of business income from foreign operations,* pp. 110-116. New York, 1958.

Manoliu, F. "La doble imposición," *Revista de economía y estadística* (Rio de Janeiro), vol. 8, no. 2, 1964, pp. 79-151.

"Summary of taxes more likely to be handled by a foreign company operating in Brazil," *Foreign tax law weekly bulletin,* vol. 14, no. 8, 1963, pp. 1-9; vol. 14, no. 9, 1963, pp. 1-6.

United States Department of Commerce. *Brazil—Information for United States businessmen.* Washington, 1961, 207pp.

United States Department of Commerce. *Establishing a business in Brazil.* Washington, 1966, 28pp.

9

Almeida, A. de. "Estradas e impostos do sul do Brasil," *Revista do arquivo municipal* (São Paulo), vol. 153, November 1952, pp. 73-83.

Baleeiro, A. "Estados, discriminação de rendas e reforma constitucional," *Revista forense*, vol. 143, 1952, p. 7. Reprinted in: *Revista de direito administrativo*, vol. 30, 1952, p. 11.

Baleeiro, A. "Taxas de defesa contra fogo: Rio Grande do Sul, Brazil, Tribunal superior," *Revista jurídica*, no. 69, 1965, pp. 64-76.

Benevolo, O. "Bases para um regime econômico a adotar na futura capital federal," *Revista brasileira dos municípios*, vol. 8, pp. 128-137.

Bernades, C. "O poder tributador e suas implicações no federalismo brasileiro," *Justitia*, vol. 39, no. 4, 1962, pp. 101-120.

Boucas, V. "Os municípios e a discriminação de rendas," *Revista de finanças públicas*, vol. 12, September 1952, pp. 3-10.

Burkinski, F. "Distribução das rendas fiscais e aproveitamento dos recursos locais," *Revista brasileira dos municípios*, vol. 14, no. 55-56, July-December 1961, pp. 134-137.

Burkinski, F. "Finanças, orçamento e contabilidade dos municípios," *Revista de finanças públicas*, vol. 13, January-February 1953, pp. 18-25.

Carvalho, O. "Relações financeiras da união com as outras órbitas de governo," *Digesto econômico*, vol. 10, January 1954, pp. 34-45.

Carvalho Mendanha, D. de. "A fiscalização financeira dos municípios pelos Tribunais de contas estaduais," *Revista brasileira de estudos políticos*, no. 13, January 1962, pp. 249-274.

Código de impostos e taxas. Alvares, Belo Horizonte, 1961, 278pp.

Delorenzo Neto, A. "A política financeira da união em relação às entidades locais. O regime de subvenções," *Revista do serviço público*, vol. 23, November-December 1959, pp. 154-163.

Donald, C. "The politics of local government finance in Brazil," *Inter-American economic affairs*, vol. 13, no. 1, 1959, p. 21.

Faria, S. "O fisco estadual e as mercadorias transferidas," *Revista de la Faculdade de direito* (Universidade da Bahia), vol. 34, 1959-61, pp. 38-57.

Ferreira, I. "Limitações tributárias municipais," *Revista do serviço público*, vol. 16, November 1953, pp. 131-136.

Gil, O. "Discrimanação de rendas," *Revista das sociedades anônimas ltda.*, vol. 7, no. 79, 1963, pp. 4-11.

Hardy, G. *Belo Horizonte property assessment* (in Portuguese). International Cooperation Administration, March 1956, 27pp. (mimeo).

Leite, A. de. *Impostas na guanabara: Estudo econômico-financeiro dos impostos estaduais e municipais.* Edições Financeiras, Rio de Janeiro, 1961, 257pp.

Machado, J. "Rendas locais na constitução federal," *Revista de administração municipal*, vol. 9, no. 50, January-February 1962, pp. 16-23.

Mello, L. de. "O problema das finanças municipais no Brasil," *Revista brasileira dos municípios*, vol. 9, July-December 1956, pp. 209-216.

Ministério de Fazenda, Comissão de Reforma. *Reforma da discriminação constitucional de rendas.* Fundação Getúlio Vargas, Rio de Janeiro, 1965.

Murray, C., and Ballão, J. *Panorama das finanças públicas do estado de São Paulo.* Escola de Sociologia e Política de São Paulo, São Paulo, 1954, 39pp.

Nattier, F., Jr. "Local taxation: Brazil." In: H. Landau, *Doing business abroad*, pp. 393-411. Practising Law Institute, New York, 1962.

Oliveira, Y. de. "Estudo da adequação de rendas municipais," *Revista de finanças públicas*, vol. 12, September 1952, pp. 13-16.

Palmer, T. "Estado de São Paulo: Elementos de história financeira," *Revista de finanças públicas*, vol. 12, June 1952, pp. 3-5; vol. 12, July-August 1952, pp. 8-11.

"Sales tax most important of all state taxes," *Conjuntura econômica* (international edition), vol. 7, November 1960, pp. 47-53.

Silva, A. "Estructura econômica financeira comparada de vinte e seis municípios de São Paulo," *Revista de administração municipal*, vol. 4, September-December 1950, pp. 41-71.

Silva, D. da. "O município e o impôsto de renda," *Revista do serviço público*, vol. 16, November 1953, pp. 124-130.

"State taxes," *Foreign tax law weekly bulletin*, vol. 13, no. 35, 1963, pp. 6-9; vol. 13, no. 36, 1963, pp. 1-3.

"States and municipalities—Their share of

the union's tax revenue," *Conjuntura econômica* (international edition), December 1960, pp. 46-51.

Tácito, C. "Taxa de bombeiros," *Revista jurídica*, no. 69, 1965, pp. 77-96.

Tieseira, C. "Tributação nos territórios federais," *Revista do serviço público*, vol. 8, December 1945, pp. 55-62; vol. 9, April 1946, pp. 21-28; vol. 9, July 1946, pp. 58-61.

Ulhôa Canto, G. de. "Study of the Brazilian tax system in view of the federal regime," *Bulletin for international fiscal documentation*, vol. 3, 1949, pp. 72-104.

Villa, F. "Notas sôbre a competência tributária dos municípios," *Revista do serviço público*, vol. 16, October 1953, pp. 102-108.

10

Boucher, H. *Estudio da mais-valia no direito tributário brasileiro*. Livraria Freitas Bastos, Rio de Janeiro, 1964.

"Regulamento do estatuto da terra," *Revista das sociedades anônimas ltda.*, vol. 10, no. 109, 1965, pp. 8-15.

Vegni-Neri, G. *Prática das transações imobiliárias*. Companhia Editôra Nacional, São Paulo, 1967, pp. 177-210.

11

Nicholls, W. *Complete texts of the law and regulations, agrarian reform law of 1960, state of São Paulo, Brazil*. Vanderbilt University, Nashville, Tenn., 1961, 29pp. (mimeo).

12

Barbieri, C. "Manutenção do capital de giro e estímulos fiscais," *Revista das sociedades anônimas ltda.*, vol. 10, 1965, pp. 14-27.

Carneiro, E., and Barbieri, C. "Como interpretar as normas sôbre estímulos fiscais," *Revista das sociedades anônimas ltda.*, vol. 10, no. 111, 1965, pp. 4-39.

Hirschman, A. *Industrial development in the Brazilian Northeast and the tax credit mechanism of article 34/18*. Paper prepared for the Agency for International Development at Harvard University, Cambridge, Mass., July 1967, 33pp.

Price, Waterhouse, Peat & Co. *Brazilian tax concessions in the northeastern region of Brazil, under law no. 4239, June 27, 1963*. São Paulo, 1963, 2pp.

13

Andrade, C. de. "O aluguel das coletorias federais," *Revista do serviço público*, vol. 24, October-November-December 1960, pp. 71-80.

Carvalho, F. de. *Administração, fisco e arrecadação*. Coelho Branco, Rio de Janeiro, 1965, 393pp.

"Department of income tax, 1951," *Foreign tax law weekly bulletin*, vol. 2, no. 32A, 1951.

Lyra Filho, J. *Da descentralização funcional do Tribunal de contas*. Departamento de Imprensa Nacional, Rio de Janeiro, 1959, 64pp.

Lyra Filho, J. "O emprêgo e o contrôle dos dinheiros públicos," *Revista brasileira de estudos políticos*, vol. 11, June 1961, pp. 198-221.

Ministério de Fazenda, Comissão de Reforma. *Arrecadação pela rêde bancaria*. Fundação Getúlio Vargas, Rio de Janeiro, 1965.

Ministério de Fazenda, Comissão de Reforma. *Cadastro geral de contribuintes*. Fundação Getúlio Vargas, Rio de Janeiro, 1966.

Ministério de Fazenda, Comissão de Reforma. *Departamento de arrecadação*. Fundação Getúlio Vargas, Rio de Janeiro, 1965.

Ministério de Fazenda, Comissão de Reforma. *Departamento de rendas internas*. Fundação Getúlio Vargas, Rio de Janeiro, 1966.

Ministério de Fazenda, Comissão de Reforma. *Processo tributário*. Fundação Getúlio Vargas, Rio de Janeiro, 1964, 161pp.

Ministério de Fazenda, Comissão de Reforma. *Serviço federal de processamento de dados*. Fundação Getúlio Vargas, Rio de Janeiro, 1966.

"New withholding tax regulations," *Foreign tax law weekly bulletin*, vol. 9, no. 41, 1959, pp. 3-5.

14

Araújo Falção, A. de. *Direito tributário brasileiro (aspectos concretos)*. Edições Financeiras, Rio de Janeiro, 1960, 387pp.

Baleeiro, A. *O direito tributário da constituição*. Instituto Brasileiro de Direito Financeiro, Edições Financeiras, Rio de Janeiro, 1959, 202pp.

Baleeiro, A. *Limitações constitucionais ao poder de tributar.* Edição Revista Forense, Rio de Janeiro, 2d edition, 1960, 430pp.

Barbosa Nogueira, R. *Da interpretação e da aplicação das leis tributarias.* Revista dos Tribunais, São Paulo, 2d edition, 1965, 138pp.

Barbosa Nogueira, R. "O princípio de legalidade ou de reserva da lei, na tributação," *Justitia,* vol. 26, 1964, pp. 136-150.

Costa, A. "Conceito de tributo, impôsto e taxa," *Revista de direito administrativo,* vol. 78, 1964, pp. 26-37.

Costa, A. "Natureza jurídica dos empréstitos compulsórios," *Revista de direito administrativo,* vol. 70, 1962, pp. 1-11. Also in: *Revista forense,* vol. 203, 1963, pp. 19-24.

Dória, A. *Princípios constitucionais tributários e a cláusula due process of law.* Thesis, Universidad de São Paulo, Emprêsa Gráfica da "Revista dos Tribunais," São Paulo, 1964, 279pp.

Dória, H. *Direito processual tributário.* J. Bushatsky, São Paulo, 1963, 351pp.

Faria, S. "Immunidade fiscal das pessôas jurídicas de direito público," *Scientia iuridica,* vol. 12, January-March 1963, pp. 9-26.

Ferreira, A. "A criação do crédito fiscal e sus condições," *Revista do serviço público,* vol. 24, October-November-December 1960, pp. 48-66.

Ferreira, A. *Direito fiscal: Aspectos doctrinários e práticos.* Edição Saraiva, São Paulo, 1961, 309pp.

Gil, O. *Direito fiscal aplicado.* Edições Financeiras, Rio de Janeiro, 1963, 388pp.

Instituto Brasileiro de Direito Financeiro. *Justiça e processo fiscal.* Rio de Janeiro, 1954, 285pp.

Instituto Brasileiro de Direito Financeiro. *Problemas de direito tributário.* Edições Financeiras, Rio de Janeiro, 1962, 154pp.

Lins, M., and Loureiro, C. *Teoria e prática do direito tributário.* Forense, Rio de Janeiro, 1961, 503pp.

Loureiro, R. *O processo executivo fiscal no direito constituído e constituendo.* Revista dos Tribunais, São Paulo, 1961, 430pp.

Melo, R. de. *Teoria e prática do processo fiscal.* Salvador Livraria Progresso Editôra, Bahia, 1957, 223pp.

Pontes, V. *A defesa do contribuiente no processo executivo fiscal.* Borsoi, Rio de Janeiro, 1962, 245pp.

Ribeiro, M. "Aspectos jurídicos do projeto de código de contabilidade pública da união," *Revista de direito administrativo,* vol. 79, 1965, pp. 38-48.

Rocha Guimarães, C. da. "O processo fiscal." In: Instituto brasileiro de direito financeiro, *Problemas de direito tributário,* pp. 97-154. Rio de Janeiro, 1962.

Sousa, M. de. "The juridical nature of the 'quinto do ouro' " (in Portuguese), *Revista da Faculdade de direito* (São Paulo), vol. 56, no. 1, 1961, pp. 299-327.

Ulhôa Canto, G. de. "Alcuni aspetti giuridico-costituzionali della parafiscalità nel Brasile," *Archivio finanziario,* vol. 5, 1956, pp. 36-41.

Ulhôa Canto, G. de. *O processo tributário.* Fundação Getúlio Vargas, Rio de Janeiro, 1965.

Vanoni, E. *Natureza e interpretação das leis tributárias.* Edições Financeiras, Rio de Janeiro, 1953, 345pp.

15

Kafka, A. "The Brazilian exchange auction system," *Review of economics and statistics,* vol. 38, 1956, p. 308.

17

Almeida, R. "La zona latinoamericana de libre comercio," *Técnicas financieras* (CEMLA), vol. 2, no. 5, May-June 1963, pp. 453-472.

Gutiérrez Kirchner, A. "El mercomún latinoamericano y la política fiscal," *Investigación fiscal,* no. 19, July 1967, pp. 15-63.

18

"Brazil law digest." In: *Martindale-Hubbell law directory,* vol. 4, pp. 2492-2505. Martindale-Hubbell, Inc., Summit, N.J., 1961.

"Brazilian income tax legislation." In: American Society of International Law, *International legal materials,* vol. 3, pp. 898-921. Washington, 1964.

Diamond, W. *Foreign tax and trade briefs.* Fallon Law Book Company, New York, loose-leaf, 1951–.

Economist Intelligence Unit, Ltd. *Economic review of Brazil.* London, irregular.

Gomes de Sousa, R. *Compêndio de legis-lação tributária.* Edições Financeiras, Rio de Janeiro, 3d edition, 1960, 164pp.
"Leis fiscais." In: J. Dias and F. Dias (eds.), *Carteira da "Revista forense,"* vol. 2, pp. 2795-3088. Edição Revista Forense, Rio de Janeiro, 2d edition, 1961.
Ministério de Fazenda, Comissão de Reforma. *Indicador da legislação fazendaria.* Fundação Getúlio Vargas, Rio de Janeiro, 1966.
Sociedades anônimas. Revista das Sociedades Anônimas, Rio de Janeiro, monthly, September 1956-.

BRITISH HONDURAS

4

"British Honduras." In: Board of Inland Revenue (Great Britain), *Income taxes outside the United Kingdom 1966,* vol. 1, pp. 243-263. H. M. Stationery Office, London, 1967.

12

"British Honduras: Tax concessions and income taxes," *Foreign tax law weekly bulletin,* vol. 16, no. 6, 1965, pp. 6-18.
Government of British Honduras. *British Honduras—Tax holidays.* 1960, 37pp.

BRITISH VIRGIN ISLANDS

1

United States Department of Commerce. *Basic data on the economy of the British Virgin Islands.* Washington, 1964, 8pp.

4

"Virgin Islands." In: Board of Inland Revenue (Great Britain), *Income taxes outside the United Kingdom 1966,* vol. 8, pp. 229-243. H. M. Stationery Office, London, 1967.

BRITISH WEST INDIES

1

Canadian Tax Foundation. *Taxes abroad: West Indies.* Toronto, 1961, 22pp.
Prest, A. *A fiscal survey of the British Caribbean.* H. M. Stationery Office, London, 1957, 136pp.

4

Foreign Tax Law Association. *Leeward Islands income tax service.* Deer Park, L.I., N.Y., loose-leaf, 1950-1953.
Foreign Tax Law Association. *Windward Islands income tax service.* Deer Park, L.I., N.Y., loose-leaf, 1948-1952.
"Montserrat." In Board of Inland Revenue (Great Britain), *Income taxes outside the United Kingdom 1966,* vol. 5, pp. 195-211. H. M. Stationery Office, London, 1967.
"St. Christopher, Nevis and Anguilla (St. Kitts)." In: Board of Inland Revenue (Great Britain), *Income taxes outside the United Kingdom 1966,* vol. 6, pp. 343-362. H. M. Stationery Office, London, 1967.
"St. Lucia." In: Board of Inland Revenue (Great Britain), *Income taxes outside the United Kingdom 1966,* vol. 7, pp. 1-23. H. M. Stationery Office, London, 1967.
"St. Vincent." In: Board of Inland Revenue (Great Britain), *Income taxes outside the United Kingdom 1966,* vol. 7, pp. 25-42. H. M. Stationery Office, London, 1967.
"West Indies." In: Board of Inland Revenue (Great Britain), *Income taxes outside the United Kingdom 1966,* vol. 8, pp. 245-252. H. M. Stationery Office, London, 1967.

8

Noyes Research Co. *Investment in the Caribbean.* Pearl River, N.Y., 1964, 132pp.

9

Hicks, U. *Development from below: Local government and finance in developing countries of the Commonwealth.* Oxford University Press, London, 1961, 552pp.
MacArthur, D. "Problems of local financing in the Caribbean." In: A. Wilgus (ed.), *The Caribbean: Natural resources.* University of Florida Press, Gainesville, Fla., 1959.

12

Caribbean Commission. *The promotion of industrial development in the Caribbean.* Port-of-Spain, 1952, 173pp.

17

Comptroller for Development and Welfare. *Financial aspects of federation in the British West Indian territories.* Barbados, 1953.

Seers, D. "Federation in the British West Indies: The economic and financial aspects," *Social and economic studies,* vol. 6, June 1957, pp. 197-214.

BURMA

1

United States Department of Commerce. *Basic data on the economy of Burma.* Washington, 1963, 8pp.

2

Knappen Tippets Abbott Eng. Co., Pierce Management, Inc., and Robert Nathan Associates, Inc. *Economic and engineering survey of Burma.* Foreign Operations Administration, 1953, vol. I, chapter IV.

Mali, K. *Financing economic development of Burma since independence.* Ph.D. thesis, Indiana, 1960.

Musgrave, R. *Fiscal policy and development in Burma.* Private paper, 1959.

Musgrave, R. *Tax policy for economic development in Burma.* Robert R. Nathan Associates, Inc., 1955 (mimeo).

United Nations. *Mobilization of domestic capital in certain countries of Asia and the Far East.* Sales No. 1951.II.F.3, Bangkok, 1951.

4

"Burma." In: Board of Inland Revenue (Great Britain), *Income taxes outside the United Kingdom 1966,* vol. 1, pp. 313-328. H. M. Stationery Office, London, 1967.

7

United States Department of Commerce. *Import tariff system of Burma.* Washington, 1962, 2pp.

8

United States Department of Commerce. *Establishing a business in Burma.* Washington, 1956, 12pp.

11

Binns, B. *Agricultural economy in Burma.* Rangoon, 1948, pp. 45-48.

12

"Burma's new investment act and rules," *Far Eastern economic review,* vol. 28, 1960, p. 113.

BURUNDI

1

Kint, R. "Le Législation fiscale au Burundi," *Revue juridique de droit écrit et coutumier du Rwanda et du Burundi,* vol. 4, 1964, pp. 149-158.

Rousseaux, R. "Le Vote du budget originaire au Burundi, au Rwanda et au Congo," *Revue juridique de droit écrit et coutumier du Rwanda et du Burundi,* vol. 5, 1965, pp. 83-90.

8

United States Department of Commerce. *Establishing a business in the Belgian Congo and Ruanda-Urundi.* Washington, 1957, 12pp.

CAMBODIA

1

Japan Tax Association. *Asian taxation 1964.* Tokyo, 1964, 139pp. Supplement, 1965, 17pp.

United States Department of Commerce. *Basic data on the economy of Cambodia.* Washington, 1965, 12pp.

3

Yoingco, A., and Trinidad, R. *Fiscal systems and practices in Asian countries.* Frederick A. Praeger, New York, 1967.

4

Foreign Tax Law Association. *Cambodia income tax service.* St. Petersburg, Fla., loose-leaf, 1962-.

7

United States Department of Commerce. *Foreign trade regulations of Cambodia.* Washington, 1965, 8pp.

United States Department of Commerce. *Import tariff system of Cambodia.* Washington, 1963, 2pp.

CAMEROON

1

Delacour, F. "Le Régime fiscal de la République du Cameroun," *Pénant: Revue de droit des pays l'Afrique,* vol. 71, 1961, pp. 95-107, 299-311.
United States Department of Commerce. *Basic data on the economy of the Federal Republic of Cameroon.* Washington, 1961, 13pp.

2

de Carbon, B. "Politique fiscale et croissance économique dans les états d'Afrique Equatoriale et Cameroun," *Banque centrale du Cameroun et de l'Afrique Equatoriale bulletin mensuel,* May 1961.
Hovine, M. "Finances publiques et croissance des économies de l'Afrique Equatoriale," *Développement africain* (Algiers), vol. 2, 1959, pp. 16-22.

4

"Methods of direct taxation in British Tropical Africa," *Journal of African administration,* vol. 2, October 1950, pp. 3-12; vol. 3, January 1951, pp. 30-41; vol. 3, October 1951, pp. 77-87.

10

Ministry of Education and Social Welfare. *West Cameroon education rating scheme: A note on the proposal.* Government Printer, Buca, 1965.

12

United States Department of Commerce. *Investment law of the Federal Republic of Cameroon.* Washington, 1962, 4pp.

CENTRAL AFRICAN REPUBLIC

1

United States Department of Commerce. *Basic data on the economy of the Central African Republic.* Washington, 1963, 12pp.

2

de Carbon, B. "Politique fiscale et croissance économique dans les états d'Afrique Equatoriale et Cameroun," *Banque centrale du Cameroun et de l'Afrique Equatoriale bulletin mensuel,* May 1961.

Hovine, M. "Finances publiques et croissance des économies de l'Afrique Equatoriale," *Développement africain* (Algiers), vol. 2, 1959, pp. 16-22.

CEYLON

1

Department of Inland Revenue. *The new tax system.* Colombo, 1959.
"Income tax in respect of companies," *Foreign tax law weekly bulletin,* vol. 15, no. 27, 1964, pp. 1-9.
Indrartna, A. "Basis of Ceylon's taxation," *University of Ceylon review,* vol. 12, April 1954, pp. 108-124.
Ramachandran, N. "Ceylon's tax system— Some recent experiments," *Public finance,* vol. 22, 1967.
Report of the Taxation commission, 1954-55. Sessional paper XVII, Government Publications Bureau, Colombo, 1955, 350pp.
United States Department of Commerce. *Basic data on the economy of Ceylon.* Washington, 1966, 12pp.
Wai, U. "Report of Ceylon taxation commission," *Public finance,* vol. 12, 1957, pp. 122-141.

2

International Bank for Reconstruction and Development. *The economic development of Ceylon.* The Johns Hopkins Press, Baltimore, 1953, pp. 88-105, 168-198.
Kanesathasan, S. "Export instability and contracyclical fiscal policy in underdeveloped export economies: A case study of Ceylon since 1948," *International monetary fund staff papers,* vol. 7, no. 1, April 1959, pp. 46-74.
Ministry of Finance, Department of National Planning. *The budget and economic development.* Colombo, 1961, 78pp.
Snodgrass, D. *Ceylon: An export economy in transition.* Yale University Press, New Haven, Conn., 1966.
United Nations. *Mobilization of domestic capital in certain countries of Asia and the Far East.* Sales No. 1951.II.F.3, Bangkok, 1951.

3

Yoingco, A., and Trinidad, R. *Fiscal systems and practices in Asian countries.* Frederick A. Praeger, New York, 1967.

4

"Ceylon." In: Board of Inland Revenue (Great Britain), *Income taxes outside the United Kingdom 1966,* vol. 2, pp. 129-198. H. M. Stationery Office, London, 1967.

Foreign Tax Law Association. *Ceylon income tax service.* Centerport, L.I., N.Y., loose-leaf, 1951–.

Jegasothy, A. *The tax base in the Ceylon income tax law.* Seminar paper, Harvard Law School, Cambridge, Mass., 1961.

5

Goode, R. "New system of direct taxation in Ceylon," *National tax journal,* vol. 13, December 1960, pp. 329-340.

Kaldor, N. *Suggestions for a comprehensive reform of direct taxation.* Sessional paper IV, Government Printer, Colombo, April 1960, 21pp.

7

Staley, C. "Export taxes in Ceylon," *Public finance,* vol. 14, 1959, pp. 249-265.

United States Department of Commerce. *Foreign trade regulations of Ceylon.* Washington, 1964, 8pp.

8

Asian African Legal Consultative Committee, Secretariat. *Foreign investment laws and regulations of member countries.* Economic Law Series No. 2, N.M. Tripathi Private Ltd., Bombay, 1965, 91pp. (mimeo).

Embassy of Ceylon. *Ceylon provides investment opportunities.* Washington, 1965.

Embassy of Ceylon. *Government policy on private foreign investment.* Washington, 1966, 14pp.

Ministry of Industries, Development Division. *Investor's guide.* Colombo, 1961.

United States Department of Commerce. *Establishing a business in Ceylon.* Washington, 1955, 8pp.

9

Hicks, U. *Development from below: Local government and finance in developing countries of the Commonwealth.* Oxford University Press, London, 1961, 552pp.

11

Department of Inland Revenue. *Tax concessions for agriculture.* Government Publications Bureau, Colombo, 1966, 27pp.

12

Embassy of Ceylon. *List of existing incentives to the private sector in Ceylon.* Washington, 5pp.

13

Kanesalingam, V. "Problems of financial administration in a new state with particular reference to Ceylon," *Public finance,* vol. 17, 1962, pp. 66-79.

18

Diamond, W. *Foreign tax and trade briefs.* Fallon Law Book Company, New York, loose-leaf, 1951–.

Sabapathillai, S. *Report of Ceylon tax cases.* Department of Inland Revenue, Colombo, 2 volumes, 1960, 1962, 578/455pp.

CHAD

2

de Carbon, B. "Politique fiscale et croissance économique dans les états d'Afrique Equatoriale et Cameroun," *Banque centrale du Cameroun et de l'Afrique Equatoriale bulletin mensuel,* May 1961.

Hovine, M. "Finances publiques et croissance des économies de l'Afrique Equatoriale," *Développement africain* (Algiers), vol. 2, 1959, pp. 16-22.

6

"Taxes de consommation: Nouveau texte," *Fiscalité de l'Afrique noire,* no. 15, 5 July 1961.

CHILE

1

"All taxes amended," *Foreign tax law weekly bulletin,* vol. 8, no. 45, 1958; vol. 10, no. 12, 1959.

Araneda Dörr, H. *Teoría del sistema tributario, nociones fundamentales.* Universidad de Chile, Santiago, 1961, 147pp.

Arthur Andersen & Co. *Tax and trade guide: Chile.* New York, 1966, 98pp.

Asociación Nacional de Empleados de Impuestos Internos. *Anuario informativo tributario, 1962.* Santiago, 1962, 608pp.

Baklanoff, E. "International taxation and mineral development: The political economy of Chile's La gran minería de cobre," *Proceedings of the National tax association 1965,* vol. 58, pp. 328-342.

Carvallo Hererra, S. *Legislación tributaria chilena.* Universidad de Chile, Santiago, 1961, 329pp.

"Chile amends tax laws," *Foreign commerce weekly,* vol. 61, no. 23, 1959.

Davis, T. "The evolution in the Chilean tax structure." In: Tax Institute of America, Inc., *Tax policy on United States investment in Latin America,* pp. 89-95. Princeton, N.J., 1963.

Latasté, A. "Notas sobre la tributación en Chile." In: Ministerio de Hacienda, Departamento de Estudios Financieros, *Desarrollo de las finanzas públicas chilenas.* Santiago, January-February 1956.

Martínez Cantor, M. *Problemas que plantea el estudio e investigación de los sistemas impositivos e los paises subdesarrollados.* Universidad de Chile, Santiago, 1961.

Matus Benavente, M. *Finanzas públicas.* Editorial Jurídica, Santiago, 2d edition, 1956, 311pp.

Ministerio de Hacienda, Comisión Técnica de Reforma Tributaria. *Proyecto de código tributario.* Santiago, 1960, 223pp. (mimeo).

Ministerio de Hacienda, Departamento de Estudios Financieros. *Desarrollo de las finanzas públicas chilenas, 1955.* Santiago, 1957.

Ministerio de Hacienda, Departamento de Estudios Financieros. *Estudio preliminar . . . sobre la estructura del sistema de ingresos fiscales chilenos.* Prepared by G. Martner, revised by A. Latasté. Ed. Universitaria, Santiago, 1952, 227pp.

Ministerio de Hacienda, Departamento de Estudios Financieros. *Experiencia fiscal chilena: Período 1940 a 1953.* Santiago, 1954, 189pp. (mimeo).

Ministerio de Hacienda, Dirección General de Impuestos Internos. *Evaluación estadística del programa presupuestario y del programa tributario del año 1959:*

Series impositivas, 1948-1959. Santiago, 1961.

Ministerio de Hacienda, Dirección General de Impuestos Internos. *Manual de estadística tributaria.* Santiago, 1958, 268pp.

Ministerio de Hacienda, Dirección General de Impuestos Internos. *Programa tributario para 1957.* Santiago, July 1957, 40pp. (mimeo).

Ministerio de Hacienda, Dirección General de Impuestos Internos. *Programa tributario para 1958.* Santiago, 1958, 57pp.

Ministerio de Hacienda, Dirección General de Impuestos Internos. *Programa tributario para 1959.* Santiago, 1959, 68pp.

Ministerio de Hacienda, Dirección General de Impuestos Internos. *El sistema tributario chileno.* Santiago, 2 volumes, 1960, 377/321pp.

"New tax law," *Foreign tax law weekly bulletin,* vol. 7, no. 36, 1957.

Niño de Zepeda, R., Saavedra S., A., and Cortés Tello, H. *Guía práctica del contribuyente.* Santiago, loose-leaf, 1959.

Nowak, N. "The Chilean tax system," *Bulletin for international fiscal documentation,* vol. 20, 1966, pp. 447-454.

Pan American Union. *A statement of the laws of Chile in matters affecting business.* Washington, 3d edition, 1962, 242pp. Supplement, 1965, 42pp.

Pérez Calderón, L., Parga Gazitua, J., and Pérez Calderón, S. (eds.). *Reforma tributaria.* Editorial Jurídica, Santiago, 1966, 536pp.

Piedrabuena Richard, E. *Finanzas públicas.* Universidad Católica, Santiago, 1962, 257pp.

Piedrabuena Richard, E. *Manual de derecho financiero (derecho tributario chileno).* Editorial Jurídica, Santiago, 1950, 405pp.

Piedrabuena Richard, E., and Casanegra, M. *Panorama impositivo chileno.* Santiago, 1961, 99pp.

Poblete M., R. *Impuestos vigentes en 1962.* Santiago, 2d edition, 1962, 144pp.

Price Waterhouse & Co. *Information guide for doing business in Chile.* New York, 1966, 50pp.

Price Waterhouse & Co. *Outline of business organization in Chile.* Santiago, February 1958, sections IV-VI, 18pp.

Price, Waterhouse, Peat & Co. *Boletín*

informativo. Santiago, February and June 1964.

Programa Conjunto de Tributación de la Organización de los Estados Americanos y del Banco Interamericano de Desarrollo. *Sistemas tributarios de América Latina: Chile.* Unión Panamericana, Washington, 1964, 106pp.

Robles Guzmán, J. *Manual para la aplicación de las leyes tributarias.* Vera y Gianni, Santiago, loose-leaf, 1956–.

Sociedad de Fomento Fabril. *Foro tributario: Versión de las intervenciones de los diferentes relatores.* Industria, Santiago, September 1959.

"Tax reform bill now law," *Foreign tax law weekly bulletin,* vol. 14, no. 47, 1964, pp. 10-13.

Torres Ahumada, O. *Crisis del sistema tributario chileno: Un análisis constructivo de nuestros problemas tributarios y sus soluciones.* Bustos y Letelier, Santiago, 1952, 95pp.

Torres Ahumada, O. *La reforma tributaria de la ley 11.575 de fecha 13 de ag. de 1954, publ. en el Diario oficial no. 22922 de fecha 14 de ag. de 1954.* Bustos y Letelier, Santiago, 1954, 126pp.

Ugas Canelo, L. (ed.). *El código tributario: Sus normas complementarias y jurisprudencia.* Universidad Católica, Facultad de Ciencias Jurídicas y Sociales, Memoria No. 8, Editorial Jurídica, Santiago, 1965, 399pp.

United States Department of Commerce. *Basic data on the economy of Chile.* Washington, 1964, 24pp.

Urzúa, E. "Circular de impuestos internos," *Revista de derecho, jurisprudencia y ciencias sociales y gaceta de los tribunales,* vol. 61, May-June 1964, p. 48.

2

Betinyani R., R. *Flexibilidad tributaria.* Trabajo presentado en la Primera Jornada de Estudios Fiscales, Santiago, June 1957.

Felix, D. "Chile." In: A. Pepelasis *et al., Economic development: Analysis and case studies,* pp. 288-323. Harper & Brothers, New York, 1961.

Felix, D. *Desequilibrios estructurales y crecimiento industrial—El caso chileno.* Instituto de Economía de la Universidad de Chile, Santiago, 1958.

Froomkin, J. "Some problems of tax policy in Latin America," *National tax journal,* vol. 10, December 1957, pp. 370-379.

Garnham Searle, S. *Análisis de la capacidad tributaria nacional.* Thesis, University of Chile, Imprenta Universo, Valparaíso, 1953, 48pp.

González Ruiz, F. *La reforma tributaria frente a la economía chilena.* Pacífico, Santiago, 1962, 85pp.

Herrera Lane, F. *Fundamentos de la política fiscal: Teoría y práctica.* Editorial Jurídica, Santiago, 1951, 221pp.

Klein & Saks. *El programa de estabilización de la economía chilena y el trabajo de la Misión Klein & Saks.* Santiago, May 1958, 249pp.

Lastasté, A., and Molina, S. "Experiencia fiscal chilena (período 1940-1953)," *Economía* (Santiago), vol. 15, April 1955, pp. 45-53.

Mamalakis, M., and Reynolds, C. *Essays on the Chilean economy.* Yale University Press, New Haven, Conn., 1965.

Martner G., G. "La inflexibilidad de la tributación interna y la codificación de las leyes impositivas," *Finanzas públicas* (Chile), January-April 1957.

Pinto Santa Cruz, A., Matus R., C., and Martner G., G. *Política fiscal y desarrollo económico.* Santiago, 1958, 37pp. (mimeo).

Tapia Moore, V. *Estudio sobre el desarrollo de las finanzas y la deuda pública.* Santiago, 1951, 226pp.

United Nations. *Informe de la misión económica de las Naciones Unidas para Chile, 1949-1950.* Sales No. 1951.II.B.6, New York, 1951, xvi/155pp.

3

"Análisis comparativo de la tributación en la Argentina, el Brasil, Chile y México." In: United Nations, *Las inversiones privadas extranjeras en la zona latinoamericana de libre comercio,* pp. 31-33. Sales No. 1960.II.G.5, México, 1960.

4

Aguilera C., A. *Ley de impuesto a la renta. I: Texto actualizado con la recopilación de dictámenes e instrucciones fijadas por el Servicio de impuestos internos, que incluye todos los suplementos del manual no. 6 de renta.* Santiago, 1966, 408pp.

Bell Escalona, E. (ed.). *La reforma tributaria: Nueva ley de la renta.* Valparaíso, 1964, 159pp.

Cárcamo Pérez, P. *Análisis del impuesto sobre la renta 1966.* Gutenberg, Santiago, 2 volumes, 1966.

Corporación de Fomento de la Producción. *Chilean income taxes in brief.* New York, 1966.

Dagnino, E., and de la Babra, F. *Explicaciones sobre la nueva ley de impuesto a la renta.* Cámara de Comercio de Santiago, Santiago, 1964, 105pp.

Espejo H., J. *Ley del impuesto sobre la renta.* Santiago, 2 volumes, 1954, 1955, 242/306pp.

"Exposición de la Sociedad de fomento fabril ante el proyecto de nuevos tributos a la industria," *Panorama económico* (Santiago), vol. 4, no. 25, March-April 1950, pp. 73-74.

Foreign Tax Law Association. *Chilean income tax service.* Centerport, L.I., N.Y., loose-leaf, 1954–1955.

Gómez Oyarzan, C. *El impuesto a la renta en Chile y en Argentina.* Thesis, Universidad de Concepción, Concepción, 1955, 98pp.

Illanes Narea, L. *Modificaciones introducidos a la ley sobre impuesto a la renta por la ley no. 13.305 de 6 de abril de 1959.* Universidad de Chile, Santiago, 1962, 150pp.

Irarrazaval Covarrubias, J. *Concepto tributario de renta.* Thesis, Universidad Católica, Santiago, 1962, 109pp.

Ministerio de Hacienda, Departmento de Estudios Financieros. *Tributación: Legislación de renta.* Santiago, 1959, 27pp.

Ministerio de Hacienda, Dirección General de Impuestos Internos. *Tributación chilena y desarrollo económico. I: Efectos de la tributación a las utilidades de las empresas sobre los incentivos a invertir.* Santiago, 1958, 36pp.

Ministerio de Hacienda, Dirección General de Impuestos Internos. *Tributación chilena y desarrollo económico. II: Régimen de amortizaciones y revalorizaciones de las empresas.* Santiago, 1958, 46pp.

Pérez Calderón, L., Parga Gazitua, J., and Pérez Calderón, S. (eds.). *Reforma tributaria: Historia fidedigna de la*

nueva ley de impuesto a la renta y de la ley no. 5427 sobre impuestos a las herencias, asignaciones y donaciones y de sus modificaciones posteriores. Editorial Jurídica, Santiago, 1966, 536pp.

Poblete M., R. *Impuestos a la renta vigentes en 1966.* Divulgación Tributaria No. 12, Santiago, 1966, 136pp.

Poblete, M., R. *Nueva ley de impuesto a la renta: Texto de la ley 15.564, comentarios, ejemplos, declaraciones año 1964.* Divulgación Tributaria No. 6, Santiago, 1964, 176pp.

Poblete Troncoso, M. *Impuestos a la renta vigentes en 1960.* Santiago, 1960, 91pp.

Rencoret Bravo, A. *Derecho tributario: El impuesto sobre la renta.* Editorial Jurídica, Santiago, 1950, 404pp.

Toretti Rivera, C. "Actual situación tributaria del abogado," *Revista de derecho, jurisprudencia y ciencias sociales y gaceta de los tribunales,* vol. 61, January-April 1964, p. 1.

6

Bell Escalona, E. (ed.). *Comentarios a la nueva ley de timbres.* Barros Arana, Valparaíso, 1963, 60pp.

Claro Valdes, R. *El impuesto a la transferencia de acciones y el mercado de capitales.* Trabajo presentado en la Primera Jornada de Estudios Fiscales, Santiago, June 1957.

Gertner Fernández, A. *El impuesto a las compraventas.* Santiago, 1959, 42pp.

Ministerio de Hacienda, Dirección General de Impuestos Internos. *Ley sobre impuestos a las compraventas, permutas y otras convenciones.* Santiago, 1957, 242pp.

Piedrabuena Richard, E. *Alternativas para la reforma del sistema de impuestos indirectos.* Trabajo presentado en la Primera Jornada de Estudios Fiscales, Santiago, June 1957.

Rosmanich Poduje, A. *El impuesto a las compraventas.* Thesis, Universidad Católica, Santiago, 1959, 168pp.

7

United States Department of Commerce. *Foreign trade regulations of Chile.* Washington, 1967, 8pp.

8

Babra Correa, F. *El sistema tributario de La gran minería del cobre.* Thesis, Universidad Católica, Santiago, 1961, 101pp.

Baklanoff, E. "Taxation of United-States-owned copper companies in Chile: Economic myopia v. long-run self-interest," *National tax journal*, vol. 14, March 1961, pp. 81-88.

Hart, A. "Tax policies in Chile." In: Tax Institute of America, Inc., *Tax policy on United States investment in Latin America*, pp. 96-110. Princeton, N.J., 1963.

Ministerio de Hacienda, Dirección General de Impuestos Internos. *Estudios sobre tratados tributarios.* Santiago, 1957 (mimeo).

Ministerio de Hacienda, Dirección General de Impuestos Internos. *Tributación chilena y desarrollo económico. IV: Estudio sobre la tributación a La gran minería del cobre.* Santiago, 1958, 41pp.

"Tax, tariff and credit problems." In: L. Ehrman, *Opportunities for investment in Chile,* pp. 58-85. Frederick A. Praeger, New York, 1966.

United States Department of Commerce. *Establishing a business in Chile.* Washington, 1966, 20pp.

United States Department of Commerce. *Foreign investment law and regulations of Chile.* Washington, 1960, 5pp.

United States Department of Commerce. *Investment in Chile: Basic information for United States businessmen.* Washington, 1960, 282pp.

9

Toro González, J. *Régimen financiero municipal.* Thesis, University of Chile, Imprenta El Esfuerzo, Santiago, 1944, 71pp.

10

Darrigrandi Aguirre, G. "Del impuesto territorial en Chile, Argentina y otras legislaciones." In: Universidad de Chile, Facultad de Ciencias Jurídicas y Sociales, *Memorias de licenciados,* vol. 13, 1951, pp. 153-203. Editorial Jurídica, Santiago, 1951.

Strasma, J. *Property taxation in Chile.* University of Wisconsin Land Tenure Center, Madison, Wisc., June 1966 (duplicated).

Torreti, C. *La tributación sobre la propiedad territorial.* Santiago, 1962, 39pp.

11

"Antecedentes y estimaciones sobre la tributación agrícola," *Panorama económico* (Santiago), vol. 7, no. 99, May 1954, pp. 218-224.

Burckhardt, K., and Escobar, R. *Agricultura y tributación—Dos ensayos.* Publicación No. 75, Instituto de Economía de la Universidad de Chile, Santiago, 1965, xiv/188pp.

Daie, J. "Tributación agrícola en Chile," *Finanzas públicas* (Chile), May-August 1958, p. 38.

Garrido Rojas, J. "Algunos criterios sobre financiamiento de la reforma agraria." In: *Seminario sobre el financiamiento de la reforma agraria.* Instituto Interamericano de Ciencias Agricolas, San José, 1964.

Instituto de Economía de la Universidad de Chile. *La tributación agrícola en Chile, 1940-1958.* Santiago, 1960, 213pp.

Maturana, S. "La tributación y el desarrollo económico de la agricultura," *Panorama económico* (Santiago), vol. 12, no. 203, June 1959, pp. 198-199.

"Structure and taxation of agriculture in Chile." In: H. Wald and J. Froomkin (eds.), *Papers and proceedings of the Conference on agricultural taxation and economic development,* pp. 337-348. Harvard Law School International Program in Taxation, Cambridge, Mass., 1954.

Ullrich, K., and Lagos, R. *Agricultura y tributación.* Instituto de Economía de la Universidad de Chile, Santiago, 1965.

12

Ministerio de Hacienda, Departamento de Estudios Financieros. *Tributación de fomento al desarrollo económico en Chile.* Santiago, 1958, 69pp.

Ministerio de Hacienda, Dirección General de Impuestos Internos. *Tributación chilena y desarrollo económico. III: Incentivos tributarios de fomento.* Santiago, 1958, 89pp.

Pavez Basso, D. "La tributación como incentivo en la formación de capital," *Economía* (Facultad de Economía, Universidad de Chile), September 1957, p. 67. Also in: *Selección de temas económicos* (Montevideo), May-June 1958, p. 28.

13

Fuenzalida Ibarra, A. *De la administración del impuesto a la renta y de las sanciones*. Universidad de Chile, Santiago, 1962, 117pp.

Instituto de Economía de la Universidad de Chile. *El proceso presupuestario fiscal chileno*. Santiago, 1959.

Lidstone, H. "Recomendaciones para la reorganización de impuestos internos," *Panorama económico* (Santiago), vol. 8, no. 110, October 1954, pp. 695-697.

Ministerio de Hacienda, Dirección General de Impuestos Internos. *Actividades de la Oficina de estudios tributarios en los meses de julio, agosto y septiembre de 1957*. Santiago, 2 October 1957, 38pp. (mimeo).

Ministerio de Hacienda, Dirección General de Impuestos Internos. *Manual de administración de impuestos*. Santiago, 1958, 109pp.

Ministerio de Hacienda, Dirección General de Impuestos Internos. *Manual de fiscalización de impuestos*. Santiago, 1958, 256pp.

Ministerio de Hacienda, Dirección General de Impuestos Internos. *Manual de supervisión*. Santiago, 1959, 43pp.

Paternost G., E. *Practical conclusions drawn from a case of reorganization in the Direction general of internal revenue*. 31 July 1956, 7pp. (mimeo).

Piedrabuena Richard, E. *Memorándum sobre los problemas prácticos y técnicos de administración de impuestos de interés fundamental para el Servicio de impuestos internos de Chile*. Ministerio de Hacienda, Santiago, n.d., 17pp. (mimeo).

Podlech Michaud, A. *Fiscalización de la administración financiera en Chile*. Thesis, University of Chile, Santiago, 1951, 141pp.

United Nations, Technical Assistance Administration. "Legislación y administración de impuestos en Chile." Doc. No. TAA/CHI/1 (restricted), 24 April 1956.

United Nations, Technical Assistance Programme. "Informe sobre administración tributaria en Chile." Prepared by E. Dougherty, 1956, 17pp.

Vélez, M. *Modernization of the Chilean internal tax administrative systems*.

Agency for International Development, USAID Mission to Chile, Santiago, 1961, 54pp.

Wainer Kopels, U. *La fiscalización de impuestos en Chile*. Ministerio de Hacienda, Dirección del Presupuesto, Santiago, 1964, 212pp.

14

Babra Lyon, S. *Teoría de la prueba de las obligaciones tributarias*. Thesis, Universidad Católica, Santiago, 1962, 73pp.

Fernandez Provoste, M., and Fernandez Provoste, H. *Principios de derecho tributario*. Editorial Jurídica, Santiago, 1952, 404pp.

Gorziglia B., A. *Facultades presupuestarias legislativas*. Thesis, Universidad Católica, Santiago, 1960, 150pp.

Rencoret Araya, H. *Introducción al estudio de la norma tributaria*. Thesis, Universidad de Chile, Santiago, 1957, 145pp.

Serrano Mahns, G. *Curso de nociones jurídico-contables*. Universidad de Chile, Santiago, 1951, 226pp.

15

Baklanoff, E. "Model for economic stagnation: The Chilean experience with multiple exchange rates," *Inter-American economic affairs*, vol. 13, Summer 1959, pp. 58-82.

Deaver, J. *La inflación chilena como un impuesto*. Universidad Católica, Santiago, 1957.

Herrera Lane, F. "La inflación chilena y la política fiscal," *Panorama económico* (Santiago), vol. 8, no. 117, March 1955, pp. 80-86. Also in: *El derecho ante la inflación*. Editorial Jurídica de Chile, Santiago, 1955.

17

Almeida, R. "La zona latinoamericana de libre comercio," *Técnicas financieras* (CEMLA), vol. 2, no. 5, May-June 1963, pp. 453-472.

Gutiérrez Kirchner, A. "El mercomún latinoamericano y la política fiscal," *Investigación fiscal*, no. 19, July 1967, pp. 15-63.

18

Bell Escalona, E. (ed.). *Jurisprudencia tributaria de la Corte suprema*. Valparaíso, loose-leaf, 1960-.

Bell Escalona, E. *Jurisprudencia tributaria de los Cortes de apelaciones.* Imprenta y Litografia Universo, Valparaíso, looseleaf, 1961–.

Bell Escalona, E. (ed.). *Todo el tributo al dia.* Valparaíso, loose-leaf, 1962–.

Charad Dahud, E. *El código tributario: Explicaciones, instrucciones oficiales de la Dirección nacional de impuestos internos.* Impresora "Horizonte," Santiago, 1965, 373pp.

"Chile law digest." In: *Martindale-Hubbell law directory,* vol. 4, pp. 2506-2519. Martindale-Hubbell, Inc., Summit, N.J., 1961.

Diamond, W. *Foreign tax and trade briefs.* Fallon Law Book Company, New York, loose-leaf, 1951–.

Economist Intelligence Unit, Ltd. *Economic review of Chile.* London, irregular.

Instituto Chileno de Derecho Tributario. *Boletín.* Santiago, irregular.

Ministerio de Hacienda, Dirección General de Impuestos Internos. *Boletín de estadística tributaria.* Santiago, annual, 1957–.

Ministerio de Hacienda, Dirección General de Impuestos Internos. *Boletín de la Dirección general de impuestos internos.* Santiago, monthly, 1953–.

Ministerio de Hacienda, Dirección General de Impuestos Internos. *Estudios tributarios.* Santiago, monthly, 1957–.

Ministerio de Hacienda, Dirección General de Impuestos Internos. *Memoria.* Santiago, annual, 1950–.

Ministerio de Hacienda, Dirección General de Impuestos Internos. *Recopilación de leyes tributarias: Textos anotados de la legislación vigente.* Editorial Jurídica, Santiago, 2 volumes, 1959.

CHINA (Mainland)

1

Chand, G. "Taxation in new China," *Indian taxation,* vol. 7, October 1956, pp. 380-386.

Chekhutov, A. *The tax system in the People's Republic of China.* Joint Publications Research Service, Washington, 15 February 1963, 204pp. (mimeo). Also: United States Department of Commerce, Washington, 1963, 204pp.

"Chinese communist taxes," *Foreign tax law weekly bulletin,* vol. 16, no. 8, 1965, pp. 10-13.

Durand, F. *Le Financement du budget en Chine populaire.* Editions Sirey, Paris, 1965, 409pp.

Ecklund, G. *Taxation in Communist China, 1950-1959.* Ph.D. thesis, University of Minnesota, Minneapolis, Minn., 1962. Also: Central Intelligence Agency, Washington, July 1961.

Kwang, C. "The budgetary system of the People's Republic of China: A preliminary survey," *Public finance,* vol. 18, 1963, pp. 253-286.

Liu, J. "China's financial problems." In: *Symposium on economic and social problems of the Far East, University of Hong Kong, 1961,* pp. 72-100. Hong Kong University Press, Hong Kong, 1962.

Mao, C. "National taxes in China, 1928-1936," *National tax journal,* vol. 7, March 1954, pp. 89-92.

Shiomi, S. "The taxation system of China," *Kyoto University economic review,* vol. 17, no. 4, October 1942, pp. 1-26.

Tao, A. *A study of tax structure in China.* National Peking University Press, Peking, 1946.

"Taxation in Communist Shanghai," *Australian accountant,* vol. 21, February 1951, pp. 58-61.

2

Cheng-Jui, L. "How China raises funds for national construction," *Peking review,* vol. 9, no. 1, 1966, pp. 19-23.

Ecklund, G. *Financing the Chinese government budget, 1950-1959.* Aldine Publishing Co., Chicago, 1960, 133pp.

Froomkin, J., and Hsia, R. "Developments in public finance in Communist China 1950-1954," *Public finance,* vol. 10, 1955, pp. 83-104.

Mah, F. "The financing of public investment in Communist China," *Journal of Asian studies,* vol. 21, November 1961, pp. 33-48.

Szczepanik, E. "Four years of fiscal policy in Communist China," *Bulletin for international fiscal documentation,* vol. 9, 1955, pp. 206-226.

Wu, Y. *An economic survey of Communist China.* Bookman Associates, New York, 1956, chapter 3.

4

"Bylaws of the consolidated industrial and commercial tax of the People's Republic of China (draft)," *Compendium of laws and regulations of the People's Republic of China*, vol. 8, 1962, pp. 285-298.

"Preparatory committee for the Tibet autonomous region adopts a resolution to abolish service tax." In: N. Ling (ed.), *Tibetan sourcebook*, pp. 284-286. Union Research Institute, Hong Kong, 1964.

"Regulations of consolidated industrial and commercial tax of the People's Republic of China (draft)," *Compendium of laws and regulations of the People's Republic of China*, vol. 8, 1962, pp. 268-284.

6

Sun, I. *Salt taxation in China*. Ph.D. thesis, University of Wisconsin, Madison, Wisc., 1953.

9

Li, C. *A study of the fiscal relations between the central, the provincial, and the local governments*. Columbia University Press, New York, 1922, 187pp.

11

Buck, J. *Land utilization in China*. University of Nanking, Nanking, 1937, pp. 326-328.

Froomkin, J. "Structure and taxation of agriculture in China." In: H. Wald and J. Froomkin (eds.), *Papers and proceedings of the Conference on agricultural taxation and economic development*, pp. 412-423. Harvard Law School International Program in Taxation, Cambridge, Mass., 1954.

Mao, C. "Land taxation and economic growth in China, 1928-1936," *Land economics*, vol. 32, 1956, pp. 180-183.

18

Joint Publications Research Service. *Collection of fiscal laws and regulations, 1958-1960: Communist China*. Washington, 1963, 306pp.

CHINA (Taiwan)

1

Crockett, J. *Taxation in China*. International Cooperation Administration, Taipei, 1 August 1960, 147pp. (mimeo).

Hsiao, C. "The taxation system in Taiwan," *Bank of China economic review*, March-April 1966, pp. 12-17.

Industrial Development and Investment Center. *Selected laws and regulations affecting industry, Republic of China*. Taipei, July 1960.

Industrial Development and Investment Center. *Taxes in Taiwan*. Taipei, 1964, 27pp.

Japan Tax Association. *Asian taxation 1964*. Tokyo, 1964, 139pp. Supplement, 1965, 17pp.

Li, M. *The tax system of Taiwan*. Ph.D. thesis, New York, 1956.

Ministry of Finance, Taxation Department. *An outline of the tax laws and regulations of the Republic of China*. Taipei, 1956, 105pp.

"Public finance and taxation." In: *China yearbook 1960-1961*, pp. 321-333. China Publishing Co., Taipei, 1961.

Seidman, J. "Taxes in Nationalist China," *Journal of accounting*, vol. 107, June 1959, pp. 20-21.

United States Department of Commerce. *Basic data on the economy of Taiwan*. Washington, 1963, 27pp.

Warren, G., and Mangerich, H. *Summary of the tax system of the Republic of China*. International Cooperation Administration, Washington, 1957, 36pp. (mimeo).

3

Yoingco, A., and Trinidad, R. *Fiscal systems and practices in Asian countries*. Frederick A. Praeger, New York, 1967.

4

Council for International Economic Cooperation. *Income tax law*. Taipei, 1965, 12pp.

Foreign Tax Law Association. *Taiwan income tax service*. St. Petersburg, Fla., loose-leaf, 1962–.

Industrial Development and Investment Center. *Income tax law*. Taipei, 1964, 115pp.

Industrial Development and Investment Center. *Regulations governing revaluation of assets of profit seeking enterprises*. Taipei, 1961, 27pp.

Lu, W. *Current Chinese industrial and commercial tax laws and regulations*.

Tax Affairs Publ., Taipei, 1952, 136pp.
"Statute on income tax rates for 1962,"
Foreign tax law weekly bulletin, vol. 13,
no. 38, 1963, pp. 1-9.

7

"Customs import tariff." In: *China yearbook, 1959-1960,* pp. 912-971. China
Publishing Co., Taipei, 1960.

8

Council for International Economic Co-
operation. *How to do business with
Taiwan.* Taipei, 1965, 12pp.
United States Department of Commerce.
Establishing a business in Taiwan.
Washington, 1967, 16pp.
United States Department of Commerce.
Investment factors in Taiwan. Washing-
ton, 1962, 17pp.
United States Department of Commerce.
Investment in Taiwan (Formosa).
Washington, 1959, pp. 119-124, 153-154.

11

United Nations, Economic Commission for
Asia and the Far East. "Experience in
Taiwan in introducing a tax element
into government aid to agricultural
producers and food transactions." Pre-
pared by T. Chang and C. Hong, Doc.
No. ECAFE/I & T/FED/11, 6 August
1953.
Young-Chi, T. "Land-use improvement:
A key to the economic development of
Taiwan," *Journal of farm economics,*
May 1962, pp. 363-372.

12

Chou, S. *The impact of fiscal incentives
on the development of manufacturing
industries in Taiwan.* Prepared for
United Nations Industrial Development
Organization, New York, 1966.
Industrial Development and Investment
Center. *Criteria of encouragement by
way of reduction or exemption of profit
seeking enterprise income tax.* Taipei,
1965, 27pp.
Industrial Development and Investment
Center. *Investment laws of the Republic
of China.* Taipei, September 1960, 64pp.
Industrial Development and Investment
Center. *Statute of encouragement of
investment.* Taipei, 1965, 32pp.
Li, K. "The new book of Taiwan's invest-

ment climate," *Bank of China economic
review,* September-October 1960, pp. 4-
8.
"Taiwan—Tax incentives," *Foreign tax
law weekly bulletin,* vol. 12, no. 9, 1961,
pp. 8-9.

13

Public Administration Service. *Financial
administration: A summary of recommendations for improvement contained
in a report October 1953.* Taiwan, 9 pp.
(offset).
United Nations, Economic and Social
Council, Fiscal Commission. "Procedures available for the review of initial
tax assessments: Reply of the government of China." Doc. No. E/CN.8/59/
Add.6, Part I, 14 August 1951, 20pp;
Part II, 20 October 1953, 14pp. (mimeo).

18

"China law digest." In: *Martindale-Hubbell law directory,* vol. 4, pp. 2520-2528.
Martindale-Hubbell, Inc., Summit, N.J.,
1961.
Council for United States Aid, Law Revision Planning Group. *Laws of the Republic of China: Second series.* China
Printing, Ltd., Taipei, 1962, 985pp.
Diamond, W. *Foreign tax and trade briefs.*
Fallon Law Book Company, New York,
loose-leaf, 1951–.

COLOMBIA

1

Afanador Pinzón, F. *La reforma tributaria
de 1960.* Thesis, Pontificia Universidad
Javeriana, Bogotá, 1965, 296pp.
Afanador Pinzón, F. *Régimen legal del
impuesto sobre la renta.* Luenmor, Bogotá, 1965, 296pp.
Albandea Pavón, J. "Régimen impositivo
colombiano," *Revista de derecho,* no. 2,
1964, pp. 72-83.
Alvarado, M. *Tratado de ciencia tributaria.* Ed. Siglio XX, Bogotá, 1941,
500pp.
Arthur Andersen & Co. *Tax and trade
guide: Colombia.* New York, 1965,
158pp.
Asociación Nacional de Industriales. *Régimen tributario: 1958-1959.* ANDI,
Medellín, 1959, 179pp.
Banco de la República. *Reforma tributaria
en Colombia.* Bogotá, 1961, 96pp.

"Budgets and tax reform," *Foreign tax law weekly bulletin,* vol. 9, no. 40, 1959.

Camacho Rueda, A. *Hacienda pública.* Publicaciones de la Universidad Externado de Colombia, Bogotá, 1965, viii/483pp.

Cruz Santos, A. *El presupuesto colombiano.* Temis, Bogotá, 4th edition, 1963, 288pp.

Harvard Law School International Program in Taxation. *World Tax Series: Taxation in Colombia.* Prepared by G. Eder, J. Chommie, and H. Becerra. Commerce Clearing House, Inc., Chicago, 1964, xxxviii/586pp.

Jaramillo, E. *Hacienda pública.* Librería Voluntad, Bogotá, 5th edition, 1953, xvi/595pp.

Jaramillo, E. *La reforma tributaria en Colombia.* Banco de la República, Bogotá, 1956, 222pp.

Lara Hernández, A., and Camacho Rueda, A. "Sobre la reforma tributaria." In: Ministerio de Hacienda, *Memoria,* Anexo II, pp. 5-72. Bogotá, 1961.

Lascarro, L. *Administración fiscal presupuesto descentralización.* Editorial Andes, Bogotá, 1965, 264pp.

Ministerio de Hacienda y Crédito Público. *Régimen fiscal nacional.* Bogotá, October 1947, 292pp.

Naar, R. "Recent economic and legal developments in Colombia," *Foreign tax law weekly bulletin,* vol. 1, no. 19, 1950, pp. 1-8.

Pan American Union. *A statement of the laws of Colombia in matters affecting business.* Washington, 2d edition, 1961, 303pp. Supplement, 1963.

Parrish, K. "Los nuevos impuestos," *Boletín semanal* (Cámara de Comercio de Barranquilla), no. 464, 11 September 1965.

Pineda Manrique, F. *Aspectos económicos del presupuesto nacional.* Thesis, Universidad Nacional de Colombia, Facultad de Ciencias Económicas, Bogotá, October 1965, 138pp.

Price Waterhouse & Co. *Information guide for doing business in Colombia.* New York, 1966, 39pp.

"La reforma tributaria de 1953," *Legislación económica* (Bogotá), nos. 30-31, 20 October 1953.

Samper Bernal, G. *Tratado de hacienda pública.* Imp. de Bogotá, Bogotá, 1955, 279pp.

Tobón, L. "Problemas fiscales," *Revista del Banco de la república,* August 1959.

Tobón Arbelaez, D., López Toro, A., and Becerra, H. *La tributación ante el desarrollo económico.* Biblioteca ANDI, Medellín, 1963, 104pp.

United Nations. *Public finance information papers: Colombia.* Sales No. 1951.XVI.8, New York, 1951.

United States Department of Commerce. *Basic data on the economy of Colombia.* Washington, 1966, 24pp.

Vega Lara, H., and Jimenez Posada, H. *Bases para una reforma tributaria.* Comité Operativo del Ingreso y la Cooperación Social, Bogotá, 1966, 43pp. (mimeo).

Wurfel, S. *Foreign enterprise in Colombia: Laws and policies.* University of North Carolina Press, Chapel Hill, N.C., 1965.

2

Casas Sanz de Santamaría, E. *La jurisdicción coactiva en la legislación colombiana, sus inconvenientes y reformas que se proponen.* Thesis, Pontificia Universidad Javeriana, Bogotá, 1963, 75pp.

Comisión de Estudios. *Asuntos económicos y fiscales 1965.* Talleres Gráficos del Banco de la República, Bogotá, 1965.

Consejo Nacional de Política Económica y Planeación, Departamento Administrativo de Planeación y Servicios Técnicos. *Plan general de desarrollo ecónomico y social. Primera parte: El programa general.* Editorial el Mundo, Ltda., Bogotá, 1962, chapter 6.

Currie, L. *Operación Colombia.* Biblioteca de Estudios Económicos, Sociedad Colombiana de Economistas, Bogotá, 1961, 82pp.

Froomkin, J. "Some problems of tax policy in Latin America," *National tax journal,* vol. 10, December 1957, pp. 370-379.

Gómez, J. "Ideas económicas y fiscales de Colombia," *Problemas colombianos,* VI. Bogotá, 1949.

International Bank for Reconstruction and Development. *The basis of a development programme for Colombia.* Sales No. IBRD.1950.2, Washington, 1950, chapters 13, 26. Summarized in: United

Nations, *Taxes and fiscal policy in under-developed countries,* pp. 57-63. Sales No. 1955.II.H.1, New York, 1954.

Joint Tax Program, Organization of American States and Inter-American Development Bank, *Fiscal survey of Colombia.* Published for The Joint Tax Program by The Johns Hopkins Press, Baltimore, 1965, xvii/276pp.

Levin, J. *Import cycle and fiscal policy in Colombia.* DM 67/29, International Monetary Fund, Washington, 8 May 1967.

Martner, G. *El desarrollo de las finanzas públicas de Colombia 1950-1960.* Dirección General del Presupuesto, Bogotá, n.d., 116pp.

Ministerio de Hacienda y Crédito Público. *Política fiscal y reforma tributaria.* Imprenta Nacional, Bogotá, 1953, 115pp.

Pérez, F. "La política fiscal del gobierno," *El mes financiero y económico* (Bogotá), vol. 10, October 1947, pp. 15-18.

Rivas Groot, J. *Asuntos económicos y fiscales.* Banco de la República, Bogotá, 1952, 265pp.

Shere, L. *A tax program for Colombia.* Pan American Union, Washington, 1960, 235pp. (mimeo).

Taylor, M., and Richman, R. "Public finance and development in Colombia," *Journal of inter-American studies,* vol. 8, January 1966, pp. 11-33.

United Nations. *Analysis and projections of economic development—III: The economic development of Colombia.* Sales No. 1957.II.G.3, Geneva, 1957, xii/454pp.

United Nations, Technical Assistance Programme. "Report and recommendations on the tax system of Colombia with a short chapter on budget presentation and procedure." Doc. No. ST/TAA/J/COLOMBIA/R.2 (restricted), 1952, 116pp.

4

Becerra, H. "Comentarios sobre la ley 81 de 1960, reorgánica del impuesto sobre la renta," *Derecho positivo,* vol. 3, 1961, pp. 171-208.

Becerra, H. "Régimen tributario de operaciones en divisas," *Revista del Instituto colombiano de derecho tributario,* vol. 1, 1965, pp. 183-194.

Camacho Rueda, A. "El impuesto sobre la renta en Colombia," *Técnica y finanzas* (Bogotá), vol. 1, April-June 1952, pp. 97-116.

"Colombia: Dividends excluded from income on which excess profits tax is based," *Foreign tax law weekly bulletin,* vol. 1, no. 29, 1951, pp. 32-33.

Devis Echandía, H. "El good will y su reglamentación en derecho colombiano: Habitualidad para efectos impositivos." In: *Doctrina y jurisprudencia.* Bogotá, 1952.

Diaz del Castillo, P. *Código tributario: Declaración de renta, patrimonio y excesso de utilidades.* Imprenta "Márquez," Cali, 1954, 236pp.

Escuela Superior de Administración Pública. *La reforma tributaria de 1960.* Imprenta Nacional, Bogotá, 3 volumes, 1961, 215/387/207pp.

"Extraordinary tax imposed," *Foreign tax law weekly bulletin,* vol. 16, no. 34, 1966, pp. 14-17.

Foreign Tax Law Association. *Colombia income tax service.* Hempstead, L.I., N.Y., 3 volumes, loose-leaf, 1950-1954.

Harvard Law School Group. *Analysis of draft law no. 462 and evaluation of comments on income tax reform.* Harvard Law School International Program in Taxation, Cambridge, Mass., 1959, 138pp. (mimeo). In Spanish in: Ministerio de Hacienda, *Memoria. Anexo III: Reforma tributaria,* pp. 217-309. Bogotá, 1959. Part reprinted in: R. Bird and O. Oldman (eds.), *Readings on taxation in developing countries.* The Johns Hopkins Press, Baltimore, 1964, pp. 236-244; revised edition, 1967, pp. 188-196.

"Income tax rules amended," *Foreign tax law weekly bulletin,* vol. 8, no. 41, 1958, pp. 1-2.

Martínez Porras, J. "Las sociedades del capital y el gravamen sobre sus dividendos," *Economía colombiana,* November 1954.

Ministerio de Hacienda, Ministerio de Minas y Petroleos, and Industria Petrolera Privada. *Informe de la Comisión de estudio sobre la participación del estado en la explotación del petroleo.* Bogotá, December 1965, 75pp.

Ministerio de Hacienda y Crédito Público, División de Impuestos Nacionales, Subdivisión de Recaudación. *Impuesto sobre la renta y complementarios año fiscal 1964.* Bogotá, 1966, ii/93pp.

Ministerio de Hacienda y Crédito Público, División de Impuestos Nacionales, Subdivisión de Recaudación. *Informe financiero año fiscal 1965.* Bogotá, 1967, 214pp.

Raisbeck, J. *Colombian income taxation.* Luis F. Serrano A., Bogotá, 2d edition, 1964, xxxii/364pp.

Ramírez, R. *Instrucciones para la declaración de la renta y del patrimonio.* Librería Colombiana, Bogotá, 22d edition, 1966.

"Regulations for the new income tax law," *Foreign tax law weekly bulletin,* vol. 12, no. 4, 1961, pp. 4-9.

"Reorgánica del impuesto sobre la renta: Ley 81 de 1960," *Revista del Banco de la república,* January 1961, p. 29.

Rodríguez Rozo, H. "La excesiva tributación de las sociedades anónimas," *Economía colombiana,* April 1958.

Tamayo, A. *Las sociedades ante la ley 81 de 1960.* Thesis, Pontificia Universidad Javeriana, Bogotá, 1962, 140pp.

"Taxation of income in Colombia," *Foreign tax law weekly bulletin,* vol. 13, no. 29, 1962, pp. 4-9.

"Taxation of income, personal property and excess profits in Colombia," *International Ref. Serv.,* vol. 2, no. 2, 1945.

Torre, A., and Marulanda U., J. *Leyes y reglamentos del impuesto sobre la renta en Colombia.* Bogotá, 1958.

"Two new income taxes," *Foreign tax law weekly bulletin,* vol. 8, no. 10, 1957.

Williams, R. *The impact of the corporate tax structure on private capital formation in Colombia.* Ph.D. dissertation, Oregon, 1964.

5

"Definition of patrimony tax in Colombia," *Foreign tax law weekly bulletin,* vol. 1, no. 50, 1951, pp. 13-26.

Martínez Rey, A. *La sucesión ante el derecho fiscal.* Pontificia Universidad Católica Javeriana, Bucaramanga, 1962, 244pp.

6

Bird, R. *Sales taxation in Colombia: Tax policy and development planning.* Economic Development Series Report No. 36, Development Advisory Service, Center for International Affairs, Harvard University, Cambridge, Mass., 1966, 47pp. (multilith). Part reprinted in: R. Bird and O. Oldman (eds.), *Readings on taxation in developing countries,* pp. 309-323. The Johns Hopkins Press, Baltimore, revised edition, 1967.

Bird, R. "Stamp tax reform in Colombia," *Bulletin for international fiscal documentation,* vol. 21, 1967, pp. 247-255.

El impuesto a las ventas en Colombia—Su aplicación práctica. Legislación Económica Ltda., Bogotá, 1966, 234pp.

Jimenez Forero, L., and Pinzon Matiz, M. *Timbre nacional y papel sellado.* Bogotá, 1964.

Lascarro, L. "El estado cantinero," *Economía colombiana,* January 1956.

Levin, J. *The effects of economic development upon the base of a sales tax: A case study of Colombia.* DM 67/47, International Monetary Fund, Washington, 28 July 1967, 68pp. (mimeo).

7

"Colombia changes coffee export tax, retention," *Foreign commerce weekly,* vol. 65, no. 10, 1961, p. 20.

United States Department of Commerce. *Foreign trade regulations of Colombia.* Washington, 1967, 12pp.

8

Eder, G. "Tax policies in Colombia." In: Tax Institute of America, Inc., *Tax policy on United States investment in Latin America,* pp. 111-127. Princeton, N.J., 1963.

Pomeranz, M. "Taxation of United States investments in Latin America," *Virginia law review,* vol. 44, 1958, pp. 205-215.

Rueda, A. "Doble tributación internacional," *Revista del Instituto colombiano de derecho tributario,* vol. 1, 1965, pp. 165-176.

"Tax law problems." In: S. Wurfel, *Foreign enterprise in Colombia: Laws and policies,* pp. 410-457. University of North Carolina Press, Chapel Hill, N.C., 1965.

United States Department of Commerce. *Establishing a business in Colombia.* Washington, 1966, 20pp.

United States Department of Commerce. *Investment in Colombia.* Washington, 1953, pp. 79-86.

9

Alvarez A., O. *Ingresos departamentales.* Escuela Superior de Administración Pública, Bogotá, 1964, 33pp. (mimeo).

Alvarez Cardona, J. *Finanzas públicas departamentales y municipales comparadas en Colombia, 1957.* Monografía 5, Centro de Estudios sobre Desarrollo Económico de la Universidad de Los Andes, Bogotá, 1960, 110pp.

Aristizabal Ospina, R. *Informe sobre el departamento de Caldas y el municipio de Manizales.* Planeación, Bogotá, 1952, 21pp.

Casas Morales, C. *Régimen tributario de los pequeños municipios colombianos.* Editorial S.J. Eudes, Bogotá, 1952, 111pp.

Consejo Nacional de Planificación. *Impuesto sobre industria y comercio.* Bogotá, 1953.

Currie, L., *et al. Plan socio-económico para el atlantico.* Imprenta Nacional, Bogotá, 1965.

Departamento Administrativo de Planificación, Subdirección de Estudios Basicos. *Resumen de los estudios adelantados hasta 1962, distrito especial de Bogotá.* Bogotá, December 1963, 104pp.

Galvis Gaitan, F. *El municipio colombiano.* Imprenta Departamental "Antonio Nariño," 1964, 442pp.

Jiménez González C., E. *Tierra y valorización. La reforma tributaria municipal, patrimonio fiscal de municipios, capacidad económica tributaria.* Bogotá, 1956.

Lopez Toro, A. *A social-economic survey of San Andres and Providence.* 1963.

Menderhausen, H. "Economic and fiscal problems of a Colombian department," *Inter-American economic affairs,* vol. 6, no. 4, 1953, p. 49.

Ministerio de Hacienda y Crédito Público, Comité de Expertos Financieros. *Anteproyecto de ley sobre delimitación de rentas y gastos de las entidades de derecho público y desarrollo de campañas antialcoholicas.* Imprenta Nacional, Bogotá, 1951, 198pp.

Municipio de Medellín, Departamento Administrativo y Planeación. *Estudio impuestos.* Medellín, n.d., 146pp.

Netzer, D. *Some aspects of local government finances.* Economic Development Series Report No. 51, Development Advisory Service, Center for International Affairs, Harvard University, Cambridge, Mass., 1966, 147pp.

10

Bird, R. "Local property taxes in Colombia," *Proceedings of the National tax association 1965,* vol. 58, pp. 481-516.

Fernández Cadavid, A. *El impuesto de valorización en Colombia.* Tip. Bedout, Medellín, 1948, 364pp.

Instituto Geográfico "Agustín Coduzzi," Departamento de Catastro. *Coeficientes para actualización de avalúos.* Bogotá, 1965, 99pp.

Instituto Geográfico "Agustín Coduzzi," Departamento de Catastro. *Plan cuatrienal para la actualización de los avalúos catastrales en Colombia.* Bogotá, 2 volumes, 1966.

Montalvo Burgos, J. *La valorización como medio de financiación del desarrollo urbano nacional y su aplicación en el municipio de Cali.* Bogotá, 1964, 119pp.

Mora Rubio, R. *Régimen de valorización municipal y renovación urbana.* Editorial ABC, Bogotá, 1966.

Restrepo U., J. *El impuesto de valorización en Medellín.* Medellín, 1957.

Rhoads, W., and Bird, R. *The valorization tax in Colombia: An example for other developing countries?* Economic Development Series Report No. 50, Development Advisory Service, Center for International Affairs, Harvard University, Cambridge, Mass., June 1966, 59pp.

11

Barlowe, R. *Land, taxes and rural economic development in Colombia.* 1960, 22pp. (mimeo).

Castro Guerrero, G. *Régimen legal del impuesto sobre le renta en la ganadería.* Pontificia Universidad Javeriana, Bogotá, 1964, 132pp.

Comité Interamericano de Desarrollo Agricola. *Tenencia de la tierra y desarrollo socio-económico del sector agricola: Colombia.* Unión Panamericana, Washington, 1966, 563pp.

Consejo Social Agrano. *Informe de la primera reunión.* Imprenta Nacional, Bogotá, 1963, 196pp.

Currie, L., *et al. Programa de desarrollo económico de Valle del Magdalena y norte de Colombia.* Bogotá, 1960.

Fadul, M. "El incentivo tributario como complemento a una reforma social agraria," *La nueva economía*, vol. 1, February 1961, pp. 52-67.

Hirschman, A. *Journeys towards progress.* Twentieth Century Fund, New York, 1963, chapter 2. Part reprinted in: R. Bird and O. Oldman (eds.), *Readings on taxation in developing countries.* The Johns Hopkins Press, Baltimore, 1964, pp. 416-435; revised edition, 1967, pp. 445-464.

International Bank for Reconstruction and Development. *The agricultural development of Colombia.* Washington, 1956, pp. 65-67 (mimeo).

World Bank Mission to Colombia. "A graduated land tax." In: R. Bird and O. Oldman (eds.), *Readings on taxation in developing countries.* The Johns Hopkins Press, Baltimore, 1964, pp. 413-415; revised edition, 1967, pp. 442-444.

12

Camacho Rueda, A. "Nuevas medidas e incentivos para la construcción de vivienda," *Comercio colombo-americano*, vol. 5, no. 20, November-December 1965, pp. 31-33.

"Colombian measures to stimulate economic development," *Bulletin of the Pan American union*, vol. 74, 1940, p. 722.

"Tax advantages in Barranquilla," *Foreign tax law weekly bulletin*, vol. 9, no. 35, 1959, pp. 1-4.

13

Controulis, T. *A breakthrough in the collection of delinquent taxes: A case study in Colombia.* Paper presented at the AID/IRS Regional Conference on Tax Administration Assistance (Panamá), Spring 1965, 9pp. (mimeo).

Controulis, T. *Country briefing paper: Colombia.* United States Treasury Department, Internal Revenue Service, Foreign Tax Assistance Program, Washington, 20 July 1966, 18pp. (mimeo).

Garzonnieto Combariza, G. *Algunos aspectos del control fiscal nacional en Colombia.* Kelly, Bogotá, 1961, 143pp.

Secretaría de la Presidencia. *Informe correspondiente al estudio # E-57C de la administración regional de impuestos nacionales de Bogotá.* Bogotá, 1962.

14

Becerra Gómez, E. *De los recursos en derecho tributario.* Thesis, Pontificia Universidad Javeriana, Bogotá, 1965, 102pp.

López Freyle, I. *Principios de derecho tributario.* Lerner, Bogotá, 2d edition, 1962, 806pp.

Parra Escobar, A. *Aspectos principales del procedimiento tributario.* Minerva, Bogotá, 1962, 107pp.

Ponbo Toro, J. *Apuntes sobre los ingresos públicos en la historia constitucional de Colombia.* Thesis, Pontificia Universidad Javeriana, Bogotá, 1964, 92pp.

15

Dunkerley, H. *Exchange rate systems and development in conditions of continuing inflation.* Economic Development Series Report No. 37, Development Advisory Service, Center for International Affairs, Harvard University, Cambridge, Mass., 1966, 74pp. (multilith).

Peñalosa Camargo, E. *El régimen del control de cambios en Colombia.* Editorial *El Gráfico*, Bogotá, 1951, 71pp.

17

Almeida, R. "La zona latinoamericana de libre comercio," *Técnicas financieras* (CEMLA), vol. 2, no. 5, May-June 1963, pp. 453-472.

Gutiérrez Kirchner, A. "El mercomún latinoamericano y la política fiscal," *Investigación fiscal*, no. 19, July 1967, pp. 15-63.

18

"Colombia law digest." In: *Martindale-Hubbell law directory*, vol. 4, pp. 2529-2540. Martindale-Hubbell, Inc., Summit, N.J., 1961.

Diamond, W. *Foreign tax and trade briefs.* Fallon Law Book Company, New York, loose-leaf, 1951–.

Economist Intelligence Unit, Ltd. *Economic review of Colombia and Venezuela.* London, irregular.

Instituto Colombiano de Derecho Tributario. *Revista del Instituto colombiano de derecho tributario.* Bogotá, 1965–.

Legislación económica. Legislación Económica Ltda., Bogotá, fortnightly, 1952–.

Ministerio de Hacienda y Crédito Público. *Memoria.* Imprenta Nacional, Bogotá, annual, 1823–.

CONGO, DEMOCRATIC REPUBLIC OF

1

Price Waterhouse & Co. *Memorandum on the formation of companies and the taxation relating thereto in the Belgian Congo.* Brussels, 28 February 1957, 12pp. (mimeo).

United States Department of Commerce. *Basic data on the economy of the Democratic Republic of the Congo (Leopoldville).* Washington, 1965, 12pp.

Wertz, J. "Esquisse de l'evolution du système fiscal congolais," *Bulletin de la Banque centrale du Congo Belge et du Ruanda Urundi,* vol. 9, 1957, pp. 347-355.

2

Leclercq, H. "Principes pour l'orientation d'une politique fiscale au Congo belge," *Zaïre,* vol. 13, no. 5, 1959, pp. 451-497.

4

Foreign Tax Law Association. *Belgian Congo income tax service.* Centerport, L.I., N.Y., loose-leaf, 1955–.

8

Organisation for European Economic Cooperation. *Taxation systems applicable to investments in the overseas countries associated with member countries of O.E.E.C.* Paris, 1960.

United States Department of Commerce. *Establishing a business in the Belgian Congo and Ruanda-Urundi.* Washington, 1957, 12pp.

18

Diamond, W. *Foreign tax and trade briefs.* Fallon Law Book Company, New York, loose-leaf, 1951–.

CONGO (Brazzaville)

1

"Régime fiscal au 1ER juillet 1965," *Problèmes d'outre-mer,* 1 and 15 August 1965, pp. 63-67.

Rousseaux, R. "Le Vote du budget originaire au Burundi, au Rwanda et au Congo," *Revue juridique de droit écrit et coutumier du Rwanda et du Burundi,* vol. 5, 1965, pp. 83-90.

United States Department of Commerce. *Basic data on the economy of the Republic of Congo (Brazzaville).* Washington, 1964, 12pp.

2

de Carbon, B. "Politique fiscale et croissance économique dans les états d'Afrique Equatoriale et Cameroun," *Banque centrale du Cameroun et de l'Afrique Equatoriale bulletin mensuel,* May 1961.

Hovine, M. "Finances publiques et croissance des économies de l'Afrique Equatoriale," *Développement africain* (Algiers), vol. 2, 1959, pp. 16-22.

8

United States Department of Commerce. *Investment law of the Republic of Congo (Brazzaville).* Washington, 1962, 12pp.

COOK ISLANDS

4

"Cook Islands." In: Board of Inland Revenue (Great Britain), *Income taxes outside the United Kingdom 1966,* vol. 2, pp. 199-220. H. M. Stationery Office, London, 1967.

COSTA RICA

1

Banco Central de Costa Rica. *Documentos relacionados con la situación fiscal de Costa Rica y con las medidas financieras propuestas para nivelar el presupuesto nacional.* San José, 1957, 48pp.

Costa, J. *Taxes in the 1954 budget of Costa Rica: A preliminary study of taxes and tax administration in Costa Rica and comments with respect thereto for consideration.* International Cooperation Administration, Washington, 1953, 18pp. (offset).

Lord, E. "Salient features of taxation in Costa Rica," *Taxes,* vol. 20, 1942, p. 585.

Pan American Union. *A statement of the laws of Costa Rica in matters affecting business.* Pan American Union, Washington, 3d edition, 1959. Supplement, 1963.

Price Waterhouse & Co. *Memorandum on taxation, exchange, etc. in Costa Rica.* México, 15 November 1954, 8pp. (mimeo).

Programa Conjunto de Tributación de la Organización de los Estados Americanos y del Banco Interamericano de Desarrollo. *Sistemas tributarios de América Latina: Costa Rica.* Unión Panamericana, Washington, 1965, 76pp.

Quesada Fonseca, J. *Análisis de algunos aspectos de la tributación costarricense.* Ministerio de Economía y Hacienda, San José, 1961, 77pp.

United States Department of Commerce. *Basic data on the economy of Costa Rica.* Washington, 1963, 18pp.

United States Department of Commerce. *Investment in Costa Rica.* Washington, 1960, 7pp.

2

May, S., *et al. Costa Rica, a study in economic development.* Twentieth Century Fund, New York, 1952.

4

Foreign Tax Law Association. *Costa Rican income tax service.* Centerport, L.I., N.Y., loose-leaf, 1954–1955.

Peat, Marwick, Mitchell & Co. *Republic of Costa Rica, income tax law.* Panamá, 48pp.

"Taxation of individuals and corporations in Costa Rica," *Foreign tax law semiweekly bulletin,* vol. 5, nos. 15-16, 1954, pp. 3-8.

5

Costa, J. *Death and gift taxes in Costa Rica.* International Cooperation Administration, Washington, 1956, 105pp. (mimeo).

6

Londoño Angel, A. "Los impuestos al consumo." In: Escuela Superior de Administración Pública América Central, *Informe del seminario regional sobre administración fiscal 5 a 9 de octubre de 1964,* pp. 115-120. San José, 1965.

Programa Conjunto de Tributación de la Organización de los Estados Americanos y del Banco Interamericano de Desarrollo. *El impuesto sobre las ventas.* Unión Panamericana, Washington, December 1966 (mimeo).

7

"Costa Rica tax on coffee," *Foreign tax law weekly bulletin,* vol. 1, no. 36, 1951, pp. 3-6.

Lynch, D. *Tariff policy in Costa Rica.* International Cooperation Administration, Washington, 1951.

United States Department of Commerce. *Foreign trade regulations of the Central American common market.* Washington, 1967, 12pp.

8

Diamond, W. *Costa Rica: Lucrative foreign investment center for United States companies.* Matthew Bender & Co., New York, 1959, 12pp.

Ministerio de Industrias. *Costa Rica: A handbook of facts for persons considering investments.* San José, 1964, 64pp.

9

Brown, D. *Financial administration study of the city of San José.* Work document, 1956, 42pp. (mimeo).

10

Costa, J. *The land tax of Costa Rica.* International Cooperation Administration, Washington, 1954, 68pp.

"Costa Rica raises real estate taxes," *Foreign commerce weekly,* vol. 63, no. 7, 1960, p. 15.

Londoño Angel, A. "Los impuestos a la propiedad territorial." In: Escuela Superior de Administración Pública América Central, *Informe del seminario regional sobre administración fiscal 5 a 9 de octubre de 1964,* pp. 73-114. San José, 1965.

12

United States Department of Commerce. *Industrial encouragement law of Costa Rica.* Washington, 1959, 7pp.

13

Fernández Pacheco, M. "Reorganización de la administración financiera de Costa Rica," *Veritas* (Buenos Aires), vol. 17, 15 February 1948, pp. 185-190.

Jiménez Castro, W. *Plan para la implantación de un sistema estadístico para el impuesto sobre la renta.* Serie Economía y Finanzas No. 414, Escuela Superior de Administración Pública América Central, San José, 1964, v/65pp.

United States Treasury Department, Internal Revenue Service, Foreign Tax Assistance Staff. *Report on tax administration in Costa Rica.* Washington, 1964 (mimeo).

17

Programa Conjunto de Tributación de la Organización de los Estados Americanos y del Banco de Desarrollo Interamericano. "La administración tributaria en Centroamérica y el proyecto de armonización fiscal," *Investigación fiscal,* no. 14, February 1967, pp. 91-176.

Watkin, V. *Taxes and tax harmonization in Central America.* Harvard Law School International Tax Program, Cambridge, Mass., 1967, chapter 8.

18

"Costa Rica law digest." In: *Martindale-Hubbell law directory,* vol. 4, pp. 2541-2549. Martindale-Hubbell, Inc., Summit, N.J., 1961.

Diamond, W. *Foreign tax and trade briefs.* Fallon Law Book Company, New York, loose-leaf, 1951–.

CUBA

1

"Bill cuts number of taxes," *Foreign tax law weekly bulletin,* vol. 10, no. 7, 1959, p. 5.

"Breakdown on tax project," *Foreign tax law weekly bulletin,* vol. 10, no. 6, 1959, pp. 7-11.

"Castro's government offers tax forgiveness," *Foreign tax law weekly bulletin,* vol. 9, no. 37, 1959, pp. 1-4.

"Evolución de los ingresos públicos," *Revista del Banco nacional de Cuba,* vol. 4, November 1958, pp. 643-656.

"La ley fiscal," *Trimestre de finanzas al día,* no. 3, 1962, pp. 3-8.

Magill, R., and Shoup, C. *The Cuban fiscal system.* n.p., New York, 1939, 127pp.

Masnata de Quesada, D. *Tributación de la industria azucarera.* Editorial Lex, Havana, 1953, 137pp.

Menocal, J. "The Cuban tax system," *National tax journal,* vol. 3, June 1950, pp. 165-172.

Menocal, J. *Derecho fiscal: Constitución,* legislación y jurisprudencia cubanas. Editorial Minerva, Havana, 1953, 302pp.

"New Cuban tax reform law in effect," *Foreign commerce weekly,* vol. 62, no. 15, 1959, p. 7.

"New tax decrees," *Foreign tax law weekly bulletin,* vol. 7, no. 36, 1957.

Pan American Union. *A statement of the laws of Cuba in matters affecting business.* Washington, 1958.

Price Waterhouse & Co. *Memorandum of Cuban taxation.* 1956, 2pp. (mimeo).

Price Waterhouse & Co. *Memorandum on taxation in Cuba.* Havana, July 1955, 13pp. (mimeo).

"Proposed new taxes," *Foreign tax law weekly bulletin,* vol. 10, no. 7, 1959.

Publicaciones Lewis (ed.). *Tax reform law, 1959* (translation). Private Commercial Service S.A., Havana, 1960.

Seligman, E., and Shoup, C. *A report on the revenue system of Cuba.* Talleres Tipográficos de Carasa y Cía, Havana, 1932, 430pp.

Tax reform law: Law no. 447, July 14, 1959. Private Commercial Service S.A., Havana, 2 volumes, 1959.

"Taxation and pending legislation," *Foreign tax law weekly bulletin,* vol. 10, no. 6, 1959, pp. 1-7.

"Taxpayers subject to registration," *Foreign tax law weekly bulletin,* vol. 10, no. 29, 1959, pp. 8-9.

2

Escobar Tamayo, F. "La reforma tributaria que Cuba necesita," *América* (Havana), vol. 41, October 1953, pp. 10-19.

International Bank for Reconstruction and Development. *Report on Cuba.* Sales No. IBRD.1951.3, Washington, 1951, chapters 34-37, 39.

3

Diez del Valle, M. "O sistema tributário cubano, estudo comparativo com o sistema braseleiro," *Revista de finanzas públicas,* vol. 13, July-August 1953, pp. 42-45.

4

Guni, F. "Las modificaciones de nuestro impuesto a la renta," *Contabilidad y finanzas* (Havana), vol. 6/7, October 1952-June 1953, pp. 176-186.

Menocal y Barreras, J. *Antecedentes del*

impuesto sobre las rentas y entradas personales en la legislación e historia cubanas. n.p., Havana, 1951, 47pp.

Publicaciones Lewis (ed.). *Income tax law and regulations* (translation). Private Commercial Service S.A., Havana, n.d.

Publicaciones Lewis (ed.). *Profits tax law and regulations* (translation). Private Commercial Service S.A., Havana, n.d. (processed).

Salles y Milanes, J. *El impuesto sobre la renta.* Editorial Lex, Havana, 1951.

6

"Consumption tax," *Foreign tax law weekly bulletin,* vol. 9, no. 21, 1958, p. 5.

"Miscellaneous taxes in Cuba," *Foreign tax law weekly bulletin,* vol. 7, no. 41, 1957, pp. 5-9.

8

"Mining concessionaires tax," *Foreign tax law weekly bulletin,* vol. 10, no. 28, 1959, pp. 3-4.

Patty, W. "Tax aspects of Cuban expropriations," *Tax law review,* vol. 16, May 1961, pp. 415-439.

"Representations to the Cuban government regarding taxation of United States government agencies in Cuba," *Foreign relations of the United States diplomatic papers,* vol. 6, 1943, pp. 259-279.

United States Department of Commerce. *Investment in Cuba.* Washington, 1957, pp. 155-162.

Wolfe, T., and White, J. "Income tax consequences of Cuban expropriations to Cuban resident aliens," *University of Miami law review,* vol. 19, 1965, pp. 591-614.

9

Garcini y Guerra, H. "Recursos municipais de carácter financeiro," *Revista brasileira dos municípios,* vol. 6, October-December 1953, pp. 323-328.

Menocal, J. *El poder fiscal municipal.* Editorial Minerva, Havana, 1953, 539pp.

10

Ruga Fontanilles, L. (ed.). *Nueva ley de impuesto de derechos reales.* Editorial Lex, Havana, 1955.

12

"Ten-year exemption," *Foreign tax law weekly bulletin,* vol. 9, no. 41, 1959, p. 2.

13

Price Waterhouse & Co. *Report to the Cuban government on fiscal administration.* 1950.

Publicaciones Lewis (ed.). *Regulations for the administration of the tax reform law, 1959* (translation). Private Commercial Service S.A., Havana, 1960 (processed).

United Nations, Economic and Social Council, Fiscal Commission. "Procedures available for the review of initial tax assessments: Reply of the government of Cuba." Doc. No. E/CN.8/59/ Add.12, 22 January 1952, 11pp. (mimeo).

18

"Cuba law digest." In: *Martindale-Hubbell law directory,* vol. 4, pp. 2550-2565. Martindale-Hubbell, Inc., Summit, N.J., 1961.

Diamond, W. *Foreign tax and trade briefs.* Fallon Law Book Company, New York, loose-leaf, 1951-.

CYPRUS

1

Kypris, P. "Taxation in Cyprus," *Bulletin for international fiscal documentation,* vol. 19, 1965, pp. 415-417.

Price Waterhouse & Co. *Information guide for doing business in Cyprus.* New York, 1967.

United States Department of Commerce. *Basic data on the economy of Cyprus.* Washington, 1963, 14pp.

4

"Cyprus." In: Board of Inland Revenue (Great Britain), *Income taxes outside the United Kingdom 1966,* vol. 2, pp. 221-258, H. M. Stationery Office, London, 1967.

Foreign Tax Law Association. *Cyprus income tax service.* St. Petersburg, Fla., loose-leaf, 1962-.

7

United States Department of Commerce. *Foreign trade regulations of Cyprus.* Washington, 1965, 8pp.

8

United States Department of Commerce, Office of Technical Services, Joint Publications Research Service. *Income tax act (on foreign persons) of 1961.* Washington, 23 November 1962, 96pp.

DAHOMEY

2

The economic and financial structure of French West Africa. Annual conference of the Economic Sections, West African Institute of Social and Economic Research, University College, Ibadan, 1953 (mimeo).

3

Mémento fiscal et social 1964, numéro spécial no. 14, 25 June 1964. A comparative survey of taxes in the West African Union and Guinea.

12

United States Department of Commerce. *Investment law in the Republic of Dahomey.* Washington, 1963, 12pp.

DOMINICA

4

"Dominica." In: Board of Inland Revenue (Great Britain), *Income taxes outside the United Kingdom 1966,* vol. 2, pp. 289-306. H. M. Stationery Office, London, 1967.

DOMINICAN REPUBLIC

1

"Desarrollo de la hacienda pública en la era de Trujillo," *Revista de la Secretaría de estado de economía y comercio,* vol. 24, September-October 1952, pp. 10-21.

Dirección General de Rentas Internas. *Conocimientos esenciales para Inspectores de rentas internas.* Ciudad Trujillo, 1951, 341pp.

González H., J. *Historia de las finanzas dominicanas.* Tip. Emilio Montalvo, Ciudad Trujillo, 1951, 76pp.

Nanita, A. "La independencia financiera," *Revista de la Secretaría de estado de economía y comercio,* vol. 30, September-October 1953, pp. 10-13.

Pan American Union. *A statement of the laws of the Dominican Republic in matters affecting business.* Washington, 3d edition revised, 1964, 300pp.

Salvador Ortiz, S. *Dominican taxation during the Trujillo era.* Editora del Caribe, Ciudad Trujillo, 1953, 34pp.

"Síntesis del sistema tributario de la República Dominicana en la era de Trujillo," *Revista de la Secretaría de estado de economía y comercio,* vol. 28, May-June 1953, pp. 2-9.

"Taxation in Dominican Republic," *Foreign tax law weekly bulletin,* vol. 13, no. 25, 1962, pp. 1-6.

United States Department of Commerce. *Basic data on the economy of the Dominican Republic.* Washington, 1957, 15pp.

United States Department of State. *Background notes: Dominican Republic.* Washington, 1965, 4pp.

4

"Dominican Republic revises profits tax, creates personal income tax," *Foreign commerce weekly,* vol. 67, no. 8, 1962, p. 318.

Foreign Tax Law Association. *Dominican Republic income tax service.* Centerport, L.I., N.Y., loose-leaf, 1954-1955.

"Second regulation—No. 8357," *Foreign tax law weekly bulletin,* vol. 3, no. 47, 1952, pp. 1-15 (on depreciation).

7

United States Department of Commerce. *Foreign trade regulations of the Dominican Republic.* Washington, 1966, 8pp.

8

Messina, M. "Trade, laws, taxes and foreign investments in the Dominican Republic," *A look at the Dominican Republic,* vol. 3, no. 2, 1958, p. 14.

United States Department of Commerce. *Establishing a business in the Dominican Republic.* Washington, 1956, 10pp.

14

Barbosa Aguinó, F. *La realidad económica como elemento esencial del principio de interpretación y aplicación de las leyes tributarias.* Dirección General de Impuesto sobre Beneficios, Ciudad Trujillo, 1959, 69pp.

18

Diamond, W. *Foreign tax and trade briefs.* Fallon Law Book Company, New York, loose-leaf, 1951-.

"Dominican Republic law digest." In: *Martindale-Hubbell law directory,* vol. 4, pp. 2571-2579. Martindale-Hubbell, Inc., Summit, N.J., 1961.

ECUADOR

1

Amador Navarro, E. *Leyes mercantiles y tributarias de la República del Ecuador.* Janer, Guayaquil, 1963, 580pp.

Banco Central del Ecuador. *Invest in Ecuador.* Quito, 1963, 42pp.

Borjay Borja, R. "Informe sobre la codificación de la ley orgánica de hacienda," *Boletín jurídico* (Ecuador), vol. 2, 1960, pp. 251-494.

Businessmen look at Ecuador. Cendes, Quito, 1965, 32pp.

Costa, J. *Taxes in Ecuador: A review of some of the Ecuadorean tax laws and their administration and proposals for reform thereof.* International Cooperation Administration, Washington, 1956, 50pp. (mimeo).

Cuevas Silva, J. *Finanzas públicas del Ecuador.* Quito, 1960, 246pp.

"Laws and taxes." In: Checchi and Company, *Expanding private investment for Ecuador's economic growth,* pp. 22-46. Washington, 1961.

"New tax rates," *Foreign tax law weekly bulletin,* vol. 14, no. 17, 1963, pp. 1-4.

Pan American Union. *A statement of the laws of Ecuador in matters affecting business.* Washington, 2d edition revised, 1955, 190pp. Supplements, 1958, 1961.

Price Waterhouse & Co. *Information guide for doing business in Ecuador.* New York, 1966.

Reyes, J. *Apuntaciones sobre problemas ecuatorianos.* Editorial Casa de la Cultura Ecuatoriana, Quito, 1957, 133pp.

"Starting a business in Ecuador," *Foreign tax law weekly bulletin,* vol. 3, no. 16, 1952, pp. 1-8.

United States Department of Commerce. *Basic data on the economy of Ecuador.* Washington, 1960, 16pp.

2

Nunn, G. *La tributación en relación con el desarrollo en el Ecuador.* Junta Nacional de Planificación y Coordinación Económica, Quito, 1961, 123pp.

Pan American Union. *Ecuador: Hacienda pública y política fiscal.* Washington, 1954, 205pp.

Special Economic Mission. *Informe de los trabajos de la Misión económica especial en el Ecuador.* Quito, 1959, chapters 6, 7, annexes F, G, and H.

4

"Ecuador extends, raises income tax," *Foreign tax law weekly bulletin,* vol. 10, no. 12, 1959, pp. 4-5.

Foreign Tax Law Association. *Ecuador income tax service.* Centerport, L.I., N.Y., loose-leaf, 1954–.

Galán Gómez, M., and Wiese, G. *Estudio sobre el proyecto de ley de impuesto a la renta.* United Nations mission, Quito, 1954.

Hayer, F. "Por que son perjudiciales los impuestos progresivos sobre la renta," *Boletín de difusión económica* (Guayaquil), October 1955, p. 38.

"Income tax laws amended," *Foreign tax law weekly bulletin,* vol. 9, no. 25, 1958, pp. 1-2.

Maldonado Aguilar, J. (ed.). *La nueva ley del impuesto a la renta.* Editorial "Don Bosco," Cuenca, 1963, 143pp.

Reyes, J. "El impuesto sobre la renta o el ingreso," *Boletín del Ministerio del tesoro* (Quito), no. 49050, 1957, p. 21.

Riofrio Villagómez, E. "Breves comentarios a la nueva ley de impuesto a la renta," *Revista de derecho,* no. 2, 1964, pp. 112-126.

Riofrio Villagómez, E. "Rendimiento comparativo de los actuales impuestos a la renta y el proyecto de nueva ley de los expertos de la ONU," *Boletín trimestral de información económica* (Quito), vol. 2, June-November 1952, pp. 14-50.

"Surcharge on income," *Foreign tax law weekly bulletin,* vol. 7, no. 36, 1957, pp. 1-2.

6

"Ecuador increases tax on imported cigarettes," *Foreign commerce weekly,* vol. 65, no. 6, 1961, p. 6.

Programa Conjunto de Tributación de la Organización de los Estados Americanos y del Banco Interamericano de Desarrollo. *El impuesto sobre las ventas.* Unión Panamericana, Washington, December 1966 (mimeo).

7

United States Department of Commerce. *Foreign trade regulations of Ecuador.* Washington, 1967, 8pp.

8

Peña Astudillo, M. "Tratado modelo sobre doble tributación," *Revista de la Cámara de comercio de Guayaquil,* 30 November 1959, p. 24.

United States Department of Commerce. *Establishing a business in Ecuador.* Washington, 1960, 12pp.

United States Department of Commerce. *Investment in Ecuador.* Washington, 1958, pp. 127-129.

9

Riofrio Villagómez, E. *Gobierno y finanzas municipales.* Imprenta Municipal, Quito, 1954, 672pp.

Riofrio Villagómez, E. *La participación de las provincias en las finanzas públicas del estado.* Casa de la Cultura Ecuatoriana, Quito, 1955, 116pp.

Smith, N. *Report of a study of the fiscal functions and recommendations for the reorganization of the Department of finance in the city of Quito, Ecuador.* 1956, 24pp. (mimeo).

12

United States Department of Commerce. *Industrial development law of Ecuador.* Washington, 1962, 10pp.

13

Costa, J. *Draft law of agencies participating in national revenues.* International Cooperation Administration, Washington, 1956.

14

Riofrio Villagómez, E. "¿Es revocable de oficio la resolución de última instancia administrativa en los tributario?" *Boletín jurídico* (Ecuador), vol. 2, 1960, pp. 1021-1034.

17

Almeida, R. "La zona latinoamericana de libre comercio," *Técnicas financieras* (CEMLA), vol. 2, no. 5, May-June 1963, pp. 453-472.

Gutiérrez Kirchner, A. "El mercomún latinoamericano y la política fiscal,"

Investigación fiscal, no. 19, July 1967, pp. 15-63.

18

Contraloría General de la Nación. *Codificación de leyes tributarias del Ecuador hasta junio 1957.* Quito, 1957, 594pp.

Diamond, W. *Foreign tax and trade briefs.* Fallon Law Book Company, New York, loose-leaf, 1951–.

Economist Intelligence Unit, Ltd. *Economic review of Peru, Bolivia, and Ecuador.* London, irregular.

"Ecuador law digest." In: *Martindale-Hubbell law directory,* vol. 4, pp. 2580-2587. Martindale-Hubbell, Inc., Summit, N.J., 1961.

Junta Nacional de Planificación y Coordinación Económica. *Codificación de la legislación tributaria del Ecuador.* Quito, 1964, 145pp.

EL SALVADOR

1

Cosciani, C., and Dougherty, J. *Informe sobre el sistema tributario de El Salvador.* United Nations (restricted).

Oldman, O. "Tax reform in El Salvador," *Inter-American law review,* vol. 6, 1964, pp. 379-420.

Programa Conjunto de Tributación de la Organización de los Estados Americanos y del Banco Interamericano de Desarrollo. *Sistemas tributarios de América Latina: El Salvador.* Unión Panamericana, Washington, 1966, 88pp.

United States Department of Commerce. *Basic data on the economy of El Salvador.* Washington, 1963, 23pp.

United States Department of Commerce. *Investment in El Salvador.* Washington, 1960, 6pp.

2

J. L. Jacobs and Co. *El Salvador: Report with recommendations on the national tax system and tax administration.* Chicago, 1950, 162pp.

Schenk, W. "Tecnología, formación de capital y política fiscal gubernamental," *Economía salvadoreña,* vol. 4, 1954, pp. 141-149.

United Nations, Technical Assistance Administration. "Les Finances publiques au Salvador." Doc. No. ST/TAA/K/El Salvador/6, 1954, 144pp.

Urbina, R., Zepeda, J., and Hidalgo, J. "El equilibrio presupuestario en El Salvador en el pasado y en el presente," *Economía salvadoreña,* vol. 11, 1962, pp. 45-105.

Wallich, H., and Adler, J. *Proyecciones económicas de las finanzas públicas: Un estudio experimental en El Salvador.* Fondo de Cultura Económica, México, 1949, 363pp.

Wallich, H., and Adler, J. *Public finance in a developing country: El Salvador, a case study.* Harvard University Press, Cambridge, Mass., 1951, 346pp.

4

Cámara de Comercio e Industria de El Salvador. "Exposición sobre el proyecto de reformas a los impuestos sobre la renta y de vialidad, presentada por la Cámara a la consideración de los señores Ministros de hacienda y economía," *Boletín,* vol. 25, January-February 1951, pp. 18-26.

Fernández, H. "El impuesto sobre la renta en El Salvador," *Economía salvadoreña,* vol. 14, 1965, pp. 77-158.

Foreign Tax Law Association. *El Salvador income tax service.* Centerport, L.I., N.Y., loose-leaf, 1951–1952.

Méndez López, H. "Historia del impuesto sobre la renta en El Salvador," *Economía salvadoreña,* vol. 3, 1950, pp. 175-181.

"Taxation of individuals and corporations in El Salvador," *Foreign tax law semiweekly bulletin,* vol. 5, nos. 15-16, 1954, pp. 1-2.

7

Froomkin, J., and Lidstone, H. "Tax problems of export economies—Taxation of coffee in El Salvador," *National tax journal,* vol. 7, September 1954, pp. 264-273.

United States Department of Commerce. *Foreign trade regulations of the Central American common market.* Washington, 1967, 12pp.

9

Public Administration Service. *Financing municipal government in El Salvador.* Chicago, 1955, 109pp.

10

Gavidia Hildalgo, V. "Procedimientos modernos de valuación de la propiedad territorial y el impuesto de vialidad serie 'A,'" *Asuntos administrativos* (San Salvador), vol. 4, March-April 1956, pp. 7-18.

13

Lidstone, H. *Report to the Minister of finance, Republic of El Salvador, on the problems of tax administration and legislation in El Salvador.* 1 April 1955.

17

Peat, Marwick, Mitchell & Co. *Economical association tax among the Republics of Guatemala, El Salvador, and Honduras.* Panamá.

Programa Conjunto de Tributación de la Organización de los Estados Americanos y del Banco de Desarrollo Interamericano. "La administración tributaria en Centroamérica y el proyecto de armonización fiscal," *Investigación fiscal,* no. 14, February 1967, pp. 91-176.

Watkin, V. *Taxes and tax harmonization in Central America.* Harvard Law School International Tax Program, Cambridge, Mass., 1967, chapter 5.

18

Diamond, W. *Foreign tax and trade briefs.* Fallon Law Book Company, New York, loose-leaf, 1951–.

"El Salvador law digest." In: *Martindale-Hubbell law directory,* vol. 4, pp. 2588-2595. Martindale-Hubbell, Inc., Summit, N.J., 1961.

ETHIOPIA

1

Oldman, O., and Demos, E. *A preliminary and partial survey of the Ethiopian tax structure.* Harvard Law School International Tax Program, Cambridge, Mass., 1966, 24pp. (mimeo).

Price Waterhouse & Co. *Information guide for doing business in Ethiopia.* New York, 1964.

Qureshi, A. *Fiscal system of Ethiopia.* International Monetary Fund, Washington, January 1955, 33pp. (mimeo).

United States Department of Commerce.

Basic data on the economy of Ethiopia.
Washington, 1967, 32pp.

2

"An economic study of Ethiopia (including income tax laws)," *Foreign tax law semi-weekly bulletin,* vol. 6, no. 65, 1956, pp. 1-9.

4

Foreign Tax Law Association. *Ethiopian income tax service.* St. Petersburg, Fla., loose-leaf, 1961–.
"The income tax laws of Ethiopia and Eritrea," *Foreign tax law semi-weekly bulletin,* vol. 4, no. 66, 1954, pp. 1-5.

6

Ministry of Finance, Excise Tax Department. *General information.* Addis Ababa, 1964, 37pp.

7

Ministry of Finance, Department of Customs. *General information concerning Ethiopian customs administration, regulations, procedure and tariff.* Addis Ababa, 2d edition, 1964, 56pp.
United States Department of Commerce. *Foreign trade regulations of Ethiopia.* Washington, 1966, 8pp.

8

United States Department of Commerce. *Establishing a business in Ethiopia.* Washington, 1967, 20pp.

9

Cobley, R. "Fiscal administration in fast-growing Addis Ababa," *Municipal journal,* vol. 68, 12 August 1960, pp. 2514-2515.

11

Jandy, E. *Changing land tenure practice and land taxation in Ethiopia.* Paper from the Conference on Land and Tax Reform in the Less Developed Countries, sponsored by the Committee on Taxation, Resources and Economic Development and the Land Tenure Center, University of Wisconsin, Madison, Wisc., August 1963.
Wolde-Tsadik, S. *Land taxation in Harage Province.* Imperial Ethiopian

College of Agricultural and Mechanical Arts Bulletin No. 48, Dire Dawa, 1966, 24pp.

FALKLAND ISLANDS

4

"Falkland Islands." In: Board of Inland Revenue (Great Britain), *Income taxes outside the United Kingdom 1966,* vol. 3, pp. 1-16. H. M. Stationery Office, London, 1967.

FIJI ISLANDS

1

United States Department of Commerce. *Basic data on the economy of the British Pacific Islands.* Washington, 1963, 24pp.

4

"Fiji." In: Board of Inland Revenue (Great Britain), *Income taxes outside the United Kingdom 1966,* vol. 3, pp. 17-48. H. M. Stationery Office, London, 1967.

7

United States Department of Commerce. *Import tariff system of the Fiji Islands.* Washington, 1963, 2pp.

FRENCH SOMALILAND

1

United States Department of Commerce. *Basic data on the economy of French Somaliland.* Washington, 1961, 4pp.

GABON

1

"Single tax." In: Direction de l'Information, *Investments in Gabon,* pp. 51-57. Libreville, 1962.
United States Department of Commerce. *Basic data on the economy of Gabon.* Washington, 1963, 16pp.

2

de Carbon, B. "Politique fiscale et croissance économique dans les états d'Afrique Equatoriale et Cameroun," *Banque centrale du Cameroun et de l'Afrique Equatoriale bulletin mensuel,* May 1961.

Hovine, M. "Finances publiques et croissance des économies de l'Afrique Equatoriale," *Développement africain* (Algiers), vol. 2, 1959, pp. 16-22.

12

United States Department of Commerce. *Investment law in the Republic of Gabon.* Washington, 1962, 12pp.

GAMBIA

4

"Gambia." In: Board of Inland Revenue (Great Britain), *Income taxes outside the United Kingdom 1966,* vol. 3, pp. 105-127. H. M. Stationery Office, London, 1967.

"Methods of direct taxation in British Tropical Africa," *Journal of African administration,* vol. 2, October 1950, pp. 3-12; vol. 3, January 1951, pp. 30-41; vol. 3, October 1951, pp. 77-87.

GHANA

1

Andic, F., and Andic, S. "A survey of Ghana's tax system and finances," *Public finance,* vol. 18, 1963, pp. 5-44.

G. H. Wittman, Inc. *The Ghana report.* New York, 1959, pp. 175-182.

Hazelwood, A. "Ghana's finances," *Bankers' magazine,* vol. 183, April 1957, pp. 321-330.

Simmonds, D. "Summary of Ghana taxation," *Bulletin for international fiscal documentation,* vol. 19, 1965, pp. 257-261.

"Taxation and business laws in Ghana," *Foreign tax law weekly bulletin,* vol. 8, no. 44, 1958, pp. 1-7.

United States Department of Commerce. *Basic data on the economy of Ghana.* Washington, 1962, 10pp.

2

Carney, D. "Income distribution, income taxation and economic development in Ghana and Nigeria," *Indian journal of economics,* vol. 41, July 1961, pp. 29-41.

Cox-George, N. "Studies in finance and development—The Gold Coast (Ghana) experience 1914-1918," *Public finance,* vol. 13, 1958, pp. 146-183.

"Public finance." In: Checci and Company, *A program to accelerate economic growth in Ghana.* Washington, 1961.

Seers, D., and Ross, C. *Report on financial and physical problems of development in the Gold Coast.* Government Printing Office, Accra, 1952, 65pp.

United Nations, Technical Assistance Programme. "Taxation and economic development in Ghana." Doc. No. TAO/GHA/4 (restricted), 26 February 1958; TAO/GHA/4/Rev.1, 1 July 1959.

3

Due, J. *Taxation and economic development in Tropical Africa.* The MIT Press, Cambridge, Mass., 1963, 172pp.

4

Brewster, S. *Ghana income taxes.* Takoradi, Gold Coast, 1954, 64pp.

"Excerpts from the income tax amendment act, 1965," *Foreign tax law weekly bulletin,* vol. 16, no. 34, 1966, pp. 2-8.

Foreign Tax Law Association. *Ghana income tax service.* St. Petersburg, Fla., loose-leaf, 1962–.

"Ghana." In: Board of Inland Revenue (Great Britain), *Income taxes outside the United Kingdom 1966,* vol. 3, pp. 159-194. H. M. Stationery Office, London, 1967.

Income Tax Department. *Report for the year 1958-1959.* Government Printing Department, Accra, 1959, 17pp.

Income Tax Department. *Report for the year 1959-60.* Government Printing Department, Accra, 1960, 10pp.

Income Tax Department. *Report for the year 1960-61.* Government Printing Department, Accra, 1961, 10pp.

"Methods of direct taxation in British Tropical Africa," *Journal of African administration,* vol. 2, October 1950, pp. 3-12; vol. 3, January 1951, pp. 30-41; vol. 3, October 1951, pp. 77-87.

Smith, A. "Income tax in Ghana," *British tax review,* January-February 1960.

7

United States Department of Commerce. *Foreign trade regulations of Ghana.* Washington, 1966, 8pp.

United States Department of Commerce. *Preparing shipments to Ghana.* Washington, 1963.

8

United States Department of Commerce. *Establishing a business in the Gold Coast.* Washington, 1964, 7pp.

9

Dennis, P. "A note on land revenue and local government in Ghana," *Journal of African administration,* vol. 9, April 1957, pp. 84-88.

Hicks, U. *Development from below: Local government and finance in developing countries of the Commonwealth.* Oxford University Press, London, 1961, 552pp.

10

United Nations, Technical Assistance Administration. "Report on valuation and rating in Ghana." Doc. No. TAA/GHA/5 and Corr. 1 (restricted), 4 April 1958.

12

Smith, A. "Tax relief for new industries in Ghana," *National tax journal,* vol. 11, December 1958, pp. 362-370.

Spangler, S. "Promoting private investment in less developed countries." In T. Farar (ed.), *Financing African development,* pp. 130-143. The MIT Press, Cambridge, Mass., 1965.

16

United Nations. *A programme for technical assistance in the fiscal and financial field.* Sales No. 1958.II.H.5, New York, 1958.

GIBRALTAR

4

"Gibraltar." In: Board of Inland Revenue (Great Britain), *Income taxes outside the United Kingdom 1966,* vol. 3, pp. 195-213. H. M. Stationery Office, London, 1967.

GILBERT AND ELLICE ISLANDS

4

"Gilbert and Ellice Islands." In: Board of Inland Revenue (Great Britain), *Income taxes outside the United Kingdom 1966,* vol. 3, pp. 215-232. H. M. Stationery Office, London, 1967.

GREECE

1

Conlon, C. "Tax revision in Greece," *Proceedings of the National tax association 1951,* vol. 44, pp. 207-212.

Dertilis, P. "Les Mesures fiscales prises en Grèce depuis l'occupation," *Bulletin for international fiscal documentation,* vol. 2, 1948, pp. 305-308.

"Greece." In: Federation of British Industries, *Taxation in Western Europe, 1963: A guide for industrialists,* pp. 130-145. London, 1963.

Industrial Development Corporation. *Guide to investment in Greece.* Athens, 1962, 109pp.

Nézis, G. "Tax system of Greece," *Bulletin for international fiscal documentation,* vol. 9, 1955, pp. 1-30, 129-148, 193-205.

Nézis, G. "Taxation of ships in Greece," *Bulletin for international fiscal documentation,* vol. 11, 1957, pp. 1-6.

"Survey of Greek taxation," *European taxation,* vol. 3, 1963, pp. 51-68.

"Taxation and social security in Greece," *Foreign tax law weekly bulletin,* vol. 14, no. 12, 1963, pp. 6-9; vol. 14, no. 13, 1963, pp. 1-9; vol. 14, no. 14, 1963, pp. 1-9.

United States Department of Commerce. *Basic data on the economy of Greece.* Washington, 1964, 14pp.

United States Department of Commerce. *Doing business in Greece.* Washington, 1963, 24pp.

United States Operations Mission to Greece. *Taxes imposed in Greece.* Athens, 1955, 18pp. (mimeo).

2

Break, G., and Turvey, R. *Studies in Greek taxation.* Research Monograph No. 11, Center of Planning and Economic Research, Athens, 1964, 250pp.

Harper, J. *Progress of fiscal reform in Greece from 1947 to 1956: A summary report.* International Cooperation Administration, Washington, 1956, 39pp. (mimeo).

Katōpodēs, P., and Constantinou, G. *Fiscalité et développement économique en Grèce.* International Bureau of Fiscal Documentation, Amsterdam, 1961, 54pp.

Katopodis, P. "Charges fiscales et revenu national: Le Cas de la Grèce," *Revue de science financière*, vol. 51, 1959, p. 721.

Michalakis, A. "Fiscal policy and economic development in Greece." In: A. Peacock, *Public finance as an instrument for economic development*, pp. 19-46. Organisation for Economic Cooperation and Development, Paris, 1964.

4

American Embassy. *Tax obligations of foreign salaried personnel working in Greece*. Athens, 1966, 8pp.

Dertilis, P. "Vue d'ensemble de l'imposition directe en Grèce jusqu'à la réforme fiscale de 1919." In: E. Morselli and L. Trotabas, *Enquête sur les tarifs d'impôts*, pp. 147-188. CEDAM, Padova, 1964.

Gavallas, G. "Taxation des sociétés imbriquées: Grèce," *Cahiers de droit fiscal international*, vol. 45, 1961, p. 143 (in English; summaries in French and German).

"Greece." In: Board of Inland Revenue (Great Britain), *Income taxes outside the United Kingdom 1966*, vol. 3, pp. 233-250. H. M. Stationery Office, London, 1967.

Industrial Development Corporation. *Taxation of industrial corporations in Greece*. Athens, 1963, 48pp.

Nézis, G. "Income tax levied on Greek limited companies and foreign corporations," *Bulletin for international fiscal documentation*, vol. 14, 1960, pp. 130-140, 193-204, 257-270. Also in: Foreign Tax Law Association, *Greek income tax service*, pp. 1-46. St. Petersburg, Fla., loose-leaf, 1961-.

Nézis, G. "The taxation of the revenue from patents, trade-marks and designs: Greece," *Cahiers de droit fiscal international*, vol. 36, 1958, pp. 166-176.

Nézis, G. "Traitement fiscal des gains en capital: Grèce," *Cahiers de droit fiscal international*, vol. 42, 1960, p. 71 (summaries in English and German).

Semidalas, A. "Régime fiscal comparé du processus de la concentration des entreprises—Rapports nationaux: Grèce," *Cahiers de droit fiscal international*, vol. 48A, 1963, p. 129.

6

Dertilis, P. "L'Impôt sur le chiffre d'affaires en Grèce." In: M. Masoin and E. Morselli (eds.), *Impôts sur transactions, transmissions et chiffre d'affaires*, pp. 201-224. Archives Internationales de Finances Publiques No. 2, Cedam Casa Editrice, Dr. A. Milani, Padova, 1959.

Organisation for European Economic Cooperation. *The influence of sales taxes on productivity*. Paris, 1958, 268pp.

Zacopoulos, P. "International double taxation in the field of turnover taxes from the legal and economic point of view (on Greece)," *Cahiers de droit fiscal international*, vol. 31, 1956, pp. 224-234.

Zarkos, G. *The sales tax system of Greece*. Ph.D. thesis, Indiana, 1960.

7

Apostolou, A. "Régime fiscal de l'importation et de l'exportation de marchandises: Grèce," *Cahiers de droit fiscal international*, vol. 47A, 1962, p. 143.

8

"Convention between the government of the kingdom of Greece and the government of the kingdom of Sweden for the avoidance of double taxation and the prevention of fiscal evasion with respect to taxes on income capital," *Revue hellénique de droit international*, vol. 16, 1963, pp. 406-420.

Gavallas, G. "Interprétation des traités de double imposition: Grèce," *Cahiers de droit fiscal international*, vol. 42, 1960, p. 217 (in English; summaries in French and German).

Nézis, G. "The international double taxation in the taxation regime of Greece," *Cahiers de droit fiscal international*, vol. 7, 1948, pp. 47-55.

Nézis, G. "Mesures fiscales destinées à faciliter le mouvement international des capitaux: Grèce," *Cahiers de droit fiscal international*, vol. 39, 1959, p. 419 (in English; summaries in French, German, and Spanish).

Tsingris, D. "Mesures unilatérales tendant à éviter la double imposition: Grèce," *Cahiers de droit fiscal international*, vol. 44, 1961, pp. 109-126 (in English; summaries in French and German).

United Nations, Economic and Social Council, Fiscal Commission. "Questionnaire on the tax treatment of foreign nationals, assets and transactions: Additional reply of the government of Greece." Doc. No. E/CN.8/46/Add.6/Corr.1, 17 April 1952, 13pp.

United Nations, Economic and Social Council, Fiscal Commission. "Questionnaire on the tax treatment of foreign nationals, assets and transactions: Reply of the government of Greece." Doc. No. E/CN.8/46/Add.6, 31 December 1948, 38pp; E/CN.8/46/Add.6/Annex 1, 12 May 1949, 4pp.

United States Department of Commerce. *Establishing a business in Greece.* Washington, 1967, 24pp.

Zacopoulos, P. "The convention between Greece and the United States for the avoidance of double taxation and the prevention of fiscal evasion with respect to taxes on the estates of deceased persons," *Bulletin for international fiscal documentation,* vol. 8, 1954, pp. 129-136.

9

Traylor, O. *Financing Greek local government.* Special Supplement, Report No. B-70, Economic Cooperation Mission, Athens, 1951, 20pp.

12

Poulopoulos, S. "Fiscal legislation and promotion of private investments in Greece," *Public finance,* vol. 11, 1956, pp. 74-93.

United States Department of Commerce. *Investment law of Greece.* Washington, 5pp.

13

Constantinou, G. "Contrôle fiscal: Des aspects juridiques, psychologiques et économiques: Grèce," *Cahiers de droit fiscal international,* vol. 39, 1959, p. 184 (summaries in German, English, and Spanish).

Nézis, G. "Struggle against tax evasion," *Bulletin for international fiscal documentation,* vol. 5, 1951, pp. 273-280.

Sarantopoulos, C. *Principes généraux de contrôle des finances publiques.* Bibliothèque de la Comptabilité Publique, Athens, 1965, 70pp.

Traylor, O. *Fiscal administrative management in the Greek Ministry of finance.* Foreign Operations Administration, Athens, 1953, 78pp. (mimeo).

14

Dertilis, P. "Les Garanties du contribuable a l'égard du fisc en Grèce." In: *Studi in onore di Achille Donato Giannini,* pp. 505-514. A. Giuffrè, Milan, 1961.

18

Diamond, W. *Foreign tax and trade briefs.* Fallon Law Book Company, New York, loose-leaf, 1951–.

"Greece law digest." In: *Martindale-Hubbell law directory,* vol. 4, pp. 2657-2666. Martindale-Hubbell, Inc., Summit, N.J., 1961.

GRENADA

1

Comptroller for Development and Welfare. *Financial aspects of federation in the British West Indian territories.* Barbados, 1953.

4

Foreign Tax Law Association. *Grenada income tax service.* St. Petersburg, Fla., loose-leaf, 1963–.

"Grenada." In: Board of Inland Revenue (Great Britain), *Income taxes outside the United Kingdom 1966,* vol. 3, pp. 251-271. H. M. Stationery Office, London, 1967.

GUATEMALA

1

Consulate General of Guatemala. *Investing in Guatemala.* New York, 1966, 17pp.

Costa, J. *Aspects of taxation in Guatemala.* International Cooperation Administration, Washington, 1961, 150pp. (mimeo).

Joint Tax Program, Organization of American States and Inter-American Development Bank. *Tax systems of Latin America: Guatemala.* Pan American Union, Washington, 1966, viii/66pp.

Pan American Union. *A statement of the laws of Guatemala in matters affecting business.* Washington, 2d edition, 1959, 274pp. Supplements, 1961, 1965.

Price Waterhouse & Co. *Information guide for doing business in Guatemala.* New York, 1963.

"Taxation in Guatemala," *Foreign tax law weekly bulletin,* vol. 8, no. 3, 1957, pp. 1-4.

United States Department of Commerce. *Basic data on the economy of Guatemala.* Washington, 1966, 24pp.

United States Department of Commerce. *Investment in Guatemala.* Washington, 1960, 12pp.

2

Adler, J., Schlesinger, E., and Olson, E. *Public finance and economic development in Guatemala.* Stanford University Press, Stanford, Calif., 1952.

International Bank for Reconstruction and Development. *Economic development of Guatemala.* Sales No. IBRD.1951.2, Washington, 1951, pp. 267-273.

Klein and Saks Economic and Financial Mission to Guatemala. *Final report, 1955-57. IV: Taxation program.*

Primer Congreso Nacional de Economistas, Contadores Públicos y Auditores de Guatemala. *Desarrollo y resoluciones.* Imprenta Universitaria, Guatemala, 1960, pp. 49-52.

4

García-Araujo P., O. *El impuesto sobre la renta en el cambio de estructura tributaria y el bien común.* Guatemala, 1965.

Guatemalan income tax law and regulations (translation). Official Gazette, Guatemala, 1964, 42pp.

"El impuesto sobre la renta y el desarrollo económico," *Monitor del Infop,* June 1954, p. 2.

Luján Muñoz, J. "Algunas sugestiones para mejorar el sistema de impuesto sobre la renta a personas jurídicas en Guatemala," *Revista Universidad de San Carlos,* vol. 66, 1965, pp. 27-53.

Menchú González, A. (ed.). *El impuesto sobre la renta.* n.p., Guatemala, 1965.

Tax on individual incomes (translation of legislative decree no. 3323). August 1953, 120pp. (mimeo).

United States Embassy in Guatemala. *Unofficial English translation of Guatemala's income tax law.* Guatemala, 1963, 26pp.

6

"Legal, notarial stamp tax established by Guatemala," *Foreign commerce weekly,* vol. 65, no. 1, 1961, p. 8.

7

United States Department of Commerce. *Foreign trade regulations of the Central American common market.* Washington, 1967, 12pp.

United States Department of Commerce. *Import tariff system of Guatemala.* Washington, 1962, 4pp.

10

Davila M., F. *Tratado de avalúo: Inmuebles rurales.* Guatemala, 2 volumes, 1966.

Lissner, W. "Tax on idle lands in Guatemala," *American journal of economics and sociology,* vol. 16, July 1957, pp. 431-432.

11

Morgan, C. *Taxation of Guatemalan agriculture.* Report to the United States Agency for International Development Mission to Guatemala, American Embassy, Guatemala, 1960, 19pp.

14

Menchú González, A. (ed.). *Código fiscal de Guatemala.* n.p., Guatemala, 1967.

Vargas O., J. *La revisión como recurso excepcional.* Thesis, Universidad de San Carlos, Guatemala, 1966.

17

Peat, Marwick, Mitchell & Co. *Economical association tax among the Republics of Guatemala, El Salvador, and Honduras.* Panamá.

Programa Conjunto de Tributación de la Organización de los Estados Americanos y del Banco de Desarrollo Interamericano. "La administración tributaria en Centroamérica y el proyecto de armonización fiscal," *Investigación fiscal,* no. 14, February 1967, pp. 91-176.

Watkin, V. *Taxes and tax harmonization in Central America.* Harvard Law School International Tax Program, Cambridge, Mass., 1967, chapter 4.

18

Diamond, W. *Foreign tax and trade briefs.* Fallon Law Book Company, New York, loose-leaf, 1951–.

"Guatemala law digest." In: *Martindale-Hubbell law directory,* vol. 4, pp. 2667-2675. Martindale-Hubbell, Inc., Summit, N.J., 1961.

Menchú González, A. *Leyes y reglamentos de índole hacendaria, fiscal, municipal y administrativa.* Propsa, Guatemala, 1966, 104pp.

GUINEA

1

United States Department of Commerce. *Basic data on the economy of the Republic of Guinea.* Washington, 1960, 12pp.

3

Mémento fiscal et social 1964, numéro spécial no. 14, 25 June 1964. A comparative survey of taxes in the West African Union and Guinea.

7

United States Department of Commerce. *Preparing shipments to Guinea.* Washington, 1963, 8pp.

12

United States Department of Commerce. *Investment law in the Republic of Guinea.* Washington, 1962, 4pp.

GUYANA

1

Chase Manhattan Bank. *British Guinea.* New York, 1965, 8pp.

Commissioner of Inland Revenue. *Annual report of the Commissioner of inland revenue for the year 1961.* Georgetown, 1964.

2

International Bank for Reconstruction and Development. *The economic development of British Guiana: Report of a mission.* The Johns Hopkins Press, Baltimore, 1953, pp. 41-48.

4

Foreign Tax Law Association. *British Guiana income tax service.* Centerport, L.I., N.Y., loose-leaf, 1952–1954.

"Guyana." In: Board of Inland Revenue (Great Britain), *Income taxes outside the United Kingdom 1966,* vol. 3, pp. 301-327. H. M. Stationery Office, London, 1967.

7

Harvard Law School International Program in Taxation. *A case study in import and excise taxation in British Guiana in 1911.* Cambridge, Mass., 1957, 23pp. (mimeo).

United States Department of Commerce. *Foreign trade regulations of Guyana.* Washington, 1966, 4pp.

HAITI

1

"Certain internal taxes suspended by Haiti," *Foreign commerce weekly,* vol. 65, no. 8, 1961, p. 18.

"Civic tax replaced by solidarity tax," *Foreign tax law weekly bulletin,* vol. 11, no. 7, 1960.

"Haiti raises taxes and fees," *Foreign commerce weekly,* vol. 63, no. 8, 1960, p. 7.

Morgan, C. *The Haitian revenue system.* United States Operations Mission to Haiti, Port-au-Prince, 1960, 45pp.

"New tax amendments," *Foreign tax law weekly bulletin,* vol. 9, no. 25, 1958, pp. 4-7.

Pan American Union. *A statement of the laws of Haiti in matters affecting business.* Washington, 2d edition revised, 1955.

Shere, L. *Joint Haitian-American industrial mission, fiscal report, 1946.* Inter-American Development Commission, Washington, 1946 (mimeo).

United Nations. *Mission to Haiti: Report of the United Nations Mission of technical assistance to the Republic of Haiti.* Sales No. 1949.II.B.2, New York (Lake Success), 1949.

United Nations. "Report on field trip to Haiti 5 to 11 June 1950." (restricted).

2

Benoit, P. *Evolution budgétaire et développement économique d'Haiti.* H. Deschamps, Port-au-Prince, 1954, 134pp.

Moore, O. "Monetary-fiscal policy and economic development in Haiti," *Public finance,* vol. 9, 1954, pp. 230-253.

United Nations, Technical Assistance Administration. "Réformes de la monnaie et des finances publiques d'Haiti." Doc. No. TAA/HAI/9 (restricted), 19 February 1957.
United Nations, Technical Assistance Administration. "Réformes de la monnaie et des finances publiques d'Haiti." Doc. No. TAA/NS/HAI/4 (restricted), 15 March 1955.

4

Bureau of Internal Revenue. *Income tax and tax exemption laws.* Imprimerie de l'État, Port-au-Prince, October 1956, 43pp.
Foreign Tax Law Association. *Haitian income tax service.* Centerport, L.I., N.Y., loose-leaf, 1951–1955.
"New income tax amendments," *Foreign tax law weekly bulletin,* vol. 12, no. 41, 1962, pp. 1-4.

7

United States Department of Commerce. *Foreign trade regulations of Haiti.* Washington, 1967, 4pp.

8

Gibbons, W. *Tax factors in basing international business abroad.* Harvard Law School International Program in Taxation, Cambridge, Mass., 1957, pp. 83-88.

12

"Haiti passes new industry law," *Foreign commerce weekly,* vol. 54, no. 19, 1955.
Landman, J. "Tax inducements for doing business in Haiti," *Taxes,* vol. 33, 1955, pp. 567-578.
"Tax exemption in Republic of Haiti," *Foreign tax law weekly bulletin,* vol. 1, no. 521, 1951, pp. 7-16.

13

"Penalty clauses tightened," *Foreign tax law weekly bulletin,* vol. 11, no. 6, 1960.
Public Administration Service. *A report on a brief survey of governmental financial administration—Republic of Haiti.* International Cooperation Administration, Washington, 1959, 63pp. (mimeo).

18

Diamond, W. *Foreign tax and trade briefs.* Fallon Law Book Company, New York, loose-leaf, 1951–.

"Haiti law digest." In: *Martindale-Hubbell law directory,* vol. 4, pp. 2676-2681. Martindale-Hubbell, Inc., Summit, N.J., 1961.

HONDURAS

1

Banco Central de Honduras. *Historia financiera de Honduras.* Tegucigalpa, 1957, 91pp.
"Labor relations and taxation in Honduras," *Foreign tax law weekly bulletin,* vol. 13, no. 30, 1962, pp. 4-9.
Ministerio de Economía y Hacienda. *El sistema tributario en Honduras.* Tegucigalpa, 1959, 176pp.
Pan American Union. *A statement of the laws of Honduras in matters affecting business.* Washington, 3d edition revised, 1965, pp. 75-84.
Programa Conjunto de Tributación de la Organización de los Estados Americanos y del Banco Interamericano de Desarrollo. *Sistemas tributarios de América Latina: Honduras.* Unión Panamericana, Washington, 1966, 61pp.
United States Department of Commerce. *Basic data on the economy of Honduras.* Washington, 1965, 20pp.
United States Department of Commerce. *Investment in Honduras.* Washington, 1961, 12pp.

2

Cosciani, C. *Informe sobre la reforma tributaria en Honduras.* Consejo Nacional de Economía, Tegucigalpa, 1962, 104pp.

4

Foreign Tax Law Association. *Honduras income tax service.* Centerport, L.I., N.Y., loose-leaf, 1954–1955.
International Monetary Fund. *Income tax legislation in Honduras.* Washington, June 1950.

6

Due, J. "The retail sales tax in Honduras: A breakthrough in taxation for economic development," *Inter-American economic affairs,* vol. 20, no. 3, 1966, pp. 55-67. Reprinted in: R. Bird and O. Oldman (eds.), *Readings on taxation in developing countries,* pp. 324-334. The

Johns Hopkins Press, Baltimore, revised edition, 1967.
Programa Conjunto de Tributación de la Organización de los Estados Americanos y del Banco Interamericano de Desarrollo. *El impuesto sobre las ventas.* Unión Panamericana, Washington, December 1966 (mimeo).
Suazo, P. "El impuesto sobre las ventas en Honduras," *Investigación fiscal,* no. 19, July 1967, pp. 115-141.

7

United States Department of Commerce. *Foreign trade regulations of the Central American common market.* Washington, 1967, 12pp.
United States Department of Commerce. *Import tariff system of Honduras.* Washington, 1962, 2pp.

8

Smith, C. "Tax havens," *Taxes,* vol. 37, 1959, pp. 615-629.
United Nations, Economic and Social Council, Fiscal Commission. "Questionnaire on the tax treatment of foreign nationals, assets, and transactions: Reply of the government of Honduras." Doc. No. E/CN.8/46/Add.21, 27 June 1951, 11pp.
United States Congress, Senate, Committee on Foreign Relations. *Tax convention with the Republic of Honduras relating to double taxation, Message from the President of the United States,* Executive K, 84th Congress, 2d Session. Washington, 1956, 22pp.
United States Department of Commerce. *Establishing a business in Honduras.* Washington, 1962, 16pp.

9

Tosco, M., *et al. Ingresos del gobierno local, 1924-25 y 1951-52.* Banco Central de Honduras, Tegucigalpa, 1953, 70pp.

17

Peat, Marwick, Mitchell & Co. *Economical association tax among the Republics of Guatemala, El Salvador, and Honduras.* Panamá.
Programa Conjunto de Tributación de la Organización de los Estados Americanos y del Banco de Desarrollo Interamericano. "La administración tribu-

taria en Centroamérica y el proyecto de armonización fiscal," *Investigación fiscal,* no. 14, February 1967, pp. 91-176.
Watkin, V. *Taxes and tax harmonization in Central America.* Harvard Law School International Tax Program, Cambridge, Mass., 1967, chapter 6.

18

Diamond, W. *Foreign tax and trade briefs.* Fallon Law Book Company, New York, loose-leaf, 1951-.
"Honduras law digest." In: *Martindale-Hubbell law directory,* vol. 4, pp. 2682-2688. Martindale-Hubbell, Inc., Summit, N.J., 1961.

HONG KONG

1

Pine, S., and Moore, R. "The commercial center of South East Asia." In: Prentice-Hall, Inc., *Tax ideas.* Englewood Cliffs, N.J., 1966.
Price Waterhouse & Co. *Information guide for doing business in Hong Kong.* New York, 1967.
Sih, S. "Public accountancy in Hong Kong," *Accounting review,* vol. 37, October 1963, pp. 708-712.
"Taxation," *Foreign tax law weekly bulletin,* vol. 14, no. 28, 1963, pp. 4-6.
United States Department of Commerce. *Basic data on the economy of Hong Kong.* Washington, 1960, 20pp.

4

Foreign Tax Law Association. *Hong Kong income tax service.* Centerport, L.I., N.Y., loose-leaf, 1952-.
"Hong Kong." In: Board of Inland Revenue (Great Britain), *Income taxes outside the United Kingdom 1966,* vol. 3, pp. 329-351. H. M. Stationery Office, London, 1967.
"A review of taxation and company law," *Foreign tax law weekly bulletin,* vol. 11, no. 41, 1961, pp. 2-8.

7

United States Department of Commerce. *Foreign trade regulations of Hong Kong.* Washington, 1962, 12pp.
United States Department of Commerce. *Preparing shipments to Hong Kong.* Washington, 1963, 8pp.

8

Lee, L., and Gregg, J. "Corporate and tax aspects of doing business in Hong Kong," *Tax executive,* vol. 13, January 1961, pp. 81-118.

Peat, Marwick, Mitchell & Co. *Notes for the use of persons and organizations considering the possibility of commencing business in Hong Kong.* Hong Kong, 1960, 10pp.

United States Department of Commerce. *Establishing a business in Hong Kong.* Washington, 1964, 18pp.

United States Department of Commerce. *Investment factors in Hong Kong.* Washington, 1962, 9pp.

18

Diamond, W. *Foreign tax and trade briefs.* Fallon Law Book Company, New York, loose-leaf, 1951–.

INDIA

1

Agarwal, S. "Towards a new taxation policy," *Modern review,* vol. 95, July 1954, pp. 24-27.

Aiyar, A. (ed.). *Indian tax laws (1965).* Company Law Institute of India, Madras, 1965.

Bagga, S. *Taxation manual: With history of amendments and short comments.* Law Book Company, Allahabad, 1962, 756pp.

Balakrishna, R. *Recent trends in Indian finance.* University of Madras, Madras, 1955, 186pp.

Bhargava, R. *Indian public finances.* Allen and Unwin, London, 1962, 263pp.

Bhargava, R. "India's taxation policy," *Public finance,* vol. 13, 1958, pp. 323-334.

Bhargava, R. *Public finance: Its theory and working in India.* Chaitanya Publishing House, Allahabad, 1954, 672pp.

Bhargava, R. *The theory and working of union finance in India.* Chaitanya Publishing House, Allahabad, 2d edition, 1967, xvii/383pp.

Coswami, B. "Indian tax system," *Modern review,* March 1954, pp. 203-207.

Dalal, R. "Tax problems in perspective," *Journal of Indian merchants' chamber,* vol. 48, September 1954, pp. 483-494.

Dalal, R., and Cooper, R. "India's fiscal relations with Pakistan," *Bulletin for international fiscal documentation,* vol. 6, 1952, pp. 1-19.

"Finances of the government of India," *Reserve bank of India bulletin,* vol. 10, March 1956, pp. 237-259.

Goode, R. "Report of India Taxation enquiry commission," *National tax journal,* vol. 9, June 1956, pp. 134-147.

Gopal, M. "Taxation in ancient India," *Canadian tax journal,* vol. 5, 1957, pp. 251-253.

Harvard Law School International Program in Taxation. *World Tax Series: Taxation in India.* Prepared by W. Brudno, C. Cobb, Jr., and N. Palkhivala. Little, Brown and Co., Boston, 1960.

"If you sin, we will punish you," *Chartered accountant* (New Delhi), vol. 6, March 1958, pp. 556-557.

Indian Investment Centre. *Taxation.* Bombay, 1964, 208pp.

Japan Tax Association. *Asian taxation 1964.* Tokyo, 1964, 139pp. Supplement, 1965, 17pp.

Jindal, K. *Thus spake their lordships.* Kittab Mahal, Allahabad, 1963, 733pp.

Kapadia, G. "Recent trends in taxation," *Chartered accountant* (New Delhi), vol. 6, November 1957, pp. 251-258.

Kapadia, G. "Taxation policy," *Chartered accountant* (New Delhi), vol. 6, March 1958, pp. 538-542.

Khot, S. *Development of tax ideas in India.* Ph.D. thesis, Illinois, 1958.

Kilachand, A. "Taxation in India and the role of private enterprise," *Journal of Indian merchants' chamber,* vol. 48, January 1954, pp. 13-18.

Lakdawala, D. *Justice in taxation in India.* Popular Book Depot, Bombay, 1946, 312pp.

Malhotra, P. "Reconstructing the Indian tax system: Some broad considerations," *Indian journal of economics,* vol. 27, October 1946, pp. 250-255.

Malik, P. (ed.). *Handbook of taxation laws of India.* Eastern Book Co., Lucknow, 4th edition, 1966.

Mukherjee, S. *Recent trends in union finance.* Brookland Private Ltd., Calcutta, 1964, xvi/514pp.

Nadar, V. "New finance bill, 1963," *Taxation* (Delhi), vol. 16, April 1963, pp. 87-89.

Palkhivala, N. *The highest taxed nation.* Manaktalas, Bombay, 1965, 93pp.

"The pattern of additional taxation, 1961-62—1965-66," *Eastern economist,* 6 March 1961.

Pershad, H. *Indian taxation during and after World War II.* Allied Publishers Private, Bombay, 1964, 264pp.

Poduval, R. *Finance of the government of India (since 1935).* Premier Publishing Company, Delhi, 1951.

Price, Waterhouse, Peat & Co. *Memorandum on the finance bill, 1966.* Calcutta.

"Professor Kaldor on Indian taxation," *Indian taxation,* vol. 7, June 1956, pp. 218-221.

Report of the Taxation enquiry commission. Manager of Publications, New Delhi, 3 volumes, 1955.

Sharma, R. *Tax circulars and press notes.* Practical Tax Publishers, Delhi, 1961, 268pp.

United Nations. *Public finance surveys: India.* Sales No. 1952.XVI.1, New York, 1951.

United States Department of Commerce. *Basic data on the economy of India.* Washington, 1965, 24pp.

Venkata, R. "Recent trends in Indian tax system," *Indian journal of commerce,* vol. 11, June-September 1958, pp. 20-38.

2

Bajpai, R. "Incidence of taxation in India," *Indian journal of economics,* vol. 33, January 1953, pp. 315-324.

Basu, S. "Fiscal and monetary policies in the context of inflationary pressure during the second plan," *Economic affairs,* vol. 2, February 1957, pp. 67-74.

Batheja, H. "Development finance," *Indian journal of economics,* vol. 10, January 1930, pp. 536-548.

Bhargava, R. "Incidence of taxation," *Indian economic journal,* vol. 2, July 1954, pp. 37-44. Also in: *Indian taxation,* vol. 5, August 1954, pp. 373-377.

Bhargava, R. "Public finance in a socialist economy," *Indian journal of economics,* vol. 39, July 1958, pp. 83-98.

Bhatia, G. "Taxation in socialistic society," *Chartered accountant* (New Delhi), vol. 6, January 1958, pp. 444-448.

Bhatia, M. "Budgetary position of the government of India since independence," *Public finance,* vol. 11, 1956, pp. 241-252.

Bhatnagar, I. "Tax reform: Major task ahead," *Modern review,* September 1963, pp. 188-194.

Bhattacharyva, K. "Fiscal and monetary policies in planning—A study of Indian problems," *Indian journal of economics,* vol. 32, April 1952, pp. 395-401.

Bose, S. *Some aspects of Indian economic development.* Ranjit Printers and Publishers, Delhi, vol. 1, 1962, chapters 7-10.

"Budget for 1964-65," *Foreign tax law weekly bulletin,* vol. 14, no. 46, 1964, pp. 5-9.

"Budget of the government of India for 1961-62," *Reserve bank of India bulletin,* vol. 15, April 1961, pp. 490-517.

Chacko, K. *The monetary and fiscal policy of India.* Vora and Co., Bombay, 1957, 386pp.

Chelliah, R. *Fiscal policy in underdeveloped countries, with special reference to India.* Macmillan, New York, and Allen and Unwin, London, 1960, vi/168pp.

Choudhry, N. "Indian taxation policy 1946-51 and private investment," *Indian economic journal,* vol. 3, July 1955, pp. 51-70.

Cirvante, V. "Post-war planning and budgetary policy in India," *Indian journal of economics,* vol. 29, October 1948, pp. 147-154.

Cutt, J. *Taxation and economic development in India.* Ph.D. thesis, Toronto, 1966.

Das Gupta, B. *Our plans and our public finance.* A. R. Mukherjee and Co., Calcutta, 1960, vi/259pp.

Dass, R. "Tax policy in India since 1947," *Indian journal of economics,* vol. 43, April 1963, pp. 325-336.

Deshmukh, C. "Financial policy in an expanding economy," *All India congress committee economic review,* vol. 7, 11 February 1956, pp. 19-20. Also in: *Business digest,* vol. 3, March 1956, pp. 5-6.

Economic Research and Training Foundation. *Union budgets: A factual study of finances of government of India (1950-1 to 1964-5).* Bombay, 1965, xii/271pp.

Federation of Indian Chambers of Commerce and Industry. *Kaldor's report on Indian tax reform—An analysis.* New Delhi, 1957.

"Finances of the plan," *Reserve bank of India bulletin,* vol. 8, December 1954, pp. 974-987.

Froomkin, J. "A program for taxation and economic development—The Indian case," *Economic development and cultural change,* vol. 6, January 1958, pp. 129-142.

Ghatalia, S. "Impact of direct taxes on the Indian economy," *Finance and commerce* (India), vol. 6, September 1963, pp. 354-362.

Ghosh, A., and Chakravarty, A. *Union budgets and prices—A projection: Trends in expenditure and income of the union government and the level of prices during the third five year plan.* Asia Publishing House, New York, 1964, 72pp.

Ghosh, O. *The Indian financial situation.* Kitab Matral, Allahabad, 1958, 140pp.

Ghosh, S. *The financing of economic development.* World Press, Calcutta, 1962, 100pp.

Gopal, M. *Financial policy of the Indian union, 1947-53.* University Press, Delhi, 1955, 132pp.

Gopal, M. "Planning of production through tax adjustment," *Indian journal of economics,* vol. 29, October 1948, pp. 155-163.

Gopal, M. *A realistic tax structure for India.* Vora and Co., Bombay, 1959, 74pp.

Gopal, M. *Studies in Indian public finance.* Rao and Raghavan, Mysore, 1963, 128pp.

Gopal, M. "Tax resources for the third plan," *Indian economic journal,* vol. 9, April 1962, pp. 382-403.

Gopal, M. *Towards a realistic tax policy for India, 1959-66.* Wesley Press, Mysore, 1958, 46pp.

Gopal, M. "Towards a realistic tax policy for India," *Indian economic journal,* vol. 6, January 1959, pp. 281-326.

Gulati, I. "Long-term planning of the budget: The need for advance tax planning," *Indian economic journal,* vol. 13, October 1965, pp. 191-198.

Gulati, I. *Resource prospects for the third five year plan.* Orient Longmans Private Ltd., Calcutta, 1960, 154pp.

Gupta, S. "Incidence of taxation in India," *Indian journal of economics,* vol. 33, January 1953, pp. 289-298.

"India—Budget speech 1960," *Bulletin for international fiscal documentation,* vol. 14, 1960, pp. 245-256.

"India—Part B of budget speech for 1953-54," *Taxation* (Delhi), vol. 6, March 1953, p. 34. Reprinted in: *Bulletin for international fiscal documentation,* vol. 7, 1953, pp. 229-233.

Jain, P. "Government's taxation policy and India's industrial development," *Journal of Indian merchants' chamber,* vol. 47, January 1953, pp. 19-25.

Kaldor, N. *Indian tax reform: Report of a survey.* Department of Economic Affairs, Ministry of Finance, New Delhi, 1956.

Khusro, A. "The incidence of taxation in India: The marginal rate of tax," *Indian journal of economics,* vol. 33, April 1953, pp. 449-459.

Kilachand, T. "Tax structure in India," *Foreign tax law weekly bulletin,* vol. 2, no. 11, 1951, pp. 3-4.

Kulkarni, N. "Incidence of taxation in India," *Indian journal of economics,* vol. 33, January 1953, pp. 325-332.

Kust, M. *Taxation for economic development: A discussion of the problem within the institutional and constitutional framework of India.* Harvard Law School International Program in Taxation, Cambridge, Mass., 1956, 207pp. (mimeo).

Lakdawala, D. "Incidence of taxation in India," *Indian journal of economics,* vol. 33, April 1953, pp. 461-471.

Lakdawala, D. *Taxation and the plan.* Popular Book Depot, Bombay, 1956, 211pp.

Lakdawala, D., and Kchambadkona, M. "Sensitivity of central taxes, 1948-49 to 1954-55," *Economic weekly,* vol. 11, December 1959, pp. 1633-1640, 1675-1681.

Lalwani, K. *Fiscal policy in India.* Artha Vanijya Bagegana Mandir (Institute of Research in Economics and Commerce), Calcutta, 1952, 32pp.

Little, I. "Tax policy and the third plan." In: P. Rosenstein-Rodan (ed.), *Pricing and fiscal policies,* chapter 3. Studies in the Economic Development of India No. 3, The MIT Press, Cambridge, Mass., and Allen and Unwin, London, 1964.

Machiraju, H. *Tax policy and economic development in India with special reference to the 1954-1959 tax reforms.* Ph.D. thesis, Indiana, 1961.

Madan, D. *Financing the second five year plan.* Gokhale Institute of Politics and Economics, Poona, 1957, 24pp.

Mills, R. "Financing India's third plan," *Far Eastern survey*, vol. 29, November 1960, pp. 162-169.

Misra, B. "Can the government of India finance a plan at present?" *Indian journal of economics*, vol. 29, January 1949, pp. 243-247.

Misra, B. "Tax structure in India," *Asian studies*, vol. 4, no. 1, February 1962.

Mukerji, K. *Levels of economic activity and public expenditure in India—A historical and quantitative study.* Asia Publishing House, New York, 1965, xv/140pp.

Mundle, A. "Trend of commerce and its effects on tax policy," *Indian journal of economics*, vol. 28, January 1948, pp. 389-395.

Nambudripad, K. "Financing the five year plan," *Journal of the University of Poona*, vol. 3, 1954, pp. 67-86.

Narrielvala, P. "Pre-budget reflections on tax structure," *Income tax journal* (India), vol. 7, no. 3, 1966, pp. 5-27.

National Council of Applied Economic Research. *Taxation and private investment.* Delhi, 1961, xi/120pp.

Niyogi, J. "Taxation structure of India," *Modern review*, October 1953, pp. 293-298.

Ojha, P. "A study of the tax structure of India with special reference to central taxes," *Journal of the University of Bombay*, vol. 24, January 1956, pp. 30-32.

Prasad, B. *Planned capital formation in India—A critique of Keynesian fiscal and monetary policies.* Vora and Co., Bombay, 1965, xiv/224pp.

Rosenstein-Rodan, P. (ed.) *Pricing and fiscal policies.* Studies in the Economic Development of India No. 3, The M.I.T. Press, Cambridge, Mass., and Allen and Unwin, London, 1964, 216pp.

Sahota, G. *Indian tax structure and economic development.* Asia Publishing House, New York, 1961, 60pp., and Asia Publishing House, London, 1961, xvi/88pp.

Samant, D. "Restrictive tax structure of the central government," *Indian journal of economics*, vol. 27, October 1946, pp. 256-263.

Sharma, K. "Concept of taxable capacity with reference to India," *Agra University journal of research*, vol. 5, January 1957, pp. 14-25.

Sharma, K. "Financial aspects of India's first five year plan," *Calcutta review*, September 1953, pp. 258-266.

Sriram, P. "Tax structure in India," *Indian journal of economics*, vol. 27, October 1946, pp. 264-269.

Srivastava, R. "Taxation in underdeveloped countries with special reference to India," *All India congress committee economic review*, vol. 16, 10 November 1964, pp. 21-24.

Taraporevala, R. "Principles of taxation for underdeveloped countries: Indian tax scene surveyed—Proposals for improvement suggested," *Commerce* (Bombay), vol. 99, December 1959.

Thirumalai, S. *Resources for the third five year plan.* Indian Merchants' Chamber Economic Research and Training Foundation, Bombay, 1961, 148pp.

Tripathy, R. *Fiscal policy and economic development in India.* World Press, Calcutta, 1958, 318pp.

United Nations. *Mobilization of domestic capital in certain countries of Asia and the Far East.* Sales No. 1951.II.F.3, Bangkok, 1951.

Vaswani, M. "Incidence of taxation in India," *Indian journal of economics*, vol. 33, January 1953, pp. 345-352.

3

"Corporate taxation: A comparative study of India, U.K. and U.S.A.," *Eastern economist*, 20 May 1960, pp. 1055-1056.

Yoingco, A., and Trinidad, R. *Fiscal systems and practices in Asian countries.* Frederick A. Praeger, New York, 1967.

4

Agarwal, M. "Voluntary disclosure of schemes," *Taxation* (Delhi), vol. 21, January 1966, pp. 1-32.

Agarwala, S. (ed.). *The income tax act (43 of 1961).* Law Book Co., Allahabad, 1961, 240pp.

Agarwala, S. (ed.). *Income tax rules, 1962.* Law Book Co., Allahabad, 1962, 229pp.

Aiyar, A. (ed.). *The income tax act, 1961.* Company Law Institute of India, Madras, 1962.

Aiyar, A. *The income tax digest.* Company Law Institute of India, Madras, 7th edition, 1958. Supplement, 1961.

Aiyar, A. *The income tax rules, 1962.*

Company Law Institute of India, Madras, 1962, 227pp.

Aiyar, A., and Ramachandran, T. *Indian income tax act, 1922*. Company Law Institute of India, Madras, 1961, 182pp.

Ambirajan, S. *The taxation of corporate income in India*. Asia Publishing House, London, 1965, xv/314pp.

Arora, G. *Taxation of industry in India*. Vora and Co., Bombay, 1956, 160pp.

Association of Indian Trade and Industry. *Income tax rates compared*. Bombay, 1955, 45pp.

Association of Indian Trade and Industry. *Taxation of bonus shares*. Bombay, 1955, 22pp.

Banerjee, A. *Income tax law and practice in India*. Knowledge Home, Calcutta, 10th edition, 1965, 496pp.

Bhargava, S. *Assessment of salaries*. Navin, Delhi, 1962, 128pp.

Bhargava, S. *Income tax law, pleadings and practice*. Taxation Publishing Co., Delhi, 1963, 562pp.

Bhargava, S. *Income-tax pleadings and practice*. Taxation Publishing Co., Delhi, 2d edition, 1955.

Bhargava, S. *Law relating to refunds ana double taxation relief*. Taxation Publishing Co., Delhi, 1961, 130pp.

Bhargava, S. *Taxation of capital gains and penalties—Depreciation, obsolescence, and losses*. Taxation Publishing Co., Delhi, 1957.

Bhatnagar, J. *Finance act, 1963 and compulsory deposit scheme act, 1963; along with: compulsory deposit (employees) scheme 1963, compulsory deposit (income tax payers) scheme, 1963 and super profits tax act, 1963*. Central Law Agency, Allahabad, 1963.

Bhatnagar, K. *A digest of income tax cases (1933-1965)*. Central Law Agency, Allahabad, revised edition, 2 volumes, 1965.

Bhatt, M. "Case for non-differential corporation tax," *Economic weekly*, vol. 11, October 1959, pp. 1441-1444.

Bhattacharya, S. *Indian income tax law and practice*. Nababharat, Calcutta, 3d edition, 1965, 562pp.

"The budget and corporate taxation," *Eastern economist*, 6 March 1961.

Central Board of Revenue. *Income tax for laymen*. Directorate of Inspection, New Delhi, 3d edition, 1955, 144pp.

Chhawchharia, B., *et al. Accountant's study on the income-tax act, 1961*. Gutcutia, Calcutta, 1962, 301pp.

Chopra, O., and Chopra, S. *Income tax law and practice*. Sarkar, Calcutta, 1964.

"The compulsory deposit scheme," *Foreign tax law weekly bulletin*, vol. 14, no. 19, 1963, pp. 2-6.

Cooper, R. "The finance bill 1953—Proposals affecting income taxation," *Economic trends*, vol. 2, April-May 1953, pp. 126-134.

Cutt, J. "Income tax evasion in India: Mr. Kaldor revisited," *Indian economic journal*, vol. 15, April-June 1967.

Dalal, R. *Business profits tax and capital gains tax*. N. M. Tripathi Ltd., Bombay, 1948.

Dalal, R. "History of income tax," *Journal of Indian merchants' chamber*, vol. 53, November 1959, pp. 321-325; vol. 53, December 1959, pp. 347-350; vol. 54, January 1960, pp. 19-22; vol. 54, February 1960, pp. 43-49; vol. 54, March 1960, pp. 73-75; vol. 54, April 1960, pp. 98-102; vol. 54, May 1960, pp. 135-138; vol. 54, June 1960, pp. 158-161; vol. 54, July 1960, pp. 191-194; vol. 54, August 1960, pp. 227-229.

Dalal, R. "Law commission's report on income tax," *Journal of Indian merchants' chambers*, vol. 55, May 1961, pp. 131-134; vol. 55, June 1961, pp. 167-170; vol. 55, August 1961, pp. 217-218.

Dalal, R. "Taxes affecting industrial and commercial enterprises in India: Reply to questionnaire," *Bulletin for international fiscal documentation*, vol. 4, 1950, pp. 217-221.

Dalal, R., and Dalal, R. *Indian excess profits tax*. Bombay, 1941, 114pp.

Damania, H. "Special provisions in income tax statutes for taxation of income of private companies," *Chartered accountant* (New Delhi), vol. 6, April 1958, pp. 579-587.

Dandeker, N. "Current profits deposits." In: Council for Economic Education (Bombay), *Taxation and foreign trade and other essays*, pp. 1-5. Asia Publishing House, London, 1962.

Dastur, S., Damania, H., and Dastur, J. *Direct tax laws 1964-65*. A. S. Pandya (for N.M. Tripathi Private Ltd.), Bombay, 1964, 680pp.

Dastur, S., Damania, H., and Dastur, J. *Direct tax laws 1966-67*. N.M. Tripathi Private Ltd., Bombay, 1966, 720pp.

Dave, M. "Vires of executive actions under fiscal laws—Income tax on salaries," *Journal of the Indian law institute*, vol. 4, April-June 1962, pp. 261-278.

Foreign Tax Law Association. *Indian income tax service*. St. Petersburg, Fla., and Hempstead, L.I., N.Y., 2 volumes, loose-leaf, 1953-1963.

"Free-of-tax and less-tax preferential dividends," *Foreign tax law weekly bulletin*, vol. 11, no. 23, 1960, pp. 3-8.

"Government clarifies income-tax surcharge calculation," *Foreign tax law weekly bulletin*, vol. 14, no. 5, 1963, pp. 7-9.

Gulati, I. "A note on the capital gains tax in India," *Public finance*, vol. 18, 1963, pp. 101-107.

Gulati, I., and Gulati, K. *The undivided Hindu family*. Asia Publishing House, New York, 1962, 96pp.

Gupta, R., and Gupta, V. *Income tax law and practice*. Agra Book Store, Agra, 24th edition, 1965, 545pp.

Haribhakti, S. "Vicarious liabilities under the income-tax act, 1961," *Taxation* (Delhi), vol. 15, August 1962, pp. 83-96.

Haribhakti, V. "Cost accounting and its importance in income-tax assessments," *Taxation* (Delhi), vol. 22, July 1966, pp. 1-11.

The income tax act (act 43 of 1961). Central Law Agency, Allahabad, 1961, 160pp.

"Income tax in the fiscal situation," *Indian taxation*, vol. 7, May 1956, pp. 176-178.

"Income tax rates compared," *Economic trends*, vol. 3, April-June 1954, pp. 105-149.

"The income-tax bill, 1961," *Taxation* (Delhi), vol. 14, June 1961, pp. 33-226.

The income-tax rules, 1962, and the income-tax (certificate proceedings) rules, 1962. Eastern Book Company, Lucknow, 1962, 206pp.

"India." In: Board of Inland Revenue (Great Britain), *Income taxes outside the United Kingdom 1966*, vol. 4, pp. 1-141. H. M. Stationery Office, London, 1967.

Indian Chamber of Commerce. *Income tax act—1961 (with supplement to 1962)*. Calcutta, 1962, 579pp.

Jain, B. *The Indian excess profits tax act, 1940*. Income-Tax Law Publishing House, Delhi, 3d edition, 1945.

Jain, B. *Indian income tax act*. Income-Tax Law Publishing House, Delhi, 1960, 468pp.

Jain, B. *The income-tax act, 1961 (act no. 43 of 1961)*. Income-Tax Law Publishing House, Delhi, 1961, 236pp.

Jain, J., and Jain, P. (eds.). *Current indian income tax act*. Law Printing Press, Delhi, loose-leaf, n.d.

Jain, S. *The new income tax act, 1961*. Modern Law Publishing House, Painpat, 1962, 504pp.

Jhunjhunwala, B. *Law of income tax in relation to companies*. Eastern Law House, Calcutta, 1961, 212pp.

Jindal, K. *Income tax, past and present*. Kitab Mahal, Allahabad, 1962, 896pp.

Kagzi, M. "Taxation of income of property held under charitable trusts," *Taxation* (Delhi), vol. 15, June 1962, pp. 65-73.

Kaka, F. "Income tax in India: Planning business transactions to cut its impact," *Journal of taxation*, vol. 24, May 1966, p. 288.

Kaldor, N. "The taxation of business profits." In: R. Bird and O. Oldman (eds.), *Readings on taxation in developing countries*. The Johns Hopkins Press, Baltimore, 1964, pp. 215-235; revised edition, 1967, pp. 155-175. Reprinted from: N. Kaldor, *Indian tax reform: Report of a survey*, pp. 63-84. Department of Economic Affairs, Ministry of Finance, New Delhi, 1956.

Kanga, J., Palkhivala, N., and Pandra, A. *The law and practice of income tax*. N.M. Tripathi Private Ltd., Bombay, 5th edition, 2 volumes, 1963, 1123/808pp.

Kapur, A. *Indian income tax act and accounts*. Ranjan and Raman, Delhi, 1961.

Khanna Kailash, C. *The super profits tax act, 1963*. Oxford Book and Stationery Co., Calcutta, 1963, 185pp.

Kharbanda, M. *Commentary on the income tax act, 1961*. Law Publishing House, Allahabad, 1963.

Kharbanda, M. *India income tax law, 1961*. Law Publishing House, Allahabad, 1962, 204pp.

Kothari, B. "Analysis of the provisions

relating to section 104 companies," *Taxation* (Delhi), vol. 21, March 1966, pp. 103-117.

Kust, M. "Income tax problems of selling goods and licensing in India," *Taxes,* vol. 35, 1957, pp. 311-321.

Lakhotia, R. *Elements of Indian income tax.* Asha Publishing House, Calcutta, 9th edition, 1965, 412pp.

Lakhotia, R. *Practical problems on income tax.* Asha Publishing House, Calcutta, 3d edition, 1963, 380pp.

Lakhotia, R. *Taxation of companies and their officers.* Asha Publishing House, Calcutta, 2d edition, 1966, 864pp.

Laumas, G. "The shifting of the corporation income tax—A study with reference to Indian corporations," *Public finance,* vol. 21, 1966, pp. 462-473.

Laumas, G. *The shifting of the corporation income tax: A theoretical and empirical study with special reference to India.* Ph.D. thesis, Wayne State University, Detroit, Mich., 1966.

Manchanda, S., *et al. The income tax act: Act 43 of 1961.* Law Publishers, Allahabad, 1961, 225pp.

Ministry of Finance. *An outline of direct taxes in India (as operative from April 1, 1960).* New Delhi, 1959, 86pp.

Ministry of Law. *The income tax act, 1961 (43 of 1961) as modified up to the 1st of August, 1963.* Government of India Press, Delhi, 1963, xii/230pp.

Nagpal, B. *Illustrated income tax law.* Law Printing Press, Allahabad, 1960, 440pp.

Nandi, K. "An analysis of the distribution of the burdens of income taxation," *Modern review,* May 1963, pp. 384-390.

Narielvala, P. "Accounting problems under the bonus act," *Income-tax journal* (India), vol. 6, no. 1, 1965, pp. 59-74.

Neuhauser, P. "The two-step method of valuation: One step backwards?" *Income-tax journal* (India), vol. 8, no. 1, 1966, pp. 1-16.

Nortcliffe, E. "Taxation in India—Income tax," *British tax review,* September-October 1960, pp. 349-363, 418-428.

Ojha, P. "Degree of progression: Income tax in India," *Indian economic review,* vol. 3, February 1956, pp. 105-110.

Parekh, C. *Income tax super tax ready reckoner 1951-52 with finance act 1951.* Parekh and Co., Bombay, 1952, 38pp.

Parliament, House of the People. *Select committee on the income-tax bill, 1961: Evidence.* Lok Sabha Secretariat, New Delhi, 1961, 223pp.

Pikale, S., and Banavali, H. *The income tax law in India.* N. M. Tripathi Private Ltd., Bombay, 1962, 276pp.

Pophale, G. *A quarter century of direct taxation in India: 1939-1964 (a historical-cum-critical survey).* Sir Purshotamdas Thakurdas Research Wing, Indian Merchants' Chamber Economic Research and Training Foundation, Bombay, 1966, xliv/475pp.

Rai, V. *Commentary on the income tax act, 1961.* Eastern Book Company, Lucknow, 1962, 206pp.

Ramachandran, V. *Income tax law in India, 1963.* Efficiency Aids, Madras, 1963, 216pp.

Ramaiya, A. *A guide to the income tax act, 1961.* Madras Law Journal Office, Madras, 1962, 573pp.

Ramaswami, C., and Kanhaiya Singh, J. "India: Allowable business expenses," *Bulletin for international fiscal documentation,* vol. 15, 1961, pp. 76-86.

Ramesch, M. "Future of the capital gains tax," *Indian economic journal,* vol. 6, October 1958, pp. 217-224.

Rao, B. "Company taxation in India: A study of super profits tax," *All India congress committee economic review,* vol. 15, 15 September 1963, pp. 31-34.

"Report of Select committee on income-tax bill 1961," *Foreign tax law weekly bulletin,* vol. 12, no. 33, 1962, pp. 1-9.

Roy, B. "Company taxation in India," *Chartered accountant* (New Delhi), vol. 6, May 1958, pp. 615-618.

Sakhalkar, S. "Effects of direct taxes on equity-investment," *Indian economic journal,* vol. 8, January 1961, pp. 284-288.

Sampath Iyengar, A. *Law of income tax.* Eastern Law House, Calcutta, 5th edition, 3 volumes, 1964.

Sarien, R., and Chawla, O. "The capital gains tax in India," *Canadian tax journal,* vol. 11, 1963, pp. 451-451.

Sharma, G. "Penalty in income-tax cases for acts of alleged omission or commission," *Taxation* (Delhi), vol. 21, January 1966, pp. 64-83.

Sharma, G. *Taxation of companies.* Taxation Publishing Co., Delhi, 1957.

Sharma, G. *Taxation of companies under the new scheme.* Taxation Publishing Co., Delhi, 1961, 208pp.

Sharma, R. *Appeals, revisions and references in income-tax.* Practical Tax Publishers, Delhi, 1966, 304pp.

Sharma, R. *Cash credits and secreted profits or investments in income-tax.* Practical Tax Publishers, Delhi, 1963, 116pp.

Sharma, R. *Deductions under the income-tax act.* Practical Tax Publishers, Delhi, 1961, 276pp.

Sharma, R. *Income-tax assessments or reassessments of income tax escaping assessment.* Practical Tax Publishers, Delhi, 1962, 132pp.

Singh, B. "Compulsory savings," *Indian economic journal,* vol. 7, April 1960, pp. 378-394.

S. R. Batliboi & Co. *India—Corporate tax and business information.* Calcutta, 1963, 34pp.

Srinivasan, K. *Income tax law.* Bharadwaja, Bangalore, 3 volumes, 1962.

Srivastava, R. "The problem of income tax arrears (India)," *All India congress committee economic review,* vol. 16, 10 September 1964, pp. 6-9.

Sundaram, V. *The law of income tax in India, being a detailed commentary of the Indian income-tax act 43 of 1961 as amended.* Madras Law Journal Office, Madras, 9th edition, 1963, 1258pp.

Taraporevala, R. "New system of direct taxation x-rayed," *Commerce* (Bombay), vol. 94, 22 June 1957, pp. 1242-1243; vol. 94, 29 June 1957, pp. 1292-1293.

"Tax credit certificate (equity shares) scheme, 1965," *Business lawyer,* vol. 5, 1966, pp. 6-31.

"Tax decision of the Supreme court of India: Territoriality of income," *Bulletin for international fiscal documentation,* vol. 8, 1954, pp. 270-280.

Viswanatha Aiyar, T. "Taxation of charities and trusts," *Proceedings of the Provincial lawyers' conference, 1963,* pp. 343-361.

5

Aiyar, A. (ed.). *The estate duty cases 1886-1958.* Company Law Institute of India, Madras, 3 volumes, 1959-1962.

Aiyar, A., and Ramachandran, T. *The expenditure-tax act, 1957.* Company Law Institute of India, Madras, 1958.

Aiyar, A., *et al. Gift tax act, 1958, and gift tax rules, 1958, with explanatory notes and statement of principles derived from American, Australian and Indian decisions.* Company Law Institute of India, Madras, 1958, 200pp.

"Annual tax on total wealth," *Indian taxation,* vol. 7, February 1956, pp. 39-42.

Balakrishna, R. "The estate duty in India," *Indian economic journal,* vol. 6, October 1958, pp. 163-171.

Bhargava, R. *The principle and problem of inheritance taxation.* Nand Kishore and Byo, Benares, 1952, 195pp.

Bhattacharya, S. *Law and practice of wealth-tax, gift-tax, expenditure-tax, surtax.* Nababharat, Calcutta, 1965, 174pp.

Bhattacharyva, S. "Expenditure tax and savings," *Arthaniti,* vol. 3, May 1960, pp. 163-169.

Central Board of Revenue. *Estate duty manual.* New Delhi, 2d edition, 1961, 333pp.

Chand, G. "The inheritance tax in India," *Indian journal of economics,* vol. 25, April 1945, pp. 436-450.

Chaturvedi, K. *The law of taxes on wealth, gift and expenditure.* Eastern Law House, Calcutta, 1965, 610pp.

Chopra, O. *An exhaustive commentary on the estate duty act 1953.* Taxation Publishing Co., Delhi, 2d edition, 1961.

Dalal, R., and Cooper, R. "Tax avoidance in India," *Bulletin for international fiscal documentation,* vol. 7, 1953, pp. 1-7.

Dalal, V. "Study of expenditure tax," *Chartered accountant* (New Delhi), vol. 7, June 1959, pp. 363-370.

Eigner, R. "Indian income, wealth, and expenditure taxes: Integration and administration," *National tax journal,* vol. 12, June 1959, pp. 151-162.

The estate duty act, with commentary. N. M. Tripathy Private Ltd., Bombay, 1960, 430pp.

"Expenditure tax," *Indian taxation,* vol. 7, February 1956, pp. 43-46.

Gopal, S. *Commentaries on estate duty act, 1953.* Eastern Book Co., Lucknow, 1960, 478pp.

Gulati, I. *Capital taxation in a developing economy (India).* Orient Longmans Private Ltd., Calcutta, 1957, 209pp.

Gupta, R., and Gupta, V. *Estate duty law and practice.* Agra Book Store, Agra, 6th edition, 1965, 303pp.

Hall, J. "Indian wealth tax—A charge on capital or income?" *Journal of business law,* vol. 1961, April 1961, p. 161.

Hicks, U. "Mr. Kaldor's plan for the reform of Indian taxes," *Economic journal,* vol. 68, March 1958.

Indian Merchants' Chamber. *The estate duty act, 1953, and the rules made thereunder.* Bombay, 1954, 34pp.

Kagzi, M. *Estate duty in India, law and practice.* Metropolitan Book Company, Delhi, 1962, xv/250pp.

Kagzi, M. "A study in estate duty," *Indian estate duty journal,* vol. 7, no. 3, 1960, pp. 33-41.

Kaldor, N. "The expenditure tax in a system of personal taxation." In: R. Bird and O. Oldman (eds.), *Readings on taxation in developing countries,* pp. 253-272. The Johns Hopkins Press, Baltimore, revised edition, 1967. Reprinted from: N. Kaldor, *Indian tax reform: Report of a survey,* pp. 7-16, 39-47. Department of Economic Affairs, Ministry of Finance, New Delhi, 1956.

Kaldor, N. "Tax reform in India," *Economic weekly,* vol. 11, January 1959. Reprinted in: R. Bird and O. Oldman (eds.), *Readings on taxation in developing countries.* The Johns Hopkins Press, Baltimore, 1964, pp. 311-318; revised edition, 1967, pp. 271-278.

Khanna, K. "An expenditure tax in India," *Bulletin for international fiscal documentation,* vol. 18, 1964, pp. 353-362.

Khanna, K. "Foreign investment and taxation in India," *Bulletin for international fiscal documentation,* vol. 19, 1965, pp. 1-18.

Lakdawala, D. "An expenditure tax," *Indian economic journal,* vol. 3, April 1956, pp. 331-340.

Lakdawala, D. "The four finance commissions in India," *Indian economic journal,* vol. 13, January 1966, pp. 498-522.

Laskar, S. *Estate duty in India.* B. C. Laskas, Calcutta, 1953, 324pp.

Mandal, G. "Kaldor on Indian tax reform," *Indian journal of economics,* vol. 37, January 1957, pp. 269-272.

Mandviwalla, N., and Cooper, R. *Handbook of estate duty.* New Book Co., Bombay, 1960, 334pp.

Minocha, A. "Wealth tax and expenditure tax," *Indian review,* vol. 59, April 1958.

Misra, B. "Wealth and expenditure taxes in India," *Canadian tax journal,* vol. 6, 1958, pp. 225-232. Reprinted from: *Economic paper,* November 1957.

Nanavati, D., and Nanavati, H. *The estate duty act.* N. M. Tripathi Private Ltd., Bombay, 2d edition, 1964, 639pp.

Narayana Row, S. *Estate duty simplified.* Madras Law Journal Office, Madras, 4th edition, 1963, 377pp.

Parekh, C. *The law and practice of wealth tax in India.* Parekh and Co., Bombay, 1958.

Prakash, O. "An Indian view of the expenditure tax," *Manchester school,* vol. 26, January 1958, pp. 48-67.

Roy, P. "Putting personal property into H.U.F. hotch-pot—Whether constitutes chargeable gift?" *Taxation* (Delhi), vol. 21, January 1966, pp. 33-45.

Sethi, R. *Wealth tax act with rules.* Law Book Co., Allahabad, 1961, 625pp.

Taraporevala, R. *Wealth and expenditure taxes.* Forum of Free Enterprise, Bombay, 1957, 24pp.

Vasa, H. "Valuation of property," *Indian estate duty journal,* vol. 7, no. 3, 1960, pp. 23-33.

6

Agarwala, S. *Law and practice relating to central sales tax act.* Central Law Agency, Allahabad, 5th edition, 1967, 524pp.

Agarwala, S. *Law and practice relating to sales tax in Uttar Pradesh.* Central Law Agency, Allahabad, 3d edition, 1963.

Agrawal, M. *Current Rajasthan sales-tax manual including the central sales tax act, 1956.* Jagdish and Co., Udaipur, 1957, loose-leaf.

Agrawal, M. *Principles of sales tax laws.* Jagdish and Co., Udaipur, 1961, 65pp.

Ahuja, S. "Progression in indirect taxation in India: 1953-59 and 1958-59," *Indian economic review,* vol. 9, February 1962, p. 52.

Aiyar, S. *The sales tax digest.* Commercial Laws of India Private Ltd., Thyagarayanagar, Madras, 4th edition, 1965, cxi/1116pp.

The central sales tax act. N. M. Tripathi Private Ltd., Bombay, 2d edition, 1966, 323pp.

Chandak, M. *The law of stamp duties in Madhya Pradesh.* Allahabad Law Publications, Allahabad, 1963, 288pp.

Chaturvedi, K. (ed.). *The central sales tax law.* Eastern Law House, Calcutta, 1965, 356pp.

Chaturvedi, K. *The principles of sales tax laws.* Eastern Law House, Calcutta, 3d edition, 1964, 1185pp.

Chelliah, R. "Taxation of consumption expenditures with special reference to India." In: R. Bird and O. Oldman (eds.), *Readings on taxation in developing countries.* The Johns Hopkins Press, Baltimore, 1964, pp. 281-290; revised edition, 1967, pp. 298-308.

Choudhary, P. *A dealer's book on central and Maharashtra sales tax laws.* Taxation Information Bureau, Bombay, 1965, 244pp.

Commentaries on excise act and rules. Law Publishers, Allahabad, 1965, 587pp.

"Future of the sales tax," *Indian taxation,* vol. 7, July 1956, pp. 253-256.

Gangadharan, A. *The general sales tax act, 1125 (Kerala).* Ernakulam, Babu, 1960, 280pp.

Ghosh, A. *Sales tax in India.* Ranjit Publishers, Delhi, 1954, 134pp.

Ghosh, H. "The rationale of salt tax in India," *Indian journal of economics,* vol. 27, April 1947, pp. 493-501.

Gopal, M., and Kumar, S. *Law and procedure of sales-tax on inter-state transactions.* Finance Budget Publications, Delhi, 1954, 244pp.

Gupte, K. *The Bombay sales tax act, 1959.* Western India Law Printing Press, Poona, 1960.

Indian Law Institute. *Interstate trade barriers and sales tax laws in India.* N.M. Tripathi Private Ltd., Bombay, 1962, xiii/87pp.

"Indirect taxes—Retrospect and prospects," *Tata quarterly,* vol. 14, October 1959, pp. 95-116.

Jain, S. "Report of the Committee on sales tax—A comment," *Journal of the Indian law institute,* vol. 6, October-December 1964, p. 474.

Kaitan, B. *Evolution of sales tax laws in India.* Pahuja, Patna, 1963, 272pp.

Krishnamurthi, K., and Mathrubutham, R.

The Indian stamp act: Act II of 1899. Madras Law Journal Office, Madras, 2d edition, 1960, 1001pp.

Lokanathan, P. *Report on the simplification and improvement of the sales tax system in Madras.* Government Press, Madras, 1958, 69pp.

Maheshwari, M. *Sixteen years Madhya Pradesh sales tax digest, 1947-1962.* Popular Law House, Jabalpur, 1963, 42pp.

Ministry of Finance. *Incidence of indirect taxation in India, 1958-59.* New Delhi, 1961.

Naida, T. "The sales-tax acts in the Indian union—An analytical study," *Supreme court journal* (India), vol. 18, 1955, pp. 1-100.

Patra, A. *The Indian stamp act, 1899.* Eastern Book Co., Lucknow, 2d edition, 1963, 1150pp.

Punjab Government. *The Punjab general sales tax act, 1948 as amended up to 31st of May, 1960.* Controller of Printing and Stationery, Chandigarh, 1960, 40pp.

Rai, S. *Commentaries on the Madhya Pradesh excise act.* Central Law Agency, Allahabad, 1963, 235pp.

Ramachandren, V. (ed.). *The Madras general sales tax act, 1959.* Business Week Press, Madras, 1960, 284pp.

Rao, M. "An analysis of sales-tax," *Modern review,* June 1955, pp. 460-461.

Sarkar, S. "Application of statistics to some problems of sales tax," *Indian economic journal,* vol. 4, January 1957, pp. 248-265.

Sarkar, S. "Sales tax has a history in India," *Indian journal of economics,* vol. 34, October 1953, pp. 93-114.

"Scope for a value-added tax in India," *Tata quarterly,* vol. 20, October 1965.

Setalvad, A. *Mulla and Pratt on the Indian stamp act.* N.M. Tripathi Private Ltd., Bombay, 6th edition, 1963, 452pp.

Singh, D. "State sales tax structure in India," *All India congress committee economic review,* vol. 15, 25 February 1964, pp. 23-28.

Singh, D. "Working of the sales tax judicial machinery in Uttar Pradesh, India," *All India congress committee economic review,* vol. 14, 30 December 1962, pp. 29-34.

Singh, S. *The laws of sales tax in U.P.* Vikshody Co., Jaipur City, 1952, 410pp.

Skukla, R. "Implications of sales tax on intra-regional trade," *Indian journal of commerce,* vol. 7, March 1954, pp. 9-18.

S. *Row's Indian stamp act.* Law Book Company, Allahabad, 3d edition, 1961, 1103pp.

"Taxability of a hire-purchase transaction under our sales tax laws," *Business lawyer,* vol. 5, 1966, pp. 1-5.

Varadarajan, N., and Krishnamurthi, K. *The law of sales tax in Madras.* Varadachary, Madras, 1961, 288pp.

Viswanatha Aiyar, T. "Sales tax and inter-state trade," *Madras law journal,* vol. 128, January 1965, p. 3.

7

Bagchi, A. "Shadow prices, controls and tariff protection in India," *Indian economic review* (n.s.), vol. 1, April 1966, pp. 22-44.

Council for Economic Education (Bombay). *Taxation and foreign trade and other essays.* Asia Publishing House, London, 1962, 106pp.

Jain, S. "Beginning of export for purposes of sales taxation—Article 286(1)(b) of the constitution and section 5 of the central sales tax act," *Journal of the Indian law institute,* vol. 5, April-June 1963, p. 302.

Jain, S. "Sale in the course of export: Need for statutory amendment," *Journal of the Indian law institute,* vol. 5, July-September 1963, p. 357.

Kraft, W., and Meyer, A. *Principles of customs law and procedure.* Sarkar & Sons, Calcutta, 1962, 502pp.

United States Department of Commerce. *Foreign trade regulations of India.* Washington, 1967, 8pp.

8

"Agreement between the government of India and the government of the Federal Republic of Germany for the avoidance of double taxation of income," *Indian journal of international law,* vol. 2, 1962, pp. 259-269.

Asian African Legal Consultative Committee, Secretariat. *Foreign investment laws and regulations of member countries.* Economic Law Series No. 2, N.M.

Tripathi Private Ltd., Bombay, 1965, 91pp. (mimeo).

Basu, G., *et al. Indian tax laws and foreigners having investments in India or having business connection in or with India.* Oxford Book Co., Calcutta, 1962, 140pp.

Bombay Chamber of Commerce and Industry. *Investment in India.* Bombay, 1961, 81pp.

Indian Investment Centre. *A guide to investing in India.* New York, 1965, 12pp.

Indian Investment Centre. *India welcomes foreign investment.* Caxton Press, New Delhi, 1965, xii/91pp.

Indian tax laws and foreigners. Oxford Book & Stationery Co., Calcutta, 1960, 40pp. Supplements, May 1963.

Kust, M. "India." In: American Management Association, *The taxation of business income from foreign operations,* pp. 103-109. New York, 1958.

"Liability of non-residents to income tax act," *Foreign tax law weekly bulletin,* vol. 11, no. 50, 1961, pp. 5-9.

Lockwood, W. "Taxes, enterprise and foreign capital in India—A review article," *Pacific affairs,* December 1958.

National Council of Applied Economic Research. *Foreign investor and tax reforms.* Occasional Paper No. 9, New Delhi, 1964, xi/44pp.

National Council of Applied Economic Research. *A study of taxation law in relation to foreign investment.* Asia Publishing House, New Delhi, 2d edition, 1958.

Peterkin, J. "The British investor and India," *The accountant,* 12 August 1961, pp. 192-196.

Pophale, G. *Tax treaties between India and foreign countries.* P. C. Manaktala and Sons Private Ltd., Bombay, 1966, 134pp.

Price Waterhouse & Co. *Information guide for doing business in India.* New York, 1967.

Rai, R. *Taxation on non-residents in India.* Metropolitan Book Co., New Delhi, 1962, 190pp.

Roy, A. "Position of foreign enterprises in Indian tax structure," *Capital,* supp., 19 December 1957.

Stanford Research Institute. *Indian taxes as they affect foreign investment.* Menlo Park, Calif.

United States Department of Commerce. *Establishing a business in India.* Washington, 1965, 20pp.

United States Department of Commerce. *Investment factors in India.* Washington, 1962, 26pp.

United States Department of Commerce. *Investment in India.* Washington, 1961, 272pp.

Venkataraman, A. *Taxation of Indian and foreign companies in India.* N.M. Tripathi Private Ltd., Bombay, 1964, 148pp.

9

Agrawala, D. *Guide to revenue law in U.P., 1940-1960.* Eastern Book Co., Lucknow, 1961, 246pp.

Balakrishna, R. "Budgetary scope for planning in Madras," *Indian journal of economics,* vol. 29, October 1948, pp. 109-116.

Bhargava, R. "Recent trends in federalism," *Public finance,* vol. 9, 1954, pp. 252-264.

Bhargava, R. *The theory and working of union finance in India.* Allen and Unwin, London, 1956, 308pp.

Bhouraskar, K. *Municipal finance in certain leading Indian states.* Local Self-Government Institute, Bombay, 1954, 262pp.

Chand, G. *Local finance in India.* Kitabistan, Allahabad, 1947.

Chand, G. "Local terminal taxation," *Indian journal of economics,* vol. 22, January 1942, pp. 624-636.

Chandavarkar, A. "Finances of state governments," *Reserve bank of India bulletin,* vol. 11, August 1957, pp. 732-750.

Das Gupta, B. *Provincial taxation under autonomy.* Oxford University Press, Calcutta, 1948.

Eapen, A. "Federal-state fiscal arrangements in India." In: United States Congress, Joint Economic Committee, 90th Congress, 1st Session, *Revenue sharing and its alternatives: What future for fiscal federalism?* vol. 1, pp. 450-475. Joint Committee Print, Washington, 1967.

Finance commission report. Government of India Press, New Delhi, 1952.

Finance commission report. Government of India Press, New Delhi, 1956.

"Finances of state governments," *Reserve bank of India bulletin,* vol. 10, May 1956, pp. 473-516.

"Finances of state governments," *Reserve bank of India bulletin,* vol. 15, June 1961, pp. 854-894.

"Finances of state governments," *Reserve bank of India bulletin,* vol. 16, October 1962, pp. 1545-1587.

Goode, R. "Federal finance in India," *National tax journal,* vol. 6, December 1953, pp. 361-371.

Gopal, M. *The finances of Mysore (1799-1811).* Bureau of Economic Research, Mysore, 1948, 69pp.

Gopal, M. *The finances of the Mysore state, 1799-1831.* Orient Longmans, Bombay, 1960, xii/267pp.

Gopal, M. "Indian federation: Financial allocation in the new union," *Canadian tax journal,* vol. 2, 1954, pp. 91-99.

Gopal, M. "Union-state financial relations in India." In: Tax Institute, *Federal-state-local tax correlation,* pp. 71-75. Princeton, N.J., 1954.

Gupta, M. *Fiscal laws of Madhya Pradesh.* New Supreme Law House, Indore, 1966, 200pp.

Gupta, S. "Financial relations between the centre and the states," *Indian journal of economics,* vol. 34, April 1954, pp. 325-335.

Hicks, U. *Development from below: Local government and finance in developing countries of the Commonwealth.* Oxford University Press, London, 1961, 552pp.

Jain, M., and Jain, S. "Intergovernmental tax immunities in India," *Journal of the Indian law institute,* vol. 2, October-December 1959, p. 101.

Jha, D. *Bihar finances (1912-13 to 1960-61).* Granthmala-Karyalaya, Patna, 1962.

Krishnaswamy, J. "Local finance in Madras state," *Journal of the University of Bombay,* vol. 24, January 1956, pp. 32-33.

Krishnaswamy, J. "Studies in local finance and taxation with special reference to Madras state," *Quarterly journal of Local self-government institute,* vol. 27, October 1956, pp. 250-295.

Kuppuswami, A. "Madras Inams assessment act (XL of 1956): A critical note," *Madras law journal,* vol. 118, February 1960, p. 8.

Malik, P. *The Uttar Pradesh revenue code.* Eastern Book Co., Lucknow, 1963.

Menezes. O. "Fiscal problems of municipal home-rule in federalism," *Indian journal of economics,* vol. 33, July 1952, pp. 31-40.

Misra, B. "Finance commission," *Public finance,* vol. 12, 1957, pp. 298-313.

Misra, B. *Indian federal finance.* Orient Longmans, Bombay, revised edition, 1954, 303pp.

Nagarajan, P. "Financial dependence of the states on the centre," *Indian journal of economics,* vol. 43, January 1963, pp. 167-173.

Nagarajan, P. "Trends in Indian federal finance," *Asian economic review,* vol. 4, August 1962, pp. 523-530.

Panigrahi, S. "The finances of Punjab government," *Indian finance,* 1952, pp. 61-64.

Premchand, A. "Financial control in Madras state," *Indian journal of public administration,* vol. 9, January-March 1963, pp. 49-63.

Prest, W. "Federal-state financial relations in India," *Economic record,* April 1960, pp. 191-219.

Rao, K. "The scope of local finance," *Indian journal of economics,* vol. 22, January 1942, pp. 832-836.

Rao, T. "Reorganization of local finance in India," *Indian journal of economics,* vol. 22, January 1942, pp. 677-688.

Report of the Local finance enquiry committee. Manager of Publications, Delhi, 1951.

Singh, B. *Federal finance and underdeveloped economy.* Hind Kitabs, Ltd., Bombay, 1952, 176pp.

Stokes, E. "Structure of state revenues in India," *Eastern economist,* 3 March 1950, p. 14.

Thomas, P. *Growth of federal finance in India.* Oxford University Press, Oxford, 1939, 550pp.

Tripathy, R. *Federal finance in a developing economy.* World Press Private Ltd., Calcutta, 1960, xvi/235pp.

Tripathy, R. *Local finance in a developing economy.* Planning Commission, Delhi, 1967, xi/496pp.

Venkataraman, K. *Local finance in perspective.* Asia Monographs 12, Asia Publishing House, London, 1965, viii/63pp.

Zacharias, C. "Reform of land revenue with special reference to Madras," *Indian journal of economics,* vol. 27, October 1946, pp. 237-244.

10

Parks, J. *The principles and practice of valuations.* Eastern Law House, Calcutta, 1965, 439pp.

Vasa, H. "The valuation of properties," *Taxation* (Delhi), vol. 16, January 1963, pp. 29-40.

11

Agarwal, M. *The Rajasthan agricultural income tax act, 1953.* Jagdish and Co., Udaipur, 1954, 352pp.

Aggarwal, O. *The Punjab land revenue act.* Metropolitan Book Co., Delhi, 6th edition, 1966, 650pp.

"Agricultural income-tax in India," *Reserve bank of India bulletin,* vol. 17, August 1963, pp. 1022-1033.

Ahuja, N. "Agricultural income tax in India," *Agricultural situation in India,* vol. 10, September 1955, pp. 433-444.

Chand, B. *Commentary on Madhya Pradesh land revenue code, 1959.* Metropolitan Book Co., Delhi, 1962.

Dvivedi, H. *Commentary on the Madhya Pradesh land revenue code.* Law Journal Publications, Gwalior, 3d edition, 1963, 925pp.

Galletti, R. "Taxation and agricultural policy," *Indian journal of economics,* vol. 22, July 1941, pp. 68-87.

Gandhi, V. *Tax burden on Indian agriculture.* Harvard Law School International Tax Program, Cambridge, Mass., 1966, xix/240pp.

Groves, H., and Madhavan, M. "Agricultural taxation and India's third year plan," *Land economics,* vol. 38, February 1962.

Gupte, K. (ed.). *Bombay land revenue code, 1879.* Bombay, 5th edition, 1962, 1060pp.

Gupte, K. *Bombay land revenue rules.* Western India Law, Poona, 8th edition, 1962, 272pp.

Irani, P. "Structure and taxation of agriculture in India and Pakistan." In: H. Wald and J. Froomkin (eds.), *Papers and proceedings of the Conference on agricultural taxation and economic development,* pp. 368-395. Harvard Law School International Program in Taxation, Cambridge, Mass., 1954.

Kansal, J. "Taxation of agricultural land in Uttar Pradesh," *Indian journal of agricultural economics,* vol. 20, no. 4, October-December 1965, pp. 88-91.

Khusro, A. "Taxation and agricultural land—A proposal," *Economic weekly* (Annual), February 1963, pp. 275-282.

Land Revenue Committee. *Land revenue reform in the Punjab.* Government Printing Press, Lahore.

Lindauer, J., and Singh, S. "Effects of the Punjab land tax," *National tax journal,* vol. 19, December 1966, pp. 427-433.

Mehrotra, J. "Problem of income tax on agricultural income," *Indian journal of economics,* vol. 17, April 1937, pp. 473-479.

Mitra, A. "Tax burden for Indian agriculture." In: R. Braibanti and J. Spengler (eds.), *Administration and economic development in India,* pp. 281-303. Duke University Press, Durham, N.C., 1963.

Nath, S. "Mysore agricultural income tax," *Mysore commerce,* vol. 11, July 1955, pp. 233-237.

Pillai, V. "A basic tax on land (the Travancore experiment)," *Indian journal of agricultural economics,* vol. 5, no. 1, March 1950, pp. 185-190.

Punjab Government, Legislative Department. *The Punjab land revenue act, 1887 as amended up to the 31st of May, 1960.* Controller of Printing and Stationery, Chandigarh, 1960, 68pp.

Qureshi, A. *The economic development of Hyderabad.* Orient Longmans, Bombay, 1947, vol. 1.

Qureshi, A. "Method of assessment of the land tax in the Indo-Pakistan subcontinent." In: H. Wald and J. Froomkin (eds.), *Papers and proceedings of the Conference on agricultural taxation and economic development,* pp. 396-411. Harvard Law School International Program in Taxation, Cambridge, Mass., 1954.

Rajamani, A. "Agricultural taxation—Resource for the third plan," *Rural India,* vol. 24, March-April 1961, pp. 95-101.

Rajamani, A. "Agricultural-nonagricultural relative tax burden," *Asian economic review,* vol. 5, November 1963, pp. 56-72.

Rangnekar, S. "The burden of land taxation in the Punjab (India) : 1927-28 to

1949-50," *Indian economic journal,* vol. 1, October 1953, pp. 166-184.

Reddy, G. "Land tax in India," *Journal of Mysore University,* vol. 12, March 1952, pp. 99-109.

Saxena, H. "Future of land tax in India," *Rural India,* vol. 16, November 1953, pp. 381-388.

Saxena, H. "Future pattern of land revenue policy in India," *Rural India,* vol. 21, January-February 1958, pp. 19-30.

Sengupta, S. "The proposed agricultural income tax in Bengal," *Indian journal of economics,* vol. 24, January 1944, pp. 212-218.

Sinha, B. "The basis of land tax: A problem in applied economics," *Indian journal of economics,* vol. 21, October 1940, pp. 158-166.

Stokes, E. *The English utilitarians in India.* 1959.

Tewari, R. "Rationalisation of our land revenue system (India)," *All India congress committee economic review* vol. 13, 7 August 1961, pp. 15-18.

United Nations, Department of Economic Affairs, Fiscal Division, and Food and Agricultural Organization. "The operation of the land tax in India and Pakistan." May 1953, 56pp.

Uppal, J. "Taxation on agricultural incomes in India," *Economic affairs,* vol. 8, January 1963, pp. 73-84.

12

Balakrishna, R. "Tax incentives in India," *Indian journal of economics,* vol. 31, October 1950, pp. 115-122.

Bhatia, R. "Conditions which facilitate private investment," *Indian journal of economics,* vol. 35, July 1954, pp. 1-9.

"India." In: International Bank for Reconstruction and Development, *Tax incentives for private industrial investment in less developed countries,* pp. 56-65. Washington, 1962.

Indian Investment Centre. *Comparative tax burden on companies under the existing and proposed tax rates and incentives.* New York, 1966, 4pp.

Indian Investment Centre. *Taxes and incentives: A guide for foreign investors.* New Delhi, New York, and Düsseldorf, June 1966, 79pp.

Kust, M. "Income tax concessions to private investment in India," *Taxes,* vol. 36, 1958, pp. 114-123.

13

Appleby, P. *Public administration in India: Report of a survey.* Manager of Publications, Delhi, 1953, 66pp.

"Kaldor on tax evasion in India," *Indian taxation,* vol. 7, September 1956, pp. 341-342.

Krishnamurti, P. "The re-organisation of the treasury system in India," *Indian journal of public administration,* vol. 8, April-June 1962, pp. 215-220.

Majumdar, B. (ed.). *Problems of public administration in India.* B. Bhawa, Bankipore, 1952, 310pp.

Report of the Direct taxes administration enquiry committee, 1958-59. Manager of Publications, Delhi, 1960, 578pp.

Review of the central excise administration in India. Manager of Publications, Delhi.

Singh, I. "Reorganizing the Indian Income tax department," *Indian journal of public administration,* vol. 1, July-September 1955, pp. 224-239.

"Tax evasion obstacles suggested," *Indian taxation,* vol. 7, November 1956, pp. 427-431.

United States Treasury Department, Internal Revenue Service, Foreign Tax Assistance Staff. *Tax administration in India.* Washington, 1964, 25pp. (mimeo).

14

Donaldson, J. "Substance-over-form argument," *Income tax journal* (India), vol. 6, no. 2, 1965, pp. 11-20.

Iyer, T. "Judicial control over taxation in India," *Year book of legal studies* (Madras), vol. 3, 1960, pp. 99-108.

Venkatachari, R. "Taxation laws and article 14 of the constitution of India," *Proceedings of the Provincial lawyers' conference, 1963,* pp. 343-361.

16

Ramineni, A. *Comparative analysis of the Kaldor Indian tax reforms and the Shoup Japanese tax reforms.* Ph.D. thesis, University of Minnesota, Minneapolis, Minn., 1961.

18

Agarwal, R. *Guide to revenue law 1950-1961.* Hind Publishing House, Allahabad, 1962, 350pp.

Diamond, W. *Foreign tax and trade briefs.* Fallon Law Book Company, New York, loose-leaf, 1951-.

"India law digest." In: *Martindale-Hubbell law directory,* vol. 4, pp. 2689-2714. Martindale-Hubbell, Inc., Summit, N.J., 1961.

Taxation. Delhi, monthly, 1948-.

INDONESIA

1

Dris, M. "Taxation in Indonesia," *Ekonomi dan keuangan Indonesia,* vol. 11, August-September 1958.

Japan Tax Association. *Asian taxation 1964.* Tokyo, 1964, 139pp. Supplement, 1965, 17pp.

"Revision of tax rates," *Foreign tax law weekly bulletin,* vol. 15, no. 39, 1965, pp. 15-17.

Slamet, M. "Fiscal law of Indonesia," *Bulletin for international fiscal documentation,* vol. 5, 1951, pp. 167-177.

Slamet, M. "Taxation in connection with structure of Indonesian society," *Bulletin for international fiscal documentation,* vol. 8, 1954, pp. 188-194.

United States Department of Commerce. *Basic data on the economy of Indonesia.* Washington, 1964, 23pp.

United States Department of Commerce. *Investment in Indonesia.* Washington, 1956, pp. 103-107, 139-150.

2

Higgins, B. *Indonesia's economic stabilization and development.* Institute of Pacific Relations, New York, 1957, xxii/ 179pp.

Paauw, D. "Financing economic development in Indonesia," *Economic development and cultural change,* vol. 4, January 1956, pp. 171-185.

Paauw, D. *Financing economic development: The Indonesian case.* Center for International Studies, Massachusetts Institute of Technology, Free Press, Glencoe, Ill., 1960, xxxiv/474pp.

Paauw, D. "The tax burden and economic development in Indonesia," *Ekonomi dan keuangan Indonesia,* vol. 7, September 1954, pp. 564-583.

Schmitt, H. *Some monetary and fiscal consequences of social conflict in Indonesia, 1950-1958.* Ph.D. thesis, University of California, Berkeley, Calif., 1958.

United Nations. *Mobilization of domestic capital in certain countries of Asia and the Far East.* Sales No. 1951.II.F.3, Bangkok, 1951.

Veen, J. "Some notes on 'The tax burden and economic development in Indonesia,' " *Ekonomi dan keuangan Indonesia,* vol. 7, 1954, pp. 766-767.

3

Yoingco, A., and Trinidad, R. *Fiscal systems and practices in Asian countries.* Frederick A. Praeger, New York, 1967.

6

Jap, K. "Sales taxation in Indonesia—A fifteen years experience," *Bulletin for international fiscal documentation,* vol. 20, 1966, pp. 189-192.

7

"A description of Indonesian import surcharges." In: Harvard Law School International Program in Taxation, *A case study on import and excise taxation in British Guiana in 1911,* pp. 20-23. Cambridge, Mass., 1957 (mimeo).

Higgins, B. "The rationale of import surcharges," *Ekonomi dan keuangan Indonesia,* vol. 6, May 1953, pp. 228-236.

United States Department of Commerce. *Foreign trade regulations of Indonesia.* Washington, 1965, 12pp.

8

Jap, K. "Foreign investment policy and taxation in Indonesia," *Bulletin for international fiscal documentation,* vol. 18, 1964, pp. 323-341.

Langen, W. de. "The Netherlands East Indies, and the taxation of limited companies with international interests," *Cahiers de droit fiscal international,* vol. 1, 1939, pp. 105-122.

Slamet, M. "Mesures unilatérales tendant à éviter la double imposition: Indonésie," *Cahiers de droit fiscal international,* vol. 44, 1961, p.127 (summaries in English and German).

United States Department of Commerce. *Foreign investment law of Indonesia.* Washington, 1958, 4pp.

9

Krishnamoorthy, S. "Decentralization in Indonesia: Financial aspects," *International studies,* vol. 2, April 1961, pp. 378-391.

Paauw, D. "The case for decentralized financing of economic development in Indonesia," *Far Eastern quarterly,* vol. 15, November 1955, pp. 77-95.

Paauw, D. "Local finance in Indonesia." In: R. Bird and O. Oldman (eds.), *Readings on taxation in developing countries.* The Johns Hopkins Press, Baltimore, 1964, pp. 361-385; revised edition, 1967, pp. 396-411.

Paauw, D. "The role of local finance in Indonesian economic development," *Ekonomi dan keuangan Indonesia,* vol. 8, January 1955, pp. 2-24.

15

Kanesa-Thansan, S. "Multiple exchange rates: The Indonesian experience," *International monetary fund staff papers,* vol. 13, July 1966, pp. 354-368.

18

Diamond, W. *Foreign tax and trade briefs.* Fallon Law Book Company, New York, loose-leaf, 1951–.

IRAN

1

United Nations. *Public finance information papers: Iran.* Sales No. 1951. XVI. 4, New York, 1951.

United Nations, Technical Assistance Administration. "La Fiscalité et les finances iraniennes." Doc. No. TAA/NS/Iran/6, 1951.

United Nations, Technical Assistance Administration. "Rapport sur les finances de l'Iran." April 1953 (mimeo).

United States Department of Commerce. *Basic data on the economy of Iran.* Washington, 1966, 16pp.

United States Department of Commerce. *Investment factors in Iran.* Washington, 1963, 8pp.

2

Brown, B. *The fiscal influence on economic development, with special reference to Iran.* Ph.D. thesis, University of Wisconsin, Madison, Wisc., 1959.

Farrakh-Pars, M. *The budgets of Iran, 1930-1959: An analysis of their financial and economic impact.* Ph.D. thesis, New York, 1960.

4

Foreign Tax Law Association. *Iranian income tax service.* St. Petersburg, Fla., loose-leaf, 1963-.

Grove, T. "Direct taxation in Iran—An outline," *Bulletin for international fiscal documentation,* vol. 20, 1966, pp. 369-379.

Rees, J. *Suggestions for the improvement of income tax laws of Iran.* United States Operations Mission to Iran, Tehran, 1961, 41pp. (mimeo).

Taylor, P. *Five reports by P. E. Taylor, income tax specialist.* United States Operations Mission to Iran, Tehran, 1954.

7

United States Department of Commerce. *Foreign trade regulations of Iran.* Washington, 1967, 8pp.

8

"Law concerning the encouragement and protection of foreign capital investments in Iran," *Iran review,* vol. 3, October 1958, p. 14.

United States Department of Commerce. *Establishing a business in Iran.* Washington, 1967, 20pp.

United States Department of Commerce. *Foreign investment law of Iran.* Washington, 1956, 4pp.

10

Taylor, P. *Prospects for budget balance and a proposal for improvement of the taxes on cultivated lands and real estate.* International Cooperation Administration, Washington, August 1956.

13

Central Treaty Organization. *Symposium on tax administration.* Office of United States Economic Coordinator for CENTO Affairs, American Embassy, Ankara, 1965, 259pp.

Rees, J. *A program of legislation for the improvement of tax administration in Iran.* United States Operations Mission to Iran, Tehran, 1957, 19pp. (offset).

United Nations, Economic and Social Council, Fiscal Commission. "Procedures available for the review of initial tax assessments: Reply of the government of Iran." Doc. No. E/CN.8/59/Add.29, 12 October 1953, 3pp. (mimeo).

United Nations, Technical Assistance Administration. "Business and financial administration and accounting in Iran." Doc. No. ST/TAA/K/Iran/2, July 1954.

18

Diamond, W. *Foreign tax and trade briefs.* Fallon Law Book Company, New York, loose-leaf, 1951-.

IRAQ

1

Food and Agricultural Organization of the United Nations, Mediterranean Development Project. *Iraq: Country report.* Rome, 1959, chapter 5.

"Oil and social change," *The economist,* 2 July 1955, 17pp. (special article).

United Nations. *Public finance information papers: Iraq.* Sales No. 1951.XVI. 6, New York, 1951.

United States Department of Commerce. *Basic data on the economy of Iraq.* Washington, 1963, 6pp.

2

Alnasrawi, A. *Financing economic development in Iraq.* Frederick A. Praeger, New York, 1966, 198pp.

El-Mutwalli, T. *The tax system of Iraq: A study of taxation in a developing country.* Ph.D. thesis, American University, Washington, 1958.

4

"Income tax," *Bulletin for international fiscal documentation,* vol. 19, 1965, pp. 456-458.

United Nations. "Income tax revision in Iraq." Prepared by O. Traylor, 1955, 44pp. (mimeo).

5

"Estates and inheritance tax." In: Foreign Tax Law Association, *Commercial law service of Iraq*, pp. 40-50. St. Petersburg, Fla., loose-leaf, 1965-.

7

United States Department of Commerce. *Foreign trade regulations of Iraq.* Washington, 1964, 8pp.

8

Asian African Legal Consultative Committee, Secretariat. *Foreign investment laws and regulations of member countries.* Economic Law Series No. 2, N.M. Tripathi Private Ltd., Bombay, 1965, 91pp. (mimeo).

United States Department of Commerce. *Establishing a business in Iraq.* Washington, 1957, 8pp.

9

United Nations, Technical Assistance Administration. "Municipal administration and taxation and finance in Iraq." Doc. No. TAA/IRQ/2 (restricted), 30 November 1956.

10

"Tax on immovable property." In: Foreign Tax Law Association, *Commercial law service of Iraq*, pp. 36-39. St. Petersburg, Fla., loose-leaf, 1965-.

11

Hammadi, S. *Agricultural taxation in Iraq.* Ph.D. thesis, University of Wisconsin, Madison, Wisc., 1957.

Harvard Law School International Program in Taxation. *The istihlak tax in Iraq.* Cambridge, Mass., 1955, 30pp. (mimeo).

Jackson, C. *Recommendations on agriculture taxation in Iraq.* 1953, 14pp. (offset).

"Law no. 60 of 1961 for agricultural land tax—13 September 1961," *Food and agricultural legislation*, vol. 11, no. 3, 1963.

Qureshi, A. *Land systems in the Middle East.* n.p., 1954.

United States Operations Mission to Iraq. *Draft of land tax law.* Baghdad, 1954, 25pp. (mimeo).

12

United States Department of Commerce. *Law for the encouragement of industrial undertakings in Iraq.* Washington, 1956, 4pp.

18

Diamond, W. *Foreign tax and trade briefs,* Fallon Law Book Company, New York, loose-leaf, 1951-.

ISRAEL

1

Bader, J. "Taxation, Israel," *Israel yearbook*, 1955, pp. 53-60.

Duesterwald-Doroth, A. "Public finance in Israel," *Bulletin for international fiscal documentation,* vol. 5, 1951, pp. 3-10.

"Israel: A digest of tax and other laws," *Foreign tax law weekly bulletin,* vol. 12, no. 47, 1962, pp. 1-9.

Klimowsky, E. "The influence of the legal form, the nature and the size of enterprises on their tax regime and vice versa," *Cahiers de droit fiscal international,* vol. 32, 1956, pp. 156-170.

Klimowsky, E. "Major tax reforms in Israel," *Bulletin for international fiscal documentation,* vol. 19, 1965, pp. 50-51.

Klimowsky, E. "Palestine and Israel: A study into their fiscal continuity in civil and criminal matters," *Bulletin for international fiscal documentation,* vol. 6, 1952, pp. 273-284.

Ministry of Finance. *A short guide to taxation in Israel.* Jerusalem, July 1959, 24pp.

Ministry of Finance. *The system of taxation in Israel.* Government Printer, Jerusalem, 1957, 36pp.

Moses, S. "The Palestine taxation system and its changes during the war," *Bulletin for international fiscal documentation,* vol. 1, 1946-1947, pp. 222-227.

State of Israel Investments Authority. *Investor's manual—Laws and regulations affecting investments.* Jerusalem, 1961, 20pp.

United States Department of Commerce. *Basic data on the economy of Israel.* Washington, 1963, 14pp.

2

Ben-Sharar, H., and Sandberg, M. "Economic institutional effects on income distribution: The case of Israel," *Public finance,* vol. 22, 1967.

Duesterwald-Doroth, A. "Problems of public finance in developing countries,"

Bulletin for international fiscal documentation, vol. 12, 1958, pp. 197-210.

Grunwald, K. "Le Budget de développement d'Israel," *Revue de science financière*, vol. 47, 1955, pp. 545-558.

United Nations. *Revenue administration and policy in Israel.* Three reports: Sales No. 1953.II.H.5, New York, 1953; Sales No. 1955.II.H.3, New York, 1954; Sales No. 1958.II.H.2, New York, 1958.

4

Alon, G. *Israel income tax commentary.* Business Diary, Haifa, 1960, 48pp.

"Capital gains tax," *Foreign tax law weekly bulletin*, vol. 15, no. 10, 1964, pp. 6-8.

"Capital profits tax," *Foreign tax law weekly bulletin*, vol. 15, no. 9, 1964, pp. 8-10.

Eichelgrun, G. *Palestine income tax guide.* Paltax Publishers, Haifa, and Sweet and Maxwell, London, 1945, 235pp.

Foreign Tax Law Association. *Israel income tax service.* Centerport, L.I., N.Y., loose-leaf, 1947–1955.

Gal-Edd, I. "When is a corporation—?" *National tax journal*, vol. 15, March 1962, pp. 53-65.

Greenstein, M. "The taxation of the revenue from patents, trademarks and designs: Israel," *Cahiers de droit fiscal international*, vol. 36, 1958, pp. 177-181.

"Income tax," *Business digest*, 21 August 1952, pp. 150-164.

"Israel." In: Board of Inland Revenue (Great Britain), *Income taxes outside the United Kingdom 1966*, vol. 4, pp. 281-301. H. M. Stationery Office, London, 1967.

"Israel's income tax laws," *Business digest*, 26 October 1950, 36pp. (reprints).

Klimowsky, E. "Capital gains taxation in Israel—Modifications," *Bulletin for international fiscal documentation*, vol. 18, 1964, pp. 455-458.

Klimowsky, E. "The onus and methods of proof in income tax law: Israel," *Cahiers de droit fiscal international*, vol. 36, 1958, pp. 422-434.

Lapidoth, A. "The taxation of lease premiums in Israel," *British tax review*, June-July-August 1965.

Lapidoth, A. "Trends in the income tax legislation of Israel," *Studies in Israel legislation problems* (Hebrew University), vol. 16, 1966, pp. 325-341.

Moses, S. *The income tax (amendment) ordinance, 1942.* Tarshish Books, Jerusalem, 1942, 93pp.

Moses, S. *The income tax (amendment) ordinance, 1943.* Tarshish Books, Jerusalem, 1943, 142pp.

Moses, S. *The income tax ordinance of Palestine.* Tarshish Pooks, Jerusalem, 1942, 355pp.

Moses, S. *The income tax ordinance of Palestine.* Bitaon Publishing Co. Ltd., Tel-Aviv, 2d edition, 1946, 537pp.

"Proposed amendments to capital profits tax," *Foreign tax law weekly bulletin*, vol. 15, no. 7, 1964, pp. 16-18.

5

"Israel: Estate tax law 1949," *Business diary*, vol. 14, 1955, pp. 308-310.

7

Pick, J. "Régime fiscal de l'importation et de l'exportation de marchandises: Israël," *Cahiers de droit fiscal international*, vol. 47A, 1962, p. 169.

Pines, D. *Direct export premiums in Israel 1952-1958.* Research Paper 16, Falk Project for Economic Research in Israel, Jerusalem, 1963, 19pp.

United States Department of Commerce. *Foreign trade regulations of Israel.* Washington, 1967, 8pp.

8

Billie, S., and Klimowsky, E. "The tax convention between Sweden and Israel in respect of death duties," *Bulletin for international fiscal documentation*, vol. 19, 1965, pp. 233-240.

Gal-Edd, I. "Mesures unilatérales tendant à éviter la double imposition: Israël," *Cahiers de droit fiscal international*, vol. 44, 1961, pp. 143-166 (in English).

Greenstein, M. "Mesures fiscales destinées à faciliter le mouvement international des capitaux: Israël," *Cahiers de droit fiscal international*, vol. 39, 1959, p. 437 (in English; summaries in French, German, and Spanish).

Klimowsky, E. "Traitement fiscal des dettes et intérêts sur dettes dans les relations internationales: Israël," *Cahiers de droit fiscal international*, vol.

42, 1960, p. 217 (in English; summaries in French and German).

Nacht, D. "Taxation on corporation by country of residence (Israel)," *Certified public accountant,* September-October 1964.

State of Israel Investment Authority. *An investor's guide to Israel.* Jerusalem, 1962, pp. 64-65.

"Unilateral measures for the avoidance of double taxation," *Cahiers de droit fiscal international,* vol. 46, 1961, pp. 76ff.

United States Department of Commerce. *Establishing a business in Israel.* Washington, 1962, 11pp.

10

Casserley, N. "Israel and Henry George," *Henry George news,* vol. 20, November 1956, p. 1.

Dar-Ziv, S. *Property tax and compensation fund law, 5721-1961: The synthesis of Israeli property taxes and compensation for war damages principles.* Seminar paper, Harvard Law School, Cambridge, Mass., 1962.

"Land betterment tax." In: D. Lankin, *Biennial survey of Israel law, 1962-1963,* pp. 41-43. "Mif'al Hashichpul," Jerusalem, 1964.

"Property tax," *Israel economist,* vol. 8, August 1952, pp. 180-182.

11

Qureshi, A. *Land systems in the Middle East.* n.p., 1954.

12

Encouragement of investments law, 1959. Israel Business Books, Haifa, 1959, 16pp.

"Fostering investment in Israel," *Israel economic forum,* vol. 12, August 1963, pp. 61-67.

Government of Israel Investment Centre. *Law for the encouragement of capital investments.* Ministry of Commerce and Industry, Jerusalem, 1963, 44pp.

Harvard Law School International Program in Taxation. *Reform of tax administration in the State of Israel: Report of the committee for the examination of the methods of assessing and collecting income tax in the State of Israel.* Translated by S. Lee and edited by M. Norr, Cambridge, Mass., 1962, 82pp.

Ilan, A. *Tax incentives for industrial development in Israel.* Prepared for United Nations Industrial Development Organization, New York, 1966.

"Law for the encouragement of capital investments," *Israel yearbook,* 1960, pp. 55-74.

13

Klimowsky, E. "Contrôle fiscal: Ses aspects juridiques, psychologiques et économiques: Israël," *Cahiers de droit fiscal international,* vol. 39, 1959, p. 201 (summaries in French, German, and Spanish).

Lapidoth, A. *Evasion and avoidance of income tax: A comparative study of English law and Israeli law.* Museum of Taxes, Jerusalem, 1966, 230pp.

Public Administration Service. *Project completion report on the Israel income tax administration project.* International Cooperation Administration, Washington, 1957 (mimeo).

14

Wilkenfield, H. "The juridical guarantees of the tax-payer vis-à-vis the fisc: Israel," *Cahiers de droit fiscal international,* vol. 33, 1956, pp. 78-97.

18

Bank Yisrael. *Report.* Jerusalem, annual, 1956– (chapter on tax policy).

Diamond, W. *Foreign tax and trade briefs.* Fallon Law Book Company, New York, loose-leaf, 1951–.

"Israel law digest." In: *Martindale-Hubbell law directory,* vol. 4, pp. 2724-2732. Martindale-Hubbell, Inc., Summit, N.J., 1961.

IVORY COAST

1

Chambre de Commerce de la République de la Côte d'Ivoire. *Le Régime fiscal.* Abidjan, 1961, 133pp.

Tixier, G., and Penouil, M. "Le Système fiscale ivoiren," *Pénant: Revue de droit des pays l'Afrique,* vol. 71, 1961, pp. 719-732.

United States Department of Commerce. *Basic data on the economy of the Republic of the Ivory Coast.* Washington, 1963, 20pp.

2

The economic and financial structure of French West Africa. Annual conference of the Economic Sections, West African Institute of Social and Economic Research, University College, Ibadan, 1953 (mimeo).

3

Mémento fiscal et social 1964, numéro spécial no. 14, 25 June 1964. A comparative survey of taxes in the West African Union and Guinea.

8

Tixier, G. "Les Problèmes de double imposition entre la France et la République de Côte-d'Ivoire," *Revue de science financière,* vol. 53, 1961, pp. 566-580.

12

United States Department of Commerce. *Investment law of the Ivory Coast.* Washington, 1961, 12pp.

JAMAICA

1

Canadian Tax Foundation. *Taxes abroad: West Indies.* Toronto, 1961, 22pp.

Comptroller for Development and Welfare. *Financial aspects of federation in the British West Indian territories.* Barbados, 1953.

Jamaican Industrial Development Corporation. *Industrial investment opportunities.* Kingston, 1965, 14pp.

Prest, A. *A fiscal survey of the British Caribbean.* H.M. Stationery Office, London, 1957, 136pp.

Price Waterhouse & Co. *Information guide for doing business in Jamaica.* New York, 1964, 34pp.

"Taxation in Jamaica," *Foreign tax law weekly bulletin,* vol. 15, no. 10, 1964, pp. 11-16.

United States Department of Commerce. *Basic data on the economy of Jamaica.* Washington, 1967, 20pp.

2

Goode, R. "Taxation and economic development in Jamaica," *Social and economic studies,* vol. 5, March 1956, pp. 19-26.

Hicks, J., and Hicks, U. *Report of finance and taxation in Jamaica.* Government

Printer, Kingston, 1955, 172pp.

Huggins, H. "Employment, economic development and incentive financing in Jamaica," *Social and economic studies,* vol. 1, 1953.

Lovejoy, R. *Alternative methods of financing the Jamaican budget.* Ph.D. thesis, Michigan, 1963.

Lovejoy, R. "The burden of Jamaican taxation," *Social and economic studies,* vol. 12, December 1963, pp. 442-448.

"Symposium on the Hicks report," *Social and economic studies,* vol. 5, March 1956, pp. 19-53.

Thorne, A. "Some general comments on the Hicks report (on finance and taxation in Jamaica)," *Social and economic studies,* vol. 5, March 1956, pp. 39-47.

4

Foreign Tax Law Association. *Jamaica income tax service.* Centerport, L.I., N.Y., loose-leaf, 1954–.

"Jamaica." In: Board of Inland Revenue (Great Britain), *Income taxes outside the United Kingdom 1966,* vol. 4, pp. 329-366, H. M. Stationery Office, London, 1967.

"Self-assessment system of income tax," *Foreign tax law weekly bulletin,* vol. 14, no. 45, 1964, pp. 2-4.

Wingfield, R. "Jamaica's income tax," *Canadian tax journal,* vol. 7, 1959, pp. 480-484.

7

United States Department of Commerce. *Foreign trade regulations of Jamaica.* Washington, 1965, 8pp.

8

Brudno, W. "Jamaica." In: American Management Association, *The taxation of business income from foreign operations,* pp. 78-80. New York, 1958.

Kaelin, W., and Vendryes, C. "Tax and business aspects of investing in Jamaica." In: Prentice-Hall, Inc., *Tax ideas.* Englewood Cliffs, N.J., 1964.

Noyes Research Co. *Investment in the Caribbean.* Pearl River, N.Y., 1964, 132pp.

Swanson, H. "Income tax aspects of investment in Jamaica," *Taxes,* vol. 33, 1957, pp. 371-380.

United States Department of Commerce.

Establishing a business in Jamaica. Washington, 1958, 8pp.

9

Hicks, U. *Development from below: Local government and finance in developing countries of the Commonwealth.* Oxford University Press, London, 1961, 552pp.
MacArthur, D. "Problems of local financing in the Caribbean." In: A. Wilgus (ed.), *The Caribbean: Natural resources.* University of Florida Press, Gainesville, Fla., 1959.
Thomas, R. "Local government financing in Jamaica, 1944-59," *Social and economic studies,* vol. 12, June 1963, pp. 141-159.

10

Hicks, J., and Hicks, U. "The taxation of the unimproved value of land." In: R. Bird and O. Oldman (eds.), *Readings on taxation in developing countries.* The Johns Hopkins Press, Baltimore, 1964, pp. 402-412; revised edition, 1967, pp. 431-441.
Holland, D. "The taxation of unimproved value in Jamaica," *Proceedings of the National tax association 1965,* vol. 58, pp. 442-470.
Morgan, D. "Land valuation and land taxation in Jamaica," *Public finance,* vol. 12, 1957, pp. 232-238.
Murray, J. *Report to the government of Jamaica on valuation, land taxation and rating.* Government Printer, Kingston, 1957, 55pp.
United Nations, Technical Assistance Administration. "A further report on land valuation in Jamaica." 1960 (restricted) (mimeo).

12

Arthur D. Little, Inc. *Memorandum on taxation as an inducement to industry prepared for the Industrial development corporation of Jamaica.* Cambridge, Mass., 23pp. (duplicated).
Caribbean Commission. *The promotion of industrial development in the Caribbean.* Port-of-Spain, 1952, 173pp.
Chen-Young, P. *An economic evaluation of the tax incentive program in Jamaica.* Ph.D. thesis, University of Pittsburgh, Pittsburgh, Pa., 1966.
Chen-Young, P. "A study of tax incen-

tives in Jamaica," *National tax journal,* vol. 20, September 1967, pp. 292-308.
Jamaica Industrial Development Corporation. *Statistical report of manufacturing enterprises approved and operating under industrial incentive laws.* Kingston, 1965 (mimeo).
McGurran, H. "Tax incentives in Jamaica," *Canadian tax journal,* vol. 4, 1956, pp. 406-408.

13

Smellie, R. *Paper on suggestions for setting up an investigating and intelligence division in the Income tax department in Jamaica.* Kingston, 1957, 10pp. (typewritten).
United States Treasury Department, Internal Revenue Service, Foreign Tax Assistance Staff. *Tax administration in Jamaica.* Washington, 1965 (mimeo).

17

Seers, D. "Federation of the British West Indies: The economic and financial aspects," *Social and economic studies,* vol. 6, June 1957, pp. 197-214.

18

Diamond, W. *Foreign tax and trade briefs.* Fallon Law Book Company, New York, loose-leaf, 1951-.

JAPAN

1

Bradshaw, C. "Selected aspects of business in Japan," *Stanford law review,* vol. 14, July 1962, pp. 639-681.
Bronfenbrenner, M. "Four positions in Japanese finance," *Journal of political economy,* vol. 58, August 1950, pp. 281-288.
Cohen, J. "Tax reform in Japan," *Far Eastern survey,* vol. 18, 28 December 1949, pp. 307-311.
Cohen, J. "Tax revision in Japan," *Taxes,* vol. 28, 1950, pp. 526-533.
"Draft of special taxation measures," *Foreign tax law weekly bulletin,* vol. 11, no. 46, 1961, pp. 1-6.
Hayashi, T. *Guide to Japanese taxes.* Ginzanishi, Chuoku, Zaikei Shōhō Shā, Tokyo, 1966, 186pp.
Hicks, U. "The reform of Japanese taxation," *Public finance,* vol. 6, 1951, pp. 199-220, 338-341.
Honjo, E. "Views in the taxation on com-

merce in the closing days of Tokugawa age," *Kyoto university economic review,* vol. 16, July 1941, pp. 1-15.

Ito, H. *Studies in public finance and taxation.* Science Council of Japan, Third Division, Tokyo, 1966, 113pp.

Japan Tax Association. *Asian taxation 1964.* Tokyo, 1964, 139pp. Supplement, 1965, 17pp.

Japan Tax Association. *Proceedings of the special meeting of Japan tax association on tax system and administration in Asian countries (April 8-16, 1963).* Tokyo, 1964, 274pp.

Matsuno, K. "A brief history of Japan's public finance," *Kobe university economic review,* vol. 9, 1963, pp. 30-39.

Matsuno, K. "The political factors in public finance," *Kobe university economic review,* vol. 6, 1960, pp. 17-26.

Report on Japanese taxation by the Shoup mission. General Headquarters, Supreme Commander for the Allied Powers, Tokyo, 4 volumes, 1949.

Second report of Japanese taxation by the Shoup mission. Supreme Commander for the Allied Powers, Tokyo, 1950, 92pp.

Shavell, H. "Postwar taxation in Japan," *Journal of political economy,* vol. 56, April 1948, pp. 124-137.

Shavell, H. "Taxation reform in occupied Japan," *National tax journal,* vol. 1, June 1948, pp. 127-143.

Shiomi, S. *Japan's finance and taxation 1940-1956.* Columbia University Press, New York, 1957, 190pp.

Shiomi, S. "The reform of the tax system," *Kyoto university economic review,* vol. 15, no. 2, April 1940, pp. 34-70.

Stead, A. (ed.). *Japan by the Japanese.* William Heinemann, London, 1904, chapter 15.

Sundelson, J. "Report on Japanese taxation by the Shoup mission," *National tax journal,* vol. 3, June 1950, pp. 104-120.

2

Chung, Y. *The role of government in the generation of saving: The Japanese experience.* Ph.D. thesis, Columbia University, New York, 1965.

Cohen, J. "Fiscal policy in Japan," *Journal of finance,* vol. 5, March 1960, pp. 110-125.

Emi, K. *Government fiscal activity and economic growth in Japan, 1868-1960.* Economic Research Series, Hitotsubashi University Institute of Economic Research, Kinokuniya Bookstore Co., Ltd., Tokyo, 1963, v/186pp.

Honjo, E. "On the financial development of Japan," *Kyoto university economic review,* vol. 5, December 1930, pp. 66-79.

Kimura, M. "Fiscal policy and industrialization in Japan 1868-1895," *Annals of the Hitosubashi academy,* vol. 6, April 1956. Also in: Science Council of Japan, *Conditions for direct taxation,* pp. 68-89. Tokyo, 1958. And in: International Economic Association, *Economic development with special reference to East Asia,* pp. 273-286. New York, 1964.

Komiya, R. "Japan." In: National Bureau of Economic Research and Brookings Institution, *Foreign tax policies and economic growth,* pp. 39-96. Columbia University Press, New York, 1966.

Kurihara, K. "Post-war inflation and fiscal-monetary policy in Japan," *American economic review,* vol. 36, December 1946, pp. 843-854.

Lockwood, W. *The economic development of Japan.* Princeton University Press, Princeton, N.J., 1954, pp. 521-528.

Pons, F. *Un cas de développement sans inflation: Le Japon.* Presses Univérsitaires de France, Paris, 1963, 136pp.

Ranis, G. "The financing of Japanese economic development," *Economic history review,* vol. 11, April 1959, pp. 440-454.

Sakurai, K. *Financial aspects of economic development of Japan from 1868 to present.* Ph.D. thesis, Syracuse University, Syracuse, N.Y., 1961.

Takeda, T. "The financial policy of the Meiji government," *Developing economies,* vol. 3, no. 4, December 1965.

Tokoyama, T. "Economic recovery and public finance in post-war Japan," *Public finance,* vol. 8, 1953, pp. 283-316.

Yamamura, K. "Tax burden on wage earners in post war Japanese economic growth," *National tax journal,* vol. 19, March 1966, pp. 58-69.

Yoingco, A. "Uses of national income in taxation with special reference to the experience of Japan in the period of the Meiji restoration." In: Joint Legislative-Executive Tax Commission (Philippines), *Taxation and socio-economic growth,* pp. 212-214. Manila, 1960.

3

Yoingco, A., and Trinidad, R. *Fiscal systems and practices in Asian countries.* Frederick A. Praeger, New York, 1967.

4

Davidson, S., and Yasuba, Y. "Asset revaluation and income taxation in Japan," *National tax journal,* vol. 8, March 1960, pp. 45-58.

Fujita, S. "Political ceiling on income taxation; tax consciousness; taxpayer's cost of compliance; distribution of the tax burden," *Public finance,* vol. 16, 1961, pp. 183-198.

Hayashi, Y. "Capital accumulation and taxation in Japan," *National tax journal,* vol. 16, June 1963, pp. 174-192.

Ikeda, K. "Establishment of income tax in Japan (historical and sociological study)," *Public finance,* vol. 12, 1957, pp. 145-170.

Ito, H. "Direct taxes in Japan and the Shoup report," *Public finance,* vol. 8, 1953, pp. 357-383. Also in: Science Council of Japan, *Essays in public finance.* Tokyo, 1954.

Kennan, K. "The income tax in Japan," *National income tax magazine,* vol. 7, January 1929, pp. 12-13, 38-40.

Kimura, M. "Taxation and capital accumulation," *Annals of the Hitosubashi academy,* vol. 4, October 1953, pp. 15-39. Also in: Science Council of Japan, *Conditions for direct taxation.* Tokyo, 1958.

Uematsu, M. *The income tax system of Japan and its administration.* Harvard Law School International Program in Taxation, Cambridge, Mass., 1962 (mimeo).

Uematsu, M., and Coleman, R. *Computation of income tax in Japanese income taxation: A study in the adjustment of theory to reality.* Harvard Law School International Program in Taxation, Cambridge, Mass., 1963, 80pp.

6

Kimura, M. "Transactions tax in Japan." In: M. Masoin and E. Morselli (eds.), *Impôts sur transactions, transmissions et chiffre d'affaires,* pp. 271-284. Ar-chives Internationales de Finances Publiques No. 2. Cedam Casa Editrice, Dr. A. Milani, Padova, 1959.

8

Kimura, M. "Mesures unilatérales tendant à éviter la double imposition: Japon," *Cahiers de droit fiscal international,* vol. 44, 1961, pp. 177-194 (in English).

Okura, M. "Taxation of foreign enterprises carrying on business operations in Japan," *Bulletin for international fiscal documentation,* vol. 19, 1965, pp. 177-192, 223-227.

Pardoe, W. "Taxation in Japan: Foreign source income of Japanese corporations and taxation of income of foreign corporations doing business in Japan." In: Tax Institute of America, Inc., *Taxation of foreign income by United States and other countries,* pp. 40-56. Princeton, N.J., 1966.

"Reshaping of taxation system on aliens," *Foreign tax law weekly bulletin,* vol. 12, no. 44, 1962, pp. 1-5.

Tanaka, H. "Comments on selected Japanese laws bearing on United States trade with and investment in Japan," *Patent, trademark and copyright journal of research and education,* vol. 7, Winter 1963-1964, p. 418.

"Taxation of profits arising from foreign investments in Japan." In: Daiichi Ginko, *Guide book for investments in Japan,* pp. 56-64. Tokyo, 1962. Also: Nationalist Foreign Trade Council, New York, 1961, 8pp.

"Treaties: Japan-New Zealand," *Bulletin for international fiscal documentation,* vol. 18, 1964, pp. 386-396.

Way, G. "New Japanese approach to the taxation of foreign individuals and enterprise," *Washington law review,* vol. 38, Spring 1963, pp. 145-168.

9

Mishikawa, K. "Local governments and their financial administration in postwar Japan," *Public finance,* vol. 18, 1963, pp. 110-119.

10

Smith, T. "The land tax in the Tokugawa period," *Journal of Asian studies,* vol. 18, November 1958, pp. 3-19.

11

Food and Agricultural Organization of the United Nations, Economic and Social Commission. "The role of agricultural land taxes in Japanese development." In: R. Bird and O. Oldman (eds.), *Readings on taxation in developing countries.* The Johns Hopkins Press, Baltimore, 1964, pp. 436-449; revised edition, 1967, pp. 478-491.

Ike, N. "Taxation and landownership in the westernization of Japan," *Journal of economic history,* vol. 7, November 1947, pp. 160-182.

Oshima, H. "The role of land taxes in Japanese development (1867-1912) and its relevance to underdeveloped countries." In: Joint Legislative-Executive Tax Commission (Philippines), *Taxation and socio-economic growth,* pp. 215-243. Manila, 1960.

16

Ramineni, A. *Comparative analysis of the Kaldor Indian tax reforms and the Shoup Japanese tax reforms.* Ph.D. thesis, University of Minnesota, Minneapolis, Minn., 1961.

Supreme Commander for the Allied Powers. *Differences between Shoup recommendation and the revised laws, and reasons for amendment of recommendation.* Tokyo, 1950, 51pp. (mimeo).

18

Ministry of Finance, Tax Bureau. *Outline of Japanese taxes.* Tokyo, annual, 1960–.

JORDAN

1

American University of Beirut, Economic Research Institute. *Business legislation in Jordan.* Beirut, 1955, 64pp. (duplicated).

United States Department of Commerce. *Basic data on the economy of Jordan.* Washington, 1964, 8pp.

2

International Bank for Reconstruction and Development. *The economic development of Jordan.* The Johns Hopkins Press, Baltimore, 1957, chapters 9, 10.

4

Arafat, C. *Suggestions for the reform of the income tax law of Jordan.* Seminar paper, Harvard Law School, Cambridge, Mass., 1960.

Foreign Tax Law Association. *Jordan income tax service.* St. Petersburg, Fla., loose-leaf, 1964–.

"New income tax law," *Foreign tax law weekly bulletin,* vol. 15, no. 47, 1965, pp. 15-17.

Nimry, S. "Taxation of corporations in the Hashemite kingdom of Jordan," *Bulletin for international fiscal documentation,* vol. 19, 1965, pp. 52-56.

7

United States Department of Commerce. *Foreign trade regulations of Jordan.* Washington, 1964, 8pp.

8

United States Department of Commerce. *Establishing a business in Jordan.* Washington, 1956, 8pp.

11

Qureshi, A. *Land systems in the Middle East.* n.p., 1954.

12

United States Department of Commerce. *Laws to encourage industry and investment in Jordan.* Washington, 1955, 4pp.

KENYA

1

"Commercial and tax legislation," *Foreign tax law weekly bulletin,* vol. 7, no. 23, 1956, pp. 1-9.

Due, J. "Reform of East African taxation," *East African economics review,* vol. 11, December 1964, pp. 57-68.

Mackenzie, K. "The development of the Kenya treasury since 1936," *East African economics review,* vol. 8, December 1961, pp. 59-72.

Report of the Taxation enquiry committee. Government Printer, Nairobi, 1947.

United States Department of Commerce. *Basic data on the economy of Kenya.* Washington, 1965, 16pp.

Woods, W. *A report on a fiscal survey of Kenya, Uganda and Tanganyika.* Government Printer, Nairobi, 1946.

2

Gill, F. "Future taxation policy in independent East Africa," *East African economics review,* vol. 9, June 1962, pp. 1-15.

International Bank for Reconstruction and Development. *The economic development of Kenya.* The Johns Hopkins Press, Baltimore, 1963, pp. 273-293.

Mwihia, F. *Decision rules for optimal tax policy with illustrations from Kenya's experience as to their practical application.* Ph.D. thesis, University of Pittsburgh, Pittsburgh, Pa., 1965.

Report of the Economic and fiscal commission. H. M. Stationery Office, London, 1961.

3

Due, J. *Taxation and economic development in Tropical Africa.* The MIT Press, Cambridge, Mass., 1963, 172pp.

4

"East Africa territories." In: Board of Inland Revenue (Great Britain), *Income taxes outside the United Kingdom 1966,* vol. 2, pp. 307-400. H. M. Stationery Office, London, 1967.

England, J. "Graduated personal tax in Kenya," *Journal of local administration overseas,* vol. 3, October 1964, pp. 204-213.

Foreign Tax Law Association. *Kenya income tax service.* Centerport, L.I., N.Y., loose-leaf, 1952–1955.

Jethna, N. "Company taxation in East Africa," *British tax review,* January-February 1965.

Jethna, N. "Low-income taxation in Kenya," *British tax review,* July-August 1966, pp. 251-267.

McNeil, R., and Bechgaard, K. *East African income tax.* Butterworth, Durban, 1960, 568pp.

Select committee on the East African income tax (management) bill, 1958. Government Printer, Nairobi, 1958.

7

United States Department of Commerce. *Foreign trade regulations of East Africa.* Washington, 1966, 8pp.

Walker, D. "A recent change in East African company taxation," *Public finance,* vol. 15, 1960, pp. 166-188.

8

"East African income tax and nonresidents," *Taxation,* 6 February 1960.

United States Department of Commerce. *Establishing a business in East Africa.* Washington, 1966, 16pp.

9

"Graduated personal tax for rural local government in Kenya," *Journal of local administration overseas,* vol. 3, January 1964, pp. 45-52.

Hicks, U. *Development from below: Local government and finance in developing countries of the Commonwealth.* Oxford University Press, London, 1961, 552pp.

"Urban problems in East and Central Africa," *Journal of African administration,* vol. 10, October 1958, pp. 215-218.

13

Altorfer, A. "Financial officers of the Ministry of local government, Kenya," *Journal of African administration,* vol. 13, January 1961, pp. 11-23.

United States Treasury Department, Internal Revenue Service, Foreign Tax Assistance Staff. *Report on tax administration in the East Africa common services organization.* Washington, 1964 (mimeo).

18

Diamond, W. *Foreign tax and trade briefs.* Fallon Law Book Company, New York, loose-leaf, 1951–.

KOREA

1

Bonnevalle, R. *Report and recommendations on the budget and related fiscal controls of the Republic of Korea.* 1952, 53pp. (mimeo).

Campbell, C., and Tullock, G. "Some little-understood aspects of Korea's monetary and fiscal systems," *American economic review,* vol. 47, June 1957, pp. 336-349.

First National City Bank of New York. *Republic of Korea.* New York, 1966, 16pp.

Hall, J. Special reports on taxation and draft tax bills. Ministry of Finance, Seoul, 1959-1960.

Japan Tax Association. *Asian taxation*

1964. Tokyo, 1964, 139pp. Supplement, 1965, 17pp.

Korean Information Service. *Guide to Korea.* Washington, 1966, 32pp.

Ministry of Finance, Taxation Bureau. *Outline of national tax, 1965.* Seoul, 1966, 86pp.

Musgrave, R. *Suggestions for the 1967 tax reform.* Cambridge, Mass., 1967, 32pp. (mimeo).

Tax Advisory Group to the Ministry of Finance. *Recommendations regarding the revision of the national tax system of Korea.* Seoul, 34pp. (mimeo).

"Taxation." In: Ministry of Foreign Affairs, Economic Bureau, *Trade and investment guide to Korea,* pp. 77-82. Seoul, 1963.

"Taxation in Korea." In: Foreign Tax Law Association, *Commercial laws of Korea,* pp. 19-40. St. Petersburg, Fla., loose-leaf, 1962–.

United States Department of Commerce. *Basic data on the economy of Korea.* Washington, 1959, 18pp.

United States Department of Commerce. *Summary of national and local taxes.* Washington, 1966, 61pp.

Wald, H. *Report and recommendations on taxation in the Republic of Korea.* 1953, 18pp. (mimeo).

2

Chough, S. *Financing of economic development in South Korea, 1954-1964.* Ph.D. thesis, University of California, Berkeley, Calif., 1967.

Kay, B. *Fiscal and taxation policy in a developing economy with special reference to the Republic of Korea.* Ph.D. thesis, University of Wisconsin, Madison, Wisc., 1958.

Musgrave, R. *Revenue policy for Korea's economic development.* Nathan Economic Advisory Group, Seoul, 1965, vii/100pp. Part reprinted in: R. Bird and O. Oldman (eds.), *Readings on taxation in developing countries,* pp. 45-51. The Johns Hopkins Press, Baltimore, revised edition, 1967.

United Nations, Korean Reconstruction Agency. "An economic program for Korean reconstruction." Doc. No. UNKRA/AG/13/Rev.1, April 1954.

3

Yoingco, A., and Trinidad, R. *Fiscal systems and practices in Asian countries.* Frederick A. Praeger, New York, 1967.

4

Ministry of Finance. *Income tax law; corporation tax law; past, present and future of internal tax; and an outline of the national tax system in Korea.* Seoul, 1963.

6

Tax Advisory Group to the Ministry of Finance. Translations of stamp and travelling tax laws, of inheritance, amusement, mining, and registration tax laws. Seoul, 1957 (mimeo).

7

United States Department of Commerce. *Foreign trade regulations of Korea.* Washington, 1967, 12pp.

11

Wald, H. "The recent experience of the Republic of Korea with tax collections in kind." In: H. Wald and J. Froomkin (eds.), *Papers and proceedings of the Conference on agricultural taxation and economic development,* pp. 424-431. Harvard Law School International Program in Taxation, Cambridge, Mass., 1954.

Wald, H. "Use of tax collections in kind to combat inflation in the Republic of Korea," *Public finance,* vol. 9, 1954, pp. 176-187.

18

Ministry of Finance, Bureau of Taxation. *Yearbook of tax statistics.* Seoul, annual, 1961–.

KUWAIT

1

Ministry of Guidance and Information. *This is Kuwait.* Nairobi, 1963, 31pp.

United States Department of Commerce. *Basic data on the economy of Kuwait.* Washington, 1963, 5pp.

United States Department of State. *Background notes: Kuwait.* Washington, 1965, 4pp.

4

"Kuwait income tax." In: Foreign Tax Law Association, *Kuwait corporation law,* pp. 77-88. St. Petersburg, Fla., loose-leaf, 1961–.

United States Department of Commerce. *Kuwait income tax law.* Washington, 1955, 8pp.

7

United States Department of Commerce. *Foreign trade regulations of Kuwait.* Washington, 1966, 8pp.

8

United States Department of Commerce. *Establishing a business in Kuwait.* Washington, 1963, 5pp.

LAOS

1

Jacoby, N. *Exploratory report on taxation in Laos.* International Cooperation Administration, Washington, March 1960.

Japan Tax Association. *Asian taxation 1964.* Tokyo, 1964, 139pp. Supplement, 1965, 17pp.

2

Jacoby, N. "Taxation in Laos: Policies for a new country with an underdeveloped economy," *National tax journal,* vol. 14, June 1961, pp. 145-162.

Souryadboy, I. *Analysis of the financial situation in Laos (15 July 1960).* Joint Public Research Service, New York, 1960, 33pp.

LEBANON

1

American University of Beirut, Economic Research Institute. *Business legislation in Lebanon.* Beirut, 1955, 75pp. (duplicated).

Himadeh, R. *The fiscal system of Lebanon.* Khayat's, Beirut, 1961, xii/120pp.

"Tax rates in Lebanon," *Foreign tax law weekly bulletin,* vol. 14, no. 16, 1963, pp. 6-9.

Tayara, A. "Fiscalité libanaise," *Bulletin for international fiscal documentation,* vol. 7, 1953, pp. 143-150.

United States Department of Commerce.

Basic data on the economy of Lebanon. Washington, 1965, 12pp.

2

Gannage, E. "Un Exemple de redistribution des revenus dans un pays insuffisamment développé: Le Liban," *Revue de science financière,* vol. 47, 1955, pp. 718-737.

Higgins, B. *Financing Lebanese development.* International Cooperation Administration, Beirut, 1960, 105pp. (mimeo).

4

Foreign Tax Law Association. *Lebanon income tax service.* St. Petersburg, Fla., loose-leaf, 1963–.

Gannage, E. *La Réforme des impôts directs au Liban et en Syrie.* Recueil Sirey, Beirut, 1947.

Hakim, S. *Lebanese income tax law.* Lebanese and Arab Documentation Office, Beirut, 1962, 28pp.

"Income tax in Lebanon," *Middle East law review,* vol. 1, 1958, pp. 239-271, 318-327.

5

"Tax laws on inheritance, wills, grants and wages," *Foreign tax law weekly bulletin,* vol. 14, no. 5, 1963, pp. 1-3.

8

United States Department of Commerce. *Establishing a business in Lebanon.* Washington, 1962, 8pp.

11

Qureshi, A. *Land systems in the Middle East.* n.p., 1954.

12

United States Department of Commerce. *Law exempting productive investment from income tax in Lebanon.* Washington, 1956, 2pp.

13

United Nations, Economic and Social Council, Fiscal Commission. "Procedures available for the review of initial tax assessments: Reply of the government of Lebanon." Doc. No. E/CN.8/59/Add.25, 5 October 1953, 5pp. (mimeo).

18

Diamond, W. *Foreign tax and trade briefs.* Fallon Law Book Company, New York, loose-leaf, 1951–.
"Lebanon law digest." In: *Martindale-Hubbell law directory,* vol. 4, pp. 2758-2767. Martindale-Hubbell, Inc., Summit, N.J., 1961.

LESOTHO

1

High Commissioner for Basutoland, the Bechuanaland Protectorate and Swaziland (Great Britain). *Report of an economic survey mission.* H. M. Stationery Office, London, 1960, 555pp.

4

"Income tax laws of Basutoland," *Foreign tax law semi-weekly bulletin,* vol. 6, no. 64, 1956, pp. 1-13.
"Lesotho." In: Board of Inland Revenue (Great Britain), *Income taxes outside the United Kingdom 1966,* vol. 5, pp. 65-87. H. M. Stationery Office, London, 1967.

LIBERIA

1

Liberian Government. *The Liberian internal revenue code.* Monrovia, 1958, 12pp.
"Tax and corporation laws of Liberia," *Foreign tax law weekly bulletin,* vol. 14, no. 26, 1963, pp. 1-9.
United States Department of Commerce. *Basic data on the economy of Liberia.* Washington, 1964.

4

Foreign Tax Law Association. *Liberian income tax service.* Deer Park, L.I., N.Y., loose-leaf, 1953–. St. Petersburg, Fla., loose-leaf, 1963–.

7

United States Department of Commerce. *Foreign trade regulations of Liberia.* Washington, 1964.

8

Diamond, W. "Advantages of incorporating in Liberia." In: Prentice-Hall, Inc., *Tax ideas.* Englewood Cliffs, N.J., 1966.

Gibbons, W. *Tax factors in basing international business abroad.* Harvard Law School International Program in Taxation, Cambridge, Mass., 1957, pp. 89-94.
Hager, L. "Taxation of foreign investment in Liberia," *Liberian law journal,* vol. 1, 1965, pp. 151-178.
United States Department of Commerce. *Establishing a business in Liberia.* Washington, 1966, 16pp.

18

Diamond, W. *Foreign tax and trade briefs.* Fallon Law Book Company, New York, loose-leaf, 1951–.

LIBYA

1

Price Waterhouse & Co. *Information guide for doing business in Libya.* New York, 1961, 11pp.
United Nations, Technical Assistance Administration. "Problems and recommendations on taxation in Libya." Doc. No. TAA/LIB/4 (restricted), 14 February 1957.
United States Department of Commerce. *Basic data on the economy of Libya.* Washington, 1961, 16pp.

2

United Nations, Department of Economic Affairs, Fiscal Division. "Report on public finance in Libya, 1944-51." (restricted).

8

United States Department of Commerce. *Establishing a business in Libya.* Washington, 1963, 11pp.

11

Qureshi, A. *Land systems in the Middle East.* n.p., 1954.

12

United States Department of Commerce. *Investment law of Libya.* Washington, 1958, 3pp.

18

Diamond, W. *Foreign tax and trade briefs.* Fallon Law Book Company, New York, loose-leaf, 1951–.

MALAGASY REPUBLIC

1

United States Department of Commerce. *Basic data on the economy of the Malagasy Republic.* Washington, 1962, 18pp.

12

United States Department of Commerce. *Investment law of the Malagasy Republic.* Washington, 1963, 5pp.

MALAWI

1

"Federation of Rhodesia and Nyasaland," *Coopers and Lybrand international tax summaries,* vol. 3, March 1960, pp. 1-15.

Garmany, J. "Revenue allocation in a federal state: The experience of Rhodesia and Nyasaland," *South African journal of economics,* March 1962, pp. 50-60.

Report of the Advisory commission on the review of the constitution of Rhodesia and Nyasaland. H. M. Stationery Office, London, Cmnd. 1148, 1960, chapter 9.

United States Department of Commerce. *Basic data on the economy of the Federation of Rhodesia and Nyasaland.* Washington, 1962, 12pp.

United States Department of Commerce. *Investment in Federation of Rhodesia and Nyasaland.* Washington, 1956, pp. 107-109.

2

Hazlewood, A., and Henderson, P. *Nyasaland: The economics of federation.* Blackwell, Oxford, 1961.

3

Due, J. *Taxation and economic development in Tropical Africa.* The MIT Press, Cambridge, Mass., 1963, 172pp.

4

"Malawi." In: Board of Inland Revenue (Great Britain), *Income taxes outside the United Kingdom 1966,* vol. 5, pp. 107-137. H. M. Stationery Office, London, 1967.

"Methods of direct taxation in British Tropical Africa," *Journal of African administration,* vol. 2, October 1950, pp. 3-12; vol. 3, January 1951, pp. 30-41; vol. 3, October 1951, pp. 77-87.

Notes on income tax and exchange control in the Federation of Rhodesia and Nyasaland. H. M. Stationery Office, London, 1961, 15pp.

9

"Urban problems in East and Central Africa," *Journal of African administration,* vol. 10, October 1958, pp. 215-218.

MALAYSIA

1

Japan Tax Association. *Asian taxation 1964.* Tokyo, 1964, 139pp. Supplement, 1965, 17pp.

Price Waterhouse & Co. *Information guide for doing business in the Federation of Malaya and the State of Singapore.* New York, 1962, 23pp.

"Tax changes," *Foreign tax law weekly bulletin,* vol. 16, no. 28, 1965, pp. 1-6.

"Tax proposals," *Foreign tax law weekly bulletin,* vol. 16, no. 27, 1965, pp. 6-18.

United States Department of Commerce. *Basic data on the economy of Malaysia.* Washington, 1966, 32pp.

2

International Bank for Reconstruction and Development. *The economic development of Malaya.* The Johns Hopkins Press, Baltimore, 1955, chapters 8, 9.

3

Yoingco, A., and Trinidad, R. *Fiscal systems and practices in Asian countries.* Frederick A. Praeger, New York, 1967.

4

Foreign Tax Law Association. *Malaysia income tax service.* St. Petersburg, Fla., loose-leaf, 1964–.

Government of the Federation of Malaya. *Income tax ordinance, 1947 and pioneer industries (relief from income tax) ordinance, 1958 (as amended to February 1, 1961).* Kuala Lumpur, 1961, 229pp.

"Malaysia, Federation of." In: Board of Inland Revenue (Great Britain), *Income taxes outside the United Kingdom 1966,* vol. 5, pp. 139-141. H. M. Stationery Office, London, 1967.

Pepper, H. "Corporate taxation in Malaysia," *Bulletin for international fiscal documentation,* vol. 19, 1965, pp. 193-201.

Pepper, H. *Personal income tax in the*

Federation of Malaya. Government Printer, Kuala Lumpur, 1963, 39pp.

"Sabah." In: Board of Inland Revenue (Great Britain), *Income taxes outside the United Kingdom 1966,* vol. 6, pp. 313-341. H. M. Stationery Office, London, 1967.

Taylor, M. "Income taxation in the Federation of Malaya," *National tax journal,* vol. 14, June 1961, pp. 198-205.

"West Malaysia." In: Board of Inland Revenue (Great Britain), *Income taxes outside the United Kingdom 1966,* vol. 8, pp. 253-281. H. M. Stationery Office, London, 1967.

6

Yah, L. "The Malayan rubber replanting taxes," *Malayan economic review,* vol. 6, October 1961.

7

Edwards, C. "The future role of import and excise duty taxation in the states of Malaya and Singapore," *Malayan economic review,* vol. 11, April 1966, pp. 29-41. Part reprinted in: R. Bird and O. Oldman (eds.), *Readings on taxation in developing countries,* pp. 381-395. The Johns Hopkins Press, Baltimore, revised edition, 1967.

Edwards, C. "The structure of import and excise duty taxation in the states of Malaya and Singapore," *Malayan economic review,* vol. 10, October 1965, pp. 83-101.

Stern, R. "The export tax on Malayan rubber—Problems and policy," *National tax journal,* vol. 16, March 1963, pp. 81-88.

United States Department of Commerce. *Foreign trade regulations of Malaysia.* Washington, 1967, 12pp.

Yah, L. "Export taxes on rubber in Malaya—A survey of post-war development," *Malayan economic review,* vol. 5, October 1960.

8

United States Department of Commerce. *Establishing a business in Malyasia.* Washington, 1964.

9

Hong, H. "The new system of revenue allocation to states and settlements in the Federation of Malaya," *Malayan economic review,* vol. 11, April 1957.

12

"Tax-free period for pioneer industries in Malaya," *Asian review* (n.s.), vol. 55, January 1959, pp. 65-69.

17

Pepper, H. "Tax harmonisation in a federation: The 1965 budget in Malaysia," *Bulletin for international fiscal documentation,* vol. 19, 1965, pp. 228-232.

18

Diamond, W. *Foreign tax and trade briefs.* Fallon Law Book Company, New York, loose-leaf, 1951–.

MALTA

1

United States Department of Commerce. *Basic data on the economy of Malta.* Washington, 1964, 8pp.

United States Department of State. *Malta's industrial development plan: Opportunities for U.S. enterprises.* Valetta.

2

Busuttil, S. *Fiscal policy in Malta.* Malta Chamber of Commerce, Valetta, 1965, xii/96pp.

4

Department of Inland Revenue. *Brief notes on the income-tax act, 1948.* Valetta, 1963, 9pp.

"Malta." In: Board of Inland Revenue (Great Britain), *Income taxes outside the United Kingdom 1966,* vol. 5, pp. 143-166. H. M. Stationery Office, London, 1967.

MARTINIQUE

4

Cotteret, J. "Fiscalité directe et sous-développement: L'Exemple du département d'outre-mer de la Martinique," *Revue de science financière,* vol. 54, 1962, pp. 461-483.

MAURITANIA

1

United States Department of Commerce. *Basic data on the economy of the Is-*

lamic Republic of Mauritania. Washington, 1963, 14pp.

3

Mémento fiscal et social 1964, numéro spécial no. 14, 25 June 1964. A comparative survey of taxes in the West African Union and Guinea.

7

United States Department of Commerce. *Preparing shipments to Mauritania.* Washington, 1962, 8pp.

12

United States Department of Commerce. *Investment law in the Islamic Republic of Mauritania.* Washington, 1962, 4pp.

MAURITIUS

2

Meade, J. *The economic and social structure of Mauritius.* Methuen & Co., London, 1961.

4

"Mauritius." In: Board of Inland Revenue (Great Britain), *Income taxes outside the United Kingdom 1966,* vol. 5, pp. 167-193. H. M. Stationery Office, London, 1967.

MEXICO

1

Albareda, J. "Aspecto fiscal de las actividades comerciales comunes," *Revista fiscal y financiera,* vol. 15, August 1955, pp. 17-28.
Albareda, J. "Cambio de domicilio fiscal," *Revista fiscal y financiera,* vol. 17, July 1957, pp. 11-17.
Albareda, J. "Conozca sus nuevas obligaciones fiscales," *Revista fiscal y financiera,* vol. 14, July 1954, pp. 14-40.
Arthur Andersen & Co. *Tax and trade guide: Mexico.* Chicago, 1967.
Beteta, R. "La reforma fiscal de 1946," *Revista fiscal y financiera,* vol. 8, February 1957, pp. 9-13.
Bustamante, E. "Las finanzas públicas de México a mediados del siglo XIX— Bases que para organizar las adoptó el Congreso extraordinario constituyente de 1856," *Revista de la Escuela de con-tabilidad, economía y administración,* vol. 9, January 1957, pp. 1-25.
Bustamante, E. "La insuficiencia de nuestro régimen tributario y las posibilidades de un régimen patrimonial complementario," *Revista de la Escuela de contabilidad, economía y administración,* vol. 10, April 1958, pp. 117-137.
Calderón Acton, V. *Análisis de la ley de ingresos de la federación.* México, 1963, 119pp.
Canadian Tax Foundation. *Taxes abroad: Mexico.* Toronto, 1958.
Cervantes Delgado, A. "La política fiscal y las reformas impositivas de 1962," *Investigación económica,* vol. 22, no. 85, 1962, pp. 55-80. Also in: *El trimestre económico,* vol. 29, July-September 1962, pp. 391-409.
Chandler, H. "Preliminary survey of Mexican revenue problem—With suggestions for reconstruction of system— 1918," *Revista de la Escuela de estudios contables,* vol. 2, July 1950, pp. 225-242; vol. 2, October 1950, pp. 287-311 (Spanish version of original 1918 report).
Chaves Flores, O. "Antecedentes históricos de los impuestos: Evolución del régimen fiscal en México," *Finanzas y contabilidad.* Reprinted in: *Revista fiscal y financiera,* vol. 13, October 1953, pp. 25-41.
Chaves Flores, O. "Evolución del régimen fiscal en México," *América* (Havana), vol. 44, August 1954, pp. 55-62.
"Código fiscal de la federación," *Investigación fiscal,* no. 13, January 1967, pp. 57-182.
Creel Luján, L. "Notes on Mexican fiscal literature," *Bulletin for international fiscal documentation,* vol. 4, 1950, pp. 91-104. In Spanish in: *Revista de la Escuela de estudios contables,* vol. 2, July 1950, pp. 189-200.
Dalton, J. "Mexican taxes," *Journal of the Bar association of the state of Kansas,* vol. 16, 1948, pp. 302-314.
"Exposición de motivos de la iniciativa de la ley orgánica del tribunal fiscal de la federación," *Investigación fiscal,* no. 15, March 1967, pp. 65-69.
"Exposición de motivos de la iniciativa de la ley que reforma y adiciona diversas leyes que rigen impuestos federales," *Investigación fiscal,* no. 15, March 1967, pp. 73-79.

"Exposición de motivos de la iniciativa del código fiscal de la federación," *Investigación fiscal,* no. 15, March 1967, pp. 49-62.

Flores Zavala, E. "La actividad tributaria en el régimen del Presidente Miguel Alemán," *Revista fiscal y financiera,* vol. 6, May 1950, pp. 28-34.

Flores Zavala, E. *Elementos de finanzas públicas mexicanas.* Porrúa, México, 6th edition, 1963, 407pp.

Flores Zavala, E. "Los impuestos a la industria de México," *Revista fiscal y financiera,* vol. 16, April 1957, pp. 35-131.

Flores Zavala, E. "La nueva legislación fiscal," *Revista de la Escuela de contabilidad, economía y administración,* vol. 6, October 1954, pp. 347-360.

Flores Zavala, E. "La política tributaria en los 6 ultimos años," *Revista fiscal y financiera,* vol. 11, October 1952, pp. 27-40.

Frangi, A. "Las tendencias actuales en las reformas presupuestarias," *Justicia* (México), vol. 25, no. 422, 1965, pp. 37-64.

García Velasco, G. *Los organismos descentralizados por función y su clasificación dentro del régimen fiscal mexicano.* Thesis, Universidad Nacional Autónoma de México, México, 1964, 116pp.

Gómez Reyes, R., and Monterrey, C. "La generalización del impuesto," *Revista fiscal y financiera,* vol. 7, October 1950, pp. 36-40.

Gómez Tagle, R. "El deber de pagar los impuestos," *Revista fiscal y financiera,* vol. 7, November 1950, p. 72.

Harvard Law School International Program in Taxation. *World Tax Series: Taxation in Mexico.* Prepared by H. Gumpel and H. Margáin, Little, Brown and Co., Boston, 1957, 428pp.

Hurtado Figueroa, J. *El régimen fiscal de los organismos descentralizados y empresas de participación estatal.* Thesis, Universidad Nacional Autónoma de México, México, 1964, 119pp.

"Ley de ingresos de la federación para el ejercicio fiscal de 1967," *Investigación fiscal,* no. 14, February 1967, pp. 71-88.

"Ley que reforma y adiciona diversas leyes que rigen impuestos federales y establece vigencia propia para disposiciones consignadas en anteriores leyes de la federación," *Investigación fiscal,* no. 13, January 1967, pp. 193-216.

Lomelí Cerezo, M. *El poder sancionador de la administración pública en materia fiscal.* Compañia Editorial Continental, México, 1961, 32pp.

Margáin, H. "La obligación ciudadana de pagar impuestos," *Revista fiscal y financiera,* vol. 15, June 1955, pp. 9-14.

Martínez de Escobar, R. *How to do business in Mexico.* Exposition Press, New York, 1960, 196pp.

"Mexican tax system reviewed," *Foreign tax law weekly bulletin,* vol. 8, no. 49, 1958, pp. 1-4.

"Mexico's tax reforms: An analysis of what they mean," *Mexican-American review,* vol. 30, January 1962, pp. 18-19.

Mireles, M. "Requisito fiscal que no llena su cometido," *Revista fiscal y financiera,* vol. 16, January 1956, pp. 43-45.

Moore, O. *Evaluación de las instituciones financieras en México.* Centro de Estudios Latino-Americanos, México, 1963, 413pp.

Morales Cuevas, S. "El nuevo sistema de tributación," *Carta semanal* (México), vol. 11, 3 July 1948, pp. 16-17.

Navarrete, A., Jr. "México: Sus finanzas públicas," *Revista de economía* (México), vol. 18, October 1955, pp. 245-247.

"New finance measures accelerate economic expansion in Mexico," *Foreign commerce weekly,* vol. 63, no. 26, 1960, p. 14.

Pan American Union. *A statement of the laws of Mexico in matters affecting business.* Washington, 3d edition, 1964, pp. 80-103.

Pani, A. *El problema supremo de México: Ensayo de crítica constructiva de la política financiera.* Inversiones A.R.P.A., México, 2d edition, 1955, 220pp.

Price Waterhouse & Co. *Information guide for doing business in Mexico.* New York, 1966, 34pp. Supplement, 1967, 9pp.

"La reforma fiscal," *Comercio exterior,* December 1961, pp. 706-710.

Remolina Roqueñí, M. de los. *Los ingresos y egresos de la federación.* Thesis, Universidad Nacional Autónoma de México, México, 1964, 138pp.

"Review of taxation in Mexico," *Foreign tax law weekly bulletin,* vol. 6, no. 71, 1956, pp. 1-9.

Río Rodríguez, C. del. "Presentación de la ley de 1815, que establece una contribución general extraordinaria," *Revista del tribunal fiscal de la federación* (número extraordinario), 1965, pp. 175-184.

Santillán López, R., and Rosas Figueroa, A. *Teoría general de las finanzas públicas y el caso de México.* Universidad Nacional Autónoma de México, México, 1962, 304pp.

Servín, A. "¿Cuánto paga usted en impuestos?" *Revista fiscal y financiera,* vol. 15, December 1954, pp. 29-37.

Somers, H. "Problemas fiscales de paises en desarrollo." In: *XXVII convención nacional de centros patronales.* México, 1964.

Torres Gaitán, R. "La política financiera de la revolución," *Revista de administración pública,* vol. 1, January-March 1956, pp. 17-35.

United States Department of Commerce. *Basic data on the economy of Mexico.* Washington, 1967, 32pp.

United States Department of Commerce. *Investment in Mexico.* Washington, 1955, chapter 11, appendixes A, C.

United States Department of State. *Background notes: Mexico.* Washington, 1965, 8pp.

Urrutia Millán, R. *Algunos aspectos fiscales y comerciales de México.* Ed. Libros S.E.L.A., México, 1966, 161pp.

Valdés Montoya, A. "Algunos aspectos del problema financiero del gobierno federal," *Investigación económica,* vol. 20, no. 78, 1960, pp. 251-261.

Yáñez Ruiz, M. *El problema fiscal en las distintas estapas de nuestra organización política.* Secretaría de Hacienda y Crédito Público, México, 6 volumes, 1958, 1959, 1961, 2984pp.

2

Aubey, R. *Mexico: A study of the financial relationship between the government and the private sector of the economy.* Ph.D. thesis, U.C.L.A., Los Angeles, Calif., 1965.

Bustamante, E. "La política fiscal y los niveles de vida," *Investigación económica,* vol. 13, no. 3, 1953, pp. 379-392.

Delgado, A. "La política fiscal y las reformas impositivas de 1962," *El trimestre económico,* vol. 29, July-September 1962.

Froomkin, J. "Some problems of tax policy in Latin America," *National tax journal,* vol. 10, December 1957, pp. 370-379.

International Bank for Reconstruction and Development. *The economic development of Mexico.* The Johns Hopkins Press, Baltimore, 1953, chapter 9.

Kaldor, N. *Report on Mexican tax reform.* México, 1960.

Margáin, H. "Derecho fiscal y desarrollo económico en México: Estudios histórico y actual," *Justicia* (México), vol. 21, no. 372, 1961, pp. 25-39.

Margáin, H. *Importancia del derecho fiscal en el desarrollo económico de México.* México, 1960, 31pp.

Margáin, H. "La industrialización frente al derecho fiscal mexicano," *Revista fiscal y financiera,* vol. 15, April 1955, pp. 47-68.

Mosk, S. "Financing industrial development in Mexico," *Inter-American economic affairs,* vol. 1, no. 1, 1947, p. 5.

Navarrete, A., Jr. "La administración financiera y el desarrollo económico de México," *Revista de economía* (México), vol. 27, April 1964, pp. 107-118.

Navarrete, I. de. *La distribución del ingreso y el desarrollo económico de México.* Instituto Mexicano de Investigaciones Económicas, México, 1960, 99pp.

Navarrete, I. de. "La política fiscal y la distribución del ingreso," *Investigación económica,* vol. 17, no. 1, 1957, pp. 43-62.

Navarrete, I. de. "El proceso de desarrollo económico y la política fiscal," *Investigación económica,* vol. 15, no. 2, 1955, pp. 229-247.

Navarrete, I. de. "The tax structure and the economic development of Mexico," *Public finance,* vol. 19, 1964, pp. 158-179.

Ortiz Mena, R. "Las nuevas funciones de las finanzas públicas," *El trimestre económico,* vol. 14, April-June 1947, pp. 34-67.

Pallares, M. "La política fiscal en la industria de transformación," *Revista fiscal y financiera,* vol. 8, February 1951, pp. 21-27.

Pérez de Ayala, J. "Nuevo sentido de una cuestión clásica: Impuestos directos, impuestos indirectos y pérdida de bienestar económico," *Moneda y crédito,* vol. 70, September 1959, pp. 49-67.

Pola Cruz, E. *El presupuesto en el estado moderno.* Thesis, Universidad Nacional Autónoma de México, México, 1965, 119pp.

Robles Quintero, S. "El financiamiento del desarrollo económico de México," *Economía política,* vol. 3, no. 2, 1966, pp. 167-178.

Robles Quintero, S. "La política fiscal en México," *Economía política,* vol. 2, no. 4, 1965.

Salera, V. "Financing economic development in Mexico," *Inter-American economic affairs,* vol. 1, no. 2, 1947, p. 97.

Salinas Lozano, R. "Política fiscal y desarrollo económico," *Investigación económica,* vol. 12, no. 2, 1952, pp. 152-166.

Soto Ponce, J. "El fisco mexicano: Su influencia en la economía," *Revista fiscal y financiera,* vol. 9, July 1951, pp. 26-28.

Zamora Bátiz, J. "La política fiscal en México y paises desarrollados," *Revista de economía* (México), vol. 23, February 1960, pp. 57-64.

3

"Análisis comparativo de la tributación en la Argentina, el Brasil, Chile y México." In: United Nations, *Las inversiones privadas extranjeras en la zona latinoamericana de libre comercio,* pp. 31-33. Sales No. 1960.II.G.5, México, 1960.

Prieto López, E. "Sistemas impositivos en México y los Estados Unidos," *Revista fiscal y financiera,* vol. 11, July 1952, pp. 24-29.

4

"Acuerdo de la Dirección general del impuesto sobre la renta," *Investigación fiscal,* no. 15, March 1967, pp. 83-85.

Albareda, J. *Conozca sus nuevas obligaciones fiscales: Impuesto sobre la renta.* Ed. de la Revista Fiscal y Financiera, México, 1955, xxiv/613pp.

Albareda, J. "Las declaraciones del impuesto sobre la renta," *Revista fiscal y financiera,* vol. 18, March 1958, pp. 5-9.

Albareda, J. "Depreciación," *Revista fiscal y financiera,* vol. 3, August 1948, pp. 13-17.

Albareda, J. "La ley del impuesto sobre la renta: Principales aspectos de su posible transformación," *Revista fiscal y financiera,* vol. 13, November 1953, pp. 10-23.

Albareda, J. "Origen del impuesto sobre la renta," *Revista fiscal y financiera,* vol. 13, July 1953, pp. 20-24; vol. 13, October 1953, pp. 41-46.

Albareda, J. "Redacción del impuesto sobre utilidades excedentes," *Revista fiscal y financiera,* vol. 16, May 1956, pp. 7-10.

Albareda, J. "Las reformas al impuesto sobre la renta: Notas complementarias," *Revista fiscal y financiera,* vol. 13, November 1953, pp. 23-26.

Albareda, J. "Revaluación y reposición de activo fijo," *Revista fiscal y financiera,* vol. 15, May 1955, pp. 9-16.

American Chamber of Commerce in Mexixo. *Income tax law and regulations.* México, irregular.

Andrade Muñoz, C. "Reformas a la ley del impuesto sobre la renta," *Revista fiscal y financiera,* vol. 14, May 1954, pp. 18-35.

Ayarzagoitia, O. "Tópicos en relación con la nueva ley del impuesto sobre la renta," *Revista fiscal y financiera,* vol. 15, September 1954, pp. 47-51.

Belaunzarán, C. "Depreciación y amortización agotamiento: Algunas explicaciones sobre los conceptos anteriores," *Revista de la Escuela de estudios contables,* vol. 1, July 1949, pp. 219-229.

Burnham, J. "Mining taxes in Mexico," *Mineral trade notes,* vol. 26, no. 4, supp., 1948.

Cárdenas, R. "El impuesto sobre la renta en la cédula II," *Revista de la Escuela de estudios contables,* vol. 2, April 1950, pp. 87-102.

Cárdenas, R. "Ley del impuesto sobre la renta: Comentarios en relación con el proyecto de reformas," *Revista fiscal y financiera,* vol. 13, December 1953, pp. 19-32.

Casas, R. "Survey of the Mexican general income tax," *Bulletin for international fiscal documentation,* vol. 18, 1964, pp. 278-289.

Castellanos Coutiño, H. "La cédula V del impuesto sobre la renta," *Revista de la Facultad de derecho de México,* vol. 13, 1963, pp. 627-652.

Confederación Patronal de la República Mexicana, Departamento Fiscal. *Impuesto sobre la renta: Manual para la aplicación de la ley.* México, 2d revised edition, 1966, 333pp.

Creel Luján, L. "War changes in Mexican income tax," *Bulletin for international fiscal documentation,* vol. 1, 1946-1947, pp. 259-263.

"Criterio no. 36 de la Dirección general del impuesto sobre la renta," *Investigación fiscal,* no. 13, January 1967, pp. 219-220.

Delgado Navarro, J. "La redistribución del ingreso y el nuevo impuesto sobre la renta," *Revista de economía* (México), vol. 16, December 1953, pp. 376-379.

"Exposición de motivos de la iniciativa de reformas y adiciones a la ley del impuesto sobre la renta, 1962," *El foro, Organo de la Barra mexicana, Colegio de abogados,* vol. 103, October-December 1962.

Flores Zavala, E. "Notas acerca del impuesto sobre la renta," *El universal* (Caracas). Reprinted in: *Revista fiscal y financiera,* vol. 13, October 1953, pp. 21-25.

Foreign Tax Law Association. *Mexican income tax reporter service.* Deer Park, L.I., N.Y., loose-leaf, 1960–.

Foreign Tax Law Association. *Mexican income tax service.* Centerport, L.I., N.Y., 3 volumes, loose-leaf, 1953–1955.

Gallegos, M. "Causantes permanentes del impuesto sobre la renta cédula V," *Revista fiscal y financiera,* vol. 5, August 1949, pp. 9-11.

García Villalobos y Gálvez, M. *El impuesto sobre la renta en las cédulas I, II, y III: Su mecanismo.* Thesis, Universidad Nacional Autónoma de México, México, 1961, 128pp.

Gómez Arriola, S. "Los anticipos a cuenta del impuesto sobre la renta en cédula uno," *Revista fiscal y financiera,* vol. 7, October 1950, pp. 26-28.

Gutiérrez Kirchner, A. *Hacia la reforma integral del impuesto sobre la renta en México.* Thesis, Universidad Nacional Autónoma de México, México, 1965, 138pp.

Guzmán Lozano, E. "Apuntes sobre los impuestos a las rentas del trabajo," *Revista de la Escuela de estudios contables,* vol. 1, January 1949, pp. 43-72.

Guzmán Lozano, E. "Notas para el estudio del impuesto sobre dividendos," *Re-*

vista de la Escuela de estudios contables, vol. 1, July 1949, pp. 163-218.

Hoyo, R. *Conferencia sustentada sobre el tema "Proyecciones generales en la elaboración y aplicación de la nueva ley del impuesto sobre la renta."* Cámara Nacional de la Industria de Transformación, México, 1965, 104pp.

Humphrey Salinas, A. *Administración del impuesto sobre la renta cuando tiende a ser personal.* Thesis, Universidad Nacional Autónoma de México, México, 1964, 94pp.

"Income tax law amended," *Foreign tax law semi-weekly bulletin,* vol. 6, no. 62, 1956, pp. 8-10.

"Impuesto sobre la renta: Revaluación de los activos," *Revista fiscal y financiera,* vol. 16, May 1957, pp. 47-55.

"Impuesto sobre la renta: Síntesis de los principales aspectos que contiene el proyecto de reformas," *Revista fiscal y financiera,* vol. 13, November 1953, pp. 55-59.

"Income taxes in Mexico," *Foreign tax law weekly bulletin,* vol. 7, no. 2, 1956, pp. 7-11.

Irezábal, R. de. "El impuesto sobre la renta de los agentes de seguros," *Revista fiscal y financiera,* vol. 7, October 1950, pp. 23-25.

Isoard, C. "Apuntes sobre las reformas a la ley del impuesto sobre la renta y su reglamento," *Revista de la Escuela de contabilidad, economía y administración,* vol. 8, July 1956, pp. 211-229.

"Jurisprudencia sobre el impuesto del 1% para la enseñanza," *El foro, Organo de la Barra mexicana, Colegio de abogados,* vol. 137, April-June 1963.

Ley del impuesto sobre la renta. Editorial Porrúa, México, 3d edition, 1964, 381pp.

López Munguía, A. "El desarrollo del impuesto sobre la renta en México, antes de su reforma en 1961," *Investigación económica,* vol. 22, no. 85, 1962, pp. 35-54.

Lumpkin, J., and Altatriste, R. "Income and gross receipts taxes in Mexico," *Arthur Andersen chronicle,* vol. 8, April 1948, pp. 149-165.

Margáin, H. "Reformas al impuesto sobre la renta," *Revista fiscal y financiera,* vol. 16, February 1956, pp. 5-17.

Margáin, H. "La reposición de los activos

fijos," *Revista fiscal y financiera,* vol. 14, July 1954, pp. 11-13.

"Mexican income tax law." In: Foreign Tax Law Association, *Mexican income tax reporter service,* pp. 3-205. Deer Park, L.I., N.Y., loose-leaf, 1960–.

"Mexican income tax law revised," *Foreign commerce weekly,* vol. 63, no. 14, 1960, p. 11.

"Mexico changes income tax laws," *Foreign commerce weekly,* vol. 55, no. 11, 1956.

"Mexico—Income tax amended," *Foreign tax law weekly bulletin,* vol. 6, no. 62, 1956, pp. 8-10.

Mireles, M. "El impuesto sobre dividendos," *Revista fiscal y financiera,* vol. 8, January 1951, pp. 39-40.

Mireles, M. "Recibos por honorarios de profesionistas," *Revista fiscal y financiera,* vol. 14, May 1954, pp. 45-47.

Montes de Oca, L. "Algunas consecuencias económicas del impuesto sobre utilidades excedentes," *Revista fiscal y financiera,* vol. 4, June 1949, pp. 18-30.

Naranjo y Elizondo, N. "Estudio analítico sobre la repartición de utilidades," *Revista mexicana del trabajo,* vol. 10, no. 1-2, 1963, pp. 29-60.

Navarrete, I. de. "El impuesto a las ganancias de capital en la teoría y en la práctica fiscal," *El trimestre económico,* vol. 30, April-June 1963, pp. 201-241.

Navarro, G. "El concepto de renta gravable," *Investigación económica,* vol. 16, no. 2, 1956, pp. 227-249.

Osorio Nieto, A. *El impuesto sobre la renta en derecho comparado.* Thesis, Universidad Nacional Autónoma de México, México, 1963, 122pp.

Palacios Dorantes, J. *Tasa complementaria de ingresos acumulados en el impuesto sobre la renta mexicano.* Thesis, Universidad Nacional Autónoma de México, México, 1964, 212pp.

Peat, Marwick, Mitchell & Co. *Memorandum on Mexican income tax.* 1965, 24pp.

Pérez Morales, E. *El régimen fiscal de la participación de los trabajadores en las utilidades de las empresas.* Thesis, Universidad Nacional Autónoma de México, México, 1965, 100pp.

Plancarte, F. "El impuesto sobre la renta y sus ultimas reformas," *Revista de la Escuela de contabilidad, economía y ad-*

ministración, vol. 8, July 1956, pp. 231-240.

"Regulations of the income tax law." In: Foreign Tax Law Association, *Mexican income tax reporter service,* pp. 901-977. Deer Park, L.I., N.Y., loose-leaf, 1960–.

Riofri, E. "La doble imposición de las sociedades por acciones y de las accionistas," *Revista fiscal y financiera,* vol. 15, July 1955, pp. 17-46.

Robles Glenn, J. *Apuntes de derecho fiscal y nueva ley del impuesto sobre la renta.* Segundo Curso de Derecho Administrativo, Facultad de Derecho, Universidad Nacional Autónoma de México, México, 1965, 366pp.

Rodríguez de la Mora, F. "¿Es conveniente el impuesto sobre la renta global?" *Revista fiscal y financiera,* vol. 13, July 1953, pp. 42-46.

Rosado Muñoz, C. "Aspectos fiscales de los planes de prestaciones para el personal," *Investigación fiscal,* no. 13, January 1967, pp. 47-54.

Rosado Muñoz, C. "Beneficios adicionales de invalidez, viudez y orfandad en los planes privados de pensiones," *Investigación fiscal,* no. 15, March 1967, pp. 39-43.

Rosado Muñoz, C. "El fisco y el financiamiento de los planes privados de pensiones," *Investigación fiscal,* no. 14, February 1967, pp. 55-65.

Ruiz Olvera, C. *La participación de utilidades y el derecho de objeción de los trabajadores a la declaración de impuestos relativa.* Thesis, Universidad Nacional Autónoma de México, México, 1963, 185pp.

Sahagún Castro, J. *La familia en un impuesto sobre la renta personal o global.* Thesis, México, 1963, 135pp.

Santos Cervantes, E. "La inconstitucionalidad del impuesto de la renta sobre las acciones preferentes," *Revista de la Escuela de contabilidad, economía y administración,* vol. 7, July 1955, pp. 239-250. Reprinted in: *Revista fiscal y financiera,* vol. 15, September 1955, pp. 71-87.

Santos Trejo, J. *La base gravable del impuesto sobre la renta.* Thesis, Universidad Nacional Autónoma de México, México, 1963, 111pp.

Secretaría de Hacienda y Crédito Público, Dirección General del Impuesto sobre la

Renta. *Ley del impuesto sobre la renta y su reglamento*. México, 1954, 1007pp.

Servín, A. "Rentas derivadas de bienes muebles y nuestro impuesto sobre la renta," *Revista fiscal y financiera*, vol. 16, June 1956, pp. 13-16.

Traducciones. *Income tax law 1954 with 1960 amd.* (translation). México (processed).

Urquidi, V. "El impuesto sobre la renta en el desarrollo económico de México," *Revista de la Escuela de contabilidad, economía y administración*, vol. 8, July 1956, pp. 199-210. Also in: *El trimestre económico*, vol. 23, October-December 1956, p. 424.

Valdés Montoya, A. "Los ingresos federales y el impuesto sobre la renta con relación al producto nacional bruto, durante 1953-1958," *Revista de economía* (México), vol. 21, October 1958, pp. 271-283.

5

Lozano Noriega, F. "La reforma fiscal mexicana y la derogación de impuestos sobre herencias, legados y donaciones," *Revista de derecho financiero y de hacienda pública* (Madrid), vol. 15, 1965, pp. 91-100. Also in: *Revista internacional de notariado*, vol. 16, no. 62, 1964, pp. 163-172; *Revista notarial* (La Plata), no. 755, 1964, pp. 1113-1120.

6

Alatriste, S. "La administración del impuesto sobre ingresos mercantiles en el distrito federal," *Revista de la Escuela de contabilidad, economía y administración*, vol. 6, October 1954, pp. 335-346.

Albareda, J. "Comentarios en torno al impuesto sobre ingresos mercantiles," *Revista fiscal y financiera*, vol. 15, April 1955, pp. 69-72.

Albareda, J. *Conozca sus nuevas obligaciones fiscales—Impuesto sobre ingresos mercantiles*. Ediciones Universales, México.

Briseño Hermosillo, R. *Impuestos sobre ventas: El impuesto federal sobre ingresos mercantiles*. Thesis, Universidad Nacional Autónoma de México, México, 1963, 243pp.

Cetina Albertos, H. "Ingresos mercantiles: El impuesto y los causantes," *Revista fiscal y financiera*, vol. 8, January 1951, pp. 20-21.

Colomo Castro, F. "La inconstitucionalidad del impuesto local al comercio de derivados del petróleo," *Lecturas jurídicas* (Chihuahua), no. 23, 1965, pp. 65-92.

Commerce Clearing House, Inc. *Mexican commercial receipts tax law, as of July 1, 1966*. Chicago, 1966, 64pp.

Domínguez Pastrana, J. *Impuestos sobre la producción*. Thesis, Universidad Nacional Autónoma de México, México, 1963, 106pp.

Flores Meza, J. "Mexico income tax law codified," *Foreign tax law semi-weekly bulletin*, vol. 4, no. 65, 1954, pp. 1-6.

García Uribe, A. "Bebidas alcohólicas: Las nuevas tarifas del impuesto sobre expendios," *Revista fiscal y financiera*, vol. 8, March 1951, pp. 22-23.

García Villalobos, R. "El impuesto sobre ingresos mercantiles," *Revista fiscal y financiera*, vol. 15, October 1955, pp. 9-14.

"Impuesto a la minería," *Revista fiscal y financiera*, vol. 17, June 1957, pp. 27-47.

"Impuestos a la minería," *Revista fiscal y financiera*, vol. 4, January 1949, pp. 53-63.

Leal Duk, L. "Estudio sobre el impuesto a las ventas en México," *Investigación fiscal*, no. 19, July 1967, pp. 97-110.

"Ley del impuesto federal sobre ingresos mercantiles," *Revista fiscal y financiera*, vol. 8, January 1951, pp. 22-38.

Mercantile revenue tax law—Ley fiscal del impuesto sobre ingresos mercantiles. Traducciones, México, loose-leaf, 1954 (English and Spanish).

Morineau, O., and Barrera Graf, J. "Reforma a la fracción XXV del artículo 18 de la ley del impuesto sobre ingresos mercantiles," *El foro, Organo de la Barra mexicana, Colegio de abogados*, vol. 4, April-June 1961, p. 19.

Peña S., S. "Como se calculan los impuestos específicos a la minería en México y notas sobre los ordenamientos legales en que se basan," *Revista minera y petrolera* (México), vol. 18, August 1952, pp. 2-4; vol. 18, October-November 1952, pp. 14-15.

"Relativo al impuesto por servicios telefónicos," *Boletín oficial de la Secretaría*

de hacienda y crédito público, vol. 11, 1965, pp. 361-370.
Vargas, L. "El impuesto sobre primas de seguros," *Revista fiscal y financiera,* vol. 7, October 1950, pp. 32-33.

7

Aguirre Prieto, J. *Los puertos libres mexicanos.* Thesis, Universidad Nacional Autónoma de México, México, 1963, 104pp.
Chayet Volchansky, I. *El régimen aduanal Mexico-Norteamericano.* Thesis, Universidad Nacional Autónoma de México, México, 1961, 181pp.
Díaz González, D. "El contrabando, perjuicios que ocasiona en las economías nacionales." In: *III congreso interamericano del ministerio publico: Ponencias,* pp. 177-230. Procuraduria General de la República, México, 1963.
Durán Rojas, E. *La regla XIV de la tarifa del impuesto general de importación.* Thesis, Universidad Nacional Autónoma de México, México, 1965, 104pp.
"Government encouragement of exports," *Comercio exterior de México,* vol. 7, October 1961, p. 8.
"Impuestos a la exportación: Revisión de la tarifa," *Revista fiscal y financiera,* vol. 13, November 1953, pp. 31-35.
Izquierdo, R. "Protectionism in Mexico." In: R. Vernon (ed.), *Public policy and private enterprise in Mexico,* pp. 241-292. Harvard University Press, Cambridge, Mass., 1964.
Ocegueda Gallardo, R. *Régimen fiscal de los puertos: Zonas y perímetros libres.* Thesis, Universidad Nacional Autónoma de México, México, 1963, 283pp.
United States Department of Commerce. *Foreign trade regulations of Mexico.* Washington, 1966, 8pp.

8

Arthur Andersen & Co. *Highlights of taxation in Mexico for United States businessmen.* Chicago, 1961.
Brudno, W. "Tax and legal aspects of investment in Mexico." In: Southwestern Legal Foundation, *Proceedings of 1960 institute of private investments abroad and foreign trade,* pp. 403-447. Matthew Bender and Co., Albany, N.Y., 1960.
Caraza, R., and Jackson, A. "Tax, legal

and practical considerations for doing business in or with Mexico," *University of Southern California 1966 tax institute,* pp. 669-710.
Chapoy Bonifaz, D. "La doble imposición internacional y las medidas para evitarla," *Investigación fiscal,* no. 13, January 1967, pp. 15-46.
Creel Luján, L. "Jurisdiction to tax in Mexico," *Bulletin for international fiscal documentation,* vol. 2, 1948, pp. 404-419.
"Double taxation and foreign investment," *Foreign tax law weekly bulletin,* vol. 8, no. 7, 1957, pp. 1-5.
Gumpel, H. "The international tax law of Mexico." In: Tax Institute of America, Inc., *Taxation of foreign income by United States and other countries,* pp. 57-73. Princeton, N.J., 1966.
Gumpel, H. "Mexico." In: American Management Association, *The taxation of business income from foreign operations,* pp. 122-128. New York, 1958.
Gumpel, H. "Taxation of American income and business in Mexico," *Taxes,* vol. 36, 1958, pp. 427-436.
Helguera, E. "Mexican taxation of foreign corporations," *Miami law quarterly,* vol. 11, Summer 1957, p. 487. Also in: *Mexico: A symposium of law and government,* pp. 76-90. University of Miami Press, Coral Gables, Fla., 1958.
Margáin, H. "Tax problems of companies operating in Mexico," *Tax executive,* vol. 10, October 1957, pp. 59-71.
"Mexico enacts tax sparing," *Foreign commerce weekly,* vol. 61, no. 9, 1959.
"Mexico—New tax sanctuary," *Foreign tax law weekly bulletin,* vol. 7, no. 41, 1957, pp. 1-2.
Miranda, F. "Foreign investment and operation in Mexico," *Arizona law review,* vol. 2, 1960, pp. 187-211.
Ryan, J. *Handbook for foreign investors in Mexico.* John Morris Ryan Publisher, México, 2d edition, 1960, pp. 171-219. Periodic supplements.
"Some aspects of taxation affecting foreign companies in Mexico," *Foreign tax law weekly bulletin,* vol. 1, no. 48, 1951, pp. 3-14.
United Nations, Economic and Social Council, Fiscal Commission. "Taxation in capital-exporting and capital-importing countries of foreign private investment in Latin America: Taxation of

foreign investment in Mexico." Doc. No. E/CN.8/69/Add.2, 3 April 1953, 38pp. (mimeo).

United Nations, Economic Commission for Latin America. "Sistema impositivo mexicano en relación con el fomento de las inversiones extranjeras." Doc. No. E/CN.12/298/Add.1, 1953.

United States Department of Commerce. *Establishing a business in Mexico.* Washington, 1965, 20pp.

9

Bolio Ontiveros, E. "Distribución equitativa de los impuestos de la federación, los estados y los municipios," *Revista fiscal y financiera,* vol. 8, February 1951, pp. 34-36.

Bustamante, E. "Los sistemas tributarios de los estados," *Revista de economía* (México), vol. 13, April 1950; vol. 13, May 1950.

Cárdenas, C. "La concurrencia federal y local en materia impositiva." In: *Memoria del Segundo congreso mexicano de ciencias sociales,* vol. 4, 1945, pp. 353-369.

Facultades de Comercio y Administración y de Economía de la Universidad de Nuevo León. "Estudio fiscal del estado de Nuevo León," *Investigación fiscal,* no. 15, March 1967, pp. 17-36.

Fernández S. Calderón, M. *Las alcabalas en México.* Universidad Nacional Autónoma de México, México, 1947.

Figueroa Torres, J. *Las finanzas públicas en el estado de Michoacán.* Universidad Nacional Autónoma de México, México, 1956, 132pp.

Gil Preciado, J. "Jalisco y las finanzas," *Revista de economía* (México), vol. 23, May 1960, pp. 147-149.

Guzmán Lozano, E. "Centralismo tributario," *Revista de la Escuela de contabilidad, economía y administración,* vol. 9, July 1957, pp. 189-206.

"Ley de coordinación fiscal entre la federación y los estados: Exposición de motivos," *Revista fiscal y financiera,* vol. 13, December 1953, pp. 33-43.

Llanos, L. *Las finanzas del estado de Nayarit y la economía regional.* Universidad Nacional Autónoma de México, México, 1954, 173pp.

Martínez Báez, A. "La división de competencias tributarias en el constituyente de 1824," *Revista del tribunal fiscal de la federación* (número extraordinario), 1965, pp. 89-130.

Mayoral Pardo, L. "La concurrencia impositiva entre federación, estados y municipios," *Revista del tribunal fiscal de la federación* (número extraordinario), 1965, pp. 131-148.

Navarro Manrique, M. *Aspectos de la concurrencia tributaria en México.* Thesis, Universidad Nacional Autónoma de México, México, 1964, 225pp.

Oldman, O. "Mexico City's property tax problems," *Proceedings of the National tax association 1965,* vol. 58, pp. 471-480.

Oldman, O., Bird, R., Aaron, H., and Kass, S. *Financing urban development in Mexico City.* Harvard University Press, Cambridge, Mass., 1967.

Reyes Mazzone, R. "Relaciones fiscales intergubernamentales," *Revista de economía* (México), vol. 23, November 1960, pp. 317-322.

Romero Kolbeck, G., and Urquidi, V. *La exención fiscal en el distrito federal como instrumento de atracción de industrias.* Treasury of the Federal District Government, México, 1952, 126pp.

Serrano Fimbres, L. *Doble imposición en la ley de ingresos del estado de Sonora.* Thesis, Universidad Nacional Autónoma de México, México, 1963, 107pp.

Servín, A. "Las técnicas impositivas locales," *Revista de economía* (México), vol. 14, April 1951, p. 79.

Vargas Aguayo, R. *Consideraciones sobre el impuesto para obras de planificación en el distrito federal.* Thesis, Universidad Nacional Autónoma de México, México, 1965.

10

Abasolo Pérez, A. *La contribución especial.* Universidad Nacional Autónoma de México, México, 1963, 48pp.

Barbosa Heldt, H. "La tributación sobre bienes inmuebles," *Revista de la Facultad de derecho de México,* vol. 12, 1962, pp. 23-32.

Lobato Macías, J. *Las contribuciones especiales: Análisis teórico y aplicación en nuestro derecho.* Thesis, Universidad Nacional Autónoma de México, México, 1964, 82pp.

Margáin Manautou, E. "Los derechos, tasas o taxas y la contribución especial,"

Foro de México, no. 112-113, 1962, pp. 14-29.

Mora Fernández, D. *El impuesto a la propiedad territorial.* Thesis, México, 1961, 146pp.

Ruiz Sánchez, J. *Impuesto predial y leyes de planificación.* Thesis, Universidad Nacional Autónoma de México, México, 1963, 133pp.

Santillán López, R. *El impuesto predial rústico.* México, 1946.

Servín, A. "La administración del impuesto predial," *Revista de economía* (México), vol. 14, November 1951, p. 342.

Zamudio, S. "Inconstitucionalidad del impuesto federal sobre inmuebles urbanos," *Revista de la Facultad de derecho de México,* vol. 13, January-March 1963, p. 177.

11

Aizenstat, A. "Structure and taxation of agriculture in Mexico." In: H. Wald and J. Froomkin (eds.), *Papers and proceedings of the Conference on agricultural taxation and economic development,* pp. 305-321. Harvard Law School International Program in Taxation, Cambridge, Mass., 1954.

Gonzales, J., and Galindo, H. "Impuestos a la agricultura: Estado de Morelos," *México D.E.R. boletín mensuel,* no. 228, May 1945, pp. 337-343.

International Institute of Agriculture. "The federal land tax and the distribution of rural landed property (México)," *Monthly bulletin of economic and social intelligence* (Rome), no. 11, 1914, pp. 141-147.

12

García Caraveo, A. *La ley fomento de industrias de transformación.* Thesis, Universidad Nacional Autónoma de México, México, 1957.

Morán de León, L. *Los regímenes fiscales enfocados a las industrias nuevas y necesarias.* Thesis, Universidad Nacional Autónoma de México, México, 1960, 100pp.

Quintana, C. "Política industrial y evaluación de proyectos." In: Escuela Superior de Administración Pública América Central, *Informe del seminario sobre el proyecto de convenio centroamericano*

de incentivos fiscales al desarrollo industrial, pp. 85-103. San José, 1962.

Ross, S., and Christensen, J. *Tax incentives for industry in Mexico.* Harvard Law School International Program in Taxation, Cambridge, Mass., 1959.

Ryan, J. (ed). *Mexican tax exemptions for business.* John Morris Ryan Publisher, México, 1960, 71pp.

Servín, A. "Las industrias nuevas o necesarias y la indulgencia fiscal," *Revista fiscal y financiera,* vol. 3, August 1948, pp. 27-30.

"Tax incentives for new or necessary industries," *Mexican economic panorama* vol. 10, September 1959.

United States Department of Commerce *Industrial encouragement law of Mexico.* Washington, 1955, 6pp.

Vásquez Tercero, H. *Fomento industrial en México: Consideraciones en torno a la ley de fomento de industrias nuevas y necesarias.* Centro de Estudios Económicos del Sector Privado, México, 1966, 163pp.

13

Albareda, J. "Instrucción pública para combatir el fraude fiscal," *Revista fiscal y financiera,* vol. 15, July 1955, pp. 13-16.

Cabrera Acevedo, L. "Aspectos sociológicos del fraude fiscal," *Revista fiscal y financiera,* vol. 11, November 1952, pp. 29-33.

Flores Zavala, E. "El fraude fiscal," *Revista fiscal y financiera,* vol. 3, November 1948, pp. 23-25.

García Coeto, A. *Estudio sobre la naturaleza y funciones del tribunal fiscal.* Thesis, Universidad Nacional Autónoma de México, México, 1964, 141pp.

Heduán Virués, D. *Las funciones del tribunal fiscal de la federación.* Compañía Editorial Continental, México, 1961, 325pp.

"Ley de justicia fiscal: Exposición de motivos," *Revista del tribunal fiscal de la federación* (número extraordinario), 1965, pp. 11-44.

"Ley orgánica del tribunal fiscal de la federación," *Investigación fiscal,* no. 13, January 1967, pp. 183-192.

López Munguía, A. "Ingresos y recaudación de impuestos," *Revista fiscal y financiera,* vol. 14, June 1954, pp. 24-34.

López Velarde, G. "El tribunal fiscal de

la federación," *Revista de la Escuela de contabilidad, economía y administración,* vol. 8, April 1956, pp. 175-182.

Margáin, H. "Organización fiscal en México," *Revista fiscal y financiera,* vol. 12, January 1953, pp. 24-31.

Ortega, J. "Codificación administrativa fiscal," *Foro de México,* nos. 110-111, 1962, pp. 47-95.

Ortiz, E. "Bases para la nueva organización de las dependencias administrativas de los impuestos interiores," *Revista fiscal y financiera,* vol. 3, September 1948, pp. 11-12.

Ortiz Parlato, J. *Dirección de auditoría fiscal federal.* Thesis, Universidad Nacional Autónoma de México, México, 1963, 167pp.

Salazar Graniel, S. "La tendencia a defraudar al fisco," *Revista fiscal y financiera,* vol. 5, July 1949, pp. 16-19.

Sánchez Dávalos, R. "Tribunal fiscal: Competencia," *Revista fiscal y financiera,* vol. 16, November 1956, pp. 31-45.

Sherwood, W. "Tax administration in Mexico," *National tax journal,* vol. 2, March 1949, pp. 63-70.

"Tax procedures: Amendment to fiscal code 1951," *Foreign tax law weekly bulletin,* vol. 1, no. 38, 1951, pp. 3-14.

14

Alegre López, G. "El estado y el contribuyente," *Revista de la Facultad de derecho de México,* vol. 11, 1961, pp. 41-58.

Briseño Sierra, H. *Derecho procesal fiscal: El régimen federal mexicano.* Robredo, México, 1964, 701pp.

Briseño Sierra, H. "Procedimientos administrativos," *Revista fiscal y financiera,* vol. 16, April 1956, pp. 49-58.

Dzib Núñez, J. *La interpretación de las leyes fiscales.* Thesis, Universidad Nacional Autónoma de México, México, 1963, 92pp.

Flores Zavala, E. "Las normas tributarias." In: Universidad Nacional Autónoma de México, Consejo Técnico de Humanidades, *Estudios sobre el decreto constitucional de Apatzingán,* pp. 539-554. México, 1964.

Garza, S. *Las garantías constitucionales en el derecho tributario mexicano.* Editorial Cultura, México, 1949.

Gutiérrez Galván, J. *Reflexiones constitu-* cionales en materia tributaria. Thesis, Universidad Nacional Autónoma de México, México, 1963, 79pp.

Guzmán Lozano, E. "Normas de derecho tributario en la constitución política de 1857," *Revista de la Escuela de contabilidad, economía y administración,* vol. 9, April 1957, pp. 113-161.

Hernández Esparza, A. *Delito de defraudación fiscal.* Thesis, Universidad Nacional Autónoma de México, México, 1962, 150pp.

Margáin, H. "The legal base of taxation in Mexico," *Foreign tax law weekly bulletin,* vol. 9, no. 11, 1958, pp. 2-7. Also in: *Mexican-American review,* vol. 26, no. 7, 1958, p. 55.

Margáin, H. "El régimen del derecho en el campo fiscal," *Revista fiscal y financiera,* vol. 16, November 1956, pp. 7-18.

Margáin Manautou, E. "Clasificación de los recursos públicos y teorías que fundamentan la percepción de los tributos," *Foro de México,* nos. 110-111, 1962, pp. 27-38.

Margáin Manautou, E. "La interpretación de la ley tributaria: Ley tributaria y su reglamento: Efectos de los impuestos," *Foro de México,* nos. 108-109, 1962, pp. 64-77.

Margáin Manautou, E. "La obligación tributaria y los sujetos de la misma en la legislación mexicana," *Foro de México,* nos. 114-115, 1962, pp. 16-29.

Margáin Manautou, E. "La ubicación del derecho fiscal en la clasificación general del derecho," *Foro de México,* no. 106, 1962, pp. 45-51.

Meillón Pérez, M. *La defraudación fiscal.* Thesis, Universidad Nacional Autónoma de México, México, 1963, 89pp.

Meillón Pérez, M. *Prescripción fiscal.* Thesis, México, 1961, 124pp.

Nava Negrete, A. *Derecho procesal administrativo.* Porrúa, México, 1959.

Ortega, J. "Los principios de la justicia tributaria en la constitución," *Revista del tribunal fiscal de la federación* (número extraordinario), 1965, pp. 149-174.

Robles Glenn, J. "Equidad y proporcionalidad en el impuesto," *Revista de la Facultad de derecho de México,* vol. 14, 1964, p. 755.

Santos Cervantes, E. "La interpretación de la ley en derecho fiscal," *Revista de la Escuela de contabilidad, economía y administración,* vol. 7, January 1955, pp. 17-28.

17

Almeida, R. "La zona latinoamericana de libre comercio," *Técnicas financieras* (CEMLA), vol. 2, no. 5, May-June 1963, pp. 453-472.

Gutiérrez Kirchner, A. "El mercomún latinoamericano y la política fiscal," *Investigación fiscal,* no. 19, July 1967, pp. 15-63.

18

Banco Nacional de Comercio Exterior. *Comercio exterior.* México, monthly.

Banco Nacional de Comercio Exterior. *Comercio exterior de México.* Editorial Cultura, México, monthly, 1938– (English).

Diamond, W. *Foreign tax and trade briefs.* Fallon Law Book Company, New York, loose-leaf, 1951–.

Economist Intelligence Unit, Ltd. *Economic review of Mexico.* London, irregular.

"Mexico law digest." In: *Martindale-Hubbell law directory,* vol. 4, pp. 2770-2787. Martindale-Hubbell, Inc., Summit, N.J., 1961.

Revista fiscal y financiera. Instituto Mexicano de Técnicos Fiscales, México, monthly.

MONGOLIA

1

Holzman, F. "The tax system of Outer Mongolia, 1911-55," *Journal of Asian studies,* vol. 16, February 1957, pp. 221-236.

United States Department of Commerce. *Collection of laws and regulations concerning state finances of the Mongolian People's Republic; decisions of the Council of ministers and Ministry of finance.* Washington, 1963, 216pp.

11

Holzman, F. "Equity of the livestock tax of Outer Mongolia," *American Slavic and East European review,* vol. 15, 1956, pp. 506-510.

MOROCCO

1

Albert, M. "Les Réformes de la fiscalité marocaine en date du 30/12/61," *Revue*

marocaine de droit, vol. 15, 1963, pp. 385-407.

Dupuy, P. "La Situation du Trésor, la situation monétaire et les aspects techniques de la politique financière," *Bulletin économique et social du Maroc,* vol. 25, no. 90, November 1961, pp. 163-174.

"Taxation in Morocco," *Foreign tax law weekly bulletin,* vol. 14, no. 18, 1963, pp. 2-9.

Thrioreau, A. *Code fiscal.* Fiduciaire Marocaine d'Éditions Techniques, Casablanca, loose-leaf.

United States Department of Commerce. *Basic data on the economy of Morocco.* Washington, 1966, 24pp.

2

International Bank for Reconstruction and Development. *The economic development of Morocco.* The Johns Hopkins Press, Baltimore, 1966, 356pp.

Rouquet la Garrigue, V. L'Évolution économique et la politique financière contemporaine du Maroc," *Annales de sciences économiques appliquées,* vol. 19, no. 2, May 1961, pp. 191-226; vol. 19, no. 3, July 1961, pp. 249-277.

Tiano, A. *La Politique économique et financière du Maroc indépendant.* Presses Univérsitaires de France, Paris, 1963, 292pp.

3

Brochier, E. "Fiscalités française, algérienne, marocaine et tunisienne," *Bulletin for international fiscal documentation,* vol. 9, 1955, pp. 271-285.

Caniot, A. "Fiscalité comparée: Algérie-Tunisie-Maroc," *Bulletin for international fiscal documentation,* vol. 6, 1952, pp. 203-219.

4

Schonseck, P. *Privilège des impôts directs au Maroc dans ses rapports avec les autres sûretés mobilières.* Éditions La Porte, Librairie de Médicis, Paris, 1961, 215pp.

6

Mengual, A. *Les Taxes sur la possession des véhicules automobiles au Maroc et en France.* Éditions La Porte, Rabat, 1962, 317pp.

7

United States Department of Commerce. *Foreign trade regulations of Morocco.* Washington, 1963, 8pp.
United States Department of Commerce. *Preparing shipments to Morocco.* Washington, 1963, 8pp.

8

Gibbons, W. *Tax factors in basing international business abroad.* Harvard Law School International Program in Taxation, Cambridge, Mass., 1957, pp. 151-156.
United States Department of Commerce. *Establishing a business in Morocco.* Washington, 1965, 12pp.

11

"L'Imposition des bénéfices agricoles dans l'union française et à l'étranger," *Statistiques et études financières, finances comparées,* no. 1, 1949, pp. 21-24.

12

"Advantages granted to some enterprises by the general legislation." In: Banque Marocaine du Commerce Extérieur, *How to invest in Morocco,* pp. 33-42. Casablanca, 1962.
Délégation Générale à la Promotion Nationale et au Plan. *Le Problème de l'investissement et la politique économique.* Rabat, 1965.
Noja, S. "Agevolazioni fiscali alle nuove imprese in Marocco," *Diritto e pratica tributaria,* vol. 34, 1963, pp. 302-309.
United States Department of Commerce. *Investment law of Morocco.* Washington, 1961, 4pp.

14

Reynal, R. *Les Particularités du droit fiscal par raport au droit privé en matière d'enregistrement au Maroc.* La Porte, Rabat, 1962, 302pp.

MOZAMBIQUE

1

"Taxation in Portuguese East Africa," *Foreign tax law semi-weekly bulletin,* vol. 6, no. 49, 1955, pp. 1-10.

2

Gersdorff, R. "La Formation de capitaux par des mesures fiscales dans l'empire portugais," *Public finance,* vol. 15, 1960, pp. 31-50 (English summary).

4

Soarez Martínez, P. "Apontamentos para o estudo de uma reforma da tributação directa na província de Moçambique," *Ciência e tecnica fiscal,* vol. 63, March 1964, pp. 7-67.

7

United States Department of Commerce. *Foreign trade regulations of Mozambique.* Washington, 1966, 8pp.

8

Organisation for European Economic Cooperation. *Taxation systems applicable to investments in the overseas countries associated with member countries of O.E.E.C.* Paris, 1960, 100pp.
United States Department of Commerce. *Establishing a business in Mozambique.* Washington, 1960, 6pp.

12

Gersdorff, R. *Mesures pour encourager la formation de capitaux privés dans l'empire portugais.* Polygraphischer Verlag, Zurich, 1958.

NEPAL

1

United Nations, Technical Assistance Administration. "The fiscal system of Nepal." Prepared by E. Himsworth, 1958.
United States Department of Commerce. *Basic data on the economy of Nepal.* Washington, 1963, 16pp.

2

Consing, A. "The economy of Nepal," *International monetary fund staff papers,* vol. 10, November 1963, pp. 504-530.

4

Foreign Tax Law Association. *Nepal income tax service.* St. Petersburg, Fla., loose-leaf, 1966-.

11

Regmi, M. *Land tenure and taxation in Nepal. I: The state as landlord: Raikar tenure.* University of California Institute of International Studies, Berkeley, Calif., 1963, xi/274pp.

Regmi, M. *Land tenure and taxation in Nepal. III: The Jagir, Rakam and Kipat tenure systems.* University of California Institute of International Studies, Berkeley, Calif., 1965, 224pp.

United Nations, Technical Assistance Administration, Economic Survey Mission. "The land revenue system of Nepal." Prepared by E. Himsworth, 1957, 32pp. (offset).

13

Cooper, J. *Improving tax administration in Nepal.* United States Agency for International Development, Kathmanda, 1964, 18pp./appendixes.

NETHERLANDS ANTILLES

1

Minister of Economic Affairs. *Investment factors.* Willemstad, 1966, 45pp.

"Taxation and other laws in the Netherlands Antilles," *Foreign tax law weekly bulletin,* vol. 13, no. 26, 1962, pp. 1-6.

United States Department of Commerce. *Basic data on the economy of the Netherlands Antilles.* Washington, 1962, 11pp.

4

Foreign Tax Law Association. *Netherlands Antilles income tax service.* St. Petersburg, Fla., loose-leaf, 1966-.

"National ordinance on profit tax, 1940." In: Government Information Service, *National ordinances regarding investment facilities in the Netherlands Antilles,* pp. 15-35. Curaçao, 1961.

"Netherlands Antilles." In: Board of Inland Revenue (Great Britain), *Income taxes outside the United Kingdom 1966,* vol. 5, pp. 237-247. H.M. Stationery Office, London, 1967.

7

United States Department of Commerce. *Foreign trade regulations of the Netherlands Antilles.* Washington, 1967, 8pp.

8

Gibbons, W. *Tax factors in basing international business abroad.* Harvard Law School International Program in Taxation, Cambridge, Mass., 1957, pp. 118-125.

Government Information Service. *It pays to invest in the Netherlands Antilles.* Curaçao, 1961, 10pp.

Insular Service for Economic Affairs and Development. *Guide for the establishment of enterprises in Curaçao.* Curaçao, 1962, 69pp.

Joseph, F., and Koppel, R. "Curaçao organizations," *Taxes,* vol. 39, 1961, pp. 485-507.

Lowe, J., Jr. "Curaçao investment companies: Some shoals in a tax haven," *Tax law review,* vol. 16, January 1961, p. 177.

United States Department of Commerce. *Establishing a business and investing in the Netherlands Antilles.* Washington, 1962, 14pp.

12

Rado, A. "Tax advantages of investment companies in the Netherlands Antilles." In: Prentice-Hall, Inc., *Tax ideas.* Englewood Cliffs, N.J., 1957.

Weissman, M. "Tax advantages of Netherlands Antilles for motion picture companies," *Southern California law review,* vol. 32, Summer 1959, p. 391.

NICARAGUA

1

Comisión Fiscal. *Informe: Consideraciones relativas a la situación fiscal de Nicaragua y la necesidad de su reforma.* Managua, 1961.

Pan American Union. *A statement of the laws of Nicaragua in matters affecting business.* Washington, 3d edition revised, 1965, pp. 107-122.

Programa Conjunto de Tributación de la Organización de Estados Americanos y del Banco de Desarrollo Interamericano. *Sistemas tributarios de América Latina: Nicaragua.* Unión Panamericana, Washington, 1966, 82pp.

United States Department of Commerce. *Basic data on the economy of Nicaragua.* Washington, 1965, 24pp.

United States Department of Commerce. *Investment in Nicaragua.* Washington, 1962, 9pp.

2

International Bank for Reconstruction and Development. *The economic devel-*

opment of Nicaragua. Washington, 1953, pp. 77-83, chapters 19-23.

4

Foreign Tax Law Association. *Nicaraguan income tax service.* Centerport, L.I., N.Y., loose-leaf, 1952–.

6

"Nicaragua increases cigarette duties," *Foreign commerce weekly,* vol. 65, no. 10, 1961, p. 23.

"Nicaragua ups consumption tax on domestic cigarettes," *Foreign commerce weekly,* vol. 65, no. 4, 1961, p. 19.

7

"Nicaragua imposes taxes on beef cattle exports," *Foreign commerce weekly,* vol. 65, no. 15, 1961, p. 12.

"Presidential decree no. 4, containing regulations of the coffee and cotton producers' tax." In: Food and Agricultural Organization of the United Nations, *Food and agricultural legislation,* vol. 1. Rome, 1952.

United States Department of Commerce. *Foreign trade regulations of the Central American common market.* Washington, 1967, 12pp.

United States Department of Commerce. *Import tariff system of Nicaragua.* Washington, 1963, 2pp.

8

United States Department of Commerce. *Foreign investment law of Nicaragua.* Washington, 1955, 2pp.

12

United States Department of Commerce. *Industrial encouragement law of Nicaragua.* Washington, 1959, 5pp.

13

United States Treasury Department, Internal Revenue Service, Foreign Tax Assistance Staff. *A tax administration modernization program for the government of Nicaragua.* Washington, 1964 (mimeo).

17

Programa Conjunto de Tributación de la Organización de los Estados Americanos y del Banco de Desarrollo Inter-

americano. "La administración tributaria en Centroamérica y el proyecto de armonización fiscal," *Investigación fiscal,* no. 14, February 1967, pp. 91-176.

Watkin, V. *Taxes and tax harmonization in Central America.* Harvard Law School International Tax Program, Cambridge, Mass., 1967, chapter 7.

18

Diamond, W. *Foreign tax and trade briefs.* Fallon Law Book Company, New York, loose-leaf, 1951–.

"Nicaragua law digest." In: *Martindale-Hubbell law directory,* vol. 4, pp. 2812-2819. Martindale-Hubbell, Inc., Summit, N.J., 1961.

NIGER

1

United States Department of Commerce. *Basic data on the economy of Niger.* Washington, 1962, 16pp.

2

The economic and financial structure of French West Africa. Annual conference of the Economic Sections, West African Institute of Social and Economic Research, University College, Ibadan, 1953 (mimeo).

3

Mémento fiscal et social 1964, numéro spécial no. 14, 25 June 1964. A comparative survey of taxes in the West African Union and Guinea.

12

United States Department of Commerce. *Investment law in the Republic of Niger.* Washington, 1963, 4pp.

NIGERIA

1

Cox-George, N. "Fiscal experiments in eastern Nigeria," *Public finance,* vol. 12, 1957, pp. 173-180.

Okigbo, P. *Nigerian public finance.* Northwestern University Press, Evanston, Ill., 1965, xiii/245pp.

Omoregie, S. "National taxation in Nigeria," *Justice of the peace,* vol. 119, 27 August 1955, p. 556.

Orewa, G. *Taxation in western Nigeria—*

The problems of an emergent state. Nigerian Social and Economic Studies No. 4; published for the Nigerian Institute of Social and Economic Research by Oxford University Press, New York, 1962, xvii/169pp.

Pim, A. "Public finance." In: M. Perham (ed.), *Mining, commerce and finance in Nigeria.* Taber and Taber, London, 1940.

Price Waterhouse & Co. *Information guide for doing business in Nigeria.* New York, 1963.

Report of the Fiscal commissioner on the financial effects of the proposed constitution. H.M. Stationery Office, London, Cmnd. 9026, December 1953.

United States Department of Commerce. *Basic data on the economy of Nigeria.* Washington, 1964, 19pp.

2

Aluko, S. "Financing economic development in Nigeria," *Nigerian journal of economics and social studies,* vol. 3, no. 1, November 1961, pp. 39-67.

Bauer, P. "The economic development of Nigeria," *Journal of political economy,* vol. 63, October 1955, pp. 398-411.

Carney, D. "Income distribution, income taxation and economic development in Ghana and Nigeria," *Indian journal of economics,* vol. 41, July 1961, pp. 29-41.

Ezenkwele, A. "The evolution of modern Nigerian finance: The problems and prospects," *Indian journal of economics,* vol. 40, July 1959, pp. 37-44.

Gustafson, D. "The monetary and fiscal background of Nigeria's six-year development plan." In: T. Farar (ed.), *Financing African development,* pp. 72-93. The MIT Press, Cambridge, Mass., 1965.

Hausman, W. (ed.). *Managing economic development in Africa.* The MIT Press, Cambridge, Mass., 1963.

Helleiner, G. *Peasant agriculture, government and economic growth in Nigeria.* Richard D. Irwin, Inc., Homewood, Ill., 1967.

Hinrichs, H. *Mobilizing government revenues for development in Nigeria.* International Bank for Reconstruction and Development, Washington, January 1966, 167pp.

International Bank for Reconstruction and Development. *The economic development of Nigeria.* The Johns Hopkins Press, Baltimore, 1955, chapter 5.

Okotie-Eboh, F. "The mobilization budget." In: *Conference on law and economic development.* Massachusetts Institute of Technology, Cambridge, Mass., 1962.

Robinson, H., *et al. The economic coordination of transport development in Nigeria.* Stanford Research Institute, Menlo Park, Calif., 1961.

Stolper, W. *Planning without facts.* Harvard University Press, Cambridge, Mass., 1966, pp. 262-275.

3

Due, J. *Taxation and economic development in Tropical Africa.* The MIT Press, Cambridge, Mass., 1963, 172pp.

4

Booth, J. "Application of the direct taxation ordinance in eastern Nigeria," *Journal of African administration,* vol. 8, April 1956, pp. 74-82.

Federal Ministry of Commerce and Industry, Publications and Information Division. *Company tax and the plantation industry.* Lagos, 1959, 4pp.

Foreign Tax Law Association. *Nigeria income tax service.* Centerport, L.I., N.Y., loose-leaf, 1952–.

"Methods of direct taxation in British Tropical Africa," *Journal of African administration,* vol. 2, October 1950, pp. 3-12; vol. 3, January 1951, pp. 30-41; vol. 3, October 1951, pp. 77-87.

"Nigeria, Federal Republic of." In: Board of Inland Revenue (Great Britain), *Income taxes outside the United Kingdom 1966,* vol. 6, pp. 1-74. H.M. Stationery Office, London, 1967.

7

Adler, J. "The economic development of Nigeria," *Journal of political economy,* vol. 64, October 1956, pp. 425-432. Reprinted in: R. Bird and O. Oldman (eds.), *Readings on taxation in developing countries.* The Johns Hopkins Press, Baltimore, 1964, pp. 484-494; revised edition, 1967, pp. 372-382.

Bauer, P. "The economic development of Nigeria," *Journal of political economy,* vol. 63, October 1955, pp. 399-408. Reprinted in: R. Bird and O. Oldman (eds.), *Readings on taxation in developing countries.* The Johns Hopkins Press, Baltimore, 1964, pp. 472-483; revised edition, 1967, pp. 360-371.

Helleiner, G. "The fiscal role of the marketing boards in Nigerian economic development, 1947-1961," *Economic journal,* vol. 74, September 1964, pp. 582-605.

United States Department of Commerce. *Foreign trade regulations of Nigeria.* Washington, 1963, 12pp.

World Bank Mission to Nigeria. "Taxes on foreign trade in Nigeria." In: R. Bird and O. Oldman (eds.), *Readings on taxation in developing countries.* The Johns Hopkins Press, Baltimore, 1964, pp. 467-471; revised edition, 1967, pp. 355-359.

8

United States Department of Commerce. *Establishing a business in Nigeria.* Washington, 1965, 20pp.

9

Aluko, S. *Federal finance and economic development in Nigeria.* Ph.D. thesis, University of London, London, 1959, 337pp.

Binns, K. *Report of the Fiscal review commission.* Federal Ministry of Information, Lagos, 1965.

Cotter, W. "Taxation and federalism in Nigeria," *British tax review,* March-April 1964, pp. 97-116.

Hazelwood, A. "New deal for Nigerian federal finance," *Banker's magazine,* vol. 85, November 1958, pp. 365-373.

Hazlewood, A. "The finances of Nigerian federation," *West Africa,* 27 August 1955. Also: Reprint Series No. 14, Oxford University Institute of Colonial Studies, Oxford.

Hicks, J. "A chapter in federal finance— The case of Nigeria." In: J. Hicks, *Essays in world economics,* pp. 216-236. Clarendon Press, Oxford, 1959.

Hicks, J., *et al. Report of the Commission of revenue allocation.* Government Printer, Lagos, 1951, 185pp.

Hicks, U. *Development from below: Local government and finance in developing*

countries of the Commonwealth. Oxford University Press, London, 1951, 552pp.

Hicks, U. "The new tax system of eastern Nigeria. A note on the eastern region of Nigeria finance law no. 1 of 1956," *Journal of African administration,* vol. 8, October 1956, pp. 202-205.

Hinrichs, H. "The impact of economic development on fiscal federalism: The Nigerian experience." In: United States Congress, Joint Economic Committee, 90th Congress, 1st Session, *Revenue sharing and its alternatives: What future for fiscal federalism?* vol. 1, pp. 552-555. Joint Committee Print, Washington, 1967.

Phillipson, S. *Administrative and financial procedure under the new constitution: Financial relations between government of Nigeria and the native administrations.* Government Printer, Lagos, 1947.

Reisman, J., and Tress, R. *Fiscal commission report.* H.M. Stationery Office, London, Cmnd. 481, 1958.

12

Aluko, S. *Fiscal incentives for industrial development in Nigeria.* Prepared for United Nations Industrial Development Organization, New York, 1966.

Investment possibilities in the eastern region of the Federation of Nigeria. Eastern Region Government Printer, July 1959.

"Legislation affecting investment," *Foreign tax law weekly bulletin,* vol. 13, no. 33, 1963, pp. 3-7.

Lewis, B. *Incentives for industrial development in Nigeria.* n.p., Ibadan, 1962.

"Taxation, incentives and handicaps." In: P. Proehl, *Foreign enterprise in Nigeria: Laws and policies,* pp. 117-136. University of North Carolina Press, Chapel Hill, N.C., 1965.

United States Department of Commerce. *Investment in Nigeria.* Washington, 1957, 182pp.

18

Diamond, W. *Foreign tax and trade briefs.* Fallon Law Book Company, New York, loose-leaf, 1951-.

Eyre and Spottiswoode, Ltd. *The laws of the Federation of Nigeria and Lagos.* London, 1959, 195pp.

PAKISTAN

1

A. F. Ferguson & Co. *Taxes in Pakistan.* Karachi, 1965, 31pp.

Department of Investment Promotion and Supplies. *Investment opportunities in Pakistan.* Manager of Publications, Karachi, 1964, pp. 27-38.

Ministry of Industries, Investment Promotion Bureau. *Investment opportunities in Pakistan.* Manager of Publications, Karachi, 1960.

"Pakistan—Budget, June 1959: Explanatory memorandum on taxation," *Bulletin for international fiscal documentation,* vol. 14, 1960, pp. 119-127.

Price Waterhouse & Co. *Information guide for doing business in Pakistan.* New York, 1964.

Price Waterhouse & Co. *Investment and taxation in Pakistan.* New York, 1960.

Qureshi, A. *Fiscal system of Pakistan.* International Monetary Fund, Washington, 1955, 65pp. (mimeo).

Taxation Enquiry Commission. *Interim report (central taxation).* Manager of Publications, Karachi, 1959.

Taxation Enquiry Committee. *Report.* Manager of Publications, Karachi, 1961.

United States Department of Commerce. *Basic data on the economy of Pakistan.* Washington, 1966, 20pp.

United States Department of Commerce. *Investment factors in Pakistan.* Washington, 1962, 12pp.

United States Department of Commerce. *Investment in Pakistan.* Washington, 1954, pp. 119-143, 207-214.

2

Ali, A. "Pakistan budgets: General and provincial," *Pakistan economic journal,* vol. 1, no. 1, July 1949, pp. 117-125.

Andrus, J., and Mohammed, A. *The economy of Pakistan.* Oxford University Press, London, 1958, chapters 18, 19.

Andrus, J., and Mohammed, A. *Trade, finance and development in Pakistan.* Stanford University Press, Stanford, Calif., 1966, xii/289pp.

Baqai, M. *Some aspects of the relationship between fiscal and monetary policy in underdeveloped countries: A case study of Pakistan.* Ph.D. thesis, Kansas, 1956.

Chowdhury, A. "The predictability and the flexibility of tax revenues in Pakistan," *Pakistan development review,* vol. 2, no. 2, Summer 1962, pp. 189-214.

Chowdhury, A. "The weight of tax revenue in the Pakistan economy," *Pakistan development review,* vol. 3, no. 1, Spring 1963, pp. 98-117.

"Economic development through private enterprise," *Karachi commerce,* vol. 12, nos. 39-40, 29 October 1960.

Fareed, Q. "Third five-year plan: Resources and financing." In: A. Qureshi (ed.), *The third five year plan and other papers,* pp. 127-134. Pakistan Economic Association, Lahore, 1965.

Griffin, K. "Financing development plans in Pakistan," *Pakistan development review,* vol. 5, no. 4, Winter 1965.

Haq, M., and Khanam, K. *Deficit financing in Pakistan 1951-60.* Monograph in Economic Development No. 3, Institute of Development Economics, Karachi, 1961, 68pp.

Huq, A. "Fiscal policy in expanding economy: Case study of Pakistan," *Public finance,* vol. 14, 1959, pp. 283-321.

Islam, N. "Financial resources and the first five-year plan of Pakistan," *Economia internazionale,* vol. 10, August 1957, pp. 493-506.

Khan, A. "Financing the second five year plan," *Pakistan development review,* vol. 1, Summer 1961, pp. 52-63.

Lewis, S., Jr. "Aspects of fiscal policy and resource mobilization in Pakistan," *Pakistan development review,* vol. 4, no. 2, Summer 1964, pp. 261-282.

Lewis, S., Jr. "Domestic resources and fiscal policy in Pakistan's second and third plans," *Pakistan development review,* vol. 5, no. 2, Summer 1965; vol. 5, no. 3, Autumn 1965, pp. 461-495.

Pakistan Planning Commission. *The second five-year plan (1960-65).* Manager of Publications, Karachi, 1960, chapter 3. Reprinted in: R. Bird and O. Oldman (eds.), *Readings on taxation in developing countries,* pp. 59-70. The Johns Hopkins Press, Baltimore, 1964.

"Pakistan steps up development program," *Foreign commerce weekly,* vol. 63, no. 10, 1960, p. 3.

Parkinson, J. "The balance of payments and fiscal policy in Pakistan," *Scottish journal of political economy,* vol. 9, no. 2, June 1962, pp. 99-109.

Sharif, M. "Resource mobilisation during the third plan." In: A. Qureshi (ed.), *The third five year plan and other papers*, pp. 114-126. Pakistan Economic Association, Lahore, 1965.

"Tax policy and second plan," *Economic observer*, vol. 14, nos. 3-4, February 1960.

United Nations, Technical Assistance Administration. "Preliminary note on the economic and financial situation of Pakistan." Doc. No. TAO/PAK/25 (restricted), 7 July 1959.

Yaqub, M. *The tax structure of a developing country: A case study of Pakistan*. Ph.D. thesis, Princeton University, Princeton, N.J., 1966.

4

Ahmad, A. *Desirability of introducing self assessment in Pakistan*. Seminar paper, Harvard Law School, Cambridge, Mass., 1963.

Baig, M. *Elements of tax laws: A concise exposition of the law and procedure of income tax in Pakistan*. Pakistan Publishing House, Karachi, 1964, 242pp.

Foreign Tax Law Association. *Pakistan income tax service*. Centerport, L.I., N.Y., loose-leaf, 1950–1955.

Gupta, C. *Income-tax law and accounts*. Adarsh-Prakashan, Agra, 1961, 166pp.

Income tax act, 1922 (corrected up to the 31st of December 1965). Manager, Government of Pakistan Press, Karachi, 1966, 244pp.

Jafar, M. *Personal taxation in Pakistan: A study of exemptions and allowances*. Seminar paper, Harvard Law School, Cambridge, Mass., 1961.

Karachi Chamber of Commerce and Industry. *Memorandum on company taxation*. Karachi, 1960, 7pp. (duplicated).

Naqvi, S. *A guide to income tax law*. Taxation House, Lahore, 3d edition, 1963, 301pp.

Naqvi, S. *The law and practice of income-tax in Pakistan*. Taxation House, Lahore, 3d edition, 2 volumes, 1964.

Naqvi, S. *The law and procedure of income-tax in Pakistan*. Taxation House, Lahore, 2d edition, 1955. Supplement, 1959.

"Pakistan." In: Board of Inland Revenue (Great Britain), *Income taxes outside the United Kingdom 1966*, vol. 6, pp.

107-205. H.M. Stationery Office, London, 1967.

Price Waterhouse & Co. *Memorandum of Pakistan income tax, etc.* Calcutta, 22 August 1956, 4pp. (mimeo).

5

Naqvi, S. *The law of gift-tax in Pakistan*. Taxation House, Lahore, 1964, 95pp.

Naqvi, S. *The law of wealth-tax in Pakistan*. Taxation House, Lahore, 1964, 134pp.

6

Butt, M., and Butt, M. *The law of sales tax (act III of 1951) as modified up to the 31st of December, 1963*. Quami Kutub Khana, Lahore, 1964, 312pp.

Central Board of Revenue. *Sales tax manual*. Manager of Publications, Karachi, 1962, 64pp.

Lewis, S., Jr., and Qureshi, S. "The structure of revenue from indirect taxes in Pakistan," *Pakistan development review*, vol. 4, no. 3, Autumn 1964, pp. 491-525.

Naqvi, S. *The law of sales-tax in Pakistan*. Taxation House, Lahore, 1955.

Radhu, G. "The rate structure of indirect taxes in Pakistan," *Pakistan development review*, vol. 4, no. 3, Autumn 1964, pp. 527-551.

Radhu, G. "The relation of indirect tax changes to price changes in Pakistan," *Pakistan development review*, vol. 5, no. 1, Spring 1965.

8

Asian African Legal Consultative Committee, Secretariat. *Foreign investment laws and regulations of member countries*. Economic Law Series No. 2, N.M. Tripathi Private Ltd., Bombay, 1965, 91pp. (mimeo).

Central Board of Revenue. *Tax in Pakistan: A brief outline with particular reference to tax concessions to new industries and incentives to foreign investment*. Manager of Publications, Karachi, 1961.

United States Department of Commerce. *Establishing a business in Pakistan*. Washington, 1966, 16pp.

United States Department of Commerce. *Foreign investment policy of Pakistan*. Washington, 1955, 3pp.

9

Akhtar, S. "Pakistan's provincial finance: West Punjab," *Pakistan economic journal,* vol. 1, no. 2, October 1949, pp. 1-11.

Bhatia, M. "Financial aspects of the constitution of Pakistan," *Indian journal of economics,* vol. 38, July 1957, pp. 119-126.

Local finance enquiry committee report. 1951.

Taxation Enquiry Commission. *Report on provincial taxation.* Manager of Publications, Karachi, 1959, 87pp.

10

"Property tax due July 1st," *Foreign tax law weekly bulletin,* vol. 15, no. 9, 1964, pp. 16-18.

11

Irani, P. "Structure and taxation of agriculture in India and Pakistan." In: H. Wald and J. Froomkin (eds.), *Papers and proceedings of the Conference on agricultural taxation and economic development,* pp. 368-395. Harvard Law School International Program in Taxation, Cambridge, Mass., 1954.

Matin, A. "Capital formation and taxation of agriculture in Pakistan," *Credit rural and cooperative,* vol. 10, no. 3, July-September 1961, pp. 1-9.

Qureshi, A. *Land systems in the Middle East.* n.p., 1954.

Qureshi, A. "Method of assessment of the land tax in the Indo-Pakistan subcontinent." In: H. Wald and J. Froomkin (eds.), *Papers and proceedings of the Conference on agricultural taxation and economic development,* pp. 396-411. Harvard Law School International Program in Taxation, Cambridge, Mass., 1954.

United Nations, Department of Economic Affairs, Fiscal Division, and Food and Agricultural Organization. "The operation of the land tax in India and Pakistan." May 1953, 56pp.

12

Central Board of Revenue. *Brochure on taxation of income and concessions to industries in Pakistan.* Manager of Publications, Karachi, 1960, ii/102pp.

13

Central Treaty Organization. *Symposium on tax administration.* Office of United States Economic Coordinator for CENTO Affairs, Ankara, 1965, 259pp.

17

Dalal, R., and Cooper, R. "India's fiscal relations with Pakistan," *Bulletin for international fiscal documentation,* vol. 6, 1952, pp. 1-19.

18

Diamond, W. *Foreign tax and trade briefs.* Fallon Law Book Company, New York, loose-leaf, 1951-.

PANAMA

1

Harrington, J. "A businessman looks at recent changes in Panama's fiscal code," *Export trade and shipper,* vol. 77, no. 14, 1958, p. 22.

Industrial Development Center of the Institute for Economic Development. *Facts for investors in Panama.* Panamá, August 1956.

Joint Tax Program, Organization of American States and Inter-American Development Bank. *Fiscal survey of Panama: Problems and proposals for reform.* Published for The Joint Tax Program by The Johns Hopkins Press, Baltimore, 1964, xviii/277pp.

Leland, S. *A report on the revenue system of Panama.* Washington, 1946, 177pp. (mimeo).

Pan American Union. *A statement of the laws of Panama in matters affecting business.* Washington, 2d edition, 1966, 237pp.

Price Waterhouse & Co. *Information guide for doing business in Panama.* New York, 1965.

"Taxation in Panama," *Foreign tax law weekly bulletin,* vol. 13, no. 31, 1962, pp. 4-9; vol. 13, no. 32, 1963, pp. 1-9.

United States Department of Commerce. *Basic data on the economy of the Republic of Panama.* Washington, 1964, 16pp.

Young, G. *Taxation in Panama: Memorandum.* Young & Young, Panamá, 1960, 14pp.

2

Tapia, A. "El financiamiento de infraestructura y obras conexas." In: *Seminario sobre el financiamiento de la reforma agraria.* Instituto Interamericano de Ciencias Agricoles, San José, 1964.

Taylor, M., and Richman, R. "Fiscal reform and development needs in Panamá," *National tax journal,* vol. 17, June 1964, pp. 173-186.

4

Fábrega, J. *Income tax law.* Panamá, 1960, 25pp.

Fábrega, J. *Law no. 52 of May 23, 1941, income tax.* Panamá, 1955.

Foreign Tax Law Association. *Panamanian income tax service.* Centerport, L.I., N.Y., loose-leaf, 1954–.

Jiménez Camacho, F. "El impuesto sobre la renta en la República de Panamá," *Investigación fiscal,* no. 14, February 1967, pp. 15-52.

Moreno y Fábrega. *Income tax law of the Republic of Panama.* Panamá, 1964, 58pp.

"Panama raises income tax, sets stamp taxes," *Foreign commerce weekly,* vol. 65, no. 8, 1961, p. 20.

Price Waterhouse & Co. *Panama income tax law as amended by law number 2 of 1953.* Ancon, Canal Zone, 1953, 20pp. (mimeo).

"Taxation of income," *Foreign tax law semi-weekly bulletin,* vol. 4, no. 28, 1953, pp. 1-5.

5

"Inheritance and gift taxes," *Foreign tax law semi-weekly bulletin,* vol. 3, no. 84, 1953, pp. 1-2.

6

Programa Conjunto de Tributación de la Organización de los Estados Americanos y del Banco Interamericano de Desarrollo. *El impuesto sobre las ventas.* Unión Panamericana, Washington, December 1966 (mimeo).

7

United States Department of Commerce. *Foreign trade regulations of Panama.* Washington, 1963, 8pp.

8

Gibbons, W. *Tax factors in basing international business abroad.* Harvard Law School International Program in Taxation, Cambridge, Mass., 1957, pp. 126-132.

Overseas Management Company of Panama, Inc. *The use of a Panama corporation in expanding world markets.* Panamá, 1958, 20pp.

"R. P. government protests abolition of 'tax havens,'" *Foreign tax law weekly bulletin,* vol. 12, no. 9, 1961, p. 9.

United States Department of Commerce. *Establishing a business in Panama.* Washington, 1958, 16pp.

11

Escartín Martín, D. "Impuesto sobre las tierras incultas," *Anuario de derecho,* vol. 4, 1959-1960, p. 55.

12

Diamond, W. *How the Colon free zone in Panama saves tax dollars for United States business.* Fallon Law Book Company, New York, 1958, 11pp.

Taylor, M. "Fiscal incentives for development in Panamá." In: R. Bird and O. Oldman (eds.), *Readings on taxation in developing countries,* pp. 208-225. The Johns Hopkins Press, Baltimore, revised edition, 1967. Reprinted from: Joint Tax Program, Organization of American States and Inter-American Development Bank, *Fiscal survey of Panama,* pp. 170-182. Published for The Joint Tax Program by The Johns Hopkins Press, Baltimore, 1964.

Taylor, M. "Tax incentives for development: Panama's experience." In: P. Kleinsore (ed.), *Public finance and welfare essays in honor of C. Ward Macy,* pp. 285-305. University of Oregon Books, Eugene, Ore., 1966.

United States Department of Commerce. *Production development law of Panama.* Washington, 1958, 8pp.

13

Comas Calvet, P. "La codificación fiscal en la República de Panamá," *Veritas* (Buenos Aires), vol. 19, 31 March 1951, pp. 447-451.

United Nations, Technical Assistance Administration. "Administración tributaria en Panamá." Doc. No. TAA/NS/PAN/1 (restricted), 7 January 1955.

18

Diamond, W. *Foreign tax and trade briefs.* Fallon Law Book Company, New York, loose-leaf. 1951–.

"Panama law digest." In: *Martindale-Hubbell law directory,* vol. 4, pp. 2842-2855. Martindale-Hubbell, Inc., Summit, N.J., 1961.

PAPUA

2

International Bank for Reconstruction and Development. *The economic development of the territory of Papua and New Guinea.* The Johns Hopkins Press, Baltimore, 1965, pp. 385-400.

4

"Papua and New Guinea." In: Board of Inland Revenue (Great Britain), *Income taxes outside the United Kingdom 1966,* vol. 6, pp. 207-242. H.M. Stationery Office, London, 1967.

PARAGUAY

1

Crockett, J., and Costa, J. *The internal taxes of Paraguay.* International Cooperation Administration, Washington, 1952, 51pp. (mimeo).

Mersan, C. "Régimen fiscal paraguayo," *Veritas* (Buenos Aires), 31 March 1946, pp. 388-389.

Pan American Union. *A statement of the laws of Paraguay in matters affecting business.* Washington, 2d edition revised, 1962, pp. 99-112.

"Paraguay increases certain tax rates," *Foreign commerce weekly,* vol. 63, no. 2, 1960, p. 8.

Price Waterhouse & Co. *Information guide for doing business in Paraguay.* New York, 1963.

United States Department of Commerce. *Basic data on the economy of Paraguay.* Washington, 1964, 12pp.

United States Department of Commerce. *Investment in Paraguay.* Washington, 1955, pp. 101-103.

4

Costa, J. *El impuesto a la renta en el Paraguay.* Ministerio de Hacienda, Asunción, 1953, 28pp.

Foreign Tax Law Association. *Paraguay income tax service.* Centerport, L.I., N.Y., loose-leaf, 1953–.

"Increase in profit tax rates," *Foreign tax law weekly bulletin,* vol. 11, nos. 5-6, 1960.

Perrell, G. "Income taxation in Paraguay," *Foreign tax law weekly bulletin,* vol. 2, no. 5, 1951, pp. 3-31.

"Taxation of income: Decree no. 9240, 1949," *Foreign tax law weekly bulletin,* vol. 1, no. 50, 1951, pp. 3-16.

"Taxation of income in Paraguay," *Foreign tax law semi-weekly bulletin,* vol. 4, no. 56, 1954, pp. 1-5.

7

Fisher, F. *The operation of the aforo system.* Asunción, 1952, 21pp. (mimeo).

Fisher, F. *The operation of the gravamen system: Ad valorem tax on exports* Asunción, 1952, 17pp. (mimeo).

United States Department of Commerce *Foreign trade regulations of Paraguay* Washington, 1966, 8pp.

8

United States Department of Commerce. *Foreign investment law of Paraguay.* Washington, 1955, 3pp.

10

Crockett, J. *The real estate tax of Paraguay.* International Cooperation Administration, Washington, 1951, 45pp. (mimeo).

13

Costa, J. *El cobro de impuestos en el Paraguay.* International Cooperation Administration, Washington, 1958, 33pp.

Costa, J. *Proposals for legislative and administrative reforms with respect to tax collection in Paraguay.* International Cooperation Administration, Washington, 1953, 27pp. (mimeo).

17

Almeida, R. "La zona latinoamericana de libre comercio," *Técnicas financieras* (CEMLA), vol. 2, no. 5, May-June 1963, pp. 453-472.

Gutiérrez Kirchner, A. "El mercomún latinoamericano y la política fiscal," *Investigación fiscal*, no. 19, July 1967, pp. 15-63.

18

Diamond, W. *Foreign tax and trade briefs*. Fallon Law Book Company, New York, loose-leaf, 1951–.

Economist Intelligence Unit, Ltd. *Economic review of Uruguay and Paraguay*. London, irregular.

PERU

1

Belaúnde, V. *La depreciación monetaria, los impuestos y las empresas*. Lima, 1960.

Benavides Correa, A. "Los efectos tributarios de la ley 4452 y la brea y pariñas," *Revista del foro*, vol. 48, no. 1, 1961, pp. 62-92.

Capuñay Mimbela, C. "Esquema del desarrollo de la actividad fiscal del Perú 1920-1960," *Revista de la Facultad de ciencias económicas y comerciales*, no. 64, January-April 1962, pp. 38-51.

Capuñay Mimbela, C. *Legislación tributaria*. Compañía de Impr. y Publ., Lima, 3d edition, 1955, 167pp.

Commission of Financial Advisers on Finances of National Government. *Report on the taxation policy of Peru*. Lima, 1931, 15pp.

Del Pozo, A., and García González, A. *Impuestos en el Perú*. Editorial Antonio Lulli, S.A., Lima, 1959.

Fajardo, J. (ed.). *Legislación tributaria del Perú*. Editorial Mercurio, Lima, 1960, 294pp.

Ferrero, R. "Finalidades y requisitos de un sistema tributario," *Boletín semanal de la Cámara de comercio de Lima*, 18 August 1954, p. 456.

Ferrero, R. "Política tributaria y sistema impositivo en el Perú," *Revista jurisprudencia peruana*, vol. 19, September 1961, pp. 1210-1215. Also in: *Revista del foro*, vol. 49, nos. 2-3, 1962, pp. 1-10.

Foreign Tax Law Association. Tax forms (translation). New York.

García Salazar, J. *Jurisprudencia tributaria*. Bolivariana, Trujillo, 1962, 216pp.

Ibérico Robles, D. *Enciclopedia tributaria*. n.p., Lima, 1963, 748pp.

Kroeber, C. "The mobilization of Philip II's revenue in Peru, 1590-1696," *Economic history review II*, vol. 10, April 1958, pp. 439-449.

Moll, B. "El sistema tributario del Perú," *Archivio finanziario*, vol. 2, 1951, pp. 162-170.

Pan American Union. *A statement of the laws of Peru in matters affecting business*. Washington, 3d edition revised, 1962. Supplement, 1965.

Price Waterhouse & Co. *Information guide for doing business in Peru*. New York, 1966.

Price, Waterhouse, Peat & Co. *Memorandum dated June 1952 on Peruvian taxation*. Lima, 1952, 15pp. (mimeo).

United Nations. *Public finance information papers: Peru*. Sales No. 1952.XVI.2, New York, 1952.

United Nations, Technical Assistance Administration. "Informe sobre la política tributaria del Perú." Doc. No. TAA/PER/9 (restricted), 25 January 1959.

United Nations, Technical Assistance Administration. "Informe suplementario sobre la política tributaria en el Perú." Doc. No. TAA/PER/9/Add.1 (restricted), 18 September 1960.

United States Department of Commerce. *Basic data on the economy of Peru*. Washington, 1965, 22pp.

United States Department of Commerce. *Investment in Peru*. Washington, 1957, pp. 143-150.

Velarde Morán, E. (ed.). *Legislación y jurisprudencia tributaria en el Perú*. Imprenta del Ministerio de Guerra, Lima, 1962, 379pp.

Velarde Morán, E. *Normas contables y legislación tributaria; disposiciones sobre balances de los libros de contabilidad, sucesiones y jurisprudencia fiscal, control de sucursales de sociedades, fraudes-estafas-irregularidades*. Ayacucho, Lima, 1956, 441pp.

2

Arthur D. Little, Inc. *A program for the industrial and regional development of Peru*. Cambridge, Mass., 1960, 198pp.

Ferrero, R. *La política fiscal y la economía nacional*. Editorial Lúmer, Lima, 1946, 77pp.

Ferrero, R. "La política tributaria mas conveniente para el país," *Revista de* seguros (Lima), November-December 1957, p. 203.

Garmendia Bravo, L. "El presupuesto, los principios presupuestarios y la planificación," *Revista de la Guardia civil de Perú*, vol. 31, no. 280, 1962, pp. 56-57.

4

Capuñay Mimbela, C. "La historia del impuesto general sobre la renta en Perú, desde su génesis hasta nuestros días," *Revista de la Facultad de ciencias económicas y comerciales*, no. 32, April 1945, pp. 28-102.

"Crítica a la reglamentación del impuesto a las utilidades profesionales," *Revista jurisprudencia peruana*, vol. 17, September 1959, pp. 957-960.

Ferrero, R. *Estudio comparado de los impuestos a la renta en el Perú y los demás países de América Latina*. Asociación de Bancos, Cámara de Comercio de Lima, Lima, 2 volumes, 1952-1953.

Foreign Tax Law Association. *Peruvian income tax service*. Centerport, L.I., N.Y., loose-leaf, 1955–1956.

"Income taxes on foreign mining," *Foreign commerce weekly*, vol. 63, no. 7, 1960, p. 11.

Nuñez Borja, H. "Los impuestos directos en el Perú," *Revista de Universidad nacional de San Augustín de Arequipa*, vol. 21, 1949, pp. 12-30.

"Peru modifies income taxes on foreign mining firms," *Foreign tax law weekly bulletin*, vol. 10, no. 49, 1960, p. 2.

"Peru repeals excess profit tax," *Foreign commerce weekly*, vol. 61, no. 4, 1959.

"Taxation of income in Peru," *Foreign tax law weekly bulletin*, vol. 1, no. 41, 1951, pp. 3-16.

5

Amézaga Carranza, D. *Legislación y jurisprudencia de impuestos de sucesión*. Lima, 1959.

7

Levin, J. *The export economies*. Harvard University Press, Cambridge, Mass., 1960, pp. 91-96.

"Reglamento aduanero de ferias internacionales," *Informativo legal Rodrigo*, vol. 5, 1965, pp. 1996-2006.

United States Department of Commerce. *Foreign trade regulations of Peru*. Washington, 1964, 8pp.

United States Department of Commerce. *Import tariff system of Peru*. Washington, 1963, 4pp.

8

"Corporation and tax laws affecting foreigners in Peru," *Foreign tax law semiweekly bulletin*, vol. 4, nos. 70-75, 1954, pp. 1-40.

"Peru increases alien income taxes," *Foreign tax law weekly bulletin*, vol. 9, no. 5, 1958, pp. 7-8.

"The taxation question in the negotiation of an over-all metals and minerals agreement between the United States and Peru," *Foreign relations of the United States diplomatic papers*, vol. 6, 1943, pp. 735-744.

United States Department of Commerce. *Establishing a business in Peru*. Washington, 1966, 28pp.

10

"Proposed new real estate taxes," *Foreign tax law weekly bulletin*, vol. 15, no. 15, 1964, pp. 2-5.

Rueda Sanchez, G. *Patente comercial e industrial y profesional y predios rusticos y urbanos*. n.p., n.d.

11

Aizenstat, A. "Structure and taxation of agriculture in Peru." In: H. Wald and J. Froomkin (eds.), *Papers and proceedings of the Conference on agricultural taxation and economic development*, pp. 322-336. Harvard Law School International Program in Taxation, Cambridge, Mass., 1954.

Blase, M., *et al.* "Fuentes de financiación de la reforma agraria." In: *Seminario sobre el financiamiento de la reforma agraria*. Instituto Interamericano de Ciencias Agricolas, San José, 1964.

Strasma, J. *Agrarian reform, land purchase, and industrialization in Peru*. University of Wisconsin Land Tenure Center, Madison, Wisc., 1966, 21pp. Translation of: "Financiamiento de la reforma agraria en el Perú," *El trimestre económico*, vol. 32, July-September 1965, pp. 484-500.

12

Boesen, R. *Investment opportunities, tax savings and other benefits for foreign*

and domestic businesses under the Peruvian industrial development law. Peruvian Times, Lima, 1960, 260pp.
"Industrial development law enacted in Peru," Foreign commerce weekly, vol. 61, no. 26, 1959.
"Tax exemptions," Foreign tax law weekly bulletin, vol. 10, no. 36, 1960, pp. 7-8.
"10-year tax holiday for eastern Peru," Foreign tax law weekly bulletin, vol. 14, no. 48, 1964, pp. 4-7.

13

Chávez Molina, J. "Reforma de la administración tributaria," Informativo legal Rodrigo, vol. 5, 1965, pp. 2052-2085.
Costa, J. Administration in the superintendency of Peru. International Cooperation Administration, Washington, 1960 (mimeo).
"Memoria del tribunal fiscal," Revista de jurisprudencia peruana, vol. 23, April 1965, pp. 406-415.

14

Belaúnde Guinassi, M. "Autonomía del derecho tributario," Revista jurídica del Perú, vol. 14, 1963, pp. 81-105.
Busto Vargas, J. del. "Lo contencioso-tributario," Revista jurídica del Perú, vol. 14, 1963, pp. 106-127.

17

Almeida, R. "La zona latinoamericana de libre comercio," Técnicas financieras (CEMLA), vol. 2, no. 5, May-June 1963, pp. 453-472.
Gutiérrez Kirchner, A. "El mercomún latinoamericano y la política fiscal," Investigación fiscal, no. 19, July 1967, pp. 15-63.

18

Diamond, W. Foreign tax and trade briefs. Fallon Law Book Company, New York, loose-leaf, 1951–.
Economist Intelligence Unit, Ltd. Economic review of Peru, Bolivia, and Ecuador. London, irregular.
"Peru law digest." In: Martindale-Hubbell law directory, vol. 4, pp. 2856-2869. Martindale-Hubbell, Inc., Summit, N.J., 1961.

PHILIPPINES

1

Alberto, A. "Parity revisited," Lyceum of the Philippines law review, vol. 9, 1965, pp. 15-20.
Alejandro, J. (ed.). The law on taxation. Arcilla Bookbinding Service, Manila, 1961, 784pp.
Alejandro, J. Notes on taxation. F. P. Agustin, Manila, 1954, 455pp. (typewritten).
Alejandro, J. Taxation. Philan Publishing Co., Manila, revised edition, 1961, 555pp.
Bureau of Internal Revenue. The Philippine national internal revenue code, updated to June 1965. Tax Service of the Philippines, Manila, 1965, 757pp.
Campos, J., Jr. "Annual survey of taxation," Philippine law journal, vol. 30, 1955, pp. 60-65.
Caparás, M. Case book for a course in taxation. Ramón Quisumbing Books, Manila, 274pp.
Collas, J., Jr. "Taxation in the Philippines," Taxes, vol. 40, 1962, pp. 448-458.
Evangelista, I. Cases and materials on taxation. Philaw Publishing Co., Manila, 1952, 499pp.
Francisco, V. Taxation. East Publishing, Manila, 1950, 547pp.
Gadioma, D. "Taxation as it affects sales finance business," Philippine tax journal, vol. 11, 1966, pp. 277-289.
Garcia, G. Notes and materials on taxation. Philan Publishing Co., Manila, 1950, 286pp.
Gonzáles, E. (ed.). A compilation of B.I.R. rulings, tax case decisions, tax laws 1963-64. Bureau of Internal Revenue, Manila, 2 volumes, 1964-1965.
"Handbook on Philippine taxes," Philippine tax journal, vol. 8, 1963, pp. 501-534.
Joint Legislative-Executive Tax Commission. Handbook on Philippine taxes. Manila, 1964, 39pp.
Kahn, I., Jr. "Anatomy of the Philippine tax system," Philippine law journal, vol. 37, September 1962, pp. 582-600.
Lim, A. "The case for tax revision," Philippine journal of public administration, vol. 6, July 1962, pp. 192-199.
Lobrin, A. Notes on the law on taxation in the Philippines. Philaw Publishing Co., Manila, revised edition, 1956, 439pp.

Lopez-Campos, M. "Annual survey of cases on taxation," *Philippine law journal,* vol. 33, 1958, pp. 303-320.

Lopez-Campos, M. "Annual survey of 1959 Supreme court decisions in taxation," *Philippine law journal,* vol. 35, 1960, pp. 841-861.

Lopez-Campos, M. "Survey of the 1960 decisions on taxation law," *Philippine law journal,* vol. 36, 1961, pp. 372-389.

Lopez-Campos, M. "Taxation—1958," *Philippine law journal,* vol. 34, 1959, p. 277.

McMicking, J. "Our tax structure and the European philosophy of taxation," *Philippine tax journal,* vol. 8, 1963, pp. 1-5.

Monk, M. "Tax structure of Philippines," *Indian taxation,* vol. 4, October 1953, pp. 433-447. Also in: *Accountants' journal,* vol. 2, September 1952, pp. 232-238.

Philippine Institute of Accountants. *Taxes: Addresses delivered at third annual accounting seminar, 1952.* Manila, 1952, 43pp.

"President Macapagal's tax message to Congress," *Philippine tax journal,* vol. 7, 1962, pp. 125-134.

"President Macapagal's tax message to Congress," *Philippine tax journal,* vol. 8, 1963, pp. 36-38.

President Macapagal's tax message to Congress," *Philippine law journal,* vol. 39, 1965, pp. 129-138.

Price Waterhouse & Co. *Information guide for doing business in the Philippines.* New York, 1966.

"Proposed revision of the national internal revenue code by stages," *Philippine tax journal,* vol. 8, 1963, pp. 137-155.

"Proposed tax code," *Foreign tax law weekly bulletin,* vol. 16, no. 5, 1965, pp. 10-18.

"Proposed tax code," *Philippine tax journal,* vol. 10, 1965, pp. 193-202.

Quiazon, T., Jr. "Recent problems in taxation," *Philippine law journal,* vol. 37, 1962, pp. 685-708.

"Revision of the tax code." In: Joint Legislative-Executive Tax Commission, *Report (1962),* vol. 4, pp. 6-22. Manila, 1963.

"Revision of the tax code," *Philippine tax journal,* vol. 9, 1964, pp. 197-203.

Rey, C. *Tax code annotated.* Central Book Supply Inc., Manila, 1959, 429pp.

Rivera, J. "Are taxes contributions or investments?" *Philippine law journal,* vol. 37, 1962, pp. 709-727.

Shere, L. *A report on tax program for the Philippines.* United States Economic Survey Mission to the Philippines, 1950 (mimeo).

Shere, L. "Tax program for the Philippines," *National tax journal,* vol. 4, June 1951, pp. 97-115.

Sycip, D. "Urgently needed: Complete and basic tax reform," *Philippine tax journal,* vol. 9, 1964, pp. 253-257.

Sycip, Gorres, Velayo & Co. *A summary of Philippine taxes affecting business.* Manila, 1964, 28pp.

Trinidad, R. "Basic approaches in the formulation of tax policies (address)," *Economic research journal,* vol. 9, September 1962, pp. 78-90.

United States Department of Commerce. *Basic data on the economy of the Philippines.* Washington, 1964, 20pp.

United States Department of Commerce. *Investment in the Philippines.* Washington, 1955, 151pp.

White, Page and Co. *Memorandum on taxation, exchange and other matters.* Manila, 31 July 1954, 5pp. (mimeo).

Yoingco, A. "Needed: Suitable tax structure for national government," *Accountants' journal,* vol. 8, March 1958, pp. 13-21.

2

Alas, A. de las. "Economic progress and taxation," *Philippine tax journal,* vol. 8, 1963, pp. 313-321.

Araneta, S. "Tax policy to increase our permanent capacity to produce through austerity." In: Joint Legislative-Executive Tax Commission, *Taxation and socio-economic growth,* pp. 28-42. Manila, 1960.

Charlesworth, H. "Economic growth and taxation," *Economic research journal,* vol. 8, June 1961, pp. 20-38.

Evangelista, I. *Philippine taxation, budgeting and fiscal policy.* Castro, Manila, 1962, 210pp.

Golay, F. *The Philippines: Public policy and national economic development.* Cornell University Press, Ithaca, N.Y., 1961, chapter 9.

Halsema, J. "Philippine financial policies," *Far Eastern survey,* vol. 18, May 1949, pp. 97-102.

Joint Legislative-Executive Tax Commission. *Taxation and socio-economic growth.* Manila, 1960, 341pp.

Joint Legislative-Executive Tax Commission and National Economic Council, Office of Statistical Coordination and Standards. *A study of tax burden by income class in the Philippines.* Manila, 1964, 122pp.

Kintanar, A. *An analysis of the effects of certain modifications in the tax structure on the rate of economic development in the Philippines.* Ph.D. thesis, Yale University, New Haven, Conn., 1960.

Medina, A. "Some uses of national income data with reference to tax policy research," *Economic research journal,* vol. 8, December 1961, pp. 157-161.

Pujat, G. "Tax measures designed to meet our changing economy," *Far Eastern law review,* vol. 7, April 1959-March 1960, p. 565.

Reyes, R. "Some tax measures to solve our economic problems," *Philippine tax journal,* vol. 8, 1963, pp. 129-136.

Yoingco, A., and Casem, A., Jr. "Philippine government expenditure and tax revenue patterns: The recent experience," *Economic research journal,* vol. 11, December 1964, pp. 180-193.

3

Yoingco, A., and Trinidad, R. "A comparative study of the individual income tax structures of selected Asian countries," *Philippine economic journal,* vol. 2, no. 2, Second Semester 1963.

Yoingco, A., and Trinidad, R. *Fiscal systems and practices in Asian countries.* Frederick A. Praeger, New York, 1967.

4

"Amendments to Philippine national internal revenue code concerning income and excise taxes," *Foreign tax law weekly bulletin,* vol. 1, no. 29, 1951, pp. 3-31.

Aranas, J. "Tax on capital gains," *Accountants' journal,* vol. 7, March 1957, pp. 16-20.

Baldonado, J. "The problems of undue accumulations," *Far Eastern law review,* vol. 9, 1962, pp. 456-462.

Balmaceda, C. "The accountant and some aspects of taxation income in Philippine

economic development," *Philippine tax journal,* vol. 9, 1964, pp. 189-193.

Bureau of Internal Revenue. *Income tax primer.* Manila, n.d., 16pp.

Castro, C. de. "Income tax problems in corporate distribution," *Far Eastern law review,* vol. 9, August 1961, pp. 91-166.

Collas, J., Jr. "The 'tax-free' merger or consolidation: A critique of republic act no. 1921," *Philippine law journal,* vol. 38, 1963, pp. 737-766.

"Corporate readjustments under sec. 35 of the tax code," *Law review* (Philippines), vol. 10, 1960, pp. 290-300.

Dikitanan, R. "The economic significance of the capital gains tax," *Economic research journal,* vol. 10, September 1963, pp. 103-108.

Enrile, J. "Capital gains tax," *Far Eastern law review,* vol. 8, December 1960, p. 437.

Enrile, J. "Income tax treatment of corporate merger and consolidation revisited," *Philippine law journal,* vol. 37, 1962, pp. 655-684.

Evangelista, I. *Philippine income, estate, inheritance, and gift tax laws.* J. R. Castro, Manila, revised edition, 1957, 491pp.

Filler, A. "Corporate distributions to the shareholder under section 83 of the tax code," *University of the East law journal,* vol. 5, 1963, pp. 257-268.

Foreign Tax Law Association. *Philippine income tax service.* Hempstead, L.I., N.Y., loose-leaf, 1952-1954. St. Petersburg, Fla., loose-leaf, 1964-.

Gadioma, D. "Corporate readjustment and non-recognition of gain or loss," *Philippine law journal,* vol. 37, 1962, pp. 404-429.

Gadioma, D. "Corporate readjustment and recognition of gain or loss," *Philippine tax journal,* vol. 7, 1962, pp. 1-29.

Gadioma, D. "Undistributed corporate surplus and tax problems involved," *Philippine tax journal,* vol. 10, 1965, pp. 65-74.

García, B. "Reinsurance premiums and the Philippine income tax laws," *Far Eastern law review,* vol. 9, May 1962, pp. 447-455.

Guloy, E. "Tax treatments of stock dividends," *Far Eastern law review,* vol. 10, 1962, pp. 105-114.

"Income tax primer: Individuals, corporations," *Central bank news digest* (Philippines), vol. 12, 15 March 1960, pp. 3-9.

Kintanar, A. "Two papers on fiscal matter: The incidence of some direct taxes in the Philippines, 1960," *Philippine economic journal,* vol. 2, no. 2, Second Semester 1963.

Molina, G. "Partnership in income taxation," *Ateneo law journal,* vol. 10, November 1960, p. 142.

Nolledo, J. "The tax treatment of prepaid income and expenses," *Far Eastern law review,* vol. 10, February 1963, pp. 297-362.

Ong, J. "Tax aspects of charitable contributions," *San Beda law journal,* vol. 8, no. 1, 1965, pp. 9-15.

Ornum, M. "Income tax aspects of depreciation," *Faculty journal* (Lyceum of the Philippines), vol. 1, 1961, pp. 78-93.

Pérez, Y. "Corporate treatment of unincorporated entities," *Philippine tax journal,* vol. 10, 1965, pp. 708-716.

"Philippine direct taxes," *Philippine tax journal,* vol. 10, 1965, pp. 208-219.

"Philippines war profit tax law: Republic act no. 55," *Foreign tax law weekly bulletin,* vol. 1, no. 49, 1951, pp. 3-20.

"Piercing the corporate veil," *Foreign tax law weekly bulletin,* vol. 16, no. 43, 1966, pp. 2-11.

"Pointers of claims for refunds of excess income tax," *Philippine tax journal,* vol. 11, 1966, pp. 168-172.

Tantuico, F., and Tantuico, F., Jr. *Rules and rulings on the Philippine income tax.* Leyte Publishing Corporation, Tacloban City, 1961, 388pp.

"Undistributed corporate surplus and tax problems involved," *Foreign tax law weekly bulletin,* vol. 15, no. 45, 1965, pp. 12-18.

Villa, R. "Loss carry-back and carry-over," *Lyceum of the Philippines law review,* vol. 9, 1964, pp. 37-56.

Villanueva, G. "Tax-free exchanges of property pursuant to corporate mergers and consolidations: The Philippines," *Ateneo law journal,* vol. 7, August 1957, pp. 18-31.

Yoingco, A., and Trinidad, R. "A study of the personal income tax system of the Philippines," *Economic research journal,* vol. 10, December 1963, pp. 140-152.

Zagala, R. "The net worth-expenditures technique of taxable income determination," *Far Eastern law review,* vol. 11, 1964, pp. 426-448.

5

Bongco, G. "Is donative intent essential in transfers for less than full and adequate consideration?" *Far Eastern law review,* vol. 10, 1963, pp. 283-296.

Bureau of Internal Revenue. *Primer on estate, inheritance and gift taxes.* Manila, n.d.

Evangelista, P. "Estate and inheritance taxes," *Accountants' journal,* vol. 4, June 1954, pp. 134-138.

Guzmán, F. de. "The tax consequences of renunciation of inheritance," *MLQU law quarterly,* vol. 13, 1964, pp. 237-260, 373-409.

Mangaliman, P. *The law of estate and inheritance and donor's and donee's gift taxation of the Philippines.* General Printing Press, Manila, 1956, 512pp.

Mangaliman, P. *The law of estate and inheritance taxation of the Philippines.* General Printing Press, Manila, 1951, 380pp.

Vega, E. "Estate and inheritance taxes: Critical branch of taxation," *Accountants' journal,* vol. 5, December 1955, pp. 252-260.

6

Evangelista, I. *Materials on business and occupation taxes, miscellaneous taxes, national tax census and others.* R. M. García Publishing House and Book Store, Manila, 1958, 315pp.

"Liability for retailers tax," *Foreign tax law weekly bulletin,* vol. 15, no. 47, 1965, pp. 1-5.

Maralit, A. "Tax aspects of excise tax on foreign exchange," *Accountants' journal,* vol. 2, September 1952, pp. 249-252.

"Philippine indirect taxes," *Philippine tax journal,* vol. 10, 1965, pp. 271-287.

Santos, G. "Double taxation in installment sales," *Far Eastern law review,* vol. 9, 1961, pp. 196-200.

Umali, R. "Present sales tax law," *Journal of Philippine institute of accountants,* first quarter 1951, pp. 12-20.

United States Department of Commerce. *Sales and compensation taxes of the Philippines.* Washington, 1960, 3pp.

7

Castro, A. "Philippine-American tariff and trade relations, 1898-1954," *Philippine economic journal,* vol. 4, no. 1, 1965.

Gunigundo, M. "The trinity in the tariff," *MLQU law quarterly,* vol. 12, 1963, pp. 397-439.

Legarda, B., Jr. "Economic objectives of export taxation in the Philippines (address)," *Philippine economy review,* vol. 9, December 1962, pp. 27-30. Also in: *Economic research journal,* vol. 9, September 1962, pp. 91-98.

"Progress in tariff revision." In: Joint Legislative-Executive Tax Commission, *Report (1962),* vol. 4, pp. 57-61. Manila, 1963.

Sadiua, M. "Decontrol (sic) and the export tax," *Philippine journal of public administration,* vol. 7, April 1963, pp. 91-101.

United States Department of Commerce. *Foreign trade regulations of the Philippines.* Washington, 1963, 8pp.

8

de Joya, A. "Formation and operation of foreign subsidiaries and branches, including the extent to which foreign subsidiaries are entitled to special treatment under the Philippine law," *International bar association conference report,* vol. 8, July 1960, p. 367.

Paras, E. "Territorial limits of taxation," *Far Eastern law review,* vol. 13, 1966, pp. 15-32.

Romulo, R. "Tax consequences of doing business in the Philippines," *Washington law review,* vol. 40, August 1965, pp. 602-644.

"Some fiscal aspects of the Laurel-Langley agreement," *Philippine tax journal,* vol. 10, 1965, pp. 327-338.

Sumulong, L. "Taxation of Filipinos with foreign sources of income and of foreigners with Philippine sources of income," *American chamber of commerce of the Philippines journal,* vol. 37, August 1962, p. 416.

United States Department of Commerce. *Establishing a business in the Philippines.* Washington, 1965, 16pp.

United States Department of Commerce. *Investment in the Philippines: Conditions and outlook for U.S. investors.* Washington, 1955, pp. 79-87, 113.

9

Blanco, G. "The problems of municipal taxation," *San Beda law journal,* vol. 1, no. 1, 1961, pp. 18-40.

Castillo, J. *The law on local taxation.* University Publishing Company, Manila, 1954, 426pp.

Fernández, P. *Handbook on municipal taxation.* Central Book Supply, Philippines, 1962, 120pp.

Fernández, P. "Relief from municipal taxation in the Philippines," *Philippine law journal,* vol. 35, 1960, pp. 1058-1081.

Fernández, P. "The taxing power of municipal corporations in the Philippines," *Philippine law journal,* vol. 36, 1961, pp. 556-598.

"Fiscal position of local government." In: Joint Legislative-Executive Tax Commission, *Report (1962),* vol. 4, pp. 40-56. Manila, 1963.

Limpingco, R. "Some limitations on the taxing power of municipal corporations," *Far Eastern law review,* vol. 10, February 1963, pp. 275-282.

10

Castillo, J. *Property-tax administration in the Philippines (1956).* Special Tax Revision Commission, Bureau of Printing, Manila, 1957, 170pp.

Enrile, J. "Tax treatment of real estate transactions," *Philippine tax journal,* vol. 10, 1965, pp. 631-665.

Monk, M., and McDiarmid, O. *Taxation of real property in the Philippines.* International Cooperation Administration, Washington, 1953, 34pp. (mimeo).

11

Ferry, D. *Agricultural taxation in the Philippines.* J.S.D. thesis, Yale University, New Haven, Conn., 1962.

12

Brinas, A. "Investment incentives in the Philippines," *Economic research journal,* vol. 4, June 1957, pp. 25-32.

Evangelista, P. "Accounting requirements and problems of our tax-exempt industries," *Accountants' journal,* vol. 5, June 1955, pp. 92-96.

Joint Legislative-Executive Tax Commission. *Tax incentives in the Philippines.* Intramuros, Manila, 1965, 16pp.

"Laws granting tax exemptions and other

privileges (1946-1963)," *Philippine tax journal,* vol. 9, 1964, pp. 308-316.

Ledesma, O. "Tax exemption: How far should it go?" *Philippine tax journal,* vol. 7, 1962, pp. 501-505.

Montinola, A. "Tax exemption and new industries," *Accountants' journal,* vol. 3, June 1953, pp. 92-98.

Monzon, L. "Taxation and incentives," *Philippine tax journal,* vol. 8, 1963, pp. 253-259.

Padernal, H. "Tax liabilities of new and necessary industries," *Philippine law journal,* vol. 35, 1960, p. 1521.

Padilla, A. "Tax incentives for economic growth," *Philippine tax journal,* vol. 7, 1962, pp. 557-564.

"Philippine tax exemption laws," *Philippine tax journal,* vol. 10, 1965, pp. 389-393.

13

"The activities and accomplishments of the Joint legislative-executive tax commission," *Philippine tax journal,* vol. 7, 1962, pp. 309-320.

Booz, Allen and Hamilton Management Consultant. *Modernization of budgeting, accounting, auditing and treasury practices of the Philippine government.* International Cooperation Administration, Washington, 1955-1957 (mimeo).

Castaneda, D. "Inventory method of investigation of Bureau of internal revenue," *Accountants' journal,* vol. 5, June 1955, pp. 97-103.

Current problems in Philippine public administration. University of the Philippines Institute of Public Administration, Manila, 1954, 99pp.

Davis, R. *Terminal report of Ray E. Davis to the Philippine Bureau of internal revenue.* International Cooperation Administration, Washington, 1958, 115pp.

Gimeno, F. "The independence of the General auditing office," *Far Eastern law review,* vol. 11, 1964, pp. 406-425.

"Joint legislative-executive tax commission," *Philippine tax journal,* vol. 6, 1961, pp. 133-146, 213-222.

Joint Legislative-Executive Tax Commission. *Survey on tax consciousness in the Philippines.* Manila, 1962, 74pp.

Lobrin, A. "Perplexing problems in tax

collection," *Philippine tax journal,* vol. 6, 1961, pp. 197-205.

Mathay, I. "Fiscal administration and recent development in the General auditing office," *Philippine journal of public administration,* vol. 5, no. 2, April 1961, pp. 118-122.

Montejo, F., Jr. "The Philippine Joint legislative-executive tax commission," *Philippine tax journal,* vol. 9, 1964, pp. 1-28.

Nable, M. "The Board of tax appeals," *Far Eastern university law quarterly,* vol. 1, 1953, pp. 35-37.

Navarro, M. "Mechanics, jurisdiction and achievements of the Court of tax appeals," *Philippine law journal,* vol. 37, 1962, pp. 445-457.

"Philippine tax administration and research," *Philippine tax journal,* vol. 10, 1965, pp. 339-345.

"Problems in Philippine tax administration," *Philippine tax journal,* vol. 11, 1966, pp. 234-253.

Stene, E. *Public administration in the Philippines.* University of the Philippines Institute of Public Administration, Manila, 1955, 415pp.

"Survey on tax consciousness in the Philippines conducted by the Joint legislative-executive tax commission," *Philippine tax journal,* vol. 8, 1963, pp. 69-98.

Tabios, B. "Application of the net-worth method and devices for ferreting out tax evasion," *Philippine tax journal,* vol. 10, 1965, pp. 503-523.

"Tax consciousness in the Philippines." In: Joint Legislative-Executive Tax Commission, *Report (1962),* vol. 4, pp. 23-39. Manila, 1963.

"Taxation: (1) Withholding agents, (2) provisions intended t plug loopholes against tax evasion," *Accountants' journal,* vol. 3, September 1953, pp. 204-210.

Umali, R. "Summary of tax-payers' remedies," *Philippine tax journal,* vol. 10, 1965, pp. 567-604.

Vega, E., and Short, R. "National tax administration in the Philippines," *Washington law review,* vol. 40, August 1965, p. 579.

Waldby, O. *Philippine public fiscal administration.* University of the Philippines Institute of Public Administration, Manila, 1954, 471pp.

14

Catangui, R., Jr. "Power to collect internal revenue taxes," *MLQU law quarterly,* vol. 12, 1963, pp. 440-451.

Catangui, R., Jr. "Power to collect taxes by distrain and levy," *Philippine tax journal,* vol. 11, 1966, pp. 133-167.

Soliven, J. "The compromising of criminal cases arising from violations of our internal revenue laws," *MLQU law quarterly,* vol. 10, 1960, pp. 483-500.

Soliven, J. "Defects of the tax court law," *Philippine tax journal,* vol. 9, 1964, pp. 317-323.

18

Diamond, W. *Foreign tax and trade briefs.* Fallon Law Book Company, New York, loose-leaf, 1951-.

Joint Legislative-Executive Tax Commission. *Annual report.* Manila, 1959-.

Joint Legislative-Executive Tax Commission. *Monthly newsletter.* Manila, 1960- (mimeo).

"Philippine Republic law digest." In: *Martindale-Hubbell law directory,* vol. 4, pp. 2870-2893. Martindale-Hubbell, Inc., Summit, N.J., 1961.

Philippine tax journal. Manila, monthly, January 1956-.

PORTUGAL

1

Alves Martins, C. "Receitas ex-ante e ex-post do estado português," *Economia e finanças,* vol. 29, no. 3, 1961, pp. 912-929.

Bastos Silva, J. "Les Impôts de l'état et les taux correspondants." In: E. Morselli and L. Trotabas, *Enquête sur les tarifs d'impôts,* pp. 303-334. CEDAM, Padova, 1964.

Caetano, M. "A reforma fiscal," *Direito,* vol. 96, 1964, pp. 4-19.

Caldeira Guimarães, J. "Alguns aspectos sociais da reforma fiscal portuguesa iniciada em 1958," *Análise social,* vol. 1, no. 4, October 1963, pp. 610-616.

Carmo e Cunha, F. do. "The Portuguese tax system," *Economia e finanças,* vol. 27, no. 3, 1959, pp. 877-950 (in Portuguese).

Federation of British Industries. *Portugal —Tax system.* London, 1963, 10pp.

Federation of British Industries. *Taxation in Western Europe, 1963: A guide for industrialists.* London, 1963, pp. 210-219.

Magalhães Godinho, V. "Les Finances publiques et la structure de l'état portugais au XVIème siècle," *Revista de economía* (Lisbon), vol. 14, no. 2, June 1962, pp. 105-115.

Martins, E. *Questionário de legislação fiscal.* Almedina, Coimbra, 8 volumes, 1964.

Monteiro, M. *A contabilidade em face da lei fiscal.* Portugália Editora, Lisbon, 2 volumes, 1964.

Pinto Babosa, A. "La fase actual de la hacienda portuguesa," *Impuestos de la hacienda pública,* vol. 21, no. 252, May 1964, pp. 365-370.

Pitta e Cunha, P. de. "The Portuguese tax reform: A brief survey," *Public finance,* vol. 21, 1966, pp. 420-430.

Pitta e Cunha, P. de, *et al.* "The Portuguese tax system, by members of the Centro de estudos fiscais," *Bulletin for international fiscal documentation,* vol. 20, 1966, pp. 265-322.

"Política fiscal," *Boletim da Direcção-geral das contribuições e impostos,* vol. 36, December 1961, pp. 1301-1342.

"Portuguese fiscal policy," *International financial news survey,* vol. 14, 26 January 1962, p. 24.

Price Waterhouse & Co. *Memorandum dated August 31, 1955 on taxation in Portugal.* Zurich, 1955, 22pp. (mimeo).

Soares, F., and Fonseca, H. *A nova reforma fiscal explicada ao comércio.* n.p., Lisbon, 1964, 127pp.

Thalez Couto, R., *et al. O sistema fazendario.* Direcção-Geral da Fazenda Nacional, Lisbon, 1964, 92pp.

United States Department of Commerce. *Basic data on the economy of Portugal.* Washington, 1966, 12pp.

2

Atlántico, B. "The fiscal system and economic development in Portugal." In A. Peacock, *Public finance as an instrument for economic development,* pp. 47-72. Organisation for Economic Co-operation and Development, Paris, 1964.

Galhardo, M. "De orientação da economia nacional através das finanças públicas," *Boletim da Direcção-geral das contribuições e impostos,* vol. 24, December 1960, pp. 2125-2136.

Pitta e Cunha, P. de. *Equilibrio orçamental e política financeira anticíclica.*

Direcção-Geral das Contribuições e Impostos, Lisbon, 1962, 150pp.

4

Barton, Mayhew & Company. *Memorandum on taxation of companies in Portugal*. Lisbon, 1961, 8pp.

Código da contribuição industrial. Atlântida, Coimbra, 1963, 325pp.

Código do impôsto profissional. Coimbra Editora, Coimbra, 1962, 104pp.

Código do impôsto profissional. Petrony, Lisbon, 1962.

Comentário ao código do impôsto profissional. Atlántida, Coimbra, 1962, 232pp.

Fernándes, M. (ed.). *Código do impôsto profissional*. Associação Comercial de Lisboa, Câmara de Comercio, Lisbon, 1963, 472pp.

Foreign Tax Law Association. *Portuguese income tax service*. St. Petersburg, Fla., loose-leaf, 1964–.

Fortuna, V. "Impôts directs portugais," *Bulletin for international fiscal documentation*, vol. 4, 1950, pp. 362-371.

Fortuna, V. "Impôts et taxes grevant les entreprises industrielles et commerciales au Portugal," *Bulletin for international fiscal documentation*, vol. 5, 1951, pp. 212-214.

Gouveia, F. (ed.). *Regime tributário das sociedades anônimas perante a reforma fiscal*. Empresa Nacional de Publicedade, Lisbon, 1964, 682pp.

Matos, J. de. "Breves considerações acerca da invocação e qualificação do acórdão do Sup. trib. adm., de 4 de dezembro de 1957 e do despacho ministerial de 1 de março de 1958, como 'documentos supervenientes' para efeito de anulação das colectas em impôsto profissional dos empregados dos organismos do coordenação económica, pagas antes de publicação dos referidos acórdão e despacho," *Revista de direito fiscal*, vol. 14, no. 1-3, 1962, pp. 5-9.

Patacas, A., and Correa Arez, M. *Código da contribuição industrial*. Machado, Porto, 1963, 256pp.

"Portugal." In: Board of Inland Revenue (Great Britain), *Income taxes outside the United Kingdom 1966*, vol. 6, pp. 243-268. H.M. Stationery Office, London, 1967.

Rodríguez Sáinz, A. "Los impuestos directos portugueses después de las re-cientes reformas fiscales," *Revista de derecho financiero y de hacienda pública* (Madrid), vol. 15, 1965, pp. 61-90.

5

Alves Valente, M. *Código do impôsto sucessorio e sisa. Livio I: Código do impôsto sucessorio*. Coleção "Reforma Fiscal" No. I, Edição de Manuel Alves Valente, Secretario de Finanças, Lisbon, 1959, 199pp.

Brito, M. de. "Simulação fiscal (com prejuízo da sisa e do impôsto sobre as sucessões e doações)," *Scientia ivridica*, vol. 11, no. 57, 1962, pp. 29-42.

Prazeres, M. *Código do impôsto do capitais*. Cruz, Braga, 1962, 136pp.

Sá Carneiro, J. *Notas ao código da sisa e do impôsto sobre as sucessões e doações*. Machado, Porto, 1962, 195pp.

6

Capelo, A. (ed.). *Impôsto sobre consumos supérfluos ou de luxo e de cerveja, refrigerantes, gasolina e tabacos*. n.p., 1961.

Código do impôsto de transacções comentado e anotado. Edição dos Autores, Lisbon, 1966, 642pp.

Fortuna, V. "La position portugaise à l'égard de l'imposition des transactions et des transmissions." In: M. Masoin and E. Morselli (eds.), *Impôts sur transactions, transmissions et chiffre d'affaires*, pp. 353-357. Archives Internationales de Finance Publique No. 2, Cedam Casa Editrice, Dr. A. Milani, Padova, 1959.

"Impôsto do pescado," *Boletim do Ministerio da iustiça*, no. 135, 1964, pp. 241-250.

Pitta e Cunha, P. de. *Os impostos sobre as transacções*. Ministerio das Finanças, Gabinete de Estudos da Direcção-Geral das Contribuições e Impostos, Lisbon, 172pp.

Pitta e Cunha, P. de. "A wholesale sales tax in Portugal," *Bulletin for international fiscal documentation*, vol. 20, 1966, pp. 441-446.

Tavares, A. *Tabela geral do impôsto do sêlo*. Edições Ática, Lisbon, 1962, 163pp.

7

United States Department of Commerce. *Foreign trade regulations of Portugal*. Washington, 1966, 8pp.

8

Duarte Faveiro, V., and Eusebio, D. "Mesures unilatérales tendant à éviter la double imposition: Portugal," *Cahiers de droit fiscal international,* vol. 44, 1961, p. 231.

United States Department of Commerce. *Establishing a business in Portugal.* Washington, 1961, 10pp.

9

Caetano, M. "Impôsto municipal 'ad valorem' sobre o pescado," *Direito,* vol. 94, January-March 1962, p. 5.

10

Alves Caetano, A. "Para o estudo económico regional da contribuição predial rústica," *Boletim da Direcção-geral das contribuições e impostos,* vols. 44-45, August-September 1962, pp. 209-232.

13

Duarte Faveiro, V. "Le Contrôle fiscal: Ses aspects juridiques, psychologiques et économiques: Portugal," *Cahiers de droit fiscal international,* vol. 39, 1959, p. 250 (summaries in German, English, and Spanish).

Duarte Faveiro, V. "For the reorganization of tax control," *Boletim da Direcção-geral das contribuições e impostos,* vol. 10, October 1959, pp. 1435-1453; vol. 11, November 1959, pp. 1631-1634 (in Portuguese).

Fernández Flores, F. "Estructura de la administración financiera y nueva organización de los servicios de la justicia fiscal," *Revista de derecho financiero y de hacienda pública* (Madrid), vol. 14, 1964, pp. 91-100.

Pardal, F. *Código das execuções fiscais.* Livraria Almedina, Coimbra, 1962, 534pp.

14

Carmo e Cunha, F. do. "Preceitos da constituição política sobre o sistema tributário português," *Boletim da Direcção-geral das contribuições e impostos,* vol. 24, December 1960, pp. 2079-2123.

Mouteira Guerreiro, A. *Direito processual tributario.* Atlántida, Lisbon, 1961, 251pp.

Oliveira, J., and Atanásio, A. (eds.). *Con-*

tencioso aduaneiro. Livraria Portugal, Lisbon, 1960, 179pp.

18

Capêlo, A. *Nova legislação fiscal.* Secretario de Finanças, Lisbon, loose-leaf.

Diamond, W. *Foreign tax and trade briefs.* Fallon Law Book Company, New York, loose-leaf, 1951-.

"Portugal law digest." In: *Martindale-Hubbell law directory,* vol. 4, pp. 2894-2899. Martindale-Hubbell, Inc., Summit, N.J., 1961.

PORTUGUESE GUINEA

2

Gersdorff, R. "La Formation de capitaux par des mesures fiscales dans l'empire portugais," *Public finance,* vol. 15, 1960, pp. 31-50 (English summary).

8

Organisation for European Economic Cooperation. *Taxation systems applicable to investments in the overseas countries associated with member countries of O.E.E.C.* Paris, 1960, 100pp.

12

Gersdorff, R. *Mesures pour encourager la formation de capitaux privés dans l'empire portugais.* Polygraphischer Verlag, Zurich, 1958.

PUERTO RICO

1

Arthur Andersen & Co. *Tax and trade guide: Puerto Rico.* New York, 1964.

Price Waterhouse & Co. *Information guide for doing business in Puerto Rico.* New York, 1965.

Tax laws of Puerto Rico. Equity Publishing Corporation, Oxford, N.H., 1962 (Supplement, 1963), 926pp.

2

Baer, W. "Puerto Rico: An evaluation of a successful development program," *Quarterly journal of economics,* vol. 73, November 1959, pp. 645-671.

Bhatia, M. *Redistribution of income through the fiscal system of Puerto Rico.* Office of the Governor, Puerto Rico Planning Board, Bureau of Economics and Statistics, San Juan, 1960, 45pp.

Department of the Treasury, Office of Economic and Financial Research. *Report on finances and economy.* San Juan, 1956, 18pp.

Descartes, S. *Financing economic development in Puerto Rico, 1941-1949.* Department of Finance, San Juan, 1950, 39pp.

"Financing economic development in Puerto Rico," *Federal reserve bank of New York monthly review,* May 1961.

Moscoso, T. "Industrial development in Puerto Rico." In: *Proceedings of the economic planning seminar of the Commonwealth of Puerto Rico, 1958,* pp. 228-231. Regional Technical Aids Center, International Cooperation Administration, México, 1960.

Noguera, J. "Public revenues: Ways to forecast and increase them." In: *Proceedings of the economic planning seminar of the Commonwealth of Puerto Rico, 1958,* pp. 369-386. Regional Technical Aids Center, International Cooperation Administration, México, 1960.

Phillips, C. *A tax program to encourage Puerto Rico's economic growth.* Planning Pamphlet No. 105, National Planning Association, Washington, 1958, 38pp.

Shere, L. *A tax program for Puerto Rico.* Department of Education Press, San Juan, 1953, 190pp.

4

Department of the Treasury. *Income tax act of 1954 (with supplements to 1960).* San Juan, 337pp.

Foreign Tax Law Association. *Puerto Rican income tax service.* Centerport, L.I., N.Y., loose-leaf, 1955–.

Goode, R. *Integration of business and individual income taxes.* Department of the Treasury and the Economic Development Administration, San Juan, 1952.

Mayoral Bigas, J. "The taxation of partnership profits under the income tax act of Puerto Rico of 1954," *Tax law review,* vol. 11, March 1956, pp. 315-325.

Novak, J. "Puerto Rican trusts as a means of distributing income realized in Puerto Rico tax-free to United States citizens not bona fide residents of Puerto Rico," *Tax law review,* vol. 16, May 1961, pp. 485-510.

Rivera, H. *Income tax development and procedure in Puerto Rico.* Ph.D. thesis, New York, 1959.

Taylor, M. *Evaluation of income tax administration in Puerto Rico.* Department of the Treasury, San Juan, 1957.

Taylor, M. *Some aspects of long-range corporate tax policy.* Department of the Treasury, San Juan, 1958.

6

Department of the Treasury. *Excise act on article of use and consumption in Puerto Rico.* San Juan, 1956, 69pp.

Hollander, J. "Excise taxation in Puerto Rico," *Quarterly journal of economics,* vol. 16, February 1912, pp. 187-213.

8

Peat, Marwick, Mitchell & Co. *Puerto Rico as a tax haven.* San Juan, 1959, 4pp.

Sugarman, N., and Scott, J. "Some second thoughts on doing business in Puerto Rico," *Taxes,* vol. 38, 1960.

Taylor, M. *A report on the taxation of foreign income with particular reference to Puerto Rico and Germany.* Department of the Treasury, San Juan, 1958.

Taylor, M. *A review of draft bills for the promotion of international trading companies.* Department of the Treasury, San Juan, 1958.

10

Public Administration Service. *Procedures for real property assessment in Puerto Rico.* Chicago, 1953, 305pp.

Public Administration Service. *Standards for assessing real property (Puerto Rico).* Chicago, 1953, 60pp.

Rodríguez, D., and Marshall, T. "Reassessment in Puerto Rico," *Public administration review,* vol. 10, Autumn 1950, pp. 245-253.

12

Baker, R. "Puerto Rico's program of industrial tax exemption," *George Washington law review,* vol. 18, April 1950, pp. 327-370; vol. 18, June 1950, pp. 443-473.

Bhatia, M. "Tax exemption in a developing economy," *National tax journal,* vol. 13, December 1960, pp. 241-249.

Economic Development Administration.

Industrial incentive act of 1963. San Juan, 42pp.

Harris, B. "Note on tax exemption and development," *National tax journal,* vol. 8, December 1955, pp. 393-399.

Mears, L. *Private investment and Puerto Rican development: Inducements and impediments.* Ph.D. thesis, California, 1954.

Prentice-Hall, Inc. *Tax advantages of doing business in Puerto Rico.* Englewood Cliffs, N.J., 1957, 22pp.

"Private investment and the industrialization of Puerto Rico," *Federal reserve bank of New York monthly review,* April 1960, pp. 68-74.

Research Institute of America, Inc. "Puerto Rico—Land of tax exemption," *Taxation report,* vol. 5, no. 22, Fall 1952.

Ross, D. "The costs and benefits of Puerto Rico's fomento programmes," *Social and economic studies,* vol. 6, September 1957, pp. 329-362.

Rudick, H., and Allen, G. "Tax aspects of operations under the Puerto Rican exemption program," *Tax law review,* vol. 7, May 1952, pp. 403-437; revised December 1959.

Stead, W. *Fomento: The economic development of Puerto Rico.* National Planning Association, Washington, 1958, 151pp.

Tax exemption as a factor of growth in a sample of locally-owned manufacturing firms. Economic Development Administration, San Juan, 1957.

Taylor, M. "Industrial tax exemption in Puerto Rico," *National tax journal,* vol. 7, December 1954, pp. 359-371.

Taylor, M. *Industrial tax-exemption in Puerto Rico.* University of Wisconsin Press, Madison, Wisc., 1957, 172pp.

Taylor, M. "Tax exemption as compared to other factors in operating and locating new industrial firms in Puerto Rico," *Social and economic studies,* vol. 4, June 1955, pp. 121-132.

Taylor, M. "What happens when exemptions end: Retrospect and prospect in Puerto Rico." In: Tax Institute of America, Inc., *Taxation and operations abroad,* pp. 170-186. Princeton, N.J., 1960. Also in: *Tax policy,* vol. 26, November-December 1959. Reprinted in: R. Bird and O. Oldman (eds.), *Readings on taxation in developing countries,* pp. 245-256. The Johns Hopkins Press, Baltimore, 1964.

18

Commerce Clearing House, Inc. *Puerto Rico tax reporter.* Chicago, loose-leaf, 1964-.

Diamond, W. *Foreign tax and trade briefs.* Fallon Law Book Company, New York, loose-leaf, 1951-.

Treasury Department. *What you should know about taxes in Puerto Rico.* San Juan, annual.

QATAR

4

"Amending certain provisions of Qatar income tax decree," *Foreign tax law weekly bulletin,* vol. 16, no. 26, 1965, pp. 11-13.

7

United States Department of Commerce. *Foreign trade regulations of the Arabian Gulf States.* Washington, 1967, 8pp.

RHODESIA

4

"Federation of Rhodesia and Nyasaland," *Coopers and Lybrand international tax summaries,* vol. 3, March 1960, pp. 1-15.

Garmany, J. "Revenue allocation in a federal state: The experience of Rhodesia and Nyasaland," *South African journal of economics,* March 1962, pp. 50-60.

Report of the Advisory commission on the review of the constitution of Rhodesia and Nyasaland. H.M. Stationery Office, London, Cmnd. 1148, 1960, chapter 9.

United States Department of Commerce. *Investment in Federation of Rhodesia and Nyasaland.* Washington, 1956, pp. 107-109.

3

Due, J. *Taxation and economic development in Tropical Africa.* The MIT Press, Cambridge, Mass., 1963, 172pp.

4

Foreign Tax Law Association. *Rhodesia and Nyasaland income tax service.* Deer Park, L.I., N.Y., loose-leaf, 1954-.

Goldin, B. "Recent trends in income tax,"

Rhodesia and Nyasaland law journal, March 1961, pp. 84-90.

"Methods of direct taxation in British Tropical Africa," *Journal of African administration,* vol. 2, October 1950, pp. 3-12; vol. 3, January 1951, pp. 30-41; vol. 3, October 1951, pp. 77-87.

Notes on income tax and exchange control in the Federation of Rhodesia and Nyasaland. H.M. Stationery Office, London, 1961, 15pp.

"Rhodesia." In: Board of Inland Revenue (Great Britain), *Income taxes outside the United Kingdom 1966,* vol. 6, pp. 269-311. H.M. Stationery Office, London, 1967.

The Rhodesian income tax service: Legislation service. Juta and Co., Ltd., Cape Town, loose-leaf, 1962-.

Silke, A. *1961 income tax legislation in the Federation of Rhodesia and Nyasaland.* Juta and Co., Ltd., Cape Town, 1961, 66pp.

5

"Death duties in Rhodesian federation," *Canadian tax journal,* vol. 3, July-August 1955, pp. 280-283.

8

United States Department of Commerce. *Establishing a business in the Federation of Rhodesia and Nyasaland.* Washington, 1962, 13pp.

9

"Urban problems in East and Central Africa," *Journal of African administration,* vol. 10, October 1958, pp. 215-218.

18

Blann, B., and White, R. *Butterworths taxation statutes service.* Butterworth and Company, Durban.

Diamond, W. *Foreign tax and trade briefs.* Fallon Law Book Company, New York, loose-leaf, 1951-.

RWANDA

1

Rousseaux, R. "Le Vote du budget originaire au Burundi, au Rwanda et au Congo," *Revue juridique de droit écrit et coutumier du Rwanda et du Burundi,* vol. 5, 1965, pp. 83-90.

8

United States Department of Commerce. *Establishing a business in the Belgian Congo and Ruanda-Urundi.* Washington, 1957, 12pp.

RYUKYU ISLANDS

1

United States Department of Commerce. *Basic data on the economy of the Ryukyu Islands.* Washington, 1963, 14pp.

4

Foreign Tax Law Association. *Ryukyu Islands income tax service.* St. Petersburg, Fla., loose-leaf, 1959-.

SARAWAK

1

"Sarawak: A tax digest," *Foreign tax law weekly bulletin,* vol. 9, no. 9, 1958, pp 1-9.

Silcock, T. *Fiscal survey report of Sarawak.* Government Printing Office, Kuching, 1956.

4

Foreign Tax Law Association. *Sarawak income tax service.* St. Petersburg, Fla., loose-leaf, 1962-.

"Sarawak." In: Board of Inland Revenue (Great Britain), *Income taxes outside the United Kingdom 1966,* vol. 7, pp. 43-66. H.M. Stationery Office, London, 1967.

SAUDI ARABIA

1

United States Department of Commerce. *Basic data on the economy of Saudi Arabia.* Washington, 1962, 8pp.

Young, A. "Saudi Arabian currency and finance," *Middle East journal,* vol. 7, Summer 1953, pp. 361-380; vol. 7, Autumn 1953, pp. 539-556.

4

Foreign Tax Law Association. *Saudi Arabian income tax service.* St. Petersburg, Fla., loose-leaf, 1963-.

"Income tax in Saudi Arabia," *Foreign tax law weekly bulletin,* vol. 14, no. 6, 1963, pp. 3-4.

"Income taxes in Saudi Arabia," *Foreign tax law weekly bulletin,* vol. 1, no. 43, 1951, pp. 1-2.

Shamma, S. *The law of income tax and zakat in the kingdom of Saudi Arabia: The royal decrees and the ministerial instructions, decisions, regulations, and notices on income tax and zakat.* Dar Al-ahad, Beirut, 1951.

United States Department of Commerce. *Income tax law of Saudi Arabia.* Washington, 1957, 4pp.

7

United States Department of Commerce. *Foreign trade regulations of Saudi Arabia.* Washington, 1966, 8pp.

8

United States Department of Commerce. *Law on investment of foreign capital in Saudi Arabia.* Washington, 1957, 8pp.

18

Diamond, W. *Foreign tax and trade briefs.* Fallon Law Book Company, New York, loose-leaf, 1951–.

SENEGAL

1

United States Department of Commerce. *Basic data on the economy of Senegal.* Washington, 1962, 18pp.

3

Mémento fiscal et social 1964, numéro spécial no. 14, 25 June 1964. A comparative survey of taxes in the West African Union and Guinea.

4

Denis, A. "Les Anciennes contributions directes au Sénégal," *Annales africaines,* no. 1, 1961, pp. 129-249.

12

United States Department of Commerce. *Investment law of the Republic of Senegal.* Washington, 1962, 6pp.

SEYCHELLES

4

"Seychelles." In: Board of Inland Revenue (Great Britain), *Income taxes out-* *side the United Kingdom 1966,* vol. 7, pp. 67-87. H. M. Stationery Office, London, 1967.

SIERRA LEONE

1

Ministry of Information and Broadcasting. *Investment opportunities in Sierra Leone.* Freetown, 49pp.

United States Department of Commerce. *Basic data on the economy of Sierra Leone.* Washington, 1962, 11pp.

2

Cox-George, N. *Finance and development in West Africa: The Sierra Leone experience.* Dobson, London, 1961, 333pp.

Cox-George, N. "Some problems of financing development in Sierra Leone, West Africa," *Public finance,* vol. 8, 1953, pp. 115-145.

3

Due, J. *Taxation and economic development in Tropical Africa.* The MIT Press, Cambridge, Mass., 1963, 172pp.

4

"Methods of direct taxation in British Tropical Africa," *Journal of African administration,* vol. 2, October 1950, pp. 3-12; vol. 3, January 1951, pp. 30-41; vol. 3, October 1951, pp. 77-87.

"Rates of income tax and personal deductions," *Foreign tax law weekly bulletin,* vol. 15, no. 16, 1964, pp. 11-14.

"Sierra Leone." In: Board of Inland Revenue (Great Britain), *Income taxes outside the United Kingdom 1966,* vol. 7, pp. 89-117. H.M. Stationery Office, London, 1967.

9

Report of a commission of inquiry into local taxation. Wann Committee, 1956.

12

"Incentives for investors," *Foreign tax law weekly bulletin,* vol. 15, no. 7, 1964, pp. 6-10.

SINGAPORE

1

Economic Development Board. *Industrial opportunities in Singapore.* Singapore, 1965, 32pp.

Hicks, U. "The finance of the city state," *Malayan economic review*, vol. 5, October 1960.

Price Waterhouse & Co. *Information guide for doing business in the Federation of Malaya and the State of Singapore.* New York, 1962, 23pp.

United States Department of Commerce. *Basic data on the economy of Singapore.* Washington, 1967, 28pp.

3

Yoingco, A., and Trinidad, R. *Fiscal systems and practices in Asian countries.* Frederick A. Praeger, New York, 1967.

4

Foreign Tax Law Association. *Singapore income tax service.* Centerport, L.I., N.Y., loose-leaf, 1951–.

Pepper, H. *Personal income tax in the Federation of Malaya.* Government Printer, Kuala Lumpur, 1963, 39pp.

"Singapore." In: Board of Inland Revenue (Great Britain), *Income taxes outside the United Kingdom 1966*, vol. 7, pp. 119-151. H.M. Stationery Office, London, 1967.

6

Bird, R. "A value-added tax for Singapore: Comment," *Malayan economic review*, vol. 12, April 1967, pp. 39-41.

McKinnon, R. "Export expansion through tax policy: The case for a value-added tax in Singapore," *Malayan economic review*, vol. 11, October 1966, pp. 1-27. Also "Correction," *Malayan economic review*, vol. 12, April 1967, pp. 36-38.

McKinnon, R. "A value-added tax for Singapore: Rejoinder," *Malayan economic review*, vol. 12, April 1967, pp. 42-46.

7

Edwards, C. "The future role of import and excise duty taxation in the states of Malaya and Singapore," *Malayan economic review*, vol. 11, April 1966, pp. 29-41. Part reprinted in: R. Bird and O. Oldman (eds.), *Readings on taxation in developing countries*, pp. 381-395. The Johns Hopkins Press, Baltimore, revised edition, 1967.

Edwards, C. "The structure of import and excise duty taxation in the states of Ma-

laya and Singapore," *Malayan economic review*, vol. 10, October 1965, pp. 83-101.

United States Department of Commerce. *Foreign trade regulations of Malaysia.* Washington, 1964.

8

United States Department of Commerce. *Establishing a business in Singapore.* Washington, 1966, 12pp.

12

"Investment allowances and pioneer industry relief in Singapore," *Taxation* (England), 10 December 1960.

"Singapore: The importance of pioneering," *Foreign tax law weekly bulletin*, vol. 12, no. 24, 1961, pp. 4-9.

17

Pepper, H. "Tax harmonisation in a federation: The 1965 budget in Malaysia," *Bulletin for international fiscal documentation*, vol. 19, 1965, pp. 228-232.

SOMALI

1

United States Department of Commerce. *Basic data on the economy of Somali (Somali Republic).* Washington, 1961, 16pp.

2

International Bank for Reconstruction and Development. *The economy of the trust territory of Somaliland.* Washington, 1957, pp. 52-61 (mimeo).

4

"Income tax law of 1957 as amended," *Foreign tax law weekly bulletin*, vol. 11, no. 14, 1960, pp. 1-9; vol. 11, no. 15, 1960, pp. 1-9.

7

United States Department of Commerce. *Foreign trade regulations of the Somali Republic.* Washington, 1967, 8pp.

8

Organisation for European Economic Cooperation. *Taxation systems applicable to investments in the overseas countries associated with member countries of O.E.E.C.* Paris, 1960, 100pp.

SOUTH AFRICA

1

South African Institute of Race Relations. *African taxation: Its relation to African social services.* Johannesburg, 1960, 29pp.

Trevor, D. "South African native taxation," *Review of economic studies,* vol. 3, June 1936, pp. 217-225.

4

"Republic of South Africa." In: Board of Inland Revenue (Great Britain), *Income taxes outside the United Kingdom 1966,* vol. 7, pp. 153-218. H.M. Stationery Office, London, 1967.

8

United States Department of Commerce. *Establishing a business in the Republic of South Africa.* Washington, 1965, 15pp.

SOUTH ARABIA

4

"South Arabia, Federation of." In: Board of Inland Revenue (Great Britain), *Income taxes outside the United Kingdom 1966,* vol. 7, pp. 219-224. H. M. Stationery Office, London, 1967.

SOUTH WEST AFRICA

1

"South West Africa: Rates of tax and taxation table," *Foreign tax law weekly bulletin,* vol. 16, no. 20, 1965, pp. 1-6.

"Tax laws of South West Africa," *Foreign tax law weekly bulletin,* vol. 13, no. 46, 1963, pp. 1-4.

United States Department of Commerce. *Basic data on the economy of South West Africa.* Washington, 1961, 12pp.

4

Meyerowitz, D., and Spiro, E. *The taxpayer's permanent volume on income tax in South Africa and South West Africa.* Taxpayer, Cape Town, loose-leaf, 1963.

"South West Africa." In: Board of Inland Revenue (Great Britain), *Income taxes outside the United Kingdom 1966,* vol. 7, pp. 225-251. H.M. Stationery Office, London, 1967.

SPAIN

1

Alegre, R. "La ley de reforma del sistema tributario y las bonificaciones fiscales de la ley de renovación de la flota mercante," *Revista de derecho mercantil,* vol. 39, 1965, pp. 207-221.

Amorós Rica, N. *Derecho tributario (explicaciones).* Editorial de Derecho Financiero, Madrid, 1963.

Amorós Rica, N. "La ley general tributaria española," *Impuestos,* vol. 22, 1964, pp. 125-133.

Aparici Pajares, R. "Nuevo instrumento de política tributaria: Las evaluaciones globales," *Semana de estudios de derecho financiero,* vol. 7, 1959, pp. 161-194.

Arcila Ramírez, L. "Hacienda pública," *Estudios de derecho,* vol. 24, 1965, pp. 325-379.

Arena, C. "Los principios económicos de la hacienda pública," *Revista de derecho financiero y de hacienda pública* (Madrid), vol. 12, 1962, pp. 9-68.

Arthur Andersen & Co. *Tax and trade guide: Spain.* Chicago, 1965.

Asociación Española de Derecho Financiero. *Memoria, 1958.* Madrid, 1959, 354pp.

Balleeiro, A. "Los empréstitos forzosos y la política fiscal," *Revista de derecho financiero y de hacienda pública* (Madrid), vol. 14, 1964, pp. 9-26.

Barrera de Irimo, A. "Revisión de la teoría de la parafiscalidad," *Semana de estudios de derecho financiero,* vol. 7, 1959, pp. 115-134.

Beltrán Flórez, L. *Hacienda pública, derecho fiscal.* Lex Nova, Valladolid, 1961, 390pp.

Bullón, P. *El sistema fiscal español actual.* Princesa, Madrid, 502pp.

Carretero Pérez, A. *El sistema tributario español.* Editorial Tecnos, Madrid, 1964, 817pp.

Carretero Pérez, A. "El sistema tributario español," *Revista de derecho administrativo y fiscal,* vol. 2, no. 4, 1963, pp. 19-32.

Cerezo, J. "Algunas consideraciones sobre el anteproyecto de ley general tributaria y de reforma del sistema tributario," *De economía* (Madrid), vol. 17, no. 80-81, January-June 1964, pp. 269-281.

Checa Santos, D. *Derecho fiscal*. Estades Artes Graficas, Madrid, 1962, 244pp.

Chemical Bank New York Trust Company. *Spain*. New York, 1963, 12pp.

Curillo Valverde, C. "Casos prácticos de aplicación de la ley," *Revista de derecho financiero y de hacienda pública* (Madrid), vol. 13, 1963, pp. 317-336.

Docavo Alberto, L. "Algunas consideraciones críticas sobre la reforma tributaria," *Impuestos de la hacienda pública*, vol. 20, no. 245, October 1963, pp. 675-678.

Federation of British Industries. *Spain— Tax system*. London, 1963, 12pp.

Federation of British Industries. *Taxation in western Europe, 1963: A guide for industrialists*. London, 1963, pp. 220-231.

"La Fiscalité en Espagne," *Statistiques et études financières, finances comparées*, no. 18, 1953, pp. 392-428.

García Añoveros, J. "La política presupuestaria y tributaria en 1961," *Revista de derecho financiero y de hacienda pública* (Madrid), vol. 12, 1962, pp. 69-116.

García Añoveros, J. "La política tributaria y presupuestaria en 1962," *Revista de derecho financiero y de hacienda pública* (Madrid), vol. 13, 1963, pp. 565-584.

García Añoveros, J. "La política tributaria y presupuestaria en 1963," *Revista de derecho financiero y de hacienda pública* (Madrid), vol. 14, 1964, pp. 63-90.

García Añoveros, J. "La política tributaria y presupuestaria en 1964," *Revista de derecho financiero y de hacienda pública* (Madrid), vol. 15, 1965, pp. 39-60.

Gella, A. "El balance fiscal," *Dirección general de lo contencioso del estado anales*, vol. 1, 1961, pp. 117-150.

Gómez Gutiérrez, A. "Procedimientos de determinación de la base y de la cuota," *Semana de estudios de derecho financiero*, vol. 7, 1959, pp. 51-84.

Luque Aldazábal, J. "Notas sobre la ley 41/1964, de fecha 11 de junio, de reforma del sistema tributario," *Pretor*, vol. 13, no. 23, 1964, pp. 69-80.

Manual de la administración. T-A-L-E, Madrid, loose-leaf.

"La marcha de la hacienda en los once primeros meses de 1961," *Moneda y crédito*, vol. 79, December 1961, pp. 93-94.

"Memorándum sobre la reforma del sistema tributario español," *Estudios económicos* (Madrid), vol. 4, no. 35, September 1963, pp. 5-44.

Menéndez, J. "Comentarios sobre algunos preceptos de nuestras leyes fiscales," *Revista general de derecho*, vol. 20, December 1963, pp. 976-986.

Menéndez Hernández, J. "El crédito documentario y sus repercusiones fiscales," *Revista de derecho español y americano*, vol. 10, no. 9, 1965, pp. 83-118.

Naharro, J. "Evolution et problèmes fondamentaux du système fiscal espagnol," *Revue de science et de législation financières*, vol. 45, 1953, pp. 744-761; vol. 46, 1954, pp. 139-158.

Navas Müller, J. "Procedimientos de liquidación del impuesto: Las evaluaciones globales," *Revista de derecho financiero y de hacienda pública* (Madrid), vol. 11, no. 41, 1961, pp. 697-721.

"La Nouvelle législation fiscale espagnole," *Impôts et sociétés*, vol. 42, no. 28, 1965, pp. 49-64.

Oliart, A. "Tasas y exacciones parafiscales," *Revista de derecho financiero y de hacienda pública* (Madrid), vol. 11, no. 41, 1961, pp. 667-696.

Ortiz Gracia, J. "Aperçu du système fiscal espagnol," *Bulletin for international fiscal documentation*, vol. 8, 1954, pp. 5-37.

Palomer Llovet, M., and Rovira Mola, A. de. *Conciertos y gremios fiscales*. Palestra, Barcelona, 1962, 555pp.

Peat, Marwick, Mitchell & Co. *Summary of Spanish taxation*. 1966, 14pp.

Pérez Escolar, R. *Las operaciones bancarias en el derecho tributario*. Vassallo, Madrid, 1963, 369pp.

Pérez Hernández, A. "Exenciones tributarias en el concordato de 1953," *Ius canonicum*, vol. 3, no. 1-2, 1963, pp. 419-506.

Perulles Bassas, J. *Manual de derecho fiscal*. Bosch, Barcelona, 1961, 549pp.

Perulles Bassas, J. "El problema de los activos ocultos," *Revista de derecho financiero y de hacienda pública* (Madrid), vol. 13, 1963, pp. 425-446.

Price Waterhouse & Co. *Information guide for doing business in Spain*. New York, 1966, 32pp.

Price Waterhouse & Co. *Memorandum on*

taxation in Spain. Barcelona, 15 July 1958, 16pp. (duplicated).

Sage, E. "Refonte du système fiscal espagnol," *Revue de science financière,* vol. 57, 1965, pp. 538-566.

Sáinz de Bujanda, F. "La gran paradoja de la ley general tributaria," *Revista de derecho financiero y de hacienda pública* (Madrid), vol. 14, 1964, pp. 269-308.

Sáinz de Bujanda, F. *Programa de derecho financiero: Cursos de hacienda pública, curso 1959-60.* Madrid, 160pp.

"El sistema tributario español," *Revista de derecho financiero y de hacienda pública* (Madrid), vol. 11, no. 41 (número extraordinario commemorativo del X aniversario). Madrid, 1961, 721pp.

"Spanish tax reforms: A progress report with a summary of direct and indirect taxes in Spain," *European taxation,* vol. 5, 1965, pp. 53-55.

Tarazona, J. "La ley general tributaria," *Moneda y crédito,* vol. 89, June 1964, pp. 5-19.

Trillo, E. "La imposición fiscal en los bancos de negocio," *Revista jurídica de Cataluña,* vol. 63, 1965, pp. 1019-1037.

United States Department of Commerce. *Basic data on the economy of Spain.* Washington, 1963, 19pp.

2

España, R. "El sistema fiscal y el plan de desarrollo," *Boletín de estudios económicos,* vol. 18, no. 59, May-June 1963.

Figueroa Martínez, E. de. "La política fiscal y la estabilización," *Semana de estudios de derecho financiero,* vol. 8, 1960, pp. 93-126.

Fuentes Quintana, E. "Los principios del reparto de la carga tributaria en España," *Revista de derecho financiero y de hacienda pública* (Madrid), vol. 11, no. 41, 1961, pp. 161-298.

Galena, T. "The place of the fiscal system in the Spanish economy." In: A. Peacock, *Public finance as an instrument for economic development,* pp. 73-86. Organisation for Economic Co-operation and Development, Paris, 1964.

Hicks, U. "The integration of the budget and the development plan with special reference to the Spanish situation," *Public finance,* vol. 17, 1962, pp. 120-153.

Kaufmann, M. "El abandono sistemático

del principio del equilibrio del presupuesto y sus implicaciones en el proceso económico y financiero de la nación," *Revista de derecho financiero y de hacienda pública* (Madrid), vol. 14, 1964, pp. 997-1008.

Marín Marín, S. "Los índices de rentabilidad y la reforma tributaria," *Dirección general de lo contencioso del estado anales,* vol. 1, 1961, pp. 37-62.

Pampliega, J. "El sector público y la economía española (años 1954, 1955, 1956 y 1957)," *Revista de economía política,* January-April 1962, pp. 95-120.

Pérez de Ayala, J. "Modelos de desarrollo, tablas 'input—output' y política fiscal," *Revista de derecho financiero y de hacienda pública* (Madrid), vol. 12, 1962, pp. 280-308.

Pérez de Ayala, J. "Nuevo sentido de una cuestión clásica: Impuestos directos, impuestos indirectos y pérdida de bienestar económico," *Moneda y crédito,* vol. 70, September 1959, pp. 49-67.

Sabater, A. "La seguridad social como factor de distribución de la renta," *Moneda y crédito,* vol. 95, December 1965, pp. 77-83.

Sampedro Saez, J., and Madroñero Peláez, A. "Estructura económica y sistema fiscal," *Revista de derecho financiero y de hacienda pública* (Madrid), vol. 11, no. 41, 1961, pp. 299-324.

Vicente-Arche Domingo, F. "Aspectos financieros del plan de establización," *Revista de derecho financiero y de hacienda pública* (Madrid), vol. 10, 1960, pp. 67-101.

4

Albiñana, C. *Impuesto industrial.* Editorial de Derecho Financiero, Madrid, 1961, 1416pp.

Albiñana García-Quintana, C. "El impuesto industrial," *Revista de derecho financiero y de hacienda pública* (Madrid), vol. 11, no. 41, 1961, pp. 449-479.

Albiñana García-Quintana, C. "Tributación normal y excepcional de la regularización de activos," *Revista de derecho financiero y de hacienda pública* (Madrid), vol. 13, 1963, pp. 249-286.

Amorós Rica, N. "Contorno, dintorno y circunstancia temporal de la ley de regularización," *Revista de derecho finan-*

ciero y de hacienda pública (Madrid), vol. 13, 1963, pp. 287-316.

Amorós Rica, N. "Traitement fiscal des gains en capital : Espagne," *Cahiers de droit fiscal international*, vol. 42, 1960, p. 44 (summaries in English and German).

Arboleya, A. *Spanish corporate taxation.* Banco Español de Crédito, Foreign Department, Madrid, 1966, 31pp.

Beltrán, L. "La progresión en el impuesto sobre las rentas del capital," *Revista de derecho financiero y de hacienda pública* (Madrid), vol. 13, 1963, pp. 9-38.

Cosciani, C. "Problemas relacionados con la imposición de las personas jurídicas," *Revista de derecho financiero y de hacienda pública* (Madrid), vol. 10, 1960, pp. 741-758.

Domínguez, M. *La evaluación global del impuesto industrial.* Bosch, Barcelona, n.d., 124pp.

Drake, J. *Impuesto industrial.* Editorial de Derecho Financiero, Madrid, 1961, 1361pp.

Fernández Cantos, J. *Contribución sobre la renta.* Maritima Fiscal, Bilbao, 1960, 423pp.

Fernández Flores, F. *Régimen fiscal de la exhibición cinematográfica.* Editorial de Derecho Financiero, Madrid, 1963, 399pp.

Fernández Pirla, J. *Comentarios a la ley de regularización de balances; su problemática económica, contable y fiscal.* Ariel, Barcelona, 1963, 279pp.

Fernández Pirla, J. "Objeto de la regularización y criterios valorativos," *Revista de derecho financiero y de hacienda pública* (Madrid), vol. 13, 1963, pp. 337-346.

Foreign Tax Law Association. *Spanish income tax service.* Centerport, L.I., N.Y., loose-leaf, 1954–.

García Añoveros, J. "El régimen tributario de la investigación y explotación de hidrocarburos," *Revista de derecho financiero y de hacienda pública* (Madrid), vol. 10, 1960, pp. 759-832.

Garrigues, J. "Revaloración de los activos en los balances mercantiles," *Revista de derecho mercantil*, vol. 29, 1960, p. 249.

"Legislación aplicable a la regularización de balances," *Revista de derecho financiero y de hacienda pública* (Madrid), vol. 13, 1963, pp. 505-564.

Meléndez Carrucini, G. *Manual de ganancias y pérdidas de capital.* Rumbos, Barcelona, 2 volumes, 1962.

Nieves Borrego, J. "Régimen administrativo de la regularización de balances y del fondo extraordinario de reposición," *Revista de derecho financiero y de hacienda pública* (Madrid), vol. 13, 1963, pp. 389-424.

Nino, J. "Un precedente del impuesto sobre la renta," *Moneda y crédito*, vol. 96, March 1966.

Ordex Gesti, J. *Praxis fiscal, impuesto sobre sociedades, evaluación global, cuota y procedimientos especiales.* Editorial Praxis, S.A., Barcelona, looseleaf, 1963.

Perulles Bassas, J. "El impuesto sobre los rendimientos del trabajo personal," *Revista de derecho financiero y de hacienda pública* (Madrid), vol. 11, no. 41, 1961, pp. 381-412.

Ramos, F. "El impuesto sobre las rentas del capital," *Revista de derecho financiero y de hacienda pública* (Madrid), vol. 11, no. 41, 1961, pp. 413-448.

Rodríguez Pérez, H. "La contribución general sobre la renta," *Revista de derecho financiero y de hacienda pública* (Madrid), vol. 11, no. 41, 1961, pp. 513-542.

Rodríguez Pérez, H. "Situación legal de los sistemas de amortización y fondos de reposición anteriores a la ley," *Revista de derecho financiero y de hacienda pública* (Madrid), vol. 13, 1963, pp. 463-474.

Rodríguez Robles, A. "El impuesto sobre sociedades," *Revista de derecho financiero y de hacienda pública* (Madrid), vol. 11, no. 41, 1961, pp. 481-512.

Rozas Zornoza, M. "La imposición mínima en el impuesto sobre sociedades," *Revista de derecho financiero y de hacienda pública* (Madrid), vol. 14, 1964, pp. 929-950.

Rozas Zornoza, M. "Impuesto sobre la renta de sociedades y demás entidades jurídicas," *Moneda y crédito*, vol. 89, June 1964, pp. 39-70.

Rozas Zornoza, M. *La liquidación de impuestos en la empresa.* Editorial ICE, Madrid, 1963, xix/831pp.

"Spain." In: Board of Inland Revenue (Great Britain), *Income taxes outside the United Kingdom 1966*, vol. 7, pp.

253-273. H.M. Stationery Office, London, 1967.

"Spain: Revaluation of assets," *European taxation*, vol. 3, 1963, pp. 127-131.

"Spanish income tax, surtax tax revised," *Foreign commerce weekly*, vol. 53, no. 9, 1955, p. 8.

"Texto único ordenado sobre impuesto de patente comercial e industrial y profesional," *Informativo*, vol. 5, 1965, pp. 2011-2051.

Turpín Vargas, J. "Los procedimientos estimativos de la base en la contribución sobre la renta con posterioridad a las reformas de 1957," *Revista de derecho financiero y de hacienda pública* (Madrid), vol. 12, 1962, pp. 713-730.

Vilarasau Salat, J. "Traslación de un impuesto sobre el beneficio de las empresas industriales y comerciales," *Revista de derecho financiero y de hacienda pública* (Madrid), vol. 12, 1962, pp. 585-600.

5

Lugo y Guillén, F. de. "Beneficios fiscales en relación con el impuesto general sobre las sucesiones," *Revista de derecho financiero y de hacienda pública* (Madrid), vol. 15, 1965, pp. 121-142.

Martín Oviero, J. "Reflexiones sobre los beneficios fiscales ante la legislación del impuesto general sobre transmisiones patrimoniales," *Revista de derecho financiero y de hacienda pública* (Madrid), vol. 14, 1964, pp. 573-628.

Maseda Bouso, M. "Impôts sur le capital." In: Institut International de Finances Publiques, *Impôts sur la fortune et inclus droits de successions: Debt management*, pp. 304-313. Brussels, 1962.

Menéndez Hernández, J. "Breve ensayo de derecho sucesorio fiscal," *Revista de derecho notarial*, vol. 11, 1963, pp. 203-242.

Menéndez Hernández, J. "Problemática jurídica del impuesto de transmisiones patrimoniales y del impuesto general sobre las sucesiones," *Revista de derecho notarial*, vol. 14, 1965, pp. 371-402.

Rodríguez Bereijo, A. "La sucesión en las relaciones tributarias," *Revista de derecho financiero y de hacienda pública* (Madrid), vol. 15 1965, pp. 23-38.

Solé Villalonga, G. "Discusión de una propuesta: El impuesto sobre el gasto personal," *Revista de derecho financiero*

y de hacienda pública (Madrid), vol. 14, 1964, pp. 877-928.

Velasco Alonso, A. "El impuesto sobre valores mobiliarios," *Revista de derecho financiero y de hacienda pública* (Madrid), vol. 11, no. 41, 1961, pp. 607-638.

6

Alonso Amat, F., and Torres Díaz, C. "Sujeto pasivo del impuesto del timbre en los documentos de formalización de ventas," *Revista de derecho financiero y de hacienda pública* (Madrid), vol. 12, 1962, pp. 653-672.

Amorós Rica, N. "Los documentos de crédito y giro en el impuesto del timbre," *Revista de derecho mercantil*, vol. 31, 1961, pp. 181-208.

Amorós Rica, N. "El impuesto de timbre," *Revista de derecho financiero y de hacienda pública* (Madrid), vol. 11, no. 41, 1961, pp. 543-574.

Amorós Rica, N. *Timbre del estado*. Editorial de Derecho Financiero, Madrid, 2 volumes, 1961.

Estrada y Segalerva, J. "El documento en la ley del timbre," *Semana de estudios de derecho financiero*, vol. 8, 1960, pp. 57-92.

Góngora Galera, F. *Impuestos sobre el gasto (contribución de usos y consumos)*. 2 volumes, 1958, 496/461pp. Appendix, 1961, 387pp.

Góngora Galera, J. "Rendimientos del impuesto sobre el gasto," *Semana de estudios de derecho financiero*, vol. 8, 1960, pp. 155-192.

Luis, P. de, and Monasterio-Guren, D. "Impuestos sobre ventas," *Moneda y crédito*, vol. 89, June 1964, pp. 83-95.

Mañas López, F. "Ensayo de síntesis y clasificación de la imposición indirecta en España," *Semana de estudios de derecho financiero*, vol. 9, 1961, pp. 94-144.

Mutén, L. "El impuesto al valor agregado ¿constituye una nueva arma tributaria?" *Boletín de la Dirección general impositiva* (Argentina), vol. 19, September 1963, pp. 370-374.

Puente Rodríguez, I. de la. "Impuesto sobre el gasto y estímulos fiscales a la exportación. Ensayo sobre implantación del T.V.A. francés en nuestro sistema fiscal," *Semana de estudios de derecho financiero*, vol. 11, 1964, pp. 579-630.

Rodríguez García, M. "Modificaciones a la

ley del timbre de 3 de marzo de 1960 y su reglamento de 22 de junio de 1956 por las últimas disposiciones tributarias," *Revista general de derecho,* vol. 17, 1961, pp. 812-822.

Trujillo Jiménez, D. "Ventas y obras en el impuesto del timbre," *Semana de estudios de derecho financiero,* vol. 10, 1962, pp. 66-89.

7

García, F. "Las transformaciones del arancel español entre 1960 y 1966," *Boletín de estudios económicos,* vol. 20, no. 66, September-December 1965.

Moya, E. "El GATT y el arancel español," *Boletín de estudios económicos,* vol. 20, no. 66, September-December 1965.

Pérez de Bricio, C. "Análisis de la evolución del nivel arancelario español," *Boletín de estudios económicos,* vol. 20, no. 66, September-December 1965.

Pérez de Bricio, C. "Derecho aduanero," *Semana de estudios de derecho financiero,* vol. 11, 1964, pp. 1169-1192.

Pérez de Bricio, C. "Exenciones y bonificaciones en el régimen arancelario español vigente," *Semana de estudios de derecho financiero,* vol. 11, 1964, pp. 631-660.

Pomata Martínez, J. "Régime fiscal de l'importation et l'exportation de marchandises : Espagne," *Cahiers de droit fiscal international,* vol. 47A, 1962, p. 111.

8

Acosta España, D. "Mesures unilatérales tendant à éviter la double imposition : Espagne," *Cahiers de droit fiscal international,* vol. 40, 1959, p. 620 (in French and Spanish).

"Agreements on double taxation." In : V. Garcés, *The legal position of the foreign investor in Spain,* pp. 125-130. La Polígrafa, Barcelona, 1964.

Albiñana García-Quintana, C. "Traitement fiscal des dettes et intérêts sur dettes dans les relations internationales : Espagne," *Cahiers de droit fiscal international,* vol. 42, 1960, p. 352 (summaries in English and German).

Banco Exterior de España. *Foreign investments in Spain.* Madrid, 1963, 116pp.

Banco Urquijo. *Tax system in Spain for foreign investors.* Madrid, 1960, 8pp.

Bastos, J. *Restrictions which might hinder the activity of foreign enterprises in Spain.* 9pp.

Finance Ministry, Information Office. *Foreign capital investments in Spain: Rules and regulations.* Madrid, 1965, 30pp.

Luis Díaz Monasterio, F. de. "Incentivos fiscales al capital extranjero," *Semana de estudios de derecho financiero,* vol. 11, 1964, pp. 305-310.

Presidencia del Gobierno, Oficina de Información. *Foreign capital investments in Spanish enterprises.* Madrid, 1961, 55pp.

Presidencia del Gobierno, Oficina de Información. *Foreign investments in Spain, 1962/1963.* Madrid, 1962, 112pp.

Rodríguez Sastre, A. "Problèmes fiscaux soulevés par les sociétés d'investissement et de placement à caractère international —Rapports nationaux : Espagne," *Cahiers de droit fiscal international,* vol. 47B, 1962, p. 64 (summaries in French, German, and English).

Sáinz de Bujanda, F. "La interpretación, en el derecho español, de los tratados internacionales para evitar la doble imposición," *Revista de derecho financiero y de hacienda pública* (Madrid), vol. 10, 1960, pp. 273-294.

"Taxation." In : V. Garcés, *The legal position of the foreign investor in Spain,* pp. 179-198. La Polígrafa, Barcelona, 1964.

"Taxation of foreign corporations in Spain," *European taxation,* vol. 1, 1 May 1961.

United States Department of Commerce. *Establishing a business in Spain.* Washington, 1963, 9pp.

United States Department of State. *Minister of finance decree reforms foreign corporation tax.* Washington, 1966, 5pp.

9

Ballester Ros, I. "Los presupuestos de las corporaciones locales de régimen común," *Revista de estudios de la vida local,* vol. 20, no. 117, May-June 1961, pp. 384-400.

Barrobes Oriol, J. "Estudio del reglamento de la hacienda municipal de Barcelona," *Revista de estudios de la vida local,* vol. 21, no. 22, March-April 1962, pp. 199-216.

Calabuig Morán, E. "El derecho tributario de la ciudad de Barcelona," *Revista de derecho financiero y de hacienda pública* (Madrid), vol. 12, 1962, pp. 673-712.

Lasuen, J. "Las haciendas municipales," *De economía* (Madrid), vol. 14, no. 69, January-March 1961, pp. 85-92.

Mahillo Santos, J. "Dinámica de los presupuestos locales," *Revista de estudios de la vida local,* vol. 21, no. 124, July-August 1962, pp. 545-555.

Martín Mateo, R. "El municipio y su hacienda," *Revista de administración pública* (Madrid), vol. 14, no. 40, January-April 1963, pp. 421-453.

Moreno Paez, L. "La modernización de la administración financiera en la ley del régimen municipal de la ciudad de Barcelona," *Revista de estudios de la vida local,* vol. 20, no. 116, March-April 1961, pp. 161-193.

10

Bas y Rivas, F. "El impuesto sobre el aumento de valor en las fincas rústicas y urbanas," *Revista de derecho privado,* February 1965, pp. 101-109.

Bas y Rivas, F. *Impuestos de derechos reales y sobre transmisiones de bienes.* Editorial Revista de Derecho Privado, Madrid, 2d edition, 2 volumes, 1961.

Bruna de Quixano, J. "Exención de los contratos de venta a plazos del impuesto de derechos reales," *Revista jurídica de Cataluña,* vol. 60, 1961, pp. 557-564.

Burgos Montero, J. "Haciá una posible reforma de la contribución rústica," *Impuestos de la hacienda pública,* vol. 20, no. 245, October 1963, pp. 653-658.

Cánovas-Coutiño, G. "Jurisprudencia sobre el impuesto de derechos reales," *Revista crítica de derecho inmobiliario,* vol. 37, 1961, pp. 855-874.

Cruz Martínez Esteruelas. "El impuesto de derechos reales y sobre transmisiones de bienes," *Revista de derecho financiero y de hacienda pública* (Madrid), vol. 11, no. 41, 1961, pp. 575-606.

Díez Gómez, A. "El nuevo reglamento del impuesto de derechos reales comparado con el anterior," *Revista de derecho notarial,* vol. 8, no. 28, 1960, pp. 283-406.

España, R. "Contribución urbana," *Moneda y crédito,* vol. 89, June 1964, pp. 21-37.

Impuesto de derechos reales. Editorial de Derecho Financiero, Madrid, 3d edition, 1962, 992pp.

Martin-Retortillo, C. "Las concesiones de transporte por carretera y el impuesto de derechos reales," *Revista de derecho mercantil,* vol. 37, 1964, pp. 277-294.

Navarro Azpeitia, F. "La plusvalía potencial en la transformación de la tierra," *Anuario de derecho civil,* vol. 17, 1964, pp. 621-644.

Pajares, R. "Contribución territorial rústica—Puntos esenciales de la reforma," *Moneda y crédito,* vol. 89, June 1964, pp. 71-82.

Puig Salellas, J. "La hipoteca unilateral pendiente de aceptación y el impuesto de derechos reales," *Revista jurídica de Cataluña,* vol. 61, 1962, pp. 781-795.

Rodríguez-Villamil, J. *Legislación del impuesto de derechos reales y transmisión de bienes.* Artes Gráficas, Madrid, 4th edition, 1959, 584pp.

Turpín Vargas, J. "La contribución urbana," *Revista de derecho financiero y de hacienda pública* (Madrid), vol. 11, no. 41, 1961, pp. 349-380.

Turpín Vargas, J. *Manual de contribución urbana.* Editorial de Derecho Financiero, Madrid, 1965, 710pp.

Vincente-Arche Domingo, F. "La imposición rústica," *Revista de derecho financiero y de hacienda pública* (Madrid), vol. 11, no. 41, 1961, pp. 325-348.

11

Alcaide Inchausti, J. "Los impuestos en el sector agrario," *Revista sindical de estadística,* vol. 17, no. 67, 3rd quarter 1962, pp. 2-6.

Domínguez, M. "El concepto de explotación agrícola en la ley de reforma tributaria de 11 de junio de 1964," *Revista de derecho mercantil,* vol. 40, 1965, pp. 59-76.

González de Rozas, H., and Jevenois y Aguirre, L. *La cuota proporcional de la contribución rústica y pecuaria, y su régimen contable.* Hermandad Sindical Nacional de Labradores y Ganaderos, Madrid, 1966, 351pp.

12

Acosta España, R. "Exenciones, subvenciones y otros estímulos fiscales," *Semana de estudios de derecho financiero,* vol. 11, 1964, pp. 151-172.

Barella Gutiérrez, J. "Consideraciones sobre las desgravaciones y exenciones concedidas, en contribución sobre la renta, a determinadas inversiones," *Revista de derecho financiero y de hacienda pública* (Madrid), vol. 13, 1963, pp. 1139-1156.

Economic and Social Development Plan. *Incentives in industrial centers.* Madrid, 1965, 38pp.

Pérez, H. "Notas sobre las exenciones fiscales de las sociedades inmobiliarias," *Revista de derecho privado*, September 1959.

13

Albiñana García-Quintana, C., and Rodríguez Robles, A. "Contrôle fiscal: Ses aspects juridiques, psychologiques et économiques: Espagne," *Cahiers de droit fiscal international*, vol. 39, 1959, p. 77 (in French and Spanish; summaries in German and English).

Benavides, J. "Los principios de organización y el sistema fiscal," *Semana de estudios de derecho financiero*, vol. 11, 1964, pp. 59-84.

Cortés Domínguez, M. "La declaración tributaria," *Revista de derecho financiero y de hacienda pública* (Madrid), vol. 13, 1963, pp. 1025-1050.

Cortés Domínguez, M. "Las estimaciones objetivas," *Revista de derecho financiero y de hacienda pública* (Madrid), vol. 14, 1964, pp. 429-466.

Giuliani Fonrouge, C. "Realidad y perspectivas de la codificación tributaria," *Revista de derecho financiero y de hacienda pública* (Madrid), vol. 14, 1964, pp. 241-268.

Juan Abad, A. de. "El control de la gestión financiera del estado," *Documentación administrativa*, vol. 40, April 1961, pp. 29-38.

"Un siglo de ley de administración y contabilidad," *Anuario de derecho y economía*, vol. 1, 1961, pp. 1-206.

14

Albiñana García-Quintana, C. "Notas sobre el ordenamiento español ante el fraude tributario," *Semana de estudios de derecho financiero*, vol. 9, 1961, pp. 277-288.

Amorós Rica, N. "Interpretación tributaria," *Revista de derecho privado*, January 1963, pp. 5-25.

Amorós Rica, N. "Los sujetos pasivos en la ley general tributaria," *Revista de derecho financiero y de hacienda pública* (Madrid), vol. 14, 1964, pp. 379-428.

"Apariencia jurídica y realidad social en el campo de las leyes fiscales," *Semana de estudios de derecho financiero*, vol. 9, 1961, pp. 329-348.

Calabuig Morán, E. "El principio de legalidad y el régimen jurídico de las tasas y exacciones parafiscales en la región ecuatorial," *Revista de derecho financiero y de hacienda pública* (Madrid), vol. 11, 1961, pp. 1295-1314.

D'Amati, N. "La fattispecie imponibile del tributo di bollo nel sistema italiano e in quello spagnolo," *Rivista di diritto finanziario e scienza delle finanze*, vol. 21-I, 1962, pp. 336-357.

García Añoveros, J. "Las fuentes del derecho en la ley general tributaria," *Revista de derecho financiero y de hacienda pública* (Madrid), vol. 14, 1964, pp. 309-342.

Larraz, J. "La contradicción metodológica de la jurisprudencia tributaria suprema," *Dirección general de lo contencioso del estado anales*, vol. 1, 1961, pp. 13-36.

Luna, A. de. "La doctrina de las leyes meramente penales y la evasión fiscal," *Semana de estudios de derecho financiero*, vol. 9, 1961, pp. 309-318.

Martín-Retortillo, C. "Naturaleza jurídico-fiscal del canon de superficie minera," *Revista de derecho mercantil*, vol. 34, 1962, pp. 433-448.

Martín Retortillo Baquer, L. "La interpretación de las leyes tributarias." In: Comisión de Homenaje al Profesor Jordana de Pozas con Motivo de su Jubilación Universitaria, *Estudios en homenaje a Jordana de Pozas*, vol. 2, pp. 385-434. Instituto de Estudios Políticos, Madrid, 1962.

Menéndez, J. "Aspectos sustantivos e instrumentales de algunos preceptos fiscales en relación con la ley de reformas del sistema tributario," *Revista general de derecho*, vol. 21, March 1965, pp. 164-173.

Perulles Bassas, J. "La interpretación y el derecho tributario." In: Barcelona Universidad, Facultad de Derecho, *Pro-*

blemática de la ciencia del derecho, pp. 709-732. Barcelona, 1962.

Sáinz de Bujanda, F. *Estructura jurídica del sistema tributario.* Editorial de Derecho Financiero, Madrid, 1961, 160pp. Also in: *Revista de derecho financiero y de hacienda pública* (Madrid), vol. 11, no. 41, 1961, pp. 9-160.

Sáinz de Bujanda, F. *Hacienda y derecho.* Instituto de Estudios Políticos, Madrid, 2 parts, 1962, 505/510pp.

Sáinz de Bujanda, F. "El nacimiento de la obligación tributaria," *Revista de derecho financiero y de hacienda pública* (Madrid), vol. 15, 1965, pp. 511-572.

Sáinz de Bujanda, F. "Reflexiones sobre un sistema de derecho tributario español," *Revista de la Facultad de derecho de la Universidad de Madrid,* vol. 7, no. 16-17, 1963, pp. 7-202.

Silva Muñoz, F. "Límites del poder tributario," *Revista de derecho administrativo,* vol. 3, 1964, pp. 59-84.

Vincente-Arche Domingo, F. "Consideraciones sobre el hecho imponible." In: Comisión de Homenaje al Profesor Jordana de Pozas con Motivo de su Jubilación Universitaria, *Estudios en homenaje a Jordana de Pozas,* vol. 2, pp. 475-538. Instituto de Estudios Políticos, Madrid, 1962.

Vincente-Arche Domingo, F. "Le fonti di diritto tributario spagnolo," *Rivista tributaria,* vol. 34, 1964, pp. 1-10.

17

Sánchez Asiaín, J. "Problemas fiscales que plantearía a España su asociación a la Comunidad económica europea," *Boletín de estudios económicos,* vol. 17, no. 55, January 1962, pp. 109-129.

18

Diamond, W. *Foreign tax and trade briefs.* Fallon Law Book Company, New York, loose-leaf, 1951-.

Moneda y crédito. Gráficas Valera, S.A., Madrid, quarterly, 1942-.

Revista de derecho financiero y de hacienda pública. Editorial de Derecho Financiero, Madrid, quarterly, June 1951-.

"Spain law digest." In: *Martindale-Hubbell law directory,* vol. 4, pp. 2931-2938. Martindale-Hubbell, Inc., Summit, N.J., 1961.

SPANISH GUINEA

1

Menéndez Hernández, J. "Consideración fiscal de varias figures sustantivas," *Revista de derecho español y americano,* vol. 6, April-June 1961, pp. 646-668.

Solé Villalonga, G. "La hacienda en la Guinea Ecuatorial," *Revista de derecho financiero y de hacienda pública* (Madrid), vol. 16, 1966, pp. 593-628.

8

Organisation for European Economic Cooperation. *Taxation systems applicable to investments in the overseas countries associated with member countries of O.E.E.C.* Paris, 1960, 100pp.

SUDAN

1

Kubinski, Z. "Indirect and direct taxation in an export economy: A case study of the Republic of the Sudan," *Public finance,* vol. 14, 1959, pp. 316-343 (summary in French).

United States Department of Commerce. *Basic data on the economy of Sudan.* Washington, 1959, 12pp.

2

Kubinski, Z. *Public finance for stability and growth in an underdeveloped export economy.* Studies on Taxation and Economic Development No. 2, International Bureau of Fiscal Documentation, Amsterdam, 1961.

Satti, S. "Some aspects of the Sudan economy," *African affairs,* January 1957, pp. 32-39.

Stone, J. *The finance of government economic development in the Sudan, 1899 to 1913.* Sudan Economic Institute, Khartoum, 1954.

4

McLoughlin, P. "Income distribution and direct taxation: An administrative problem in low-output African nations—A case study of the Sudan," *Economia internazionale,* vol. 16, no. 3, August 1963, pp. 529-538.

7

United States Department of Commerce. *Foreign trade regulations of the Sudan.* Washington, 1966, 8pp.

8

United States Department of Commerce. *Establishing a business in Sudan.* Washington, 1962, 7pp.

9

Buchanan, L. "Local government in the Sudan since 1947," *Journal of African administration,* vol. 5, July 1953, pp. 154-156.

11

Tunley, H. "Revenue from land and crops." In: J. Todhill (ed.), *Agriculture in the Sudan.* Oxford University Press, London, 1954.

SURINAM

1

Government of Suriname. *Investment and taxation in Suriname.* Paramaribo, 1961, 62pp.

"Suriname—Summary of taxation for new investors," *Foreign tax law weekly bulletin,* vol. 12, no. 18, 1961, pp. 5-9.

"Taxation in Surinam," *Foreign tax law weekly bulletin,* vol. 16, no. 9, 1965, pp. 3-17.

United States Department of Commerce. *Basic data on the economy of Surinam.* Washington, 1967, 12pp.

2

Andic, S. *Fiscal survey of Surinam: Planning, economic development, and fiscal requirements.* Ph.D. thesis, Michigan, 1967.

4

Foreign Tax Law Association. *Dutch Guinea income tax service.* Centerport, L.I., N.Y., loose-leaf, 1954-.

7

United States Department of Commerce. *Foreign trade regulations of Surinam.* Washington, 1967, 4pp.

8

Organisation for European Economic Co-operation. *Taxation systems applicable to investments in the overseas countries associated with member countries of O.E.E.C.* Paris, 1960, 100pp.

SWAZILAND

4

"Income taxation in Swaziland," *Foreign tax law semi-weekly bulletin,* vol. 6, no. 63, 1956, pp. 1-13.

"Swaziland." In: Board of Inland Revenue (Great Britain), *Income taxes outside the United Kingdom 1966,* vol. 7, pp. 275-298. H.M. Stationery Office, London, 1967.

SYRIA

1

American University of Beirut, Economic Research Institute. *Business legislation in Syria.* Beirut, 1955, 80pp. (duplicated).

"Arrêté no. 630 du 18.5.1954: Comportant le cahier des changes générales pour les marchés et adjudications du Ministère de la défense nationale," *Recueil des lois et de la législation financière de la République Arabe Syrienne,* vol. 17, no. 8, 1965, pp. 1-84.

Code fiscal Syrien. Recueil des Lois Syriennes et de la Législation Financière, Damas, loose-leaf, 1962 (mimeo).

Décret législatif no. 85 du 21 mai 1949; loi no. 112 du août 1958. Recueil des Lois et de la Législation Financière de le République Arabe Syriennes, Damas, 1962, 34pp.

Qureshi, A. *Fiscal system of Syria.* International Monetary Fund, Middle Eastern Department, Washington, 1955.

United Nations, Technical Assistance Administration. "Finances publiques." Doc. No. TAA/SYR/8 (restricted), 7 August 1958.

United States Department of Commerce. *Basic data on the economy of Syrian Arab Republic.* Washington, 1963, 8pp.

United States Department of State. *Background notes: Syria.* Washington, 1965, 8pp.

2

Asfour, E. *Syria: Development and monetary policy.* Harvard University Press, Cambridge, Mass., 1959, vi/158pp.

Chatti, B. *The fiscal system in Syria with*

emphasis on its role in the economic development of the country. Thesis, American University, Washington, 1957.
International Bank for Reconstruction and Development. *The economic development of Syria.* The Johns Hopkins Press, Baltimore, 1955, chapter 9 and annex B.

4

"Les Dispositions relatives a l'impôt sur le revenue," *Recueil des lois et de la législation financière de la République Arabe Syrienne,* vol. 15, no. 2, 1963, pp. 4-29.
Foreign Tax Law Association. *Syrian income tax service.* St. Petersburg, Fla., loose-leaf, 1963–.
Gannage, E. *Le Réforme des impôts directs au Liban et en Syrie.* Recueil Sirey, Beirut, 1947.
United Nations, Technical Assistance Administration. "Etude sur les impôts sur le revenu et la fortune en Syrie." Doc. No. TAA/SYR/9 (restricted), 7 August 1958.

7

United States Department of Commerce. *Foreign trade regulations of the Syrian Arab Republic.* Washington, 1965, 8pp.

11

Qureshi, A. *Land systems in the Middle East.* n.p., 1954.

18

Diamond, W. *Foreign tax and trade briefs.* Fallon Law Book Company, New York, loose-leaf, 1951–.

TANZANIA

1

Due, J. "Reform of East African taxation," *East African economics review,* vol. 11, December 1964, pp. 57-68.
East Africa High Commission, Statistical Department. *Public finance in Tanganyika: An analysis.* Government Printer, Dar Es Salaam, 1956, 46pp.
"Review of taxation and laws," *Foreign tax law weekly bulletin,* vol. 11, no. 10, 1961, pp. 1-9; vol. 11, no. 11, 1961, pp. 1-9.
United States Department of Commerce.

Basic data on the economy of Tanzania. Washington, 1966, 20pp.
Woods, W. *A report on a fiscal survey of Kenya, Uganda and Tanganyika.* Government Printer, Nairobi, 1946.

2

Gill, F. "Future taxation policy in independent East Africa," *East African economics review,* vol. 9, June 1962, pp. 1-15.
Hicks, U. "The revenue implications of the Uganda and Tanzania plans," *Journal of development studies,* vol. 2, no. 3, April 1966.
International Bank for Reconstruction and Development. *The economic development of Tanganyika.* The Johns Hopkins Press, Baltimore, 1961, pp. 244-247, 325-330.
Report of the Economic and fiscal commission. H.M. Stationery Office, London, 1961.

3

Due, J. *Taxation and economic development in Tropical Africa.* The MIT Press, Cambridge, Mass., 1963, 172pp.

4

"East Africa territories." In: Board of Inland Revenue (Great Britain), *Income taxes outside the United Kingdom 1966,* vol. 2, pp. 307-400. H.M. Stationery Office, London, 1967.
Foreign Tax Law Association. *Tanganyika income tax service.* Centerport, L.I., N.Y., loose-leaf, 1951–.
Jethna, N. "Company taxation in East Africa," *British tax review,* January-February 1965.
McNeil, R., and Bechgaard, K. *East African income tax.* Butterworth, Durban, 1960, 568pp.
Select committee on the East African income tax (management) bill, 1958. Government Printer, Nairobi, 1958.
Walker, D. "A recent change in East Africa company taxation," *Public finance,* vol. 15, 1960, pp. 166-188.

7

United States Department of Commerce. *Foreign trade regulations of East Africa.* Washington, 1966, 8pp.

8

"East African income tax and nonresidents," *Taxation* (England), 6 February 1960.

United States Department of Commerce. *Establishing a business in East Africa.* Washington, 1966, 16pp.

9

Hicks, U. *Development from below: Local government and finance in developing countries of the Commonwealth.* Oxford University Press, London, 1961, 552pp.

Lee, E. *Local taxation in Tanganyika.* University College, Dar Es Salaam, 1964, 67pp.

Lee, E. *Local taxation in Tanganyika.* University of California, Berkeley, Calif., 1965, 77pp.

Lee, E. *Local taxation in Tanzania.* Institute of Public Administration (Dar Es Salaam) Study No. 1, Oxford University Press, New York, 1966.

"Urban problems in East and Central Africa," *Journal of African administration,* vol. 10, October 1958, pp. 215-218.

13

United States Treasury Department, Internal Revenue Service, Foreign Tax Assistance Staff. *Report on tax administration in the East Africa common services organization.* Washington, 1964 (mimeo).

18

Diamond, W. *Foreign tax and trade briefs.* Fallon Law Book Company, New York, loose-leaf, 1951–.

THAILAND

1

Board of Investment. *Brief information concerning investment in Thailand.* Bangkok, 1959, 40pp.

Board of Investment. *Outline of revenue taxes.* Bangkok, 1962.

Chase Manhattan Bank. *Thailand.* New York, 1964, 20pp.

Report of the financial adviser covering the years B.E. 2484 (1941) to B.E. 2493 (1950). Bangkok, 1951, 116pp.

United States Department of Commerce.

Basic data on the economy of Thailand. Washington, 1966, 32pp.

United States Department of Commerce. *Investment factors in Thailand.* Washington, 1962, 14pp.

United States Department of Commerce. *Summary of investment factors in Thailand.* Washington, 1959, 6pp.

2

Chakkaphak, P. *The major economic and financial problems of Thailand.* Ph.D. thesis, New York, 1959.

International Bank for Reconstruction and Development. *A public development program for Thailand.* The Johns Hopkins Press, Baltimore, 1959.

International Cooperation Administration, Office for Private Enterprise. *Expanding private investment for Thailand's economic growth.* Bangkok, 1959, 202pp.

Loftus, J. "Problems of fiscal management in a developing economy," *Thai journal of public administration,* vol. 2, no. 1, July 1961, pp. 136-150.

United Nations. *Mobilization of domestic capital in certain countries of Asia and the Far East.* Sales No. 1951.II.F.3, Bangkok, 1951.

4

Foreign Tax Law Association. *Thailand income tax service.* Centerport, L.I., N.Y., loose-leaf, 1948–.

Lyman, A. "Income tax in Thailand: Comparison," *American bar association journal,* vol. 30, October 1954, pp. 857-859.

"Outline of business taxes," *Foreign tax law weekly bulletin,* vol. 15, no. 3, 1964, pp. 14-18.

Public Administration Service. *Administration of withholding tax payments under the personal income tax law.* Report No. M-3, Revenue Department, Ministry of Finance, Bangkok, December 1957, 16pp. (mimeo).

7

Sanittanont, S. *Thailand's rice export tax: Its effect on the rice economy.* Ph.D. thesis, University of Wisconsin, Madison, Wisc., 1967.

United States Department of Commerce. *Foreign trade regulations of Thailand.* Washington, 1964, 8pp.

8

Asian African Legal Consultative Committee, Secretariat. *Foreign investment laws and regulations of member countries.* Economic Law Series No. 2, N.M. Tripathi Private Ltd., Bombay, 1965, 91pp. (mimeo).

United Nations, Economic and Social Council, Fiscal Commission. "Questionnaire on the tax treatment of foreign nationals, assets and transactions: Reply of the government of Siam." Doc. No. E/CN.8/46/Add.5, 31 December 1948, 4pp.

United States Department of Commerce. *Establishing a business in Thailand.* Washington, 1967, 20pp.

9

Dhipayamontri, D. "The municipal development fund in Thailand," *Thai journal of public administration,* vol. 1, no. 4, April 1961, pp. 153-156.

10

Ingram, J. *Land taxation in Thailand.* Unpublished article, University of North Carolina, Chapel Hill, N.C., 1959.

12

Kosin, O. *Thailand's new law to promote industrial development.* Board of Investment, Bangkok, 1962, 11pp.

United States Department of Commerce. *Industrial promotion act of Thailand, 1962.* Washington, 1962, 9pp.

13

Alexander Grant and Co. *Program for technical assistance to improve financial administration in the government of Thailand.* 1955, 111pp. (offset).

Howell and Co. *Organization chart and brief description of functional assignments proposed for the reorganisation of the department of revenue.* Bangkok, 6 December 1954, 33pp. (mimeo).

Howell and Co. *Revenue, customs, excise and statistical administration in Thailand.* Ministry of Finance, Bangkok, 6 volumes, 1955, 658pp.

Public Administration Service. *Report on revenue accounting and other fiscal practices of the revenue department.* Report No. A-2, Ministry of Finance, Bangkok, 1957, 65pp. (mimeo).

18

Diamond, W. *Foreign tax and trade briefs.* Fallon Law Book Company, New York, loose-leaf, 1951–.

TOGO

1

"Loi no. 57-36 du 11 septembre 1957 sur le régime fiscal particulier des entreprises agrées." In: *Pénant: Afrique investissements,* pp. 149-154. La Documentation Africaine, Paris, 1962.

United States Department of Commerce. *Basic data on the economy of the Republic of Togo.* Washington, 1961, 12pp.

2

The economic and financial structure of French West Africa. Annual conference of the Economic Sections, West African Institute of Social and Economic Research, University College, Ibadan, 1953 (mimeo).

3

Mémento fiscal et social 1964, numéro spécial no. 14, 25 June 1964. A comparative survey of taxes in the West African Union and Guinea.

TONGA

4

"Tonga." In: Board of Inland Revenue (Great Britain), *Income taxes outside the United Kingdom 1966,* vol. 8, pp. 1-9. H. M. Stationery Office, London, 1967.

TRINIDAD

1

Canadian Tax Foundation. *Taxes abroad: West Indies.* Toronto, 1961, 22pp.

Chemical Bank New York Trust Company. *Trinidad and Tobago.* New York, 1965, 3pp.

Comptroller for Development and Welfare. *Financial aspects of federation in the British West Indian territories.* Barbados, 1953.

First National City Bank. *Basic data on the economy of Trinidad and Tobago.* New York, 1965, 10pp.

Fitzpatrick, Graham & Co. *Summary of*

fiscal and other provisions affecting enterprises in Trinidad and Tobago. Trinidad, 1961, 19pp.

Prest, A. *A fiscal survey of the British Caribbean.* H.M. Stationery Office, London, 1957, 136pp.

Price Waterhouse & Co. *Information guide for doing business in Trinidad and Tobago.* New York, 1963.

"Retroactive tax bill passed," *Foreign tax law weekly bulletin,* vol. 15, no. 2, 1964, pp. 16-19.

Trinidad and Tobago Industrial Corporation. *Why foreign investment is attracted to Trinidad and Tobago.* Port-of-Spain, 1962, 20pp.

United States Department of Commerce. *Basic data on the economy of Trinidad and Tobago.* Washington, 1965, 16pp.

4

Fitzpatrick, Graham & Co. *Notes on the income tax amendment act of 1963.* Trinidad, 1963, 17pp.

Fitzpatrick, Graham & Co. *Summary of the main provisions of the income tax company law, and other legislation affecting the operation of business enterprises in Trinidad and Tobago.* Trinidad, 1961, 26pp.

Foreign Tax Law Association. *Trinidad income tax service.* Centerport, L.I., N.Y., loose-leaf, 1950-1954. St. Petersburg, Fla., loose-leaf, 1964–.

"Recent income tax amendments," *Foreign tax law weekly bulletin,* vol. 14, no. 23, 1963, pp. 1-9.

"Trinidad and Tobago." In: Board of Inland Revenue (Great Britain), *Income taxes outside the United Kingdom 1966,* vol. 8, pp. 11-51. H.M. Stationery Office, London, 1967.

7

United States Department of Commerce. *Foreign trade regulations of Trinidad and Tobago.* Washington, 1965, 5pp.

8

Noyes Research Co. *Investment in the Caribbean.* Pearl River, N.Y., 1964, 132pp.

United States Department of Commerce. *Establishing a business in Trinidad.* Washington, 1960, 8pp.

9

Hicks, U. *Development from below: government and finance in developing countries of the Commonwealth.* Oxford University Press, London, 1961, 552pp.

MacArthur, D. "Problems of local financing in the Caribbean." In: A. Wilgus (ed.), *The Caribbean: Natural resources.* University of Florida Press, Gainesville, Fla., 1959.

12

Caribbean Commission. *The promotion of industrial development in the Caribbean.* Port-of-Spain, 1952, 173pp.

General Statistical Office. *Pioneer manufacturers: Survey of the finances of 52 pioneer establishments 1958/1959.* Statistical Studies and Papers No. 8, Trinidad, 1961.

17

Seers, D. "Federation in the British West Indies: The economic and financial aspects," *Social and economic studies,* vol. 6, June 1957, pp. 197-214.

18

Diamond, W. *Foreign tax and trade briefs.* Fallon Law Book Company, New York, loose-leaf, 1951–.

TUNISIA

1

Sebastiani, J. *Les Finances publiques tunisiennes.* Tunis, 3 volumes, 1954.

"Tax amendments in Tunisia," *Foreign tax law weekly bulletin,* vol. 16, no. 48, 1966, pp. 13-15.

"Tax system of Tunisia," *Foreign tax law weekly bulletin,* vol. 14, no. 44, 1964, pp. 1-17.

United States Department of Commerce. *Basic data on the economy of Tunisia.* Washington, 1959, 12pp.

3

Brochier, E. "Fiscalités française, algérienne, marocaine et tunisienne," *Bulletin for international fiscal documentation,* vol. 9, 1955, pp. 271-285.

Caniot, A. "Fiscalité comparée: Algérie-Tunisie-Maroc," *Bulletin for international fiscal documentation,* vol. 6, 1952, pp. 203-219.

4

Foreign Tax Law Association. *Tunisian income tax service.* St. Petersburg, Fla., loose-leaf, 1964–.

Sitbon, M. "Impôts et taxes grevant les entreprises industrielles et commerciales en Tunisie," *Bulletin for international fiscal documentation,* vol. 4, 1950, pp. 127-130.

6

Sitbon, M. *Précis de taxes sur le chiffre d'affaires en Tunisie.* Éditions de la Fiscomptor, Tunis, 1965, 178pp.

7

United States Department of Commerce. *Foreign trade regulations of Tunisia.* Washington, 1965, 8pp.

8

United States Department of Commerce. *Establishing a business in Tunisia.* Washington, 1958, 8pp.

11

Qureshi, A. "Structure and taxation of agriculture in Tunisia." In: H. Wald and J. Froomkin (eds.), *Papers and proceedings of the Conference on agricultural taxation and economic development,* pp. 349-367. Harvard Law School International Program in Taxation, Cambridge, Mass., 1954.

12

Kalnins, A. *L'Aide de l'état tunisien aux entreprises industrielles.* Librairie "Publicia," Tunis, 1959, 49pp.

TURKEY

1

Blakey, R., and Blakey, G. "Tax system of Turkey," *Taxes,* vol. 33, 1955, pp. 225-230.

Blough, R. *Possibilities for improving the fiscal system of the Turkish republic.* Economic Cooperation Administration, Chicago, 1949 (mimeo).

Hall, J. *Report on Turkish internal finance.* International Cooperation Administration, Washington, 1960, 65pp.

Hauser, G. "Fiscal survey of Turkey." In: A. Peacock (ed.), *Public finance as an instrument for economic develop-*

ment, pp. 87-112. Organisation for Economic Co-operation and Development, Paris, 1964.

Kayra, C. *A guide to the Turkish system of taxation.* Union of Chambers of Commerce, Industry and Commodity Exchanges of Turkey, Ankara, 1956, 75pp.

Presthus, R., Yasa, I., and Turner, A. *Financial and personal aspects of Ankara Belediye.* Public Administration Institute for Turkey and the Middle East, Ankara, 1955, pp. 17-24 (mimeo).

"Tax reform bills," *Foreign tax law weekly bulletin,* vol. 14, no. 52, 1964, pp. 14-18; vol. 15, no. 26, 1964, pp. 3-5.

United States Department of Commerce. *Basic data on the economy of Turkey.* Washington, 1962, 19pp.

United States Department of Commerce. *Investment factors in Turkey.* Washington, 1963, 12pp.

United States Department of Commerce. *Investment in Turkey.* Washington, 1956, pp. 131-133.

United States Department of Commerce. *Turkey—Summary of tax legislation.* Washington, 1953.

2

Dikmen, M. "Problems of financing the investments provided for in the Turkish five-year plan," *Public finance,* vol. 19, 1964, pp. 5-24 (in Turkish; summaries in English and French).

Gürsan, I. "Fiscal policy in Turkey," *European taxation,* vol. 6, 1966, pp. 126-129.

International Bank for Reconstruction and Development. *The economy of Turkey.* Washington, 1951, chapter 10.

4

"Corporation taxation," *Foreign tax law weekly bulletin,* vol. 13, no. 46, 1963, pp. 4-9.

Dikmen, M. "L'Impôt sur le revenue en Turquie—Un essai d'imposition des revenus dans un pays insuffisamment développé," *Public finance,* vol. 20, 1965, pp. 51-75 (summaries in English and German).

Hirsch, E., and Hirsch, A. "Tax reform and the burden of direct taxation in Turkey," *Public finance,* vol. 21, 1966, pp. 337-363.

Sur, F. "La Réforme de l'impôt sur le

revenue en Turquie," *Revue de science et de législation financières,* vol. 44, 1952, pp. 113-132.

"Survey of individual and corporate income taxation in the Republic of Turkey," *European taxation,* vol. 6, 1966, pp. 197-224.

6

Organisation for European Economic Cooperation. *The influence of sales taxes on productivity.* Paris, 1953, 268pp.

7

United States Department of Commerce. *Foreign trade regulations of Turkey.* Washington, 1967, 8pp.

8

Cullu, T. "How foreigners are taxed in Turkey," *Foreign tax law weekly bulletin,* vol. 1, no. 33, 1951, pp. 3-8.

Ervardar, F. "The taxation of foreign enterprises in Turkey," *Bulletin for international fiscal documentation,* vol. 20, 1966, pp. 485-487.

Kisagün, A. "Ouvertures de succursales et d'agences en Turquie par les sociétés étrangères et leurs modes d'exploitation: Turquie," *International bar association conference report,* vol. 8, July 1960, p. 428.

"Representations by the United States regarding taxation of American colleges in Turkey," *Foreign relations of the United States diplomatic papers,* vol. 4, 1942, pp. 834-835.

Turkish Consulate General. *General information for prospective foreign investors in Turkey.* New York, 1964.

United Nations, Economic and Social Council, Fiscal Commission. "Questionnaire on the tax treatment of foreign nationals, assets and transactions: Reply of the government of Turkey." Doc. No. E/CN.8/46/Add.14, 5 October 1949, 23pp.

United States Department of Commerce. *Establishing a business in Turkey.* Washington, 1959, 15pp.

9

Dikmen, M. "Considérations sur le système de recettes des autorités locales en Turquie." In: Institut International de Finances Publiques, *Centralisation*

et *décentralisation des finances publiques,* pp. 102-119. La Haye, 1964.

Feyzioglu, B. "Centralisation et décentralisation des finances publiques en Turquie." In: Institut International des Finances Publiques, *Centralisation et décentralisation des finances publiques,* pp. 120-151. La Haye, 1964.

Kurnow, E. *Problems in local government finance in the United States and Turkey; a comparative study.* Ankara University, Faculty of Political Sciences, and New York University Graduate School of Public Administration and Social Service, Ankara, 1956, 18pp.

Traylor, O. *Turkish local government and methods of financing.* Mutual Security Administration/Greece, 1953, 55pp. (mimeo).

Ulkinen, I. "Les Finances locales turques," *Revue de science et de législation financières,* vol. 46, 1954, pp. 801-830.

Yavuz, F. *A survey on the financial administration of Turkish municipalities.* Servinç Matbaasi, Ankara, 1962, viii/27pp.

12

"Turkey readies tax incentives for investors," *European taxation,* vol. 3, 1963, pp. 123-124.

United States Department of Commerce. *Investment law of Turkey.* Washington, 1956, 3pp.

13

Central Treaty Organization. *Symposium on tax administration.* Office of United States Economic Coordinator for CENTO Affairs, American Embassy, Ankara, 1965, 259pp.

"Crack down on tax dodgers," *Foreign tax law weekly bulletin,* vol. 14, no. 45, 1964, pp. 6-8.

Martin, J. "Some aspects of national budget administration in Turkey," *Revue de la Faculté des sciences économiques de l'Université d'Istanbul,* vol. 14, October 1952-July 1953, pp. 59-68. Also in: *Public finance,* vol. 8, 1953, pp. 29-41.

Martin, J., and Cush, F. *Administration of the Turkish Ministry of finance.* Ministry of Finance, Ankara, 1951, 172pp. (mimeo).

United Nations, Economic and Social Council, Fiscal Commission. "Procedures available for the review of initial tax assessments: Additional reply of the government of Turkey." Doc. No. E/CN.8/59/Add.8/Part II, 13 August 1952, 7pp. (mimeo).

16

Martin, J. "American investigations of Turkish finances," *Proceedings of the National tax association 1951,* vol. 44, pp. 222-225.

18

Diamond, W. *Foreign tax and trade briefs.* Fallon Law Book Company, New York, loose-leaf, 1951–.
"Turkey law digest." In: *Martindale-Hubbell law directory,* vol. 4, pp. 2978-2984. Martindale-Hubbell, Inc., Summit, N.J., 1961.

UGANDA

1

"Digest of taxes in force," *Foreign tax law weekly bulletin,* vol. 7, no. 46, 1957, pp. 1-9; vol. 7, no. 47, 1957, pp. 1-8.
Due, J. "Reform of East African taxation," *East African economics review,* vol. 11, December 1964, pp. 57-68.
Report of the Uganda fiscal commission. Government Printer, Entebbe, 1962.
Tax enquiry report, 1964/65. Entebbe, 1966.
United States Department of Commerce. *Basic data on the economy of Uganda.* Washington, 1966, 20pp.
Woods, W. *A report on a fiscal survey of Kenya, Uganda and Tanganyika.* Government Printer, Nairobi, 1946.

2

Commonwealth development and its financing: Uganda. H.M. Stationery Office, London, 1966, 66pp.
Elkan, W. "Uganda." In: A. Pepelasis *et al., Economic development: Analysis and case studies,* pp. 237-244. Harpers, New York, 1961.
Ghai, D. *Income elasticity of the Uganda tax structure.* Ph.D. thesis, Yale University, New Haven, Conn., 1966.
Gill, F. "Future taxation policy in independent East Africa," *East African*

economics review, vol. 9, June 1962, pp. 1-15.
Harris, D. *Development in Uganda, 1947 to 1955-56, as illustrated by an analysis of the revenue and expenditure of the protectorate during this period.* Wisbech (for the government of Uganda), 1956, 22pp.
Hicks, U. "The revenue implications of the Uganda and Tanzania plans," *Journal of development studies,* vol. 2, no. 3, April 1966.
International Bank for Reconstruction and Development. *The economic development of Uganda.* The Johns Hopkins Press, Baltimore, 1961, pp. 49-55.
Report of the Economic and fiscal commission. H.M. Stationery Office, London, 1961.
Walker, D., and Ehrlich, C. "Stabilization and development policy in Uganda," *Kyklos,* vol. 12, 1959, pp. 341-353.
Zulu, J. *An economic study of the postwar African experience with taxation, with special reference to the Republic of Uganda.* Ph.D. thesis, Colorado, 1965.

3

Due, J. *Taxation and economic development in Tropical Africa.* The MIT Press, Cambridge, Mass., 1963, 172pp.

4

"East Africa territories." In: Board of Inland Revenue (Great Britain), *Income taxes outside the United Kingdom 1966,* vol. 2, pp. 307-400. H.M. Stationery Office, London, 1967.
Jethna, N. "Company taxation in East Africa," *British tax review,* January-February 1965.
McNeil, R., and Bechgaard, K. *East African income tax.* Butterworth, Durban, 1960, 568pp.
Select committee on the East African income tax (management) bill, 1958. Government Printer, Nairobi, 1958.
Walker, D. "A recent change in East African company taxation," *Public finance,* vol. 15, 1960, pp. 166-188.

7

United States Department of Commerce. *Foreign trade regulations of East Africa.* Washington, 1966, 8pp.

8

"East African income tax and nonresidents," *Taxation* (England), 6 February 1960.
United States Department of Commerce. *Establishing a business in East Africa.* Washington, 1966, 16pp.

9

Badenoch, A. "Graduated taxation in the Teso district of Uganda," *Journal of local administration overseas,* vol. 1, no. 1, January 1962, pp. 15-22.
Elkan, W. "Central and local taxes on Africans in Uganda," *Public finance,* vol. 13, 1958, pp. 312-320.
Hicks, U. *Development from below: Local government and finance in developing countries of the Commonwealth.* Oxford University Press, London, 1961, 552pp.
Kennedy, T. "The finance of urban local government in Uganda," *South African journal of economics,* vol. 29, no. 2, June 1961, pp. 103-116.
"Urban problems in East and Central Africa," *Journal of African administration,* vol. 10, October 1958, pp. 215-218.

13

United States Treasury Department, Internal Revenue Service, Foreign Tax Assistance Staff. *Report on tax administration in the East Africa common services organization.* Washington, 1964 (mimeo).

18

Diamond, W. *Foreign tax and trade briefs.* Fallon Law Book Company, New York, loose-leaf, 1951–.

UNION OF SOVIET SOCIALIST REPUBLICS

1

"La Fiscalité dans l'Union des Républiques Socialistes Soviétiques," *Statistiques et études financières,* vol. 13, no. 151, supp., July 1961, pp. 1035-1092.
Surányi-Unger, T. "A theory of taxation on Soviet lines," *Finanzarchiv,* vol. 21, no. 1, April 1961, pp. 120-134.

2

Holzman, F. "Financing Soviet economic development." In: National Bureau of Economic Research, *Capital formation and economic growth.* Princeton, N.J., 1955. Part reprinted in: R. Bird and O. Oldman (eds.), *Readings on taxation in developing countries,* pp. 71-87. The Johns Hopkins Press, Baltimore, 1964.
Holzman, F. *Soviet taxation: The fiscal and monetary problems of a planned economy.* Harvard University Press, Cambridge, Mass., 1955, 376pp.

4

Hoy, G. "The abolition of income tax in the USSR: Procedure for the dismantling of the personal income tax structure in the USSR; progress made so far," *Canadian tax journal,* vol. 9, November-December 1961, pp. 436-440.

6

Pettibone, P. "The Soviet turnover tax," *Public finance,* vol. 19, 1964, pp. 361-379.

9

Kamins, R. " 'Democratic centralism': Local finance in the Soviet Union," *National tax journal,* vol. 15, December 1962, p. 353.

UNITED ARAB REPUBLIC

1

American University of Beirut, Economic Research Institute. *Business legislation in Egypt.* Beirut, 1955, 97pp. (duplicated).
Arthur D. Little Inc. *Factors influencing investment in Egypt.* Cambridge, Mass., 1954, 79pp.
"Egyptian public finances in the fifties," *Middle East economist,* no. 3, March 1962, pp. 98-105.
Fanner, W. "Taxation in Egypt," *Foreign tax law weekly bulletin,* vol. 1, no. 34, 1951, pp. 3-17.
Labib, G. "L'Assujettissement des personnes publiques aux impôts et l'évolution socialiste de l'économie nationale," *Egypte contemporain,* vol. 53, no. 310, October 1962, pp. 71-74.
Lotz, J. "Taxation in the United Arab Republic," *International monetary fund staff papers,* vol. 13, March 1966, pp. 121-153.
Mourad, M. "Étude comparative du système fiscal de la R.A.U.," *Egypte con-*

temporain, vol. 52, no. 306, October 1961.

"Taxation reforms in the Egyptian region," *Arab review,* vol. 1, December 1960, pp. 58-60.

United Nations. *Public finance information papers: Egypt.* Sales No. 1951. XVI.7, New York, 1951.

United Nations, Technical Assistance Administration. "The Egyptian revenue system." Doc. No. TAA/EGY/10 (restricted), 9 January 1957.

United Nations, Technical Assistance Administration. "Egyptian taxation." Prepared by O. Traylor, 1955, 223pp. (mimeo).

United States Department of Commerce. *Basic data on the economy of the United Arab Republic (Egypt).* Washington, 1967, 20pp.

2

"Fiscal policy in Egypt," *International financial news survey,* vol. 6, 10 July 1953, pp. 9-10.

Kardouche, G. *The U.A.R. in development: A study in expansionary finance.* Frederick A. Praeger, New York, 1966, xviii/170pp.

Khallaf, H. "Financing economic development in Egypt," *Middle East economic papers,* 1955, pp. 27-46.

Leith-Ross, F. "Financial and economic developments in Egypt," *International affairs,* vol. 28, January 1952, pp. 29-37.

Marzouk, G. "Monetary and financial analyses in the Egyptian region," *Egypte contemporain,* vol. 51, no. 300, April 1960, pp. 5-25.

Mead, D. *Growth and structural change in the Egyptian economy.* Yale University Press, New Haven, Conn., 1966.

Sitton, S. *Aspects et problèmes du financement interne en Egypte.* Institut de Science Economique Appliquée, Paris, 1957, 41pp.

4

Foreign Tax Law Association. *Egyptian income tax service.* Centerport, L.I., N.Y., loose-leaf, 1955–.

Ibrahim, M. *L'Assujettissement des sociétés anonymes en Egypte aux impôts sur le revenue.* Imp. Université du Caire, Cairo, 1954, 504pp.

7

United States Department of Commerce. *Foreign trade regulations of the United Arab Republic.* Washington, 1966, 8pp.

8

Rahman, A. *Egyptian income taxation of nonresident aliens and foreign corporations and its effects on Egyptian economic growth.* Ph.D. thesis, Indiana, 1960.

United States Department of Commerce. *Establishing a business in Egypt.* Washington, 1961, 4pp.

United States Department of Commerce. *Law on investment of foreign capital in Egypt.* Washington, 1955, 2pp.

Yousef, N. "Taxation with regard to the earnings of limited companies with international interests: The case of Egypt," *Cahiers de droit fiscal international,* vol. 1, 1939, pp. 77-79.

9

Hujayr, M. "En marge des nouvelles lois fiscales (estimation de la capacité contributive de la Province Sud de la République Arabe Unie)," *Économie et finances de la Syrie et des pays arabes,* vol. 3, no. 32, August 1960, pp. 55-65.

11

Qureshi, A. *Land systems in the Middle East.* n.p., 1954.

Serafy, S. *Egyptian land taxation and land reform.* Paper from the Conference on Land and Tax Reform in the Less Developed Countries, sponsored by the Committee on Taxation, Resources, and Economic Development and the Land Tenure Center, University of Wisconsin, Madison, Wisc., August 1963.

13

Aly, D. "L'Evasion fiscale en Egypte: Causes et remèdes," *Bulletin for international fiscal documentation,* vol. 7, 1953, pp. 100-105.

United Nations. "Egyptian tax organization and administration." Prepared by O. Traylor, 1955, 45pp.

18

Diamond, W. *Foreign tax and trade briefs.* Fallon Law Book Company, New York, loose-leaf, 1951–.

UPPER VOLTA

1

United States Department of Commerce. *Basic data on the economy of Upper Volta.* Washington, 1965, 8pp.

2

The economic and financial structure of French West Africa. Annual conference of the Economic Sections, West African Institute of Social and Economic Research, University College, Ibadan, 1953 (mimeo).

3

Mémento fiscal et social 1964, numéro spécial no. 14, 25 June 1964. A comparative survey of taxes in the West African Union and Guinea.

12

United States Department of Commerce. *Investment law in the Republic of Upper Volta.* Washington, 1963, 4pp.

URUGUAY

1

Azzini, J. "Características generales de las finanzas públicas en el Uruguay," *Revista de economía, finanzas y administración* (Montevideo), vol. 11, January-April 1952, pp. 27-60.

Azzini, J. "The tax system of Uruguay," *Public finance,* vol. 11, 1956, pp. 112-129.

Azzini, J., and DeMarco, H. *El sistema tributario del Uruguay.* Universidad de la República, Instituto de la Hacienda Pública, Montevideo, 1955, 26pp.

Azzini, J., and Gnazzo, E. *La fiscalidad uruguaya en el último decenio.* Universidad de la República, Instituto de la Hacienda Pública, Montevideo, 1956, 59pp. Also in: *Revista de la Facultad de ciencias económicas y administración* (Montevideo), vol. 2, December 1955, pp. 365-418.

Bank of London and South America. *Tax reform.* London, 1960.

Giampietro Borrás, G. *Las tasas en la hacienda pública.* Facultad de Derecho, Montevideo, 1959.

Hall, J. *Reformas del régimen impositivo.* Informe al Gobierno de la República Oriental del Uruguay, Montevideo, 29 November 1955, 5pp. (mimeo).

Ibarra San Martín, R. *Los impuestos finalistas en el Uruguay.* Imprenta Cordón, Montevideo, 1959, 116pp.

Ibarra San Martín, R. "Los impuestos finalistas en el Uruguay," *Revista de la Facultad de ciencias económicas y administración* (Montevideo), vol. 2, September 1959, pp. 1077-1188.

Luba, R. "Un plan realista de reforma impositiva," *Selección de temas de finanzas públicas* (Montevideo), nos. 18-19, 1961, p. 31.

National Foreign Trade Council, Inc. *Uruguayan tax law.* New York, 1961, 13pp.

Pan American Union. *A statement of the laws of Uruguay in matters affecting business.* Washington, 4th edition revised, 1963, pp. 95-123.

Popelka, V., and Vilarrubi, R. *Régimen impositivo del Uruguay.* Librería Amalio M. Fernandez, Montevideo, 1962, 43pp.

Posadas Belgrano, G. *Derecho tributario.* Medina, Montevideo, 1959.

Price Waterhouse & Co. *Information guide for doing business in Uruguay.* New York, 1966.

Programa Conjunto de Tributación de la Organización de los Estados Americanos y del Banco Interamericano de Desarrollo. *Sistemas tributarios de América Latina: Uruguay.* Unión Panamericana, Washington, 1967, x/83pp.

"Unificación de criterios fiscales." In: *Anibal R. Abadie-Santos: Documentos—Escritos,* pp. 149-162. Homenaje de "Jurisprudencia" a su fundador, Ed. Adolfo Amit, Montevideo, 1961.

Universidad de la República, Instituto de la Hacienda Pública. *Selección de temas de finanzas públicas.* Montevideo.

Universidad de la República, Instituto de la Hacienda Pública, Oficina de Impuestos Internos. *Impuestos vigentes.* Montevideo, 1965.

United States Department of Commerce. *Basic data on the economy of Uruguay.* Washington, 1963, 8pp.

"Uruguay takes steps to control inflation in fight for stabilization," *Foreign commerce weekly,* vol. 65, no. 16, 1961, p. 13.

Valdés Costa, R. *Curso de finanzas.* Centro Estudiante de Derecho, Montevideo, vol. 1, 4th edition, 1964, 195pp., vol. 2, 3d edition, 1966, 141pp.

Valdés Costa, R. *Ley de recursos no. 12,804: Texto, antecedentes y coordinación con el derecho vigente.* Facultad de Derecho y Ciencias Sociales, Montevideo, 1960, 541pp.

Valdés Costa, R. "Panorama del sistema tributario uruguayo," *Revista de derecho, jurisprudencia y administración,* vol. 57, July-December 1960, pp. 165-174.

Zerbino Cavajani, J. *Summary of Uruguayan taxation.* Arthur Young & Co., Montevideo, 1961, 24pp.

2

Teichert, P. *Industrial development policy in Uruguay.* Ph.D. thesis, Texas, 1955, 307pp.

Welinder, C. "La inflación y la distribución de los impuestos," *Selección de temas de finanzas públicas* (Montevideo), nos. 20-21, 1960, p. 127.

4

Arbenoiz, J. "Impuesto a la renta,"*Revista de la Asociación de escribanos del Uruguay,* vol. 49, 1963, pp. 185-225.

Azzini, J., and Gnazzo, E. *La imposición a las sociedades en el Uruguay.* Universidad de la República, Instituto de la Hacienda Pública, Montevideo, 1957, 20pp.

Bulante Rios, A. "Estudio de algunas situaciones particulares normativas sobre el impuesto a las ganancias elevadas," *Revista de economía, finanzas y administración* (Montevideo), vol. 11, September-December 1952, pp. 241-257.

Cámara Nacional de Comercio. "Impuestos que afectan la actividad industrial y comercial, creados o modificados por la ultima ley de recursos presupuestales," *Revista de la bolsa de comercio* (Montevideo), vol. 55, May 1953, pp. 21-30.

Carámbula, A. *Sociedades comerciales de familia en el derecho tributario.* n.p., Montevideo, 1961, 139pp.

de Marco, H. "Tratamiento de las utilidades de las sociedades anónimas en los impuestos a la renta y a las sociedades de capital." In: Instituto Uruguayo de Derecho Tributario, *Semana tributaria, 1961,* pp. 69-79. Montevideo, 1961.

Echegorry, F. "El concepto de empresa en el impuesto a las ganancias elevadas," Universidad de la República, Instituto de la Hacienda Pública, Montevideo, 1957, 32pp.

Foreign Tax Law Association. *Uruguayan income tax service.* St. Petersburg, Fla., loose-leaf, 1960-.

Griziotti, A. "Quali le migliori imposte per le industrie?" *Revista de economía* (Montevideo), vol. 6, December 1952-February 1953, pp. 527-538.

Hughes, C. *Excess profits tax; Uruguay's law no. 10,957.* Imprenta "Gaceta Comercial," Montevideo, 1945, 10pp.

"Impuesto a la renta," *Revista de la Facultad de ciencias económicas y administrativas,* no. 20, July 1962, pp. 115-186.

Instituto Uruguayo de Derecho Tributario. *Semana tributaria 1961: Aplicación del impuesto a la renta.* Montevideo, 1961, 156pp.

Lombardo, O. "Normas de valuación del activo fijo y mercaderías." In: Instituto Uruguayo de Derecho Tributario, *Semana tributaria, 1961,* pp. 31-40. Montevideo, 1961.

Noboa, R. "Clasificación de las rentas en las distintas categorías." In: Instituto Uruguayo de Derecho Tributario, *Semana tributaria, 1961,* pp. 41-53. Montevideo, 1961.

O'Farrell and Freira. *Memorandum on company, company taxation and banking laws in Uruguay.* Montevideo, 2d edition, February 1959, pp. 9-10 (mimeo).

Peirano Facio, J. "Sujeto pasivo." In: Instituto Uruguayo de Derecho Tributario, *Semana tributaria, 1961,* pp. 54-68. Montevideo, 1961.

Pesce Barcelo, P. "El impuesto adicional a las sociedades anónimas—Su ilegalidad," *Revista de economía* (Montevideo), vol. 6, September-November 1953, pp. 901-923.

Pravia, M. "Liquidación de la tasa básica proporcional." In: Instituto Uruguayo de Derecho Tributario, *Semana tributaria, 1961,* pp. 80-91. Montevideo, 1961.

Quijano, C. "Anotaciones sobre el impuesto a la renta," *Revista de economía* (Montevideo), vol. 9, March-May 1957, pp. 656-698.

Rodoszkowiez, S. *La imposición a los pagos del estado.* Universidad de la

República, Instituto de la Hacienda Pública, Montevideo, 1957, 51pp.

Rodríguez, L. "Concepto de renta; incremento del patrimonio." In: Instituto Uruguayo de Derecho Tributario, *Semana tributaria, 1961,* pp. 12-21. Montevideo, 1961.

Schvarzer, N. "El impuesto a los réditos en el Uruguay," *Impuestos,* vol. 22, 1964, pp. 69-77.

Universidad de la República, Instituto de la Hacienda Pública. *Problemas de legislación y técnica tributaria nacionales: Ganancias elevadas, ventas y transacciones.* Montevideo, 1957, 50pp.

"Uruguay establishes income tax law," *Foreign commerce weekly,* vol. 65, no. 9, 1961, p. 15.

Valdés Costa, R. "Concepto de renta en la legislación tributaria," *Revista de derecho, jurisprudencia y administración,* vol. 58, 1962, pp. 1-11.

Valdés Costa, R. "El impuesto a la renta en el Uruguay," *Impuestos,* vol. 22, 1964, pp. 1-13.

5

Belgrano, G. *El impuesto substitutivo del de herencias a las sociedades anónimas.* Medina, Montevideo, 1953, 195pp.

Berchesi, N. "Personal property tax as a substitute for the inheritance tax: Uruguay." In: Institut International de Finances Publiques, *Impôts sur la fortune y inclus droits de succession: Debt management,* pp. 281-283. Brussels, 1962.

Posadas, L. de. "La defraudación del impuesto de herencias luego de la ley no. 12,804," *Sociedades anónimas, revista de derecho comercial,* vol. 16, 1961, pp. 403-414.

Quijano, C. "El impuesto substitutivo," *Revista de economía* (Montevideo), vol. 5, December 1951-February 1952, pp. 68-74; vol. 5, March-May 1952, pp. 141-163.

Sosa Marghieri, A. "El impuesto substitutivo de herencias," *Revista de la Facultad de ciencias económicas y administración* (Montevideo), vol. 2, November 1952, pp. 3-47.

6

Bardallo, J., Lopez, M., Patron, J., and Rodriguez Pozzi, L. *Timbres y papel sellado.* Centro Estudiantes de Derecho, Montevideo, 1961, 238pp.

Larraud, R. "El impuesto de sellos en Uruguay y Argentina," *Revista notarial* (La Plata), no. 755, 1964, pp. 1221-1254.

Oliver, L., and Gnazzo, E. "L'Impôt uruguayen sur les ventes et sur les transactions." In: M. Masoin and E. Morselli (eds.), *Impôts sur transactions, transmissions et chiffre d'affaires,* pp. 383-402. Archives Internationales de Finances Publiques No. 2, Cedam Casa Editrice, Dr. A. Milani, Padova, 1959.

Peirano Facio, J. *El impuesto a las ventas.* Universidad de Montevideo, Montevideo, 1955, 469pp.

Peirano Facio, J. *Impuestos: A las ventas, suntuarios, a las transacciones agropecuarias, internos, tributo de sellos y timbres, a las transmisiones inmobiliarias.* Montevideo, 1963, 86pp.

Strace, S. "El impuesto suntuario," *Revista de economía, finanzas y administración* (Montevideo), vol. 11, May-August 1952, pp. 137-146.

7

González, A. "Removido aduanero y cabotaje," *Justicia uruguaya,* vol. 41, 1960, pp. 35-44.

González, A. *Tratado de derecho aduanero uruguayo.* Biblioteca de Publicaciones Oficiales de la Facultad de Derecho y Ciencias Sociales de la Universidad de la República, Montevideo, 3 volumes, 1962, 925pp.

"Sobre franquicias aduaneras." In: *Anibal R. Abadie-Santos: Documentos—Escritos,* pp. 273-284. Homenaje de "Jurisprudencia" a su fundador, Ed. Adolfo Amit, Montevideo, 1961.

United States Department of Commerce. *Foreign trade regulations of Uruguay.* Washington, 1966, 8pp.

8

Gibbons, W. *Tax factors in basing international business abroad.* Harvard Law School International Program in Taxation, Cambridge, Mass., 1957, pp. 157-167.

"Problema de las utilidades de las sucursales de casas extranjeras." In: Instituto Uruguayo de Derecho Tributario, *Semana tributaria, 1961,* pp. 122-130. Montevideo, 1961.

United States Department of Commerce. *Establishing a business in Uruguay.* Washington, 1962, 19pp.

9

Azzini, J. *Ingresos municipales.* Thesis, Universidad de República, Tall. L.I.G.U., Montevideo, 1946, 126pp.

Gnazzo, E. *Contribución al estudio de las finanzas locales.* Universidad de la República, Instituto de la Hacienda Pública, Montevideo, 1959.

10

Giampietro Borrás, G. "Valor imponible de la nuda propiedad, el usufructo y el uso en la ley 12.804 de 30 de noviembre de 1960," *Justicia uruguaya,* vol. 43, 1961, pp. 163-178.

12

Schiaffino Espalter, A. "Franquicias para el pago de impuestos," *Sociedades anónimas, revista de derecho comercial,* vol. 18, 1963, pp. 409-424.

Vaz, D. "El sistema del descuento impositivo y los incentivos tributarios," *Revista del Colegio de abogados del Uruguay,* vol. 4, no. 1-4, 1963, pp. 23-37.

14

Abal, J. "Función de la reglamentación: Concepto de fuente y de empresa." In: Instituto Uruguayo de Derecho Tributario, *Semana tributaria, 1961,* pp. 92-101. Montevideo, 1961.

Azzini, J. *La fuente de la obligación tributaria en tasa.* Universidad de la República, Instituto de la Hacienda Pública, Montevideo, 1955, 9pp.

Carámbula, A. "Admisión fiscal de deudas," *Justicia uruguaya,* vol. 41, 1960, pp. 45-79.

Gelsi Bidart, A. "Efectos de la sentencia fiscal en material civil en el derecho uruguayo," *Justicia uruguaya,* vol. 43, 1961, pp. 1-9.

Gelsi Bidart, A. "Juicio ejecutivo fiscal y medidas cautelares," *Revista del Colegio de abogados del Uruguay,* vol. 3, no. 1-4, 1962, pp. 1-17.

Giampietro Borrás, G. "Acerca de las inmunidades tributarias de las personas estatales," *Revista de la Facultad de derecho y ciencias sociales* (Montevideo), vol. 1-3, 1962, pp. 305-336.

Valdés Costa, R. "Contencioso tributario 'Uruguay,'" *Boletín del Instituto de derecho comparado de México,* vol. 13, September-December 1960, p. 49.

Valdés Costa, R. "Obligatoriedad y ejecución de las leyes impositivas," *Revista de economía* (Montevideo), vol. 5, September-November 1952, pp. 412-428.

17

Almeida, R. "La zona latinoamericana de libre comercio," *Técnicas financieras* (CEMLA), vol. 2, no. 5, May-June 1963, pp. 453-472.

Gutiérrez Kirchner, A. "El mercomún latinoamericano y la política fiscal," *Investigación fiscal,* no. 19, July 1967, pp. 15-63.

18

Boletín del Instituto uruguayo de derecho tributario. Librería-Editorial Juan A. Peri, Montevideo, annual.

Diamond, W. *Foreign tax and trade briefs.* Fallon Law Book Company, New York, loose-leaf, 1951–.

Economist Intelligence Unit, Ltd. *Economic review of Uruguay and Paraguay.* London, irregular.

"Uruguay law digest." In: *Martindale-Hubbell law directory,* vol. 4, pp. 2985-2997. Martindale-Hubbell, Inc., Summit, N.J., 1961.

VENEZUELA

1

Arthur Andersen & Co. *Tax and trade guide: Venezuela.* Chicago, 1966, 135pp.

Benson, J. *Report on Venezuelan tax, labor, corporation law.* Fallon Law Book Company, New York, 1964, 959pp.

Benson, J. "Tax and legal aspects of trade and investment in Venezuela." In: Southwestern Legal Foundation, *Proceedings of 1960 institute on private investments abroad and foreign trade,* pp. 449-477. Matthew Bender and Co., Albany, N.Y., 1960.

Carrillo Batalla, T. *Introducción a las finanzas públicas.* Arte, Caracas, 1961, 194pp.

Carrillo Batalla, T. *Legislación fiscal.* Editorial Jurídica Venezolana, Caracas, 4 volumes, 1962.

Embassy of Venezuela, Information Service. *Résumé of Venezuelan legislation on business, labor and taxation, as published in "Venezuela up-to-date."* Washington, 1952, 45pp.

Espinosa, A. *El problema fiscal en Venezuela.* Impresores Unidos, Caracas, 1946, 58pp.

Franco, G. "Consideraciónes sobre la política fiscal y sus fundamentos teóricos," *Boletín del Banco central de Venezuela,* nos. 131-133, January-March 1956.

La Financiera Venezolana, S. A. *Review of Venezuelan tax law.* Caracas, 1953, 10pp.

Ley orgánica de la hacienda nacional. La Torre, Caracas, 1960, 117pp.

Llovera Llovera, B. "La reforma Cárdenas (en el sistema fiscal de Venezuela)," *Boletín informativo* (Caracas), vol. 8, April 1951, pp. 3-12.

Loreto, L., *et al.* "Venezuela's tax legislation as recently revised," *Venezuela up-to-date,* vol. 7, no. 8, 1957.

Luzardo, R. *Venezuela, business and finances.* Prentice-Hall, Englewood Cliffs, N.J., 1957, 167pp.

Martínez, A., and Leáñez, F. "Análisis del desenvolvimiento fiscal en el periodo 1958-61," *Revista de hacienda,* vol. 25, January-March 1962, pp. 23-36.

Mayobre, J. "Situación fiscal y reforma impositiva en Venezuela," *Comercio exterior* (México), January 1959, p. 28.

Pan American Union. *A statement of the laws of Venezuela in matters affecting business.* Washington, 3d edition, 1962.

Price Waterhouse & Co. *Information guide for doing business in Venezuela.* New York, 1963.

Shoup, C., *et al. The fiscal system of Venezuela: A report.* The Johns Hopkins Press, Baltimore, 1959, 491pp.

Tamayo, L. "Elementos de finanzas públicas venezolanas," *Revista de hacienda,* vol. 11, December 1946, pp. 53-100.

Tinoco, P. "Observaciones a la reforma tributaria," *Boletín de la Cámara de comercio de Caracas,* no. 637, December 1966, pp. 19352-19373.

United Nations. *Public finance surveys: Venezuela.* Sales No. 1951.XVI.2, New York, 1951.

United States Department of Commerce. *Basic data on the economy of Venezuela.* Washington, 1967, 32pp.

United States Department of Commerce.

Investment in Venezuela. Washington, 1953, pp. 81, 140-146.

"Venezuela revises tax laws," *Foreign commerce weekly,* vol. 61, no. 3, 1959.

"Venezuelan tax developments," *Oil and gas tax quarterly,* vol. 10, October 1960, p. 32.

2

Basso, J. "Sistemas tributarios y desarrollo económico," *Economía y administración* (Maracaibo), vol. 4, no. 1-2, January-June 1965, p. 93.

Carrillo Batalla, T. "La estructura de la economía latinoamericana y las políticas monetaria y fiscal," *Mundo económico* (Caracas), no. 9, October-November 1961, pp. 12-16.

"Economic development in Venezuela in the 1950's," *Economic bulletin for Latin America,* vol. 5, March 1960, pp. 21-61.

Malave Mata, H. "El sistema tributario venezolano y el sector petrolero," *El trimestre económico,* vol. 31(2), no. 122, April-June 1964, pp. 788-816.

Sarda, J. "Monetary and fiscal policy and the balance of payments in Venezuela," *Inter-American economic affairs,* vol. 5, no. 2, 1951, pp. 47-66.

Silva, C. "La presión tributaria en Venezuela," *Revista de hacienda,* vol. 22, December 1958, pp. 25-41.

Wattles, M. "Financing Venezuela's development," *American journal of economics and sociology,* vol. 12, April 1954, pp. 239-245.

4

Arcaya, M. *Regulation of the income tax law of Venezuela.* Translation Service, Caracas, 1949, 44pp.

Cárdenas Becerra, H. "El impuesto sobre la renta en Venezuela," *Boletín informativo del Ministerio de hacienda* (Caracas), vol. 1, June 1950, pp. 15-50.

Cover, G. *Venezuelan income tax of 1948, and regulations of the same law decreed in 1949.* Avila Gráfica, Caracas, 1950.

Donis, R. "Los inversionistas y hombres de negocios ante el impuesto sobre la renta venezolano," *Revista de hacienda,* vol. 26, October-December 1962, pp. 39-44.

Donis, R. "Lo que a usted le conviene recordar en materia de impuesto sobre la renta," *Revista de hacienda,* vol. 25, April-June 1962, pp. 27-42.

"Exposición de motivos del proyecto de reforma de la ley de impuesto sobre la renta," *Revista de hacienda,* vol. 20, December 1955, pp. 55-75.

Foreign Tax Law Association. *Venezuelan income tax service.* Centerport, L.I., N.Y., loose-leaf, 1951–1956.

Garay, J. (ed.). *La nueva ley de impuesto sobre la renta.* Ramirez & Garay, Caracas, 1967, 167pp.

"Income tax rates slightly raised in Venezuela," *Venezuela up-to-date,* vol. 9, no. 2, 1959.

Instituto Mexicano de Técnicos Fiscales. "El impuesto sobre la renta en Venezuela," *Revista fiscal y financiera,* vol. 4, March 1949, pp. 16-18.

Jurado-Blanco, C. *Anotaciones a la ley de impuesto sobre la renta.* Tipografia Vargas, Caracas, 6th edition, 1953.

Lazo, O. *Recopilación de jurisprudencia y doctrina judicial del impuesto sobre la renta en Venezuela.* Ediciones Legis, Buenos Aires and Caracas, 4 volumes, 549/537/408/521pp.

"Main changes in the Venezuelan income tax law," *Venezuela up-to-date,* vol. 9, no. 3, 1953.

Pérez de la Coba, C. "The Venezuelan income tax structure and the oil industry," *Venezuela up-to-date,* vol. 7, no. 2, 1956.

Price Waterhouse & Co. *Summary of Venezuelan income tax decisions and rulings to December 31, 1950.* Caracas, 15 August 1952, 16pp. (mimeo).

Shoup, C., *et al.* "Schedular and global income taxes." In: R. Bird and O. Oldman (eds.), *Readings on taxation in developing countries.* The Johns Hopkins Press, Baltimore, 1964, pp. 180-184; revised edition, 1967, pp. 132-136. Reprinted from C. Shoup *et al., The fiscal system of Venezuela: A report,* pp. 101-106. The Johns Hopkins Press, Baltimore, 1959.

Shoup, C., *et al.* "Taxation of corporations and dividends." In: R. Bird and O. Oldman (eds.), *Readings on taxation in developing countries.* The Johns Hopkins Press, Baltimore, 1964, pp. 187-198; revised edition, 1967, pp. 176-187. Reprinted from: C. Shoup *et al., The fiscal system of Venezuela: A report,* pp. 111-

125. The Johns Hopkins Press, Baltimore, 1959.

Sillery Lopez de Ceballos, R. *Apuntaciones sobre la prescripción en materia de impuesto sobre la renta.* Caracas, 1966.

Tinoco, P. *Comentarios a la ley de impuesto sobre la renta de Venezuela.* n.p., Madrid, 2 volumes, 1955.

Travieso Paul, J. *Memorandum: The income tax law of 1956.* Caracas, 17pp. (mimeo).

"Venezuela and the U.S. income tax laws compared," *Venezuela up-to-date,* vol. 9, November 1959, p. 13.

"The Venezuelan income tax—Structure and the oil industry," *Foreign tax law weekly bulletin,* vol. 7, no. 8, 1956, pp. 1-9.

"Venezuelan taxation of oil and gas income," *Oil and gas tax quarterly,* vol. 6, 1957, pp. 75-85.

6

Pietri, A. "El impuesto adicional sobre las regalías de petróleo," *Revista de derecho y legislación,* vol. 43, April-June 1954, pp. 104-131.

"Venezuela establishes travelers' exit tax," *Foreign commerce weekly,* vol. 65, no. 12, 1961, p. 14.

7

United States Department of Commerce. *Foreign trade regulations of Venezuela.* Washington, 1964, 8pp.

8

Baker, W. "Venezuela." In: American Management Association, *The taxation of business income from foreign operations,* pp. 117-121. New York, 1958.

Gibbons, W. *Tax factors in basing international business abroad.* Harvard Law School International Program in Taxation, Cambridge, Mass., 1957, pp. 168-177.

Gibbons, W., *et al.* "Tax policies of Venezuela." In: Tax Institute of America, Inc., *Tax policy on United States investment in Latin America,* pp. 163-171. Princeton, N.J., 1963.

Gumucio, F. "Introducción a la elaboración de convenios entre Venezuela y los Estados Unidos para evitar la doble imposición internacional," *El trimestre económico,* vol. 30(1), no. 117, January-March 1963.

Murphy, E., Jr. "Hydrocarbon concessions in Venezuela and Bolivia: Considerations for the tax lawyer." In: Southwestern Legal Foundation, *Ninth institute on oil and gas law and taxation,* p. 461. Matthew Bender and Co., Albany, N.Y., 1958.

Tinoco, P. "Unilateral measures for the avoidance of double taxation: Venezuela," *Cahiers de droit fiscal international,* vol. 44, 1961, p. 263 (summaries in French and German).

United States Department of Commerce. *Establishing a business in Venezuela.* Washington, 1964, 19pp.

9

Shoup, C., Harriss, C., and Vickery, W. *The fiscal system of the Federal district of Venezuela: A report.* Baltimore, 1960, x/162pp.

10

Báez Finol, V. *El impuesto predial rural —Su institución en Venezuela.* Estudios Especiales, Consejo de Bienestar Rural, Caracas, 1961.

Bas y Rivas, F. "Usufructo, uso y habitación en el impuesto de derechos reales," *Revista de derecho privado,* vol. 94, February 1961.

15

Silva, C. "La incidencia del régimen venezolano de cambios diferenciales," *El trimestre económico,* vol. 22, April-June 1955.

17

Almeida, R. "La zona latinoamericana de libre comercio," *Técnicas financieras* (CEMLA), vol. 2, no. 5, May-June 1963, pp. 453-472.

Gutiérrez Kirchner, A. "El mercomún latinoamericano y la política fiscal," *Investigación fiscal,* no. 19, July 1967, pp. 15-63.

Strasma, J. "Armonización tributaria y la integración," *Mundo económico* (Caracas), no. 31, December 1966, pp. 73-74.

18

Diamond, W. *Foreign tax and trade briefs.* Fallon Law Book Company, New York, loose-leaf, 1951-.

Economist Intelligence Unit, Ltd. *Economic review of Colombia and Venezuela.* London, irregular.

Ministerio de Hacienda. *Boletín informativo de Ministerio de hacienda.* Caracas, monthly, August 1938-.

Ministerio de Hacienda. *Revista de hacienda.* Caracas, quarterly, 1936-.

Ministerio de Hacienda, Administración General del Impuesto sobre la Renta. *Boletín del impuesto sobre la renta.* Caracas, semiannual, 1942-.

"Venezuela law digest." In: *Martindale-Hubbell law directory,* vol. 4, pp. 2998-3009. Martindale-Hubbell, Inc., Summit, N.J., 1961.

VIET-NAM

1

Brookings Institution, Economic Specialist Group. *Tax reform in Vietnam: Immediate measures and basic requirements.* Washington, January 1961, 57pp. (duplicated).

Jonas, G. (ed.). *Conference on investment conditions in Vietnam: A symposium.* American Friends of Vietnam, New York, 1958, 98pp.

Lindholm, R. *An analysis of Viet-Nam tax system and recommendations.* Michigan State University Viet-Nam Advisory Group, Saigon, 300pp. (mimeo).

Lindholm, R. "Taxation in South Vietnam," *Public finance,* vol. 14, 1959, pp. 236-247.

Lindholm, R. (ed.). *Vietnam, the first five years.* Michigan State University Press, East Lansing, Mich., 1959, 365pp.

Michigan State College, Special Mission to Indochina. *Report of the mission for public administration, public information, police administration, and public finance and economics, Indochina.* Saigon, 1954, 53pp. (mimeo).

Secretary of State for Finance. *Codes fiscaux, impôts fonciers—des patentes— et sur les revenues.* Nha In Cac Cong-Bao, Saigon, 1956.

Snyder, W. *A comparison of Vietnamese government revenues and expenditures for fiscal years 1954, 1955, 1956.* Michigan State University Viet-Nam Advisory Group, Saigon, 1957 (mimeo).

Snyder, W., and Murphy, M. *An analysis of revenues and expenditures of Viet-*

namese governmental agencies having budget autonomy, fiscal year 1956. Michigan State University Viet-Nam Advisory Group, Saigon, 1957, 60pp.

Taylor, M. *The tax system of Viet-Nam: A summary.* Michigan State University Viet-Nam Advisory Group, Saigon, 1960.

Tenenbaum, H. *Summary of principles and recommendations included in R. W. Lindholm's "Analysis of Viet-Nam's tax system."* International Cooperation Administration, Saigon, 1956.

United States Department of Commerce. *Basic data on the economy of Viet-Nam.* Washington, 1963, 21pp.

3

Yoingco, A., and Trinidad, R. *Fiscal systems and practices in Asian countries.* Frederick A. Praeger, New York, 1967.

4

Taylor, M. "Some aspects of income taxation in Vietnam," *Malayan economic review,* vol. 4, October 1959, pp. 70-78.

Taylor, M. *The taxation of income in Viet-Nam.* Michigan State University Viet-Nam Advisory Group, Saigon, 1959, 96pp.

6

Taylor, M. *The patente (business license tax) in Viet-Nam.* Michigan State University Viet-Nam Advisory Group, Saigon, 1959, 104pp.

Taylor, M. *The system of excise taxes in Viet-Nam.* Michigan State University Viet-Nam Advisory Group, Saigon, 1960, 105pp.

Taylor, M. *The system of indirect taxes in Viet-Nam.* Michigan State University Viet-Nam Advisory Group, Saigon, 1960, 118pp.

8

United States Department of Commerce. *Establishing a business in Viet-Nam.* Washington, 1958, 12pp.

9

Cole, D. *Financing provincial and local government in the Republic of Viet-Nam.* Ph.D. thesis, University of Michigan, Ann Arbor, Mich., 1959.

Cole, D. *Report on taxation in the provinces of South Viet-Nam.* Michigan

State University Viet-Nam Advisory Group, Saigon, 1956, 95pp./tables.

Cole, D., and Da, B. *Summary of village finances in the south region of Viet-Nam.* National Institute of Administration and Michigan State University Viet-Nam Advisory Group, Saigon, 1957, 48pp. (mimeo).

Cole, D., and Nguyen, B. *Provincial and local revenue in Viet-Nam.* Michigan State University Viet-Nam Advisory Group, Saigon, 1957 (mimeo).

Thach, U., and Cole, D. *Financial activities of the provinces, prefecture and municipalities of Viet-Nam in 1956.* National Institute of Administration and Michigan State University Viet-Nam Advisory Group, Saigon, 1957, 43pp.

10

Taylor, M. *The taxation of real property in Viet-Nam.* Michigan State University Viet-Nam Advisory Group, Saigon, 1959, 112pp.

12

Cole, D. *Tax exemption for new investment in Viet-Nam.* Michigan State University Viet-Nam Advisory Group, Saigon, 1960, 26pp. (mimeo).

VIRGIN ISLANDS

1

Division of Trade and Industry. *Facts about doing business in the U.S. Virgin Islands.* St. Thomas, 1963, 14pp.

12

Government Information Center. *Virgin Islands tax incentive act.* New York, 1962, 23pp.

WESTERN SAMOA

4

"Western Samoa." In: Board of Inland Revenue (Great Britain), *Income taxes outside the United Kingdom 1966,* vol. 8, pp. 283-302. H. M. Stationery Office, London, 1967.

YUGOSLAVIA

1

Murko, V. "Les Tarifs d'impôts en Yugoslavia." In: E. Morselli and L. Trotabas (eds.), *Enquête sur les tarifs d'impôts,* pp. 381-398. CEDAM, Padova, 1964.

2

Dupont, C., and Keesing, F. "The Yugoslav economic system and instruments of Yugoslav economic policy: A note," *International monetary fund staff papers,* vol. 8, no. 1, November 1960, pp. 77-84.

Pejovich, S. "Taxes and the pattern of economic growth: The case of Yugoslavia," *National tax journal,* vol. 17, March 1964, pp. 96-100. Also in: *Cahiers de l'Institut de science économique appliquée,* 150 supp., June 1964, série G, no. 20, pp. 227-235.

6

Murko, V. "L'Impôt sur les transactions et les transmissions en Yougoslavie." In: M. Masoin and E. Morselli (eds.), *Impôts sur transactions, transmissions et chiffre d'affaires,* pp. 405-437. Archives Internationales de Finances Publiques No. 2, Cedam Casa Editrice, Dr. A. Milani, Padova, 1959.

7

"The new customs law and the development of customs system in Yugoslavia," *Commercial information* (Yugoslavia), vol. 12, August 1959, pp. 17-19.

United States Department of Commerce. *Foreign trade regulations of Yugoslavia.* Washington, 1965, 8pp.

11

Brashich, R. *Taxation in Yugoslavia's agriculture.* Mid-European Studies Center of the National Committee for a Free Europe, Inc., New York, 23 November 1953, 27pp. (mimeo).

13

Hackett, A. "Le Contrôle des comptes publics dans la République Populaire Fédérale de Yugoslavie," *Bulletin de liaison et d'information de l'administration centrale des finances,* no. 17, June-August 1962, pp. 41-47.

ZAMBIA

1

Committee To Review Native Taxation (Northern Rhodesia). *Report.* Government Printer, Lusaka, 1948, 15pp.

"Federation of Rhodesia and Nyasaland," *Coopers and Lybrand international tax summaries,* vol. 3, March 1960, pp. 1-15.

Garmany, J. "Revenue allocation in a federal state: The experience of Rhodesia and Nyasaland," *South African journal of economics,* March 1962, pp. 50-60.

Report of the Advisory commission on the review of the constitution of Rhodesia and Nyasaland. H.M. Stationery Office, London, Cmnd. 1148, 1960, chapter 9.

United States Department of Commerce. *Basic data on the economy of the Federation of Rhodesia and Nyasaland.* Washington, 1962, 12pp.

United States Department of Commerce. *Investment in Federation of Rhodesia and Nyasaland.* Washington, 1956, pp. 107-109.

3

Due, J. *Taxation and economic development in Tropical Africa.* The MIT Press, Cambridge, Mass., 1963, 172pp.

4

"Methods of direct taxation in British Tropical Africa," *Journal of African administration,* vol. 2, October 1950, pp. 3-12; vol. 3, January 1951, pp. 30-41; vol. 3, October 1951, pp. 77-87.

Notes on income tax and exchange control in the Federation of Rhodesia and Nyasaland. H.M. Stationery Office, London, 1961, 15pp.

"Zambia." In: Board of Inland Revenue (Great Britain), *Income taxes outside the United Kingdom 1966,* vol. 8, pp. 303-347. H.M. Stationery Office, London, 1967.

9

"Urban problems in East and Central Africa," *Journal of African administration,* vol. 10, October 1958, pp. 215-218.

10

Lund, F. "Valuation for rating in Northern Rhodesia," *Journal of Association of rating and valuation officers,* 1956.

18

Blann, B., and White, R. *Butterworths taxation statutes service.* Butterworth and Co., Durban.

94